MATCHDAYS

THE HIDDEN STORY OF THE BUNDESLIGA

Ronald Reng

Translated by James Hawes

SIMON &
SCHUSTER

London · New York · Sydney · Toronto · New Delhi

A CBS COMPANY

First published in Germany as *Spieltage*, by Piper Verlag GmbH, 2013

First published in Great Britain by Simon & Schuster UK Ltd, 2015
A CBS COMPANY

1 3 5 7 9 10 8 6 4 2

Simon & Schuster UK Ltd
1st Floor
222 Gray's Inn Road
London WC1X 8HB

www.simonandschuster.co.uk

Simon & Schuster Australia, Sydney
Simon & Schuster India, New Delhi

A CIP catalogue record for this book
is available from the British Library

ISBN: 978-1-47113-647-4
Ebook ISBN: 978-1-47113-649-8

Typeset in the UK by M Rules
Printed and bound by CPI Group (UK) Ltd, Croydon, CR0 4YY

CONTENTS

'Hello, Höher speaking.'

'Hello. This is Ronald Reng. I believe you tried to call me?'

'Mr Reng, thanks for calling back. Mr Reng, I have to meet you.'

'For what reason?'

'I can't talk about it on the phone.'

'Right.'

'You know who I am, don't you?'

'Well, to be honest, I'm not quite . . .'

'Heinz Höher.'

'Oh, well of course I know who you are, then: you used to manage Bochum and Nuremberg.'

'Sorry, perhaps I should have introduced myself properly.'

'Not at all. But as you know, I live in Barcelona. That's a fair way from Nuremberg. I come back to Germany quite often, maybe I should just get in touch next time I'm there?'

'I don't know.'

'It seems like the most sensible thing.'

'Yes, the most sensible thing.'

And then, an hour later:

'Hello?'

'Mr Reng, it's me, Höher.'

'Mr Höher?'

'Mr Reng, I've just booked a flight to Barcelona. I'm coming this Thursday.'

'This Thursday!'

'And I am staying until Tuesday.'

'Till Tuesday!'

'Please, just give me a couple of hours of your time. I want to tell you something. I have to tell you something.'

At 38, he's young for a manager: Heinz Höher.

SHEET-ICE IN THE
PENALTY BOX

At about ten in the evening, Heinz Höher tells his wife that he's going out for a while. She doesn't ask where he is heading to. She is quite accustomed to him rarely explaining what he is up to.

The thermometer in Bochum, at the heart of Germany's coal and steel belt, is hovering around zero. All day long the city council has been battling snow and ice. Now, 180 tons of salt and sand later, all those drifts and heaps are freezing over again. Last night, there were 65 car crashes in Bochum: an 18-year-old rammed head-on into a lamp-post; a 20-year-old was fired through his windscreen straight into the wall of a garage.

Heinz Höher opens up the driver's door of his silver Mercedes 190. In the windows of the flats round about, TV screens are still glowing here and there, although the closing ceremony of the Innsbruck Winter Olympics has already been and gone. Some Austrian got one of the last gold medals this afternoon, in the ski-jump. Heinz Höher could not remember the name, although he did watch the event.

He's at the stadium in less than 15 minutes, despite the terrible conditions. He drives to his own, private rules. His main ambition is never to be first in the queue at a red light. But these rules aren't about racing, they're just designed to fill up drive-time by setting himself random missions. One time, he decided that he had to do a 300-mile motorway journey to Bochum at a steady ton. No bursts of speed allowed, just cruise at 100mph for the whole three hours.

At the darkened stadium, his helpers arrive right on time. August Liese and Erwin Höffken are the backroom staff who organise everything for the VfL Bochum first team, be it a new striker or a crate of beer. They don't need floodlights: the snow that blankets the pitch reflects enough light to illuminate the night. Two days from now, Tuesday at 7.30pm, Bochum are playing their great local rivals, Schalke 04, in the Bundesliga and Heinz Höher, now in his fourth year as manager, has carefully prepped his team for the derby – except that now, he's going to make sure it doesn't happen.

Liese and Höffken know where old Rickenberg, the groundsman, keeps his buckets. They go to the showers, and fill them with water. There's only one shower-room in the Bochum stadium, so after the final whistle both teams just have to shower down together, the winners and the losers, the foulers and the fouled. Unbelievable, for the Bundesliga; unbelievable, even for a local league, in this modern age, 1976!

The three of them drag the buckets onto the pitch. The cold bites into their hands. Heinz Höher feels like the metal handle of the bucket is getting welded to his fingers. Must be way below zero now. They make for the penalty area to their right. Heinz Höher hasn't actually got a real plan. All he thought was, they would cover the pitch with ice. Now he sees what a job that's going to be. He chucks the water from his bucket, and watches as a small puddle forms in the snow. How many buckets are they going to need for the whole pitch? 10,000? 100,000? Without a word between them, the three men hurry back and forth between the showers and the penalty area. That's over 150 metres for every bloody bucket, for every little puddle. At least the freezing wind is actually turning the puddles to ice.

By midnight, all they've managed is to ice over both the penalty areas. And that's going to have to do.

The following morning, there's no change to the answering machine at the box-office at Bochum: 'A number of Standing Tickets are still available for the home game against Schalke 04 on Tuesday, 17 February at 7.30pm. End of message. Thank you for your call.'

The club is expecting a crowd of 20,000. The sports editor of one local newspaper, Franz Borner, writes: 'When it comes to derbies against Schalke, Bochum have often taken it to the next level. So here's what I say, and may our boys treat it as an order: take it to the next level, Bochum – and take out the Schalkers!' What the hell is Borner on, shouting his head off like this? He's been getting on Höher's nerves for months with his demands.

In the living room of Höher's family home, 26 Kaulbachstraße, the grey plastic telephone rings. You can get brightly coloured telephones these days, but the post office wants one mark ten extra per month for them. It's Liese on the phone: the city officials are meeting at the stadium at midday to see if the pitch is playable.

There's still a cold wind blowing down from the Alps over the Nordrhein-Westfalen region, but sleet and snow are only due to fall here and there, and the temperature could rise as high as 5°C. Most Bundesliga games on Tuesday and Wednesday look to be safe.

'Don't worry,' says Liese, 'the ice on the boxes will hold out, and Ottokar's got the city officials in the palm of his hand.'

'Who said I was worried?' answers Heinz Höher.

Ottokar Wüst is the president of Bochum and he was sitting right there in their usual pub, the Gasthaus Mense, on Sunday morning, when Heinz Höher had his big idea: what if we make sure the game never happens?

Without knowing he had the president on his side, he'd never have dared do it. As a boy Heinz Höher was instilled with a strong and firm belief in authority. He hadn't a real idea of exactly how Konrad Adenauer, Germany's post-war chancellor, ran the country – but he would never hear word against him. The club's president was his most important and most trusted ally, his helper and his protector.

Ottokar Wüst owned the biggest menswear shop in town; silver-haired rather than grey, he was rarely seen in public dressed in anything but a suit and tie. At board meetings of VfL Bochum, he always let everyone have their say on every matter of importance, always took an open vote on everything – and then he did just as he wanted.

So there they were on that Sunday morning in the Gasthaus Mense on the Castroper Straße, just three minutes on foot from the stadium: Höher and Wüst, with Liese and Höffken, discussing the situation. And what wild ideas precisely, asked Wüst, might be hiding behind Höher's mysterious words about *making sure the game never happened*? Wüst had this particular way of speechifying, his words seemed to stand to attention and – strange but true – his sentimental pomposity went down really well with Bochum's working-class supporters and the players. The tables in Mense were of rough wood that had never seen a tablecloth, and they were set with beer-mugs even on Sunday mornings.

From a purely sporting point of view it would have been logical to play the game. Heavy going on a snowy pitch would favour Bochum's physical style, and lying as they were, fourth from bottom, only one point clear of the relegation zone, they were desperate for a win. But just the same, the manager could straightaway see what a cute move it would be if they could just get the game put off. Because in just three weeks, on 7 March 1976, Bochum's stadium on the Castroper Straße was closing down for a whole four months. Complete renovation: for the rest of the season, all their home games would have to be played somewhere else. And that meant that if Tuesday's derby against Schalke could be postponed, it wouldn't take place until spring – and it would be played in Borussia Dortmund's vast new stadium, which held 54,000 spectators, compared to the 20,000 at most who would come to Bochum on a Siberian evening in February.

In Dortmund they could make 400,000 marks, maybe half a million.

The all-time record takings at the Castroper Straße stood at 150,000 marks, against Bayern Munich. Like every club in the Bundesliga, Bochum lived almost entirely on the cash that came in at the turnstiles – well, where else would a football club get money from?

It wasn't Heinz Höher's job to worry about things like that – a manager should concentrate on the task in hand, shouldn't he? But naturally, the figures were always in his head. If he woke up on a Saturday and it was raining, his first thought was *shit, that'll be 3000 less in the crowd today, that's 18,000 marks we're down*. A club like Bochum really felt a loss like that, and as manager you felt it too, the whole time: the money that just wasn't there. The club's budget for the whole year was 3.5 million marks and they had to go to extraordinary lengths to make it stretch: such as, their hotel bills where almost never paid on time and sometimes never paid at all. *Half a million*, he thought. *Half a million in cash for one single game!*

About 11.30 on Monday, 16 February 1976, Heinz Höher pulls on his navy-blue flares. Over them, he wears a reefer-jacket with shoulder tabs, the same colour. His wife chose it for him. There was a time when he didn't mind going shopping. But now he fends off his wife's attempts to make him buy clothes with panic-stricken cries of 'I've already got everything I want!' She thinks it's because of the stress of a manager's life. Her friends tell her it's just what happens to men, when they get old.

But he's only 37 and that's young, for a manager. He doesn't trouble himself in the slightest about his appearance, but he still looks good in a devil-may-care sort of way. It must be something to do with the look he gives you: eyes narrowed under bushy blonde eyebrows.

He throws his white scarf loosely over his shoulder, French-style, and leaves his coat unbuttoned as he heads off for the pitch inspection with the city officials. Surely they're going to have to cancel the game. There is just no way the ice in those penalty boxes can have melted yet. But what if they ask how come it's *only* the penalty boxes that are iced up?

For 35 years only the four men involved knew about the sabotage at Bochum's stadium. Erwin Höffken took the secret with him to the grave. August Liese and Ottokar Wüst also passed away before November 2011, when Heinz Höher decided that the story mustn't die with them. He tells his wife, Doris, that he is travelling to Barcelona. What's he doing in Barcelona, his children and friends ask her. But she doesn't know either.

Heinz Höher is 73 by now. He arrives in Barcelona with a neon-yellow 1980s Adidas rucksack on his back. Inside it is a whole stack of documents: 50-year-old newspaper articles about his own time as a player with MSV Duisburg; reports on Juri Judt, who Höher discovered as a Russian immigrant kid and trained up, single-handed, to become a professional and a German Under-21 international; letters from banks about his debts running into millions; Internet search results about alcoholism. One man's whole life in the world of football, stuffed into a single rucksack. He now feels a vague but intense need to divest himself of the lot, and he's chosen to tell his story to a German football writer living in Barcelona who he's never even met. But he feels close to him because he's read his books. Heinz Höher has always recognised and understood himself better in the books he read than in dialogue. He's always found it easier to express himself in writing than in words.

And so we begin to talk, and soon after that first evening in Barcelona the letters start too. At the same time the first announcements of books covering the Bundesliga's 50-year anniversary begin to appear, the best of the anecdotes, the most memorable matches, the biggest stars. With every letter from Höher a nagging discrepancy seems to grow, between what he experienced as a protagonist in five Bundesliga decades, and the snippets we are invited to accept as seemingly representative in anniversary books about 50 years of the Bundesliga. Would we not learn so much more about the Bundesliga by telling the story of a single man, rather than yet again summoning up all the characters, goals and tables?

At the start of the 1963 Bundesliga season, Heinz Höher was a winger as famous for his elegant play as he was for his dodgy work-rate. He was the great white hope of Germany's manager Sepp Herberger. In 1984, at FC Nuremberg, the players mounted a coup against him, and for the only time in German football, a club president sacked half the squad instead of the manager. He collapsed on the training field after misusing drugs, and he wrote a book for children. When he landed up on the dole, the way it always happens in any manager's career, he earned his money by playing cards. People who've met him often say they find it pretty hard to follow his train of thought: Heini Höher lives and thinks on some different level from the rest of us, they say. They think he's a little bit strange. I often get the feeling that he's highly intelligent.

In his 50 years in the Bundesliga, he has experienced some pretty bizarre things – and been responsible for some of them, such as those iced-over penalty boxes at Bochum. Listening to the story of this unusual life, I found myself for the first time really understanding what the Bundesliga actually felt like back in those different eras, how football has changed, and how football can change a person.

On Monday, 16 February 1976, at midday, the thin coating of snow on the pitch at the Castroper Straße seems unchanged. There are just a few footprints in the snow – it must have been the groundsman, obviously. The city council's officials poke about in the snow with the toes of their shoes and stamp their heels down hard, staring at the pitch in what looks like concentration. Here are Dr Johannes Freimuth, top sports administrator for the region, Walter Mahlendorf, boss of sport for the City of Bochum, and Max Merkel, manager of Schalke 04. Heinz Brämer, head of finance at Bochum, uses the unusual chill of the day as an excuse to show off his Russian fur hat. The only man wearing a light-coloured coat is Ottokar Wüst, resplendent in his usual trench-coat. Heinz Höher digs his hands into his pockets. They all await Max Merkel's decision. Merkel doesn't know it, but he is the only one of them with an interest in okay-ing the game: Schalke are on a roll, going for a hat-trick of wins after beating Duisburg 3-1 and Essen 5-1.

'This pitch is just about fit for the Winter bloody Olympics,' says Merkel. Everybody laughs loudly. Does Merkel notice that the others aren't just laughing at his narky little bit of wit? Does he hear the relief?

The media are informed about the decision to postpone the game. Heinz Formann, sports editor of the *Westdeutsche Allgemeine* newspaper, types as follows into his Triumph Adler: 'Schalke Manager Max Merkel declared "You could use that pitch for figure-skating, but not for football." That should be enough for anyone who was thinking that Bochum would happily have put off the game. On the contrary, Bochum really wanted to offer the fans one more real home game before the stadium is closed for renovation.' His friend, manager Heinz Höher, has assured him of this.

The first Friday of April 1976 is a lovely, mild spring evening. There's a 21km tailback on the motorway between Bochum and Dortmund. The phrase 'must-see' hasn't even been invented in 1976, but the postponed game between Bochum and Schalke is just that. The move to the Dortmund stadium has given the derby an extra-special flavour, something exotic, almost the feel of a cup final. Rainer Holzschuh, the reporter from *Kicker*, then as now Germany's biggest football magazine, estimates the crowd at between 50,000 and 54,000. It would've been a full house if all the fans had made it through the traffic jam in time. According to Bochum's official figures, attendance was 41,000 – well, the tax-man doesn't have to be told *exactly* how much money was taken. But it was certainly a good 450,000 marks that flowed into the coffers of VfL Bochum that evening, as much as in four ordinary home games.

They lose 4-1, but no one on the club's board seems to mind too much. Ottokar Wüst accompanies Heinz Höher into the press briefing-room: here in Dortmund it's a real conference room with a podium and neat rows of seating, not just any old room with a table shoved into it and a few old chairs, like at Bochum. At one point, the reporters are puzzled, because Wüst declares: 'I heartily thank Heinz Höher for his great courage in giving up home advantage for a game as tough as one against Schalke.' Courage? What courage? But, surely, the game was only postponed because of all that ice and snow . . .? Well, whatever. The reporters don't let anyone see that they didn't get it.

Heinz Höher just sits there with an expressionless face, showing no reaction to Wüst's heartfelt thank you. He smiles the way he always does, when he's particularly delighted, inwardly.

A spectacular winger, famous for his dribble and his mid-match time-outs: Heinz Höher – seen here, sitting, at a friendly in Bonn, 1959 – played as an amateur international.

1963:

A LIFT-SHARE INTO
THE BUNDESLIGA

In the mornings, Heinz Höher would drive from Leverkusen to Cologne, sit in a café near the cathedral and wait until it was time to drive home again. He did it for his mother. He told himself that she'd feel better if she could keep on believing that her youngest son was hard at it, studying Sport and English at Cologne University.

Heinz Höher considered himself highly ambitious. It was just that other people sometimes found it difficult to see this ambition, off the football pitch. When he was doing his A-levels at home in Leverkusen, he had set himself one great task: to pass without doing a stroke of work. To his teachers, his results seemed way under his potential, with lots of marks just 'satisfactory' or 'adequate'. He was happy. He had achieved what he had set out to do.

Now it was August 1963 and soon he would be 25: people would slowly start to talk of him as an eternal student. But he was confident that somehow and sometime, he'd get his degree the same way as he'd got his A-levels. It was just that at this very moment he saw no reason to go to lectures. This very moment had already being going on for two years.

Considering that no respectable person was supposed to sit in a café at 11 o'clock in the morning, the café was surprisingly busy. He looked at the young married women with their Brigitte Bardot ponytails and their collarless dresses. When he looked away, they probably looked at him, too. His hair was always freshly blonded-up. Until recently, he used to put the white peroxide solution onto his hair with a toothbrush. The narrow brush was ideal for getting the fluid out of the little bottle. Now there were real colourings made from chamomile: his little sister Hilla had told him the secret, which she'd heard from Waldtraut, the wife of Werner Röhrig, his team-mate at Bayer 04.

Sometimes he brought a book with him to the café. He tried Dostoevsky, even though to be honest it wasn't his taste. He preferred just to sit there.

You're the only man I know who has never done a single stroke of work, said Fredy Mutz, Leverkusen's old keeper. It was meant to be sarky but it came out full of admiration. Look at Heinz, stone me, said the other players when he was out of hearing range, nothing worries him. He wasn't just a student of the high art of doing sod-all, nor just the only college-boy in a team of guys who worked as book-binders, laboratory drudges and warehousemen – he was also Leverkusen's undisputed star, a flying winger who got the crowd shouting Oohs and Aahs with his passes. The Leverkusen fans also loved to boo and whis-tle whenever a pass of his went astray. They found it hard to imagine that a player like him couldn't get it right every time, they were sure it was just because he couldn't be bothered.

At home, after poor games like that, he wrote letters to himself. Once he began with the title: 'I, footballer.' Underneath this, he wrote: some people think I'm real class. Others say I'm feeble, cowardly, all show. These others are the majority. The letter ended by saying that he would show these others. When he read it a week later he was shocked at how short-lived his vows had been.

Like every respectable bachelor, Heinz Höher still lived at home. In 1959, his brother Manfred had built the whole family house on the Moltkestraße, by the city park, in the new and, in its own opinion, sophisticated part of Leverkusen. The family bed-shop in the high street, Höher's Bedding, which had been founded by their father and taken over by Manfred, was known to everyone in Leverkusen for sheets, pillows and curtains. Their dad had died just before the new family house had been finished, and the elder brothers were now far away; Johannes was married and Edelbert had emigrated to America, but their mother, their sister and Heinz moved in together with

Manfred. For the first time in his life, he had a room all to himself. Their mum let him lie in till 9 o'clock every morning. After all, he was studying and training so hard.

'These are my resolutions,' he wrote in one of these letters to himself, and under Point 6 it said: 'Show more warmth to mum. Think about the fact that she too was once a girl of 21.'

As for girls of 20, the gossip in Leverkusen said that Heinz Höher, the star of Bayer 04, had found love. Several people claimed to have seen him with an elegant young lady from the dye-works, short black hair and long legs, but they obviously couldn't be engaged yet or they'd let themselves be seen more openly together.

Thanks to football, money wasn't an issue. What with bonuses for winning and back-handers, he was making about 2000 marks a month at Bayer 04. A worker in the dye-factories made 500, a chemical engineer 1200.

Actually, the law stated that there was a maximum wage of 400 marks for a soccer player. After all, sporting clubs were legally defined as 'institutions for the common good', not companies who employed professionals. Heinz Höher got the extra payments from club official Peter Röger, stuffed into little brown envelopes.

Other people might have said: not a bad life to be going along with. At 24 years of age, Heinz Höher didn't think much about how life was going to go along at all, one way or the other, when suddenly the life he had played himself so well into was blown apart by the founding of the Bundesliga.

'We need an all-German league to be able to compete at the international level' – so wrote national manager Sepp Herberger. That was in 1936, in a letter to Felix Linnemann, the official in charge of football in the Reich League of Physical Exercise.

Everywhere else in Europe, in England, in Spain, in Italy, everywhere that football was played passionately and excellently, the top clubs faced each other every weekend, and the players were treated as professionals so that they could prepare themselves accordingly. In Germany, 26 years after Herberger's plea, players still trained three times a week after work, and the best clubs still played in five separate regional divisions, whose top teams then met each summer, at the end of the season, in a knockout competition to establish the German champions.

The establishment of the Bundesliga was unavoidably delayed by the Second World War. But 17 years after the end of that war, in the land of the economic miracle, it was now being blocked by those favourite topics of German thought: money, and morality.

Germany had piled guilt high upon its head in the Second World War; out of this had come a national desire to just not risk any more bad moral moves. Even apolitical issues such as the founding of the Bundesliga were looked at through the lens of morality. 'The men from the age of the goalposts' was what people called those who warned against the Bundesliga. These men loudly insisted that if you introduced the idea of profits into their noble sport it would lead uncontrollably to materialistic decadence.

Herberger said, 'It makes me want to laugh when I hear these old-timers talking about how they brought their own goalposts onto the pitch, puffing out their chests about their own idealism. They only brought the goalposts out because there was no one else to do it for them. And they only didn't take money because there was no money there to take. That's the long and short of it.'

But even among the clubs and regional football federations, where Herberger's sense of urgency was perfectly well understood, many people still stood against the idea of a nationwide elite league. This was because the German Inland Revenue had declared that if football became a real profession in this new league, the clubs would of course have to pay tax, national insurance, pensions and so on like any other firm. Thus many initiatives between 1955 and 1960 came to grief thanks to the top clubs themselves: they wanted a Bundesliga – but they didn't want to pay for it.

In the face of all these reservations when the Bundesliga was founded on 28 July 1962, it passed the National Committee of the German Football Union with an overwhelming majority – and as the most tangled compromise imaginable. The new National League would begin in August 1963, but not with full professionals, rather with what they called 'licensed players'. These were completely different from actual professionals, claimed the founders of the Bundesliga: they were only sort of a little bit professional. In order to set this idea in stone, the German Football Union set the maximum wage of these so-called licensed players at 1200 marks. The maximum transfer fee was set at 50,000 marks per player and no club was allowed to buy more than three players from other clubs.

The footballing officials proudly declared to their moral republic that this was the way to avoid a lunatic situation like that in Italy, where Modena had just offered the German international Albert Brülls an annual wage of 150,000 marks – and they hoped that they would thus persuade the Revenue to leave them in peace.

Heinz Höher interpreted the new situation to mean: the players would get significantly higher wages in the new Bundesliga, and on top of that they would surely also get significantly better backhanders on top.

There was just one problem: Bayer 04 Leverkusen weren't going to make it into the new Bundesliga. You could see that even eight months before it began. Forty-four clubs had applied for the 16 places. Leverkusen wouldn't make the cut because until June 1962 they had only played in the second division of the old system. Heinz Höher told himself that he'd stick with Bayer 04 and try to get promoted next year. Sometimes, he even believed himself.

He was almost 25. That was no age to be going off on adventures. Looking at things realistically, he had maybe five years left in top-flight football. Only the clever and wise were still playing on after 30.

If he'd been 20, he could have changed clubs. In the inaugural game at Bayer's new stadium on the Bismarckstraße in 1958, he had sown panic in the ranks of the Kaiserslautern defenders, and by way of rewarding himself for this grand performance, when the final whistle came, he deliberately made sure that he ended up near to Kaiserslautern's World Cup medal-winning star Fritz Walter. The way he'd played that day, for once in his life he could talk to the great man as star to star. Maybe Fritz Walter would even pay him a compliment.

Do you fancy playing for us? asked Fritz.

Heinz Höher felt like he was floating on air.

Fritz Walter's offer was one of the greatest moments of his career. But Heinz Höher never got round to taking it up. It was enough for him to know that he was getting offers.

Switching clubs was something for members of the national team who got Italian gold thrown at them, or for chancers who couldn't walk down their own home town streets any more – though everyone was saying that this would all change now the Bundesliga was founded. Well-off clubs would lure the best players from Bremen to Nuremberg or from Saarbrücken to Braunschweig. But why would he bother, he asked himself? In Leverkusen he had everything, after all: friends, family, his Doris (who very few people knew about still); he had his bed made for him, plenty of money, the admiring glances of the girls in the City Bar and the captain's armband on Sundays in the stadium.

If you bump my backhander up from 5000 to 12,000, I'll stay, he would jovially declare to Bayer's chairman Peter Röger as they had their first beer in the Gasthaus Krahne after weekday training. His fellow players didn't drink as much as they had done three or four years ago, and in one of his letters to himself, Heinz Höher too had resolved: 'No alcohol for two days before a game from now on, and generally take great care of hydration!'

'No woman the day before a game!' he also wrote underneath.

Heini, I hear what you're saying, but we can't pay you 12,000 cash in hand, said Röger. And soon afterwards, the club took an official stand on the matter: Bayer 04 were not going to be throwing money at their players just because some other clubs were bankrupting themselves for the new Bundesliga. And that applied to all players, even to their captain, their amateur international, the hero of the club who wore the number seven.

Being turned down like that doesn't bother me, Heinz Höher told himself. If they don't want me any more, fine, I go. No one would notice any anger in him, he swore to himself, he was bigger then they were.

While Heinz Höher was wondering how best to go about changing clubs, he remembered the day half a year ago, in June 1962, when he walked into the empty house in the Moltkestraße. His mother was out at church or somewhere else, and she had left a note for him on top of the shoe-rack in the hall:

My darling Heini,
  There's a fish in the fridge. Put it in the water with the lemon. When the water boils, it's ready. I hope you can manage that.
Letters up in your room.
  Mother

He'd grabbed the post from his room before he cooked the fish. There in his hand was a letter with a foreign stamp. It was from FC Metz, addressing itself to him on an A5 sheet of paper with a red letterhead that looked like the bill from a restaurant. They'd seen him playing for the German Amateur XI against France in Merlebach, said the letter, and would be glad to interest him in an engagement with them. 'Please be so kind as to inform us if you would be interested in coming to France and joining FC Metz as a professional, and if so under what conditions.'

He kept the letter as proud evidence of his class and never answered. Now, eight months later, he was angry with himself for having being so impolite.

He couldn't sit around waiting for another letter like that to come, he had to take active steps to find a new club. There was no way he could stay at Leverkusen now; he talked to Manglitz and that nutter Klima about it: Bayer 04 wasn't going to raise their pay or their back-handers either, even though they'd said that they were ready to stay in Leverkusen in the second divison and give up on the dream to play in the newly established Bundesliga. Right then, we're off, they'd said: Manfred Manglitz, the keeper, and Uwe Klimachefski, the half-back. He'd have to go too, then.

Heinz Höher sent an application to Bayern Munich. On tour with the German Amateur National team he'd got to know one of Bayern's players, Werner Olk. He asked him to get his letter to Wilhelm Neudecker, club president of Bayern. A few days afterwards, Heinz Höher received a letter from Munich.

Munich, 5 February 1963

Dear Mr Höher,

Our professional player Mr Werner Olk has forwarded us your most friendly letter.

In my capacity as president of FC Bayern Munich, and following discussions with the chairman of our players' committee as well as with our manager Mr Schneider, I am able now to inform you that we would be delighted to have you as a member of our team.

Sadly, the conditions for entry into the new Bundesliga are most challenging for us, too. On the other hand, I am convinced that even if we are not accepted for this coming season we will soon play ourselves up into the top league.

I suggest that we take up this conversation in a few weeks' time once the situation has cleared itself up.

With sporting greetings
Wilhelm Neudecker

Heinz Höher felt a bit better straight away. Other teams still rated him. But Neudecker was right. It was by no means certain that Bayern Munich would be accepted into the new Bundesliga. People were saying that each city was going to be permitted only one team in the new league, and the strongest team in Munich was TSV 1860. Heinz Höher decided to see if he couldn't find a better place to go than Bayern Munich.

The summer before, an opponent at Wuppertal tried to persuade him to come over to them. He was called Erich Ribbeck. He could at least go and take a look. Heinz Höher went as a spectator to a training session at Wuppertal. After a short time, he started to wonder how he could disappear again without being noticed. Zapf Gebhardt, their manager, was getting the players to run laps. With medicine balls under their arms. What century was he living in?

Six months before the start of the Bundesliga, looking for a new club was an exciting pastime for Heinz Höher, and one which was perfectly suited for carrying out during his alleged visits to Cologne University. He sat in the café near the cathedral, studied the pages of *Kicker* or *Das Sport Magazin*, and asked himself which club could use an inside-forward like him, with a great dribble and an accurate pass. It had been snowing in the Bergisches Land, training was still largely cancelled, it gave him the feeling that the summer, and the Bundesliga, were still way off.

The snow was sensational. Snow in the Bergisches Land, when had they last had that? The innocent beauty of the fields covered in that white sheet drove people crazy. They simply had to get out and feel the snow. Come on, let's go skiing, said his sister-in-law, Ruth. Heinz Höher was immediately up for it. Even though he didn't own any skis, or know how to ski.

There was an old pair of skis in the cellar at Heinz Wachtmeister's place. Wachtmeister's parents ran the patisserie on the Ebertplatz, since they came from Soest to Leverkusen after the war. They'd been forced to rent the cellar-bar underneath it into the bargain. They didn't let anyone see how insulted they were that established master pastry-chefs like them were being forced to run a mere pub. That pub turned out to be the salvation of them. Leverkusen was a tough place for a patisserie. The few citizens who thought themselves important enough to sit in a patisserie putting the world to rights over coffee and cake thought so much of themselves that they went to Cologne to do it. But

their little goldmine, as Wachtmeister's dad christened the pub, did a
roaring trade.

When you walked into the bar, the smoke bit into your eyes. Card-
players narrowed their eyes as they smoked their cigarettes without
using their hands. They needed their hands to smack down a trump on
the table. At the bar you could always find Mac Scheller, correspondent
of the Western Germany radio station. It was he who had taught Heinz
Höher that the whole point of beer was to sober oneself up again after
a decent session on the schnapps. I shall now sober myself up again
with beer, said Mac Scheller, who could put away 70 small glasses of
beer when he was really working at sobering up.

Heinz Wachtmeister, the pastry cooks' son, was one of those young
people in Leverkusen who weren't spectators of football any more but
now called themselves *Fans*. Heinz Wachtmeister and a dozen or so
other young men even went together to Bayer's away games. 'Bravo
Heini!' they would shout after one of his sweetly struck passes, and
Heinz Höher would look around in astonishment: who could that be,
shouting out his name?

He borrowed Wachtmeister's skis. They were made of wood, and by
the look of them, they hadn't been used for at least 15 years. The bind-
ings were leather straps. Even though the hills of the Sauerland were
closer, his brother Manfred and Manfred's wife Ruth insisted that they
should drive to the Westerwald. If they were going on a trip for once,
they might as well do it properly.

After an hour and a half's drive they reached the top of the hill. The
trees were dripping wet. The snow stuck, soft and soggy, to their shoes.
On the piste, which was hardly 300 metres long, you could see a few
brown-green patches of grass poking through.

But it had been an effort to come here. So now they would just give
it a go.

Heinz Höher got about 50 metres, maybe 150, he couldn't exactly
tell at which point he stopped kind-of skiing, and started just tumbling
down the slope. One way or another, when he finally came to rest, flat
on his back, he couldn't get up again.

The doctor said he'd been lucky: he'd only hyper-extended the ligaments in his right knee, not torn them. But when Heinz Höher went
back into training with Bayer Leverkusen three weeks later he wished
those ligaments had actually been torn. Because then he could have
taken the time to really recuperate. That would surely have been

better than this weird feeling that he was playing football while some-thing just wasn't right.

His burst out of the blocks was gone. In football, just being fast is nothing, being able to run a good 100m time isn't what matters, it's being able to hit that explosive burn in a fraction of a second. Whoever has that, gets to the ball first, or passes it fastest – and wins.

After his skiing accident, Heinz Höher trained like a madman to get his killer burst back. He loved training hard, loved the feeling after-wards that he had done everything he could so that he could drink a couple of beers and a shot without a guilty conscience.

He had a punchball in the cellar. Although he hardly ever turned up to his sports degree at Cologne these days, he'd already got to know training methods from various sports in the first semesters. His fists drummed on the punchball, his feet danced this way and that, and being a boxer in his imagination gave him wings. When he was playing football, he always felt worried when he wasn't on the ball. If he had the ball, he feared no one on earth, he would take it and dribble it straight at the toughest defender, he felt that he was the boss. But when he wasn't on the ball, when he was supposed to have a go at an opponent, he always felt this fear that the duel was going to hurt him.

His body was soon in great shape. But that kick-start eluded him. Or was he just imagining it? These days, when *Kicker* reported on Leverkusen's games, he was basically just another name in the team line-up. How would he ever get noticed by another club if his name was never in the papers?

Heinz Höher heard that Bayer Leverkusen's old trainer Raymond Schwab had a new job. This career was so new in Germany that it didn't even have a name yet. The broadsheet *Die Zeit* ran a 200-line article in which it attempted to enlighten its educated readers about this latest curiosity from the world of modern sport: there, it described Schwab as a 'football trader'. By now there were three men in Germany who made their living as football traders.

'What precisely does your business involve?' *Die Zeit* asked Schwab.

'I find clubs for players, and players for clubs.'

'Are you busy?'

'My phone never stops ringing.'

'Is it a good business to be in?'

'If a contract's signed I get a modest percentage. My overheads are high.'

Raymond Schwab, who wore his black hair combed back wit in the proper fashion, had tried his luck after the war as a boxing moter. In those days, it was no great leap from setting up box matches to managing a top soccer team. A sports teacher was suppose to be a master of all trades and Schwab's greatest talent could be deployed anywhere: he could really talk the talk. In 1951, when he was manager at Leverkusen, he'd cut an innovative deal about a bonus for achieving promotion: if he got Bayer 04 into the first division, there would be a benefit match for which he would choose the opponents and from which he would take the gate money. Leverkusen went up, and played that benefit match against Schalke 04. Schwab stuffed a good 5000 marks in his pockets, half a year's wage, and handed in his notice.

Shortly afterwards, Schwab founded a new export business: German footballers for Italy. As early as 1952 he sent Karl-Heinz Spikofski to Catania and Horst Buhtz to AC Turin.

'Human traffic', that's what it was, raged the German national man-ager, Herberger. For Heinz Höher, it was a bit of luck. Within a few weeks, Schwab had found a club interested in him, Stuttgart. Not that it was necessary to actually call yourself an agent in order to act as a go-between for footballers. All you had to do was sit down in the evening after your day's work with the sports magazine in front of you, highlight the most interesting players, and sit down at your typewriter.

'Dear Mr Höher,' wrote a certain Hans-Günther Wolf to him from Saarbrücken, keeping it, as any decent agent well might, to elegant hints: 'I possess excellent contacts to a team in Saarbrücken which is currently seeking a few players. Please take this letter as an invitation to consider whether you might possibly be interested in changing your club. Arrangements would be made for the furtherance of your career.'

Saarbrücken's interest in him, however, ended after their first meet-ing. In a letter of six lines, Rainer Lehnhof, their chief executive, respectfully informed Heinz Höher that 'our club is determined to fulfil the legal statutes concerning licensed professionals and is there-fore not in a position to meet your financial demands.' You could talk about backhanders as openly as that, without actually saying the word.

Stuttgart, on the other hand, were seriously interested in Heinz Höher. On 9 March 1963, their vice-chairman Konrad Rieker announced in a letter to Höher that a representative of the club would attend the first division match between Leverkusen and Schalke. Rieker's secretary, who typed up his letters, wasn't quite sure how to spell his first name: sometimes she spelt Konrad with a C, sometimes with a K. Well, Christian names didn't matter much, in football: Mr Vice-president Rieker's letters went off to Honoured Mr Höher and never ended without sporting greetings.

Would you go with me to Stuttgart? Heinz Höher asked this question during a walk in the city park to a young lady whose name, Doris, was now linked with his in Leverkusen. Even though she still wasn't wearing an engagement ring, it seemed okay for her to visit him in the Moltkestraße. His mother acted as though she just didn't notice anything.

He'd suddenly appeared before her one lunch-hour in the works canteen at Bayer. Of course she knew who he was. She's already seen him when he was a boy in Saint Hildegarde's church. Doris worked in sales at Bayer, her dad worked there too, her family lived in one of the rented flats belonging to the dye-works. Her figure was so gracious that they had once asked her to do some modelling work for a Bayer advertisement.

She never wanted to leave Leverkusen. And now he was asking her to go to Stuttgart. Doris swallowed hard. Then she said yes and it felt as though she was saying 'I do'.

Leverkusen drew 0-0 with Schalke. Heinz Höher was roundly booed by the fans, some of whom thought he'd been going over the top with his endless dribbling, and some of whom thought he'd just been standing about doing nothing.

After the game he waited expectantly, day by day, for news from Stuttgart, and at the same time feared to hear that news. His brother Manfred already had a phone installed in the bed-shop on the high street. But VfB Stuttgart never got in touch.

Schwab, the football trader, could have quickly found out what the problem was. But Heinz Höher didn't call him. He was too ashamed of his poor performance against Schalke. After 14 days, he couldn't stand it any more. He wrote to vice-president Rieker, in order to apologise very politely for his inadequate play against Schalke. He wrote that he could not hold it against Rieker if Stuttgart's interest in him had faded after that sad display, but wished to also to point out to Rieker that it had simply been one of those inexplicable days, when his legs would not obey the orders of his brain.

He never got furious with anything so much as with himself. 'Have you already forgotten,' he wrote to himself, 'the vows you made on 12 September 1959 when you felt your face grow red and the floor sink away beneath your feet before the Olympic qualification game against East Germany because you didn't make the team-sheet?

1) don't stand there looking about from right to left!
2) get stuck into every game as though it were an international!
3) put on muscle in every training session!'

He would show them all, next Sunday against Wuppertal. He even considered stopping going to the pub every evening from Monday till Thursday. But then, he only drank a couple of beers and a shot while playing cards.

Leverkusen lost 4-2 to Wuppertal, the fans booed, and at the end of the week he got his answer from Konrad Rieker:

Dear fellow-sportsman Höher,
    I was delighted to get your friendly letter of 2 April 1963 and even more pleased to see in it your openness and self-criticism. It was indeed this which most impressed me in your note.

Rieker went on to explain that there was a very good reason why Heinz Höher had had no news from Stuttgart since the announcement that their representative would visit the game against Schalke. The mother of Mr Schnaitmann, Stuttgart's chairman of the team committee, had sadly passed away the day before the intended journey up west and Mr Schnaitmann had accordingly been obliged to postpone his visit.

VfB Stuttgart, said the letter, continued to have a lively interest in winning him for their team. It was a principle of the club that it would not allow itself to be influenced either in a positive or negative way by variations in performance within a single game, on the contrary, it judged things on the basis of ability and constant achievement. 'Both of which you demonstrate, for it would be impossible otherwise to explain your presence in the German national amateur team and in the senior league team at Bayer Leverkusen.' In order to explain precisely the plans of the gentlemen from Stuttgart, Konrad Rieker would shortly be getting in touch once again by telephone.

Doris didn't ask again how things stood with the move to Stuttgart. Her own home life had told her that it was usually easier if you just said yes and waited to see what happened.

The season was coming to an end and in three months the Bundesliga would begin. Rieker kept on holding out the prospect of visits from the gentleman from Stuttgart, but these were always put off again. Höher heard nothing more from Bayern Munich, and he didn't ask, either. As the third best team in their region, after FC Nuremberg and 1860 Munich, Bayern were not making the cut for the Bundesliga and hence bound to play in the second division.

On the occasion of Leverkusen's final game of the 1962-63 season, against Aachen, Ernst Schnaitmann from Stuttgart did indeed condescend to observe Höher's play.

Heinz Höher often felt that he had played badly on occasions when everybody else was impressed. It was the footballers' disease: as elite sportsmen, the goal they set themselves was to achieve perfection every time. Two or three little mistakes in a game loomed larger to them than an otherwise perfectly fine performance. But against Aachen, Heinz Höher was satisfied with himself, even though they lost 2-1. He had created a couple of really sweet moments.

On 21 May 1963, ten days after that game, Konrad Rieker wrote him a brief, clear note: 'Having taken into consideration all the questions and possibilities, VfB Stuttgart has now come to the conclusion that it would not be possible to create the satisfactory preconditions for your move.'

But hadn't he had a good game against Aachen?

It was only much later that he heard on the footballing grapevine just what Schaitmann had reported back to Stuttgart: Höher, he said, had run himself offside at least five times. They already had plenty of players as thick as that down in Stuttgart.

The last season of the old first division was at an end. Heinz Höher said farewell to his team-mates.

Who are you shifting to?

Nothing's certain yet.

Oh, come on, what crazy offers are they making you?

Heinz Höher just smiled.

He lay late in bed, trained with his punchball in the cellar, waited in the park by the swimming pool for Doris to knock off work, and in the evenings he played cards in the gold-mine or at the back of old Schramm's bakery. And so the weeks passed – weeks in which not a single team made any approach to him. In Heinz Höher's own opinion, one of his great strengths was his ability to hide feelings such as despair from everyone else.

Just a few days before the start of the new season, Heinz Höher, who in everyone else's opinion took life as it came in an incredibly laid-back way, was approached by SV Meiderich. To everybody's surprise, this team from a suburb of Duisburg had just been awarded a place in the Bundesliga.

Legally speaking, Leverkusen had no right to a transfer fee because Höher was still theoretically an amateur, but when they started cutting up rough about the move, a creative solution to the problem was found. Meiderich also signed up Leverkusen's talented keeper, Manfred Manglitz – and paid double for him.

Heinz Höher suggested that Manglitz, who lived in Cologne, could bring him to the training sessions, and thus save their new team some travel money. Meiderich's chairman, Walter Schmidt, took up the suggestion with enthusiasm: what a very sensible footballer! Heinz Höher did not feel it necessary to explain to Schmidt or Manglitz why exactly he wanted a lift-share into the Bundesliga. He'd lost his licence for six months for being drunk at the wheel.

Meiderich manager Rudi Gutendorf climbs onto World Cup winner Helmut Rahn, and one team plus 5000 supporters watch in astonishment: so this is modern training.

Year Zero:

THE LANDLORD'S TEAM

For his first training session at SV Meiderich, new manager Rudi Gutendorf brought two things with him with which to impress team and spectators alike: a fast car and an overweight centre-forward.

Stone me, thought keeper Manfred Manglitz when he saw Gutendorf roll up in a shining white Mercedes 190 SE with red leather upholstery. The spectators shuffled back, as if forming up in guard of honour for Gutendorf. It was a warm day in the hot July of 1963, which was making up for the dreadful summer the year before, the coolest summer in 111 years, when only one day had reached over 25°C. What a beast to turn up to Meiderich, this working-class town, in a Mercedes, thought Manglitz. He liked people who had it and flaunted it. He himself always played wearing the latest fashion in caps.

It smells weird here, thought Heinz Höher, who had set off extra early with Manglitz so as not to be late on the first day. Heinz Höher asked himself if it really smelt so strongly in Leverkusen too, it must do, what with all the fumes that Bayer sent up into the air. But it had never troubled him at all. It was just the way things were.

A few minutes after Gutendorf turned up in his sports car, the curious onlookers in the stadium car park surged forward once again. Another Mercedes was turning into the car park from the Westender Straße. Gutendorf's mighty new centre-forward had appeared: the Boss was here.

As Helmut Rahn climbed out of his car, the crowd saw a man who looked older than you should at 34, his skin creased, heavy-set. But the crowds, and his new team-mates, still saw in him the man they all wanted to see: the Helmut Rahn who, nine years before, in the World Cup final against Hungary, had fired in the long-range goal that sealed Germany's 3-2 victory.

I'm actually sitting next to Helmut Rahn, thought Horst Gecks to himself as he sat in the changing room. Gecks was a 20-year-old fly-weight winger, only 5 foot 9 and 9 stone, and even in his thoughts, he only dared to whisper it: I am sitting next to Helmut Rahn. Apart from a single 31-year-old defender, they were all at least 10 years younger than Rahn. As boys, they had watched, wide eyed, as he scored *that* goal in 1954, that moment when radio reporter Herbert Zimmermann shouted the words which made the young West Germany actually feel, for the very first time, like a real nation: 'Rahn's way out, but surely he must shoot, he shoots . . . Goooaaaal!'

Heinz Höher had stood, 16 years of age, in front of the Birkhäuser pub, trying to get a peek through the window at the television screen; the pub was packed for the broadcast of the World Cup final. Helmut Rahn would never be just their team-mate. He would always be their hero too.

The fact that at 34 years old Rahn clearly had his heroic days behind him was neither here nor there. The Boss was still the Boss.

But really, the Bundesliga came too late for the world champions of 1954. Fritz Walter worked as a representative for Adidas, his brother Ottmar Walter had transformed himself into the owner of a petrol station with the merry advertising jingle: 'If you want to thank Ottmar, tank with Ottmar!' Apart from Helmut Rahn only three of the World Cup-winning side were still playing: Hans Schäfer at Cologne, Max Morlock at Nuremberg and Heinz Kwiatkowski as reserve keeper at Dortmund.

The Bundesliga felt like a new beginning: it was a place for new names, a new age.

In Meiderich, the club committee was considering whether they could demand a mark to watch training sessions. They swiftly abandoned the idea for fear of provoking a popular uprising. In Meiderich, a town of 70,000 inhabitants separated from Duisburg only by the Wedau river, the players worked side by side with the spectators at the Phoenix Rheinrohre steelworks. The club could never allow itself to forget just how hard the spectators worked for their money.

Nevertheless, the committee still felt gloomy at the thought of the money they could have made, with a little effort, in those first three training sessions. The year before, Meiderich had played their games before an average crowd of 8500. Now 5000 fans were making the pilgrimage to an ordinary training session, to feel the new era and to see the Boss.

Gutendorf's first training exercise was to make the players run the length of the pitch together, 100 metres there, 100 metres back. And they all had to do it while playing keep-up with the ball. None of them had ever seen an exercise like it.

Under Gutendorf's predecessor Willy Multhaup, Tuesday training at Meiderich had simply consisted of playing ten against ten over the full pitch. On Wednesdays, centre-forward Werner Krämer came begging to him, saying, Guv, it was 14-15 yesterday, go on please, let's play with the same teams again, we want to have our revenge. Well okay, Multhaup had sighed. So for the whole of every week they simply played. Multhaup wandered about on the touchline and chatted with the watching pensioners. On Sundays, he would appear at the match sporting a monocle, cufflinks, and shoes of Italian leather. Willy Multhaup, born right at the start of the 20th century, was one of the most successful and most highly regarded managers in Germany.

Gutendorf was 37 years old and last year, as manager of Marl-Hüls, he had achieved bottom of the table in the Western Region of the first division. But at his interview, he had impressed Mr Dr Schmidt, chairman of Meiderich, with his youthful energy, his modern ideas, and his air of a man of the world. He had already worked in Switzerland, and, at the behest of the German Foreign Ministry, in Tunisia, as a track-suited aid-worker. Gutendorf then had to take a walk, while Mr Dr Schmidt reported back to the rest of the board about their applicant. There followed dinner in the zum Marienbildchen restaurant, during which, as per old footballing tradition, Gutendorf's contract was written out on the back of a menu. When nothing was left on the table except the empty glasses, Gutendorf demanded that an extra clause be inserted on the menu. If they won the Bundesliga he would get a bonus of 100,000 marks; if they came second he'd get 30,000.

Mr Gutendorf, said Mr Dr Schmidt, we'll be happy if we just don't go down, and he wrote the clause in, because it really was a good joke.

Then Gutendorf persuaded them to sign up Helmut Rahn.

But, argued Mr Dr Schmidt, you've already signed up a first-class inside-right, Heinz Höher.

It wasn't a question of getting a first-class forward, said Gutendorf, and took a deep breath: what they needed was an attraction, someone whose name would make the air crackle with energy, who would make the whole of Germany look wonderingly at this unknown little place called Meiderich, someone who would fill the stadium for them.

The committee was impressed. This manager had a new way of looking at things.

'At first I was against signing up Rahn, not, be it noted, on sporting grounds,' said Mr Dr Schmidt to the journalists who surrounded him as he presented Rahn to the public. The reporters sniggered at the little phrase 'not, be it noted, on sporting grounds'. Rahn's liking for a drink was part of his legend.

'But,' Mr Dr Schmidt continued, 'of the sixteen clubs in the Bundesliga we are, well, let's put it carefully, certainly not the most prominent. So we had to do something to, now, how shall I put it, take us up a notch.'

The Bundesliga made Meiderich part of the big wide world. Rahn, Höher and Manglitz were the first players they'd ever brought in from outside their own home patch. They came from a radius of 75km, from Essen, Cologne, Leverkusen. Up until then, everyone who had ever played for Meiderich had come from Obermeiderich, Mittelmeiderich or, possibly, the neighbouring town of Hamborn.

Horst Gecks, the fleet-footed left-winger from Mittelmeiderich, had played handball until 16 years of age. It was only in the summer holidays that he walked each day the three kilometres to Meiderich's training ground. There, the kids were allowed to play out the rough-and-tumble street championship of Meiderich: Kanalstraße versus Gelderblomstraße, Weizenkamp versus Herbststraße. The landlord of the club-house bar, Hugo Hesselmann, stood in his doorway and watched them play.

The training ground was made from rough cinder. Horst Gecks tore his legs to shreds. At night, his grazes wept and stuck fast to his bed-sheets. And the next day he played again. One day, the landlord spoke to him. He should have a try for Meiderich. The landlord was the talent scout for the club and he himself trained their first youth XI. With Gecks, Danzberg, Heidemann, Lotz, Nolden, Krämer, Versteeg, 20 men who almost all knew each other from school, and who had almost all gone through youth training with the landlord, Meiderich stormed into the Bundesliga. Some people found it hard to believe.

'Where exactly is Meiderich?' national captain Uwe Seeler asked. Alemannia Aachen went to the courts to contest Meiderich's nomination for the new elite league. How on earth could this ramshackle suburban club be preferred over Alemannia, with its rich tradition?

Even Meiderich's players were soon repeating Aachen's conspiracy theories as though they were facts: defender Dieter Danzberg told the story of how the Aachen crowd had once poured a pint over the head of Franz Kremer, president of FC Cologne and an influential figure in creating the Bundesliga. 'After that,' claimed Danzberg, 'Kremer told our president: "I'm not having that Aachen lot in the Bundesliga. If you can make third place in the regional league, I give you my guarantee that it'll be Meiderich that get into the Bundesliga!"'

No doubt the truth was more prosaic. The German football commission which decided the 16 places in the Bundesliga tried, in the finest bureaucratic way, to please every regional federation. In the Lower Rhine Football Union, Meiderich, the club from a suburb of Duisburg, was demonstrably the strongest club in sporting terms. Alemannia Aachen was part of the Middle Rhine Football Union, and that meant they were up against FC Cologne.

The choice of clubs for the Bundesliga inevitably led to injustices. FC Saarbrücken were let in because they were the only well-known and halfway financially viable team in the Federal State of Saarland, though they could only make fifth place in the regional league, even in the sparsely inhabited south-west. Bayern Munich didn't make the cut: they were above Stuttgart, Karlsruhe and Eintracht Frankfurt in the Southern Region, but their third place in that division still meant that they were only the third strongest Bavarian team. The whole point was to ensure that the new top-flight division should be born as a genuine league of the whole country, not as a league of the teams which happened to be best at that moment.

On Friday, 23 August 1963, the Meiderich team met at the Hauptbahnhof in Duisburg. They had 17 second-class tickets to Karlsruhe waiting for them. With the 14 players travelled the manager, the head of the match committee and the physio. If any player were to be seriously injured, the SC Karlsruhe team doctor would look after him. All the clubs in the Bundesliga had made a gentleman's agreement that the home doctor would also look after the visiting players in case of need, because after all you couldn't expect doctors to go up and down the whole length of the country every weekend, doctors were busy people. And in any case you hardly ever needed doctors. When Manglitz the keeper dislocated a finger while stopping a shot at the very first training session in Duisburg, manager Gutendorf went up to him, took one look at his dangling finger and yanked it back into place with a single jerk. Stone me! thought Manglitz. And for the next few weeks he kept on training as an outfield player.

Heinz Höher loved the trips when the team set off on the day before a game. It always gave him the feeling that something special, something grand was coming up. Up till now, he'd only made journeys like this to amateur international or junior international games. In the Western First Division, they had always just driven to the away stadium on the bus, got out and warmed up.

On the train to Karlsruhe, the other passengers were knocking on the window of their compartment all the way. 'Helmut Rahn, it's Helmut Rahn!' The Meiderich team spent the night in a family-run B&B in Karlsruhe.

One of the players had bought the *Neue Ruhr Zeitung* along to read on the journey, and Heinz Höher took a look inside. The *NRZ* was a paper with a fresh, open feel; it printed investigative reports and caused much shaking of heads among experienced journalists by sometimes even carrying interviews with football managers. How could one give so many column inches, and so much importance, to the words of such uncultured men? On the occasion of the start of the Bundesliga the *NRZ* published an open letter to the teams in the new league:

Dear Bundesliga clubs

It is with great pleasure that we note that most of you are in an optimistic frame of mind, rather than in mourning for the time when players carried the goal-posts onto the pitch themselves and the box office receipts were counted up in a soup-dish. Farewell, farewell, we leave all that to the good old real amateurs!

The name of the game is realism. In the future, more must be done to attract the greatest possible number of spectators (aka money). Up until now, the way the top clubs advertise themselves has been like something out of the footballing Middle Ages. You've relied on the eager press, you've covered advertising hoardings with posters which have hardly changed in their layout for 50 years.

A change in this respect, too, would be practical and therefore to be recommended. You club bosses, take a look around abroad for once to see the way they do it there!

Visit clubs in England, in Italy, in Spain!

That's where we'll all learn what it means to have professional football at our clubs. So it's all aboard for tomorrow's opening of the Bundesliga! We've all helped create it and we'll be right there at the front when it comes to getting over the problems of this first part of the season.

Sincerely

NRZ

Horst Gecks, the flyweight winger, wasn't in the line-up, so he drove to Karlsruhe next day in his car, together with four fans from Meiderich. The club gave him two complimentary tickets; the other three fans had to buy their own, 6.50 marks to sit in the uncovered stand.

Half of the team were fated to be mere spectators at each game. Only 11 players were needed. The only back-up that made the journey with them was a second keeper plus one defensive and one attacking substitute in case one of the starting 11 should get sick or fall down the hotel steps. But if nothing unforeseen happened, those three players just sat the game out in the stands. Substitutions were forbidden.

For a long time, people had been debating whether it might at least be allowed to replace the keeper in case of a serious injury. But that would destroy the purity of the sport. If the keeper got injured, he went out and staggered about as best he could while an outfield player took his place in goal. Once, Heinz Höher was so badly fouled in an Olympic qualification game that it split him open to the raw shinbone, and national manager Georg Gawliczek yelled: if you go off the pitch it'll be me who operates on you and I'll do it right here! The blood poured from Höher's leg but he kept on running and saw the whole game out for fear of Gawliczek.

In the weeks leading up to the start of the first season of the Bundesliga, Manfred Manglitz and Heinz Höher often put on the kind of cynicism that footballers frequently mistake for coolness: on their drives to the training sessions they declared to each other that if only those idiots in Leverkusen had paid up, they'd have stayed. I mean, what was so special about this new Bundesliga? But on Saturday, 24 August, shortly before 5 o'clock, in the floodlit Wildpark stadium in Karlsruhe, no one could say that any more. Over 40,000 spectators packed the ground for the first match of the Bundesliga. In Leverkusen, in the old, regional first division, it had been like Christmas if they played in front of 20,000.

The Meiderich team almost all wore boots made by Hummel. This sporting goods firm from Kevelaer had promised 25 marks to every player who put on their boots for the first game of the Bundesliga. Heinz Höher found that the Hummel boots fitted badly. He wanted to wear his usual Adidas boots, but he didn't want to give up on the 25 marks. For more than an hour he sat in his hotel room and scratched the Adidas stripes off his boots with scissors and a file, then glued the Hummel logo on them.

In the changing room he naturally stole glances in the direction of Helmut Rahn. His gaze was drawn to Rahn's lower legs. The Boss wasn't putting on shinpads. I never bother, said Rahn, they just put me off.

The match-ball was black and white. An invention made for the sake of television. The old brown leather ball was harder to see on the box.

The Meiderich players weren't sure whether or not television was going to show a report of the game, maybe they would because of Helmut Rahn. People said there was going to be a new programme on Channel 2 called *Aktuelles Sportstudio*, maybe they'd be able to catch it somewhere in a pub before taking the night train home.

If those Karlsruhe blokes say hello in the tunnel before the game, just glare back at them! were Gutendorf's last words to them before the whistle, or maybe he actually said it before a different game, his players could never remember exactly, but they recalled that Gutendorf always had some words of wisdom, or some order like that, ready at the tip of his tongue.

There was nobody who could realistically judge the respective strengths of Karlsruhe and Meiderich before the game, because the two teams, playing in the South and West divisions respectively, had simply never met before. But after a few minutes of play even someone who knew nothing about football could see that the team everyone had tipped as the most likely for relegation was simply too good for Karlsruhe. Meiderich were all over them. Werner Krämer, the inside-right, and Heinz Höher, the inside-left, made mazy runs, passed out to the wings, offered themselves by return of post for the one-two into free space, took the ball on and dribbled goalwards. If either of them sat back for a moment the fans thought they were just taking a rest for once. But then they would suddenly knife a pass from deep to split the Karlsruhe defence in two. After 37 minutes the score was 0-3. Werner Krämer had made a thundering solo run to score Meiderich's first ever goal in the Bundesliga and the Boss had converted a through-ball from Heinz Höher for the third. Helmut Rahn was playing outside-right, a position which in theory involved a heavy load of running, but he only took part in the game at chosen moments and when he stood there afterwards, breathing heavily, his little bit of a belly could clearly be seen. But when he actually played you could see that however much a footballer's form may come and go, class will always be class.

Up in the press-box, *Kicker*'s reporter, Waldemar Rink, seemed to take personal offence. 'The men from Karlsruhe,' he wrote, 'played like they'd taken the day off sick.'

Meiderich again grabbed the initiative in the second half. Every time Werner Krämer's opposite number, Rolf Kahn, tried to move up into an attacking role, Krämer just said thank you for the extra space this left; no sooner had Kahn come forward, the Karlsruhe attack broke down, the ball was lost and was heading back, via Krämer, towards the Karlsruhe goal. Kahn's signature gesture of frustration, a show of the teeth above his jutting chin, only became famous decades later, in the person of his son Oliver, the German international goalkeeper, who inherited his father's angrily grinding lower jaw.

At the final whistle it was 4-1. Werner Krämer, who no one called Werner, they all just shouted Eia, had scored twice. 'Krämer directed the game brilliantly while also acting as goalscorer with a mighty shot, with excellent support from the blond-haired Höher,' wrote Rink in *Kicker*. 'Höher's technical brilliance was convincing,' declared the upmarket *Süddeutsche Zeitung*, which had deigned to run a report of the match to mark the start of the Bundesliga. Heinz Höher got his share of praise from all sides. But he himself did not share the general enthusiasm about his showing. On the outside, everything seemed fine, but in his heart he was, for some mysterious reason, unhappy. Maybe it was because Gutendorf had played him out on the left wing, rather than the right, as if giving a signal that here in Meiderich, he was no longer the star he had been in Leverkusen, but just the supporting act for Krämer and Rahn? Or was it because of what happened when Sepp Herberger visited them in the dressing-room after the match?

Germany's manager congratulated each one of them individually, with a silent shake of the hand. To Heinz Höher, he spoke. 'Heinz,' he said, just that one word, with warmth in his voice, followed by a short smile and a squeeze of the hand, and off he was to the next man. It was no secret that Herberger was there to watch Eia Krämer. Heinz Höher couldn't suppress the thought: he won't be coming for your sake, ever again.

It had been back in 1958 when Sepp Herberger first invited Heinz Höher to come for training with the national team in Grünwald, and Höher had to get permission from his school to go. At 20 years of age, he was still in the upper sixth at the Carl-Duisberg-Gymnasium, because in the meantime he had tried to start two apprenticeships and broken them both off in boredom.

At the training camp with the national side in Grünwald they practised the basic techniques: heading a ball suspended on a rope, shooting with the instep, passing with the side of the foot, one repetition after the other. The only way to get better was by endless repetition, said Herberger. His assistant, Helmut Schön, threw the ball to Heinz Höher at waist height so he could practise volleying on the turn. Heinz Höher swivelled his body halfway around and took a mighty kick. He hit the ball cleanly mid-air with his instep and as he did so, the speed of his foot multiplied together with the speed of the ball and it blasted straight into the top corner of the net. Sepp Herberger took Heinz Höher by the shoulder. Your volley on the turn is the best of the lot, said the national manager. Heinz Höher was confused. Why was Herberger saying that? Albert Brülls had a far better volley on the turn.

Over the following days, as that sentence echoed about in his head, Heinz Höher thought he understood what it meant: Herberger thought a lot of him, Herberger was counting on him. In the evenings, alone in his room, that praise grew ever more significant in Heinz Höher's daydreams: maybe Herberger wanted to train him up to be Fritz Walter's successor!

On one of their free afternoons, they took a trip to the Zugspitze. At 9.15pm, their bus was going to pick them up from the ski station in Garmisch, at the foot of the mountain, and take them back to the training school. Three minutes before it left Heinz Höher climbed in, he'd been wandering through the place with another young player till the last minute. Look at that, said Herberger, the youngest ones come in last, yet again. Heinz Höher took it with an embarrassed smile. He hadn't actually been late, had he, he asked himself. As he clambered into his seat, he looked at his watch just to check. There was a bang. Herberger had smashed his fist on the window by his head.

How dare you look at your watch, roared Herberger, are you trying to be clever? I have never seen such cheek in all my life! What an arrogant lack of respect!

But the storm passed. Herberger named him for the international against Scotland in Glasgow on 6 May 1959.

Can I have your passport please, asked the general secretary of the German FA, Georg Xandry, at the training camp in Duisburg.

I've already sent it in to get a visa for the Under-21 international in Poland in two weeks' time, said Höher. He had his ID card with him.

Oh yes, of course, said Xandry, and took the ID card.

On the day of the flight, Xandry went to the Lufthansa desk at Düsseldorf airport, carrying the stack of passports, to book seats for the team. It didn't take long. When he came back he said now, there's a problem. They wouldn't let Heinz Höher into Great Britain without his actual passport. There was nothing he could do about it.

While the national team flew to Glasgow, Heinz Höher sat alone in the suburban train to Düsseldorf's historic city centre, had a couple of beers and a shot, and, while he was doing so, fell in with a group of 10 or 12 fashion models. He had a pretty good evening after all.

Heinz Höher continued to receive Herberger's round-robin letters to the national team ('Dear Comrades and Friends!') and was named in the 40-strong longlist for the 1962 World Cup in Chile. 'He liked you,' says Herberger's assistant coach Dettmar Cramer when he meets Heinz Höher again five decades later – they are now 88 and 74. 'He just loved your volley on the turn. He wanted someone who could do more than just run and battle.'

One particular image comes back into Cramer's mind: in the great Hall of Schloss Oberhausen, 1961, the amateur international teams from Germany and the Netherlands were sitting down to the obligatory banquet after an international game. For starters they had rolls of smoked ham stuffed with egg salad and asparagus, and after their steaks the pudding was Fürst Pückler Eis with cream. Of course, Cramer doesn't remember all that, but that's what it says on the heavyweight invitation card, embossed with the emblem of the German FA, which Heinz Höher has kept by him. After the meal, Herberger, Cramer and the Dutch manager sat down together to coffee and fine biscuits.

Your boy Höher, now there's someone I could do with, I haven't got anyone like him, he's something special, said the Dutch manager. Sepp Herberger turned to Cramer and said: See?

'He just wasn't quite sure that you had the mental strength,' says Dettmar Cramer, five decades later, to Heinz Höher.

After that first Bundesliga game in Karlsruhe in 1963, Heinz Höher had a sneaking suspicion of what Herberger had meant by a lack of mental strength. No matter how he tried, or how hard he trained, he could never get rid of that inconsistency in his performance.

Unlike everyone else at Karlsruhe that day, he didn't have the feeling that something great was just beginning. Herberger's visit had reminded him of what had already finished. Heinz Höher's international career ended after that first international against Scotland in which he never played.

But there you go, he said to himself, and now it was about time to go for a beer with the team.

The train back to Duisburg didn't leave Karlsruhe till 11pm. They had time for some fun, and they wanted it too. It was a big thing to be out so far from home, even Frankfurt was a foreign country to them, thought Manfred Manglitz, if we're in Karlsruhe for once let's see what it's got to offer. So they went to a whore-house.

'But we didn't do any whoring', says Manglitz.

In the brothel they were playing the latest hits, 'I want a cowboy for my husband', the players drank beer and laughed to hide their nervous excitement whenever the girls talked to them. The sports editors of the three local newspapers, which were reporting the Meiderich game, had come along with them. They belonged there. Their manager, Rudi Gutendorf, an authority on all aspects of life, took the chance to talk about prostitutes in Tunisia, ivory-skinned Arabesses and girls from central Africa with extended earlobes, their skin so dark that it shone blue. Let's just say, their manager explained, they were the most unbelievable whores.

He didn't just have ideas – he was alive with ideas: Wim Thoelke, first great presenter of *Das aktuelle Sportstudio*.

Meanwhile, Still in Year Zero:

THE SECRETARY PLAYS DISC-JOCKEY

In a barn in Eschborn, on the edge of the Taunus mountains, a railway station clock was ticking inexorably forward. At 9.20pm, while Meiderich's Bundesliga debutants were enjoying themselvs in a brothel, over half a million Germans were watching as the second-hand on the clock advanced. On the dot of the third beat of the accompanying jingle, the TV cameras swung from the station clock onto an advertising hoarding. This announced the international track-athletics competition between Great Britain and West Germany, the big horse-racing week at Iffezheim and the Bundesliga games in Saarbrücken, Frankfurt and Munich. And now the host, Heribert Meisel, was delighted to welcome his viewers to the first edition of *Das aktuelle Sportstudio*. They'd given him the barn at the edge of the Taunus as a temporary studio.

The railway station clock was supposed to show just how up to date and on the ball the programme was. It was a symbol – at any rate that's what the sports editor of German TV's Channel 2 thought – for movement and urgency. The directors never asked themselves whether viewers could actually tell that the clock came from a railway station anyway. Hardly any of them had the slightest idea about television. And that, although they didn't know it, was the luckiest thing for them. In their enthusiasm, and with the blessed ignorance of pioneers, they dared to have a go at things which a trained TV director would never have tried.

In the winter of 1962, a second German television channel had been founded straight off the cuff. There simply weren't enough experienced TV people to run it. A few adventurous TV journalists, most of them young, such as the 28-year-old Karl Senne from WDR, had allowed themselves to be tempted away from the regional stations which together produced the first, until then the only, national TV channel. In any case, it was mainly to be newspaper journalists doing the sports programme at Channel 2. They were journalists too, after all. In overall charge of sport were Horst Peets from *Die Welt* and Willi Krämer, who had indeed worked for a time at the *Neue Ruhr Zeitung*, but whose main qualification was more likely his experience as a combat swimmer in the Second World War. These two hired just whoever they liked, among them the former chief executive of the German Handball Association, a man by the name of Wim Thoelke, and Dettmar Cramer, one of Sepp Herberger's coaches. They soon all agreed: they were going to do something completely new, something never seen before. The dawn of the new Bundesliga on 24 August 1963 seemed to be the ideal start-date for a brand-new TV format.

What if we invited sportsmen to be on the programme?

What, bring them here to the studio, to the barn?

Yes, let's give the audience the idea that the sportsmen are sitting with them, at home, on the sofa. Let's make them feel: in *Sportstudio* I'm really getting to know the stars.

No one in TV ever invites guests actually onto the programme.

So let's do it!

No one ever said: they won't let us do that. We can't do that.

Their pioneering spirit was fired by the fact that they had been sent away from the station's headquarters in Mainz – which was still under construction – to this village in the Taunus. They were the boys out there in the trenches, they said. Their studio lot was an old farmyard. Their offices consisted of a few huts in the fields. Anyone who came to the studio, to their barn, when it rained, had to drive through puddles as big as a car. In their first winter here, their temporary studio, with its draughty, wood-plank walls, had already earned the nickname Tele-Siberia.

In Eschborn there was a pub where the chips tasted like they had been recycled from the plates of yesterday's guests. So the young programme makers in the group, who gathered around Karl Senne and Wolfram Esser and who were making themselves a name within the organisation as a Rhein-Ruhr mafia, preferred to meet in the afternoons in what they called Schnitzelsville. In the neighbouring village of Steinbach there was a little restaurant where the schnitzels were bigger than the plates. They could sit there for ever and talk about the *Sportstudio* that they were going to make. After work, they met again and talked late into the night about their *Sportstudio*.

Wim Thoelke's suggestions were amazingly bold. He was a classic larger-than-life figure. He rarely had only one thing on the go. As chief executive of the German Handball Association, and later of the Bavarian Transport Association, he'd also worked on the side as a radio reporter and a financial advisor. He had founded a charter airline and had patented trousers with an expandable waistband for men whose stomachs went up and down in size. He wasn't yet 35 years old. Thoelke didn't just have ideas, he spouted them.

He wanted to invite the entire German and Swiss national tug-of-war teams to the Eschborn studio to fight it out there. They had to have music in the show, it couldn't just be a sports programme, it had to be entertainment too.

Wim the Teak, the younger ones called him. Thoelke was the only one who had a carpet and a teak desk in the huts at Eschborn. Suddenly, even before *Sportstudio* had started broadcasting, his younger colleagues saw him on the TV screen. He was playing anchorman for the Channel 2 news programme *Today*. How had he got that job?

Thoelke, whose body was neither broad nor fat, but powerful, who could be sharp-tongued one minute and charming the next, was chosen by Channel 2's chief of sport, Peets, as the host of *Das aktuelle Sportstudio*. But for the first edition they needed an experienced hand and a big name. They hired the Austrian radio sports commentator Heribert Meisel. On 24 August 1963, the railway clock had done its ticking, and after the host Heribert Meisel had navigated his way through a few sections of the programme, he handed over to the secretary of Channel 2's sports editing team. The camera swung around onto Uschi Stöhr, a young, pretty and, of course, blonde woman. As the TV audience watched, Uschi carefully laid a disc on the turntable, then scratched the needle into place, and Stevie Wonder's hit 'Fingertips' rang out. As the song played, the camera stayed tight on the revolving turntable.

*

For the experienced TV people from Germany's Channel 1 TV who just happened, naturally, to have turned on to see what their new colleagues were getting up to, it was physical pain to watch. Such incredible amateurishness!

These beginners were committing deadly sins against television. There were cameras, cameramen and cables in the picture and, to make it worse, it was obvious that these young fellows were deliberately giving people these glimpses behind the curtains. They were putting music in a sports programme! And now, for the first time in any German TV show, never mind whether it was about politics, sport or culture, they were actually letting guests appear on the programme. How did these idiots think they were going to preserve their journalistic integrity, and not lower themselves to the level of sportsmen?

The long-jumper Wolfgang Klein and Fritz Ewert, the Cologne goalie, had been invited. Ewert had just played his first Bundesliga game for Cologne in Saarbrücken, and they'd had exactly 2½ hours from the final whistle to the start of the programme, to get him into the studio. Given a journey of 183 km, that was just about on. But if the goalie ended up racing straight from his car onto the set, that wouldn't be a drama – it would be fantastic. It would underline the workshop atmosphere of the programme. It would let the viewers see what real, hard work it was.

The reporters at the games in Saarbrücken, Munich and Frankfurt had two cameras each, the lead camera in the commentary box and an extra camera behind one of the goals. If they were lucky, the goals were scored at the right end. If they were unlucky, the cameraman might be changing the film magazine at the very moment the only goal was scored.

On that opening day, they didn't carry reports about either of the two most exciting matches of the first day of the Bundesliga, Karlsruhe vs Meiderich and Werder Bremen's 3-2 victory over the champions, Borussia Dortmund, but none of the editors fretted about it. The pressure of time was just too great to be angry about anything and, young as they were, they were too high on themselves and on their new kind of journalism to worry about anything so banal as missing the odd event.

Once Karl Senne had done his piece about the horses at Iffezheim, Dettmar Cramer, the national team's assistant coach turned TV journalist, rounded off the programme with an overview of the Bundesliga.

The day's results were written up by hand on a folding whiteboard. Cramer stood beside it and gave expert opinion on games he hadn't seen. Channel 1's *Sportschau* programme had never shown any pictures, because matches in the Bundesliga didn't begin until 5pm, which was too late for any clips from them to be shown between 6pm and 7pm. It would never have occurred to anybody to take TV into account when setting the kick-off time. Kick-off time depended on the length of daylight. Starting at 5pm in August, it got earlier and earlier until it reached 2.15pm in January and then, month by month, it started getting later in the afternoon again.

Dettmar Cramer spoke sentences like this: With their dribblings, Höher and Eia Krämer forced the Karlsruhe forwards so far back into their own half that even if they won the ball, Karlsruhe were unable to create any danger, because when they switched to the attack they were too far from the Meiderich goal. He hoped that fans would enjoy their football more if they could learn its secrets from him.

Over lunch in Schnitzelsville, the Rhein-Ruhr mafia declared that no one understood Cramer, he would have to learn that he was addressing hundreds of thousands of people, not 11 footballers. Cramer watched these youngsters drinking beer at lunchtime and felt alien, alone; how could he ever have thought that sportsmen and journalists had anything in common simply because the phrase 'sports journalism' existed?

On Saturday night, when Dettmar Cramer was done, the secretary Uschi Stöhr came on screen again and played some lively music, which was supposed to leave everyone in a good mood at the end. The first edition of *Das aktuelle Sportstudio*, which had been supposed to run for 90 minutes, came in at two hours and 32 minutes.

Sometimes the girls in the nightclubs doubtless whispered: 'Look, it's the Meiderich foot-ballers.' Heinz Höher's colleague Manfred Manglitz makes the most of the night.

The 1960s:

'MOTORSCOOTERBABE'

The Meiderich players seldom went straight home after matches. After they got back from away games they packed their kit bags into the left-luggage lockers at Duisburg Station. A few new clubs had opened up in town.

Any nightclub worth its salt didn't call itself a dance hall any more but gave itself an English name, or a least a name which you might take for English – like the Shirkin in Meiderich. Even Benny Quick, who very few people knew was actually called Rolf Müller, appeared in the Shirkin. When he shouted out the ba baba baba in his rock 'n' roll hit 'Motorscooterbabe', the crowd let out a high-pitched scream and the wildest ones even sang along: 'Sundays we drive off to the fair, you on my pillion, the wind in your hair.'

Happy was the guy who got a girl up on the dance-floor in time for this one: 'We take every corner at maximum speed, you are my girl, you're all that I need ... oh oh motorscooterbabe!' Actually, though, Horst Gecks, the small Meiderich winger, preferred to dance with men. Girls couldn't carry him standing on their shoulders, and that was the best thing about rock 'n' roll: when his partner lifted him high in the air and he, Horst Gecks, then sprang down from six feet up in the air, flipping over in a *salto mortale*. And off they went again: left foot kicks forward, right foot goes back. Horst Gecks always had to make sure that there was enough room on the dance-floor for him to make his *salto*. When the band struck up Bill Haley, they all rushed to the dance-floor at once. Apart from Heinz Höher, who leaned at the bar with his elbow on the counter and a beer in his hand.

I've forgotten how to dance since I met you, said Doris to him. But even love couldn't bring him to have a go. He couldn't imagine how his body would ever be lissom and light enough for dancing, at any rate he never felt it was. What made him want to dance, at least inwardly, was beer, a couple of beers and a shot; at first he felt a pleasant dizziness in his head and then a kind of lock-gate opened in his mind, his thoughts and feelings flowed easily now, sometimes they even made it through to the outside world.

Heinz Höher wore his bottle-blond fringe down over his forehead in a daredevil way, the hair on the side of his head was at least 4cm long, shamelessly long, although of course he didn't let it grow right down over his ears like those new music stars from England. I'll pay for you to have your hair cut decently for once, said Uncle Willie every time he came to visit. The other Meiderich players wore their hair to Uncle Willie's taste, nicely clipped short on the sides and with the hair on top properly parted or combed back. Heinz Höher had grown used to standing out in his Leverkusen days, and he didn't mind if he did.

On Saturday nights in the club in Duisburg, some of the other guests even recognised them, and no doubt many a girl whispered to her friend: hey, those are the Meiderich players. When the waiter wanted to tot up the bill for the beer, the schnapps and the champagne, the footballers said: Helmut's paying. And what waiter would ever dare go up to World Cup winner Helmut Rahn and ask him to settle up?

SV Meiderich was growing bigger than its home town. They played their home games in Duisburg, where a new 6500-seater stand had been specially built. The clubs who had the most seating would soon rule the Bundesliga so the experts prophesied. This was because the income of the clubs with those big, roofed, seated stands was four times that of the others. SV Hamburg could use the city's Volksparkstadion with its 30,800 seats. At prices between 4 and 10 marks that meant they made three times the money of Schalke or Eintracht Frankfurt, who both had only 4200 seats.

Thirty-six thousand spectators came to Meiderich's first home game in Duisburg, a 3-1 victory over Frankfurt. The euphoria lasted a little while. By mid-September it started to turn into agitation. Helmut Rahn became the first player in the new Bundesliga to be sent off. In the game against Hertha, the defenders, like most defenders, kept on hacking away hard at his legs. When Hertha's Harald Beyer fouled him like that and then just stood there right in front of him, staring, Rahn lowered his eyes – then butted his forehead straight into Beyer's face.

Sending a player off the pitch was intended for just such unsportsmanlike behaviour. Fouling was something else. The spectators booed when Heinz Höher pulled back his head from a high ball in midfield instead of jumping for it. What they didn't hear was the silence at his back. That was the worst thing, when it went quiet behind him, when all of a sudden he couldn't hear his opponent behind him. That was when an outside-forward like Höher knew: he was already in the air, any second now he was going to ram his studs into your heel or his elbows into the back of your neck. If iron-shod thugs like Hertha's Otto Rehhagel really went too far, the forward might actually get a free kick now and then. But so long as the forward wasn't actually hospitalised, it was pretty well all right.

The other Meiderich players were in complete sympathy with Rahn's head-butt. They'd seen his calves and shins. They glowed with every shade of blue, yellow, green. Once, Rahn had given Gecks, his neighbour in the changing room, a private viewing: you could stick a finger into his calf, and watch it half disappear. That was how much liquid had gathered in the swellings of his maltreated lower legs.

In the week after his sending-off, Rahn didn't appear for training. The blinds were shut in the house in Essen where he had been born, where he lived all his life, and where he went to the pub. Even the manager, Gutendorf, didn't know where he was; he hastily let it be known that he had given Rahn time off to get over the disappointment of his dismissal.

Rahn's fan-mail didn't let up. Among the pile of letters he found a demand for 1200 marks. It looked as if the idea of fobbing the waiter off with 'Helmut's paying' hadn't actually worked that well.

Defender Dieter Danzberg, who knew a few tough young guys in Meiderich, went along with his muscled-up pals to visit the club's owner, and got him to lower the team's bill significantly. The players got the rest together.

Helmut Rahn's sending-off was a blow for manager Rudi Gutendorf, but it was also an opportunity. With the Boss banned from the field, the trainer had to, and could, experiment after two successive defeats against Münster and Hertha.

For decades, German teams, like almost all European teams, had played in the same formation, the so-called WM system made famous by Arsenal in the 1920s and 1930s. The five forwards made up a W on the field. The defence formed an M with two full-backs, a centre-half in the middle and two half-backs in front.

Sometimes the W was stretched a bit. For example, in the World Cup final in 1954 against Hungary, the German manager Sepp Herberger pulled his inside-right, Fritz Walter, somewhat deeper than was strictly permitted by the method.

At the World Cup final in 1958 in Sweden the Brazilians, with a young star by the name of Pelé, had electrified the European reporters, because it looked as though they were using a different formation, with four defenders, two midfielders and four forwards. At the press conference before the World Cup final the European reporters questioned Brazil's fat, sweating manager, Vicente Feola, again and again about this new formation, but he didn't seem to understand what they were on about. What did they mean with all these numbers, Feola asked, as the terms 4, 2 and 4 buzzed around his head. Germany's manager Herberger, who had come along to take this unique opportunity to hear a top South American manager setting things out, kicked his assistant, Dettmar Cramer, under the table. Now those journalists could see for once just how pseudoscientific they were being, trying to lay down set rules for tactics and formations!

Oh, said Feola at last, you mean four defenders, two midfielders, four forwards? We don't count, in Brazil. We just play. But if you insist on dividing up the 11, then you should call it a 4-2½-3½ system. The left-winger Zagalo turned into a midfielder when the opposition got the ball.

That caused a sensation in Germany too: a player taking on two roles. Here at home, the players stayed in their own zones and played man-to-man, ten miniature battles fought out on the pitch, the full-backs covered the opposing wingers, the inside-right took on the opposing left half-back, and so on. If their team lost the ball the forwards were allowed to just stand about. They weren't expected to do defensive work. The five defenders, on the other hand, could wait in their own half. Their job was just to defend.

The discovery of the Brazilian system meant that the German dogma of W and M began to weaken. Eintracht Frankfurt often played 4-2-4 in 1963, and in some Bundesliga clubs the outside-halves, and even the full-backs, took part in the attack.

But when Rudi Gutendorf tried a tactical expriment in an away game at Bremen, he didn't move on into the future, he went back into the past. He revived the reviled old idea of a double centre-half.

Gutendorf abolished the left outside-half, thereby freeing a player who he installed in the middle of the defence, playing beside the centre-half. If any opposing forward found space, the new extra defender could immediately make a second barrier between him and the goal.

The only people who took any pleasure in this extremely defensive set-up were the popular journalists. *Bild Zeitung* christened it 'Rudi's Rearguard'. Soon that gave rise to Gutendorf's nickname, 'Rearguard Rudi'. Decades went by, but that memorable nickname stuck, and somewhere along the way it led to the widely held error that Rudi Gutendorf had himself invented this lock-up system. Even today, 50 years later, there are books and articles telling us that Rudi's Rearguard landed in 1963 as a sensational tactical innovation which changed the direction of the game. Nothing could be further from the truth.

Ever since the 1930s, using a second centre-half had been a well-known, and commonplace, tactic in case of need. Heinz Höher had occasionally experienced it at Leverkusen: after a couple of poor results, an outside-half would sometimes be sacrificed to strengthen the defence. And it's hard to claim that anyone in 1963 found Gutendorf's new system sensational.

'It's only day five of the new Bundesliga, and already a term we'd all gladly see banned from the vocabulary of German football has been called back to life,' began the *Süddeutsche Zeitung*'s report of the 1-1 draw between Meiderich and Werder Bremen: 'Meiderich used the reviled double centre-half method, which meant that a game played before a crowd of 20,000 was reduced to a horribly low quality.'

When the reporters from *Kicker* and *Sport-Magazin* went as usual to meet the manager for an interview at the door of the changing-room, they found Werder's Willy Multhaup fearing for the future: 'If this sort of defensive tactic, with a double centre-half, spreads any further, we'll soon be playing to empty terraces! The spectators are our bread and butter, and we're going about things the right way to make them sick of it!'

Heinz Höher, who thanks to Rahn's absence was allowed to switch from left wing to right wing again, like in the Leverkusen days, didn't bother himself much about Gutendorf's tactical trickery. True, he was vaguely thinking about becoming a sports teacher or a manager himself one day, but there was no way that this misled him into thinking that managers were anything special. Football was a game for players. Almost all the Meiderich players agreed with him about that. It wasn't the manager's tactical finesse that interested them, but his cute girl-friends – wherever they played away, there seemed to be one waiting there for him, how the hell did he do it?

Girls were obviously a topic on the journeys to the training ground with Manfred Manglitz – girls and Adenauer. In a few weeks, in October 1963, Adenauer was going to step down as Chancellor of Germany at the age of 87, so he had declared, and Heinz Höher had trouble imagining that any successor would be able to lead them so securely through the future. Manglitz took everything in life a little more lightheartedly, including Adenauer. On those car journeys he could switch from talk of Adenauer straight to the female athletes of Leverkusen and then segue flawlessly to the new boots which had been specially developed for goalkeepers by a Swiss firm called Künzling, with five studs rather than four on the front sole to give better grip when jumping and a collar that reached up over the ankle-bone so that the keeper wouldn't slip over so easily.

In Italy, they'd even designed gloves especially for goalies. Manglitz's mum had been on holiday on the Adriatic and had brought a pair back, gloves made of high-quality material, the fingers covered with strips from the rubber facing of a table-tennis bat in order to give more grip. But after five training sessions the rubber had already been worn smooth, and before long it detached itself from the gloves.

Every year on around 15 March, Manglitz went to the shops and equipped himself with five pairs of woollen gloves at 3.95 marks each. Winter was over, gloves would now disappear from the shelves for six months, and he needed some in case it rained during a match. When that happened, Manglitz went and got sand from the long-jump pit, and rubbed it into the woollen gloves to give himself a better grip on the slippery ball. When it was dry, he naturally played with bare hands, though always in a peaked cap.

In the week after the game against Bremen they had to drive to four training sessions for the first time. The Bundesliga was just five weeks old, and the training regime had evolved more quickly in those five weeks than in the 20 years before. Many teams suddenly doubled the players' training regimes to four or five sessions per week. This was often only possible with some creative thinking, since the majority of the newly created professional players continued to work at their old jobs. There was thus a sudden rise in the number of Bundesliga players who also ran newsagents. There was no problem in leaving such businesses to a wife, an uncle or an employee for a couple of hours while they went to training. In Kaiserslautern they trained in shifts: manager Günther Brocker offered one session for players who were free in the mornings and an afternoon session for the rest.

In Meiderich, the players got up at five in the morning. From six in the morning till two in the afternoon they worked, like almost everyone else in Meiderich, in the Phoenix steelworks. After half an hour's break in the afternoon, they went to training. Eia Krämer was a locksmith at Phoenix, Horst Gecks was a salesman in the materials department, Dieter Danzberg delivered the post around the works. Defenders Werner Lotz and Hartmut Heidemann toiled away forging steel in the blast furnaces. Heinz Höher was still described as a student. He had now officially taken two years' break from his college studies.

On the sixth matchday of the Bundesliga, Heinz Höher took part in the 3-0 victory against 1860 München in front of a crowd of 20,000 umbrella-toting spectators. For the first time, he really played a blinder, not just in other people's eyes, but in his own, too. And from then on, he was off the team.

'He just loved your volley on the turn.' At this training session for the national squad in Grünwald, 1959, Heinz Höher (third from right, front row) was allowed to sit next to Germany's great manager, Sepp Herberger.

From 1963 back to 1944:

MEMORIES

After the wedding breakfast, Heinz Wachtmeister would have gladly left his own wedding. All the other men were off, after all. The top game in the Bundesliga was coming up, Cologne against Meiderich. Could he really not go along too, Heinz Wachtmeister asked the ladies, with whom he was now sitting all alone and bereft, in the living room of his parents' house in Leverkusen, while his mother prepared the best china for coffee and cake from their own patisserie. He got what he'd expected: a barrage of appalled female protests.

Heinz Höher left the wedding along with the other men. It wasn't just a good friend's big day, but his sister's too. Heinz Wachtmeister, the pastry cooks' son who had lent him the skis on that ill-fated trip to the Westerwald, had just married Höher's sister Hilla.

Heinz Höher had left the most uncomfortable duties to his brothers Johannes and Manfred. It was they who had sat Heinz Wachtmeister down a few weeks before the wedding day of 26 October 1963, and had asked him, the way any responsible family should: so, how do you see things going, how do you plan to support our sister? A man who had a patisserie and a pub was surely in permanent danger of falling into debt, that was the way the sons of Höher's Beds saw things. Hilla was appalled. Did her brothers think they still had to watch out for her? She was 21!

Heinz Höher acted more generously than his brothers. He lent the newly married couple his yellow VW beetle convertible for their honeymoon in the Bavarian forest. He didn't bother to mention that at the moment he couldn't drive it anyway, because he'd lost his licence. And that didn't alter the fact that Heinz Höher was charmingly generous. He didn't throw his money about, but he gave it unhesitatingly if one of his family or his friends asked for a favour.

As his sister slipped beneath the plank-hard duvet of the Bavarian village inn, at 7 o'clock in the evening, because there was nothing else to do in November in the Bavarian forest, Hilla thought about how differently her brother treated money. He carried loose notes in his trouser pockets. While she and her husband always asked each other can we afford to buy that?, her brother just went and bought stuff. In her honeymoon bed, she could still hear the farmers playing cards in the bar below.

Heinz Höher was one of a dozen guests from the wedding, and one of the 42,000 spectators who were at the Müngersdorf stadium to watch SV Meiderich take on FC Cologne, comfortable leaders of the Bundesliga. He was relaxed, quiet but interested, no one was going to see that he was upset. Although someone among the men from the wedding, if he were listening very carefully, might have noticed that Heinz Höher sometimes said 'the Meiderich boys'. And not 'we'.

Rudi Gutendorf's double centre-half ploy meant that one forward had to be sacrificed. Heinz Höher had drawn the short straw. Where once an inside-forward and an outside-forward had played down the left wing, a single forward now had to do the job of both. That meant they needed a player with outstanding endurance and stamina. The manager tried out Horst Gecks, Werner Kubek and Gustav Walenciak in this new role, but not Heinz Höher. His team-mates had no trouble understanding this decision: Heinz would run like crazy for 60 minutes, said Horst Gecks, and then stand like this: his hands on his hips, his head hanging, his tongue lolling out of his mouth. Heinz, he could really have a crap game now and then, said Manfred Manglitz; he was an intellectual footballer, whereas I was a player up from the streets.

In Cologne, on Hilla Höher's wedding day, Meiderich played with an eight-man defence for most of the match and nearly defeated the league leaders. There were just two minutes to go when Cologne's Wolfgang Overath managed to equalise for 3-3.

Heinz Höher had trained a few times with Overath a couple of years before at the training school of their regional football federation in Hennef. Back then, he'd told the youngster great tales about the City

Bar. And now he was sitting in the stands, while Overath was seen as a great discovery in the Bundesliga.

Back home after the wedding celebrations, Heinz Höher had a couple of beers and a shot and made a vow: he was going to make it back into the team. He was going to train like mad. Then he drank another couple of beers and a shot.

At Meiderich training sessions, nobody noticed he'd secretly put a lead vest on, under his tracksuit top. In the mornings, while the others were slaving away in the Phoenix steelworks, he trained in Leverkusen with Olympic decathlon gold medallist Willi Holdorf. The sports stars in Leverkusen all knew each other.

One time, he almost ran Holdorf over for a joke. As Heinz Höher turned out of the Kaiserstraße into the Hauptstraße, he saw Holdorf standing with his wife in front of the newspaper kiosk across the other side of the road. He drove straight at Holdorf and braked at the last minute, calculating that last minute a tad finely. Holdorf didn't think it was that funny.

In the mornings, in the Bayer stadium, he had Holdorf set him training programmes intended for top-flight athletes: pyramid sprinting, 3×100m, 2×200m, one 300m, and then 2×200m again, 3×100m, all of it with only one or two minutes pause between the sprints. Soon, Heinz Höher could run 200 metres in under 24 seconds. But the kick that he had lost while skiing in the Westerwald just wouldn't come back, he felt. Maybe that was why he had been dropped at Meiderich?

In the next seven months, Gutendorf used him only twice in the Bundesliga, against Nuremberg and Frankfurt. Heinz Höher played in the travelling XI.

Every Sunday, the day after the Bundesliga matches, SV Meiderich drove out into the backwoods to make some money. They could easily charge 1500 marks to put out an XI in places like Dinslaken, Hilden or Lünen. It was also supposed to be a good kind of training for the players who hadn't got a match the day before. But the fee would be halved if the team's stars didn't appear, so players like Helmut Rahn had to be on for at least 45 minutes, even though his Achilles tendons were already painful. Manglitz, the keeper, usually played the second half as an outside-forward.

But as far as Horst Gecks could tell, it didn't seem to bother Heinz Höher that he was now performing only at country fêtes in places like Dinslaken. Heinz, Manfred Manglitz realised for himself on their communal drives to the training sessions, now he was a cool customer. He never got worked up, he never complained.

Heinz Höher also played Cool Heinz when, in the winter of 1963, Doris had some news for him. She was pregnant. They knew what that meant: they would have to get married. The friends she told about it said 'everyone knows a girl's a fool / if she's still not wed and her belly's full'. Heinz Höher thought the fools were the ones spouting old rhymes.

He had somehow pictured it differently, becoming a father, how could he put it: more planned. But at least the question of whether he should ask Doris to marry him had now answered itself.

Anyone with half-decent eyesight at the wedding in the spring of 1964 could tell straight away why Doris's wedding-dress was so stretched over her belly. But most people naturally acted as if they couldn't see a thing.

It was all done in the proper way. Now called Heinz and Doris Höher, right after the wedding they moved in together into a flat rented from Krämer the roofing contractor, on the first floor of 110 Hauptstraße. It was the same flat, 25 metres away from the family bed shop, in which Heinz Höher's brothers, Johannes and Manfred, had both lived with their wives after their weddings. For Heinz Höher, a married man and a reserve player, it was a move back into his child-hood. He had grown up in the Hauptstraße. It made him think, not so much about what had just happened to him, as about how things had been, back then.

At six years old, he had watched Leverkusen burn and had thought to himself how awesomely beautiful those flames looked, reaching high to heaven. He was standing on the edge of the woods at Wermelskirchen, where the family had been evacuated. It was over 20km to Leverkusen, but the fires lit the entire horizon. The allied bombers dropped over 12,000 incendiary bombs on the dye-works, where thousands of slave-labourers were forced to produce oil and gas for Hitler's war. Heinz Höher had no real picture of the suffering which resulted from the air-raid of 26 October 1944. He was born in 1938, and for him the Second World War remained a dramatic piece of stage-scenery with no actual pain. The only thing that troubled him was a clip round the ear that he never understood.

His dad had been called up by the Nazis as leader of a paramedical centre. Leader, thought Heinz, that must be an important man, and every fortnight, when his dad came home for a Saturday or Sunday, he would ask: When are you going to meet Hitler at last, did you meet Hitler this time? Dad acted as though he hadn't heard a word. So Heinz went on asking. Did Hitler visit you? If he shakes your hand you're never allowed to wash it again. Suddenly, Dad's arm shot out, it was 1944 or '45 by now, and he smacked his son in the face with the flat of his hand. Then he sent him out of the room without a word.

Heinz Höher never again asked his dad about the Nazis or the war.

When they returned from Wermelskirchen to Leverkusen in the summer of 1945, they found their home and their bed shop on the Hauptsraße by and large undamaged. Johannes, the oldest brother, wasn't with them. He was a French PoW.

The family arranged itself over the three storeys of no. 90a. Their actual flat was on the first floor, where his three-year-old sister slept in the bedroom with his parents. The lack of space meant that his two brothers, Manfred and Edelbert, were shipped upstairs to a third-floor room with the Paaß family. Heinz shared a room on the second floor, where Frau Walter lived, with Edith the house-maid. His parents told him to call Frau Walter Auntie; it wasn't proper for him to be living with a woman he wasn't related to. From the back window, he could look down into the neighbouring yard and see the butcher Odenthal cutting pigs' throats and simply ripping the creatures' legs wide apart so that the blood poured out more easily. Every now and then a pig or a cow would escape the butcher and then all the children would run out after it, into the Hauptstraße, yelling in delight.

Johnny Braun had an air gun. They lay in wait with it at a window ledge belonging to Rötzel the watchmaker. Johnny was his friend, he often let him take a shot. In Rötzel the watchmaker's yard there were so many rats that he always hit one or other of them.

The rats were everywhere. At school, Itti told them about how a rat had clambered up into his trouser-leg. When he screamed, he said, his dad jumped up and choked the rat right there on his leg, inside his trousers.

On Saturdays, Heinz Höher waited for two hours at Kämpgen's bakery. The queue was several hundred metres long, right back to the Kaiserstraße. When he reached the shop itself, his mother or one of his elder brothers would take over, to do the actual buying of the bread; on Saturdays there was white bread instead of rye-bread stretched out with wood-shavings.

On Sundays, Heinz Höher had to sit all afternoon on the staircase in no. 90a Hauptstraße. There was a gang from Manfort who regularly came ringing on all the apartment-block doors on Sundays. If someone upstairs opened the door by pressing on their switch, the boys from Manfort would rush in and pinch the lightbulbs from the lamps in the hall. Heinz Höher was on guard.

He and his sister Hilla never felt that they had it tough. Their parents were busy in their business, upholstering chairs, sewing curtains, sometimes even repairing a leather football. Their dad was in charge of the balls at Bayer 04. Mum put food on the table every day, and on Fridays they even had fish, well, maybe the fish was actually only every couple of months, but it was burned into Heinz Höher's memory that Friday was fish day. Heinz and Hilla considered their family rich. Their elder brothers never told them about how they had to go to the landlord and plead on their parents' behalf for the rent to be put off.

In 1947, a man appeared at their door. This is your brother Johannes, his mother said. Hilla sat on his lap. At five years old, she was seeing him for the first time in her life. Johannes' trousers were horribly scratchy. During his imprisonment as a PoW, he had worked for a French farmer and had taught the farmer's little daughter to count.

Every Sunday, Mum sent Heinz and Hilla to the Sacred Heart church, a brown, brick-built place that looked like just another Bayer factory building. In the holidays, she demanded of her children that they go to Mass every other day. Heinz said he wasn't going. The chaplain who brought them up in the Catholic faith at school had given him a clip round the ear because he wasn't listening. Heinz swore that in revenge, he was never going to the 8.30am school Mass on Thursdays again. But what if God found him out? He thought up a compromise which he hoped would satisfy God as well as his own pride: during Mass, he went into the Holy Mary chapel in the side wing of the church. That way, he could avoid taking part in the service without actually being absent.

He was aware that the bombed-out house at no. 94 Hauptstraße was pulled down, that Christmas trees were sold in the gap where it had stood, and that a new house was then built on the site. But he didn't realise how life was getting better. In 1948, Johannes and Manfred took him along to the Müngersdorf stadium in Cologne. The first German Championship final since the end of the war was played there. Nuremberg, with Max Morlock in their team, won 2-1 against

Kaiserslautern, who had Fritz and Ottmar Walter, and Heinz Höher knew what he wanted to be: a footballer. Johannes and Manfred were both semi-professionals at Bayer 04, and later played for Preußen Dellbrück in the Western First Division. They revealed to him how much they got paid: 160 of the newly created Deutschmarks. Edelbert, their other brother, was different: he sang and acted. He wore glasses.

When Krämer the roofing contractor built a new house at the start of the 1950s at 110 Hauptstraße, their father jumped in quickly to rent it. The family needed more space. Grandad Hermanns and Uncle Paul had by now moved in with them too. Heinz was shifted into a room with them. Paul, who was mildly hydrocephalic and had a club foot, stuttered terribly. Except when he sang. He was a pillar of the church choir with his beautiful, clear voice.

At 110 Hauptstraße, warm water came flowing from the taps. Manfred and Edelbert had folding beds which disappeared behind curtains during the day, so that there was now even a living room. Everybody shared the bathroom, even Josefine, their newest housemate. She had just married Johannes.

There were 22 years separating Johannes, the eldest child, born in 1922, and Hilla, the youngest. Surely, as the smallest, and as the only girl amidst her siblings, with her translucent skin and her long, blonde hair, she had every right to be the spoiled little chick in this nest? But it was little Heinz who got the role.

Dad said that no one was to leave the table until the last person had finished eating, but when Heinz got up in the middle of the meal because the food bored him, Dad said nothing. When Heinz came home from training with the schoolboys of Bayer 04, he was allowed to just chuck his kit bag into the corner of the room. Mum cleared it up.

His parents seemed to think that the most important part of raising children was to teach them not to whinge or to complain, but to just get on with things.

Heinz was allowed to skip school on Mondays. This was something he had learned from his father. In the shop, Dad was a model citizen with perfect manners, but in the midst of his family he changed into a gentle but sickly man who often didn't get up at all on Mondays. On Sundays, after football, beer was fetched home in stone mugs from the Gasthaus Krahne. At sometime or other, about 14 or 15 years of age, Heinz Höher began to say that he didn't feel well on Monday mornings. First his mother came to his bedside to see how he was, and then

Dad came too; they couldn't see anything wrong with him, but if their little Heinz said that he didn't feel well, his parents didn't want to make a drama out of it. He stayed in bed and read *Through the Wilds of Kurdistan*, 560 pages in a single day.

On Sundays, Dad showed everybody just who he was. He was one of the first men in Leverkusen to buy a car. On Sundays, after church, the Mercedes 170 V was brought out. The kids took their places on the bench seat in the rear, and then the family went for their Sunday walk – in the car. They drove through the Bergisches Land, where Dad cruised slowly through the villages. In the back, Edelbert sang songs. They never stopped, they never got out. The whole pleasure of the thing was, after all, the ride.

The kids rode their bikes on the autobahn in the direction of Remscheid. The bridge at Wermelskirchen had been bombed in the war and had still not been rebuilt. No cars could get through. Heinz and his friends rode to the destroyed bridge, then took the forest track beneath it and came back up again onto the autobahn on the other side of the valley.

On Sundays, a sudden stillness descended on the house. The men were all out at the football. Disconcerted by this silence, Mum decided that she had better worry about her daughter. Hilla was allowed to buy a piece of cake, and Mum offered to play Nine Men's Morris with her. It was the only time that anyone in the Höher household talked about anything other than the business or football.

An important part of Heinz Höher's charm was that he was quite clearly the most talented footballer in a talented family. At 14, he was playing with the 18-year-olds in Bayer's youth XI. They went to their away games in an open lorry belonging to Meeser's vegetable wholesalers. When they set off for home, especially if they'd won, they had to keep their heads down in the back of the truck: their opponents lobbed stones and bottles at them as they left.

To Hilla, it wasn't just unfair that her brother was so spoilt, it was also understandable. After all, he was so charming, so witty in his answers and, unlike her, he never just answered with a flat No when his parents wanted him to do something.

She had often got a clip round the ear from Mum even out in the street. A clip round the ear is what kids need, said Mum. And Hilla thought she was right. In spite of the shame of getting a clip round the ear in the street, she kept on rebelling against her mother's every rule and her every piece of advice. She just couldn't help it. She was 13 or 14. In her eyes, everything about her mother was wrong. Her mother was so old. Just look at the way she dressed, her elasticated tights for her varicose veins, her sensible shoes, her scarf and her perm. And the ridiculous things she got up to. Mum went to courses in breathing techniques, in rhetoric; any old course the church community arranged, she went to it. After morning Mass on Sundays, she sometimes brought homeless people back, to feed them, much to Dad's annoyance.

At the dining-table, Mum happily told them all about her courses, demonstrated her new breathing techniques, although she knew that they would all just laugh at her again. Heinz laughed too. He secretly thought the world of his mother.

One time, she was suddenly standing there in her nightdress in front of him and Hilla, in the middle of the day. Be quiet now, she said, accusingly but calmly. Your dad really needs his lie-in. She never once said that she herself needed anything.

Hilla and Heinz enjoyed passing the time by wrangling. He would whistle a tune. She would say, shut up, you're whistling it all wrong. He would whistle louder, and more wrongly. On Fridays they were allowed to buy *Hörzu*, the radio and TV listings magazine, from the kiosk. It was vital that he got the 50 pfennigs from Mum before Hilla could, so that he could get to the kiosk first and then sit down happily in front of his sister, on the sofa, to read the serial 'Lost Child 312', in which a family torn apart by the war was finally reunited. On one occasion, Hilla asked Uncle Paul to give her 50 pfennigs. She bought her very own copy of *Hörzu*. Heinz boiled with rage. Reading that serial was only half as much fun with Hilla sitting opposite him and reading her very own magazine, now completely freed from her dependence on him, the owner of *Hörzu*.

His friends liked his little sister. That just made things worse. The boys' school and the girls' school were next to each other in the Schulstraße, and Hilla was allowed to regularly cross over into the secret world of boys, to get the atlas which she shared with her brother. Heinzchen, your sister's coming! his friends called. Get out of here! he hissed as he stuffed the atlas into her hands. To her, his hissing was music to accompany her triumphal march out of the classroom.

At some point in time, the last rubble from the war was got rid of, but that didn't mean anything, because by then they were too old to still be playing on bomb-sites. They battled out their street-games on the Schulstraße, every day from 3pm until it got dark, with real leather balls now, not bundles of old socks tied up into a roundish clump. Sometimes, Uncle Hans came to visit. Then he would tell them what it had been like in the concentration camp, where he been sent for political resistance, but when he started up with his stories again, Grandad Hermanns would leave the room, he couldn't stand that stuff, he said, and the kids should leave too.

Uncle Hans visited them because he needed money. He borrowed 50 marks and then immediately lost 20 of them playing cards with Heinz and Grandad Hermanns. The big events though, and not just for the Höher family but for all of Leverkusen, were the visits of Uncle Willie and Aunt Minna. They came from America. Uncle Willy had emigrated in the 1920s. He came back regularly to Leverkusen, to show his former neighbours just how well he'd done in the land of infinite possibilities. Uncle Willie had his gigantic light-blue Buick brought over on the transatlantic liner, so that the folks in Leverkusen could get a look at a real car for once. The Buick gleamed and glittered as it stood there on the Hauptstraße, seeming to take up the entire width of the street. Aunt Minna glittered like the car, she was hung all over with rings and chains. From the boot, Uncle Willie produced innumerable suitcases and hatboxes. When Hilla tried on her presents, those beautiful, bright, shining clothes from America, she felt ashamed. How grey their lives seemed, in Leverkusen.

But even there, the palette of colours was getting stronger by the day. The ice-cream café Santin opened in the Hauptstraße. Lots of Italians were coming to work in Germany now, explained the *Leverkusen Advertiser*, and declared that they were guests of Germany. The youths swarmed around the ice-cream café. They wanted to see Antonietta and Laura, the daughters of the ice-cream maker from the Val di Zoldo. Hilla got right up close to them, so that she could stare with astonishment at their long eyelashes and their slim sandals. All the boys in town were head over heels with Antonietta and Laura. Heinz Höher was the only one who wasn't. Everybody else could be crazy about the same thing, or do the same stuff, that wasn't his way.

When Heinz Höher, now newly married, went back to the home of his childhood at 110 Hauptstraße in the spring of 1964, he remembered something. Every Friday, he went to the kiosk across the road and bought *Hörzu*.

Pictures like this one get rarer, now: suddenly, Heinz Höher, here playing in the Bundesliga against Preußen Münster, is only playing in the reserves.

Still the 1960s:

COLD

On Saturday afternoons, Heinz Höher became a television reporter in his own living-room. He turned the commentary down on *Sportschau* and recorded his own commentary on the match reports from the Bundesliga into the microphone of an old tape-recorder. He was looking for something to busy himself, to distract himself from his own troubles. It was now the spring of 1964 and he found himself completely banished from the first XI at Meiderich, who hadn't lost a game for weeks.

Every Friday the question came up again: Höher or Gecks; Höher or Kubek; Höher or Walenciak – and every Friday someone else was chosen ahead of him again. Rudi Gutendorf, who loved his players, as well as the girls, was saddened by having to hurt Höher. But Heinz Höher didn't accept the sympathy of his manager. In difficult situations, an icy coldness overcame him. He'd always been proud of this.

For once, let's try some different way of making this horrible decision about who's going to start and who stays at home, said Gutendorf one day. He got defenders Dieter Danzberg and Hans Cichy to duel it out by seeing how far they could clear the ball from the edge of the box. Danzberg hit it almost 50 metres, Cichy a good 5 metres less. Danzberg played, Cichy didn't.

Gutendorf knew that this was modern sports psychology: transparent competition, combined with a bit of fun for the whole team. And in any case, now and then a good manager simply had to do something crazy.

The first season of the Bundesliga was nearing its end and all over the country conclusions were being drawn. 'It was a real surprise to see how low the fitness levels are in the South German teams,' wrote the soccer journalist Hans Schiefele in the *Süddeutscher Zeitung.* 'Is this because of the way they play? Because of their tactics? The idiosyncrasy of the Southern German way, its playfulness and often overcomplication, have been revealed by the Bundesliga as barely fit for purpose.' The impression of sickly southern teams was at least partly reduced by late runs which saw Eintracht Frankfurt come in third and Stuttgart fifth. But the burden of Schiefele's complaint remained: after a year with a truly national league, people in Hamburg and Munich, in Dortmund and Kaiserslautern, still saw each other as mutually foreign footballing lands, each with its own styles and ideas: the stylish south, the cool, tactical north, the physical west. Meiderich, with Rudi's Rearguard and their surprise attacks on the break, were something no opponent could understand. They irritated everyone, sometimes even their own fans.

Only 15,000 of those fans turned up to the last game against Kaiserslautern at Duisburg's Wedau stadium. Right up to the 60th minute they booed and whistled their own side, which was yet again playing a defensive game – and which was on course, unbelievably enough, to finish second behind the champions, Cologne.

But no one changes their mind as quickly as a stadium full of football fans. When Meiderich won 3-0, the same fans who had just been booing their own team stormed the field, swinging home-made flags knocked up from bed-sheets and bamboo sticks, to cheer the runners-up of the Bundesliga. The Walsum Colliery Brass Band struck up a triumphal march.

Heinz Höher stood beaming among the spectators, who were these days mostly wearing pullovers and blouson jackets rather than suits, ties and hats. He had been allowed to play in the previous two games. But he didn't let his own pleasure last for long. And he likewise quickly suppressed the knowledge that there was a celebratory dinner in the Duisburger Hof. Heinz Höher claims that after the victory at Kaiserslautern he just went with Horst Gecks to have a couple of beers and a shot, no one recognised them in the pub, no one talked to them, and then he drove home. It's as though, looking back, he wants to deny himself any pleasure in a season which he associates primarily with his personal failure to make the team.

In the second season of the Bundesliga, Meiderich came to realise that they'd done themselves no favours by winning that sensational runner-up place. They were now bound to be measured against such incredible success. In competition with their own glorious past, they could only be the losers. Catcalls became their constant companions.

Heinz Höher was sometimes in the line-up, more often out of it. Eia Krämer, the first rising star of the Bundesliga, came only sporadically to training for several weeks in a row. He was busy building a house in Meiderich. Gutendorf turned a blind eye. Carting tiles about, brick-work, painting, well, in the end that was a kind of training too. The manager himself fought with the new club chairman, Willi Tiefenbach, who came from the club's hockey division, about that 30,000 mark bonus for coming second. It had just been a joke, a clause written down on a menu! claimed Tiefenbach.

For the new season, the team now had a Brazilian player, the first Brazilian in the Bundesliga, Raoul Tagliari, straight from the country who had won successive World Cups in 1958 and 1962, the homeland of joyous play and sheer brilliance. When the Bundesliga was born, there were only five foreign players in it: two Yugoslavs, one Austrian, one Turk, one Dutchman. The Germans believed that tempting players in from abroad was something that only fanatical southern Europeans did. And now suddenly, here was a Brazilian. Unfortunately, being Brazilian was Tagliari's main talent: he only ever played nine Bundesliga matches. Gutendorf said that he hadn't brought Tagliari to Germany anyway, he had supposedly just appeared one day at the training ground.

The days of sainthood were over now, at Meiderich. Helmut Rahn could only hobble about, these days. His Achilles tendon was chroni-cally inflamed. The only way he could help his team-mates now was as a car dealer. He got Werner Kubek an Opel coupe within a week, although the normal delivery-time was half a year. Heinz Höher ordered a car from the Boss too.

Rahn wanted to bring the car to Leverkusen on Monday at 10 o'clock. Doris Höher was nervous. Would the World Cup winner like her coffee? She hoped the baby wouldn't scream the whole time.

They had christened their son Markus. It hadn't been a completely straightforward birth, for a moment the baby seemed to be in danger of oxygen starvation. Heinz Höher only knew about it from the way his wife described things, he himself had naturally not been at the birth. Fathers were allowed to visit the maternity ward on the second day, the nurses held aloft a baby from some crib or other, and then the fathers were asked to please go home again.

Doris had given up her job, the same way Heinz's sister Hilla had broken off her teacher training with the birth of her first child. People said that there were uncaring mothers about who took up work again despite having children, but Doris and Hilla had never met one. In the West German Civil Law Codex, paragraph 1356 stated: 'A housewife shall run a household in the way that she thinks best. She has the right to go out to work, inasmuch as this is consistent with her marital and familial duties.'

Nothing changed in Heinz Höher's life. Apart from the fact that there was now a pram there too when he went walking with Doris, and that he occasionally even pushed the pram himself, despite the appalled looks of some older people. After training, he still liked to stay in Duisburg for a couple of beers and a shot. In the evenings, he went out to play cards in the pub, or stayed in with Doris and Markus. He decided all these things on the spur of the moment and without consulting his wife at all. He had no idea how else to do it.

There were times when Doris asked herself if it was really that great, the way he just decided everything for himself, that he spoke so little about his thoughts and dreams. But then she asked herself, what did she want then? She had a family with a wonderfully handsome, generous husband, she was housewife of a smart flat in Leverkusen, and didn't have to count every penny. She had everything that she had always wanted. A perfectly normal life. If only Helmut Rahn would actually come at last.

He came at 12.

A man can be a couple of hours late once in a while, said the Boss.

Yes, said Heinz Höher, but you're a day and two hours late.

Rahn had come on Tuesday, not, as arranged, on Monday,

Heinz Höher kept in his head another image of the Boss from that spring. The night before the home game against Cologne, he was sharing a bedroom with Rahn and Eia Krämer in the Hotel Angermund. Suddenly, he woke up, because the manager was standing in the room screaming, get dressed and get out of the hotel, you swine are no longer members of the team!

Under Rahn's bed was a whole battery of beer bottles which the Boss and Krämer had still been trying to hide when Gutendorf came hammering at the door. The manager had heard them laughing and talking.

The whole team pleaded on behalf of the three players. They begged the governor to show mercy. In the end, Gutendorf's fear of defeat was stronger than his sense of his educational duty. He needed Rahn and Krämer. They did play against Cologne and helped to snatch a valuable 2-2 draw. Only Heinz Höher didn't make the team, as had been foreseen. Yet he was the only one of them who had genuinely not touched a drop, just slept. He never drank before games. Though he did from Saturday night until Wednesday evening.

It was about at this time that Heinz Höher found the mental bond to his team had dissolved. While Meiderich had been flying high, he had been suffering in isolation, psychologically offside. In the second season, his own feelings and those of the team were in sync once again: they were united in misery. They drifted aimlessly, mid-table. In this atmosphere of gloom, the team's image of their own manager, who had impressed everybody so much, stone me, what a bloke, with his sophistication and his new methods, began quietly to slide.

Gutendorf's authority finally disappeared on the day after John F. Kennedy died. On the morning of 23 November 1963, the players were sitting in the breakfast room of the Hotel Angermund, before the home game against Borussia Dortmund, all talking over each other's heads. Tell the landlord to turn the radio on, have they caught the killer, was it the Russians, now you'll see there'll be war again, give me a look at the paper will you . . .

Rudi Gutendorf walked into the room in his coat and scarf and said he'd been to the stadium really early to check the pitch. They should screw in their long studs, he said.

Every one of the players – they all backed each other up on this later – immediately knew that this wasn't the truth, that Gutendorf had no doubt spent the night with a woman again.

He was lying to them. Their readiness to believe that he was right about everything sank.

The outside world continued to show respect for Gutendorf, for the new way of playing that he'd brought in with Meiderich, despite their shrinking tally of victories. 'That's modern football for you,' said the manager of Germany's 1954 World Cup winners, Sepp Herberger, in praise of the way they caught opponents on the counter with that sudden switch from mass defence to scything attack.

'We need to strike the word *or* from the dictionary of football,' Herberger had been one of the first to demand: 'a player can't be a forward *or* a defender any more, he has to be an forward *and* a defender.' The way Meiderich pulled together, with the forwards defending and the defenders attacking, seemed to him the way ahead. Meiderich's players had nothing against that. It was just that they didn't believe Gutendorf had all that much to do with the way they played.

Attacking *and* defending, they'd taught themselves that in the training sessions under Gutendorf's predecessor, Willy Multhaup. Basically, Multhaup had done nothing except let them play on, while he chatted away with the pensioners. But in this sort of training game, freed up from any kind of straitjacket, they unconsciously developed an instinct for interpreting their positions more freely; for attacking *and* defending.

Of course, Gutendorf helped this way of playing along, for example by playing experienced wingers Hartmut Heidemann and Johann Sabat as outside-halves. It was just that after the day when John F. Kennedy died, the players had less and less time for all this talk of how great their manager was.

Gutendorf himself saw tactical cunning as only a minor part of his job. The manager's real task, thought Gutendorf, was to create the right atmosphere – a warlike and absolute conviction of victory. Before Bundesliga games, the players would often find him thoughtful and rational, then he would disappear swiftly to the toilets, and shortly afterwards he'd be talking like a machine-gun: don't shake hands with your opponents, glare at them, shove them out of the way!

Not feeling up for it? he'd ask a player now and then, well, take this. He'd stick a tablet in their hand. The players didn't ask what sort of tablets they were.

It must be those bloody tablets, shouted outside-half Johann Sabath, when he saw one of his team-mates lying on the ground and foaming at the mouth during a game against Dortmund.

That lot are all doped up! yelled Dortmund's Lothar Emmerich, who'd overheard Sabath.

There was a lot of talk about doping. In Italy, the manager of AC Bologna had been banned back in 1964 for doping five of his players. UEFA announced in the spring of 1965 that doctors from neutral countries would be carrying out tests on the semi-finalists in the European Cup. But there was no rule book which actually defined what doping was. What precisely doping consisted of was never explained in the newspapers. It was a darkly mysterious word, best spoken in a hushed tone: doping.

It was almost always a question of uppers, amphetamines. In Leverkusen, Heinz Höher had heard certain players banging on end-lessly about how great it was, this Roniacol, and how it was even better for sex. But actually, these players didn't seem to be getting what Heinz Höher considered that much sex, so their song of praise to amphetamines didn't make him inquisitive.

At the offices of *Kicker* in Nuremberg, the editors debated the Bologna case. Everyone was saying doping this, doping that, but no one ever actually explained: what is doping? It was set out for their readers by Mr Professor Doktor Mellerowicz, Head of the Institute for Performance Medicine, who, as former German 100m champion, was also experienced in the practice of sport: 'No doping substance on earth can produce an increase in the natural performance of a sportsman who is training properly.' All doping substances did was to cover up for nat-ural tiredness, and this could lead to acute over-exertion and hence to a chronic exhaustion of the organism. And for this reason he, Mr Professor Doktor Mellerowicz, advised as follows: *Keep Away From Doping!*

Meanwhile a certain hockey player was giving Rudi Gutendorf a hard time.

Stop playing Rudi's Rearguard, ordered Wilhelm Tiefenbach, the former leader of the hockey division of Meiderich who had now risen to the rank of club president, it's turning the spectators away.

Gutendorf would have loved to reply: get back to your hockey-sticks. But he held his tongue. Tiefenbach was a nobody, he was just trying to make a name for himself at Gutendorf's expense. But after the wretched 1-1 draw against Borussia Neunkirchen on 20 February 1965, Gutendorf was running out of arguments. Like the hockey player, thousands of their spectators had had enough of the ultra-defensive play. The *Süddeutsche Zeitung*'s correspondent reported overhearing the following conversation: 'The man was standing at the bar of the new station restaurant. Gloomily, he knocked back his third brandy. "That bloody Rearguard business," he said, "I paid ten marks, froze my arse off, and didn't see a single bit of real football."'

Tiefenbach summoned the manager again. It couldn't go on like this. He had arranged a friendly against Hamborn 07 to make things up with the fans. He demanded that Gutendorf put up his first-choice XI for the game.

Like hell he was going to tire out his best players on a Sunday bloody friendly.

Mr Gutendorf, you will produce your first XI for this match. That is an order.

So produce it yourself, arsehole!

Well, said Gutendorf, considering the way that conversation went, it hardly came as a surprise to be sacked that very evening.

In the Bundesliga, managers were kicked out more easily than before. At almost exactly the same time as Gutendorf, the managers of Stuttgart and Kaiserslautern got fired. 'If you're manager of a team sitting anywhere from 12th to 16th place, you're sitting on the electric chair,' said Kurt Sommerlatt. He'd just been sacked by Karlsruhe. In the Bundesliga, everything was bigger, including fear and panic in the face of failure.

But the real basis of all this sudden changing of managers was a deep belief in the mystique of The Manager. Ever since Sepp Herberger's World Cup triumph in 1954, when his leadership, tactical genius and choice of players had really shown the effectiveness of a talented manager, German football clubs had believed that a manager was a sort of magician. If a team was doing badly, if the manager wasn't getting results, they always hoped that a new one could change everything for the better in the twinkling of an eye, just like that.

For Gutendorf, the end at Meiderich was just a start. Rudi's Rearguard was a brand from then on. Within days, he was appointed manager of Stuttgart. Soon afterwards, he took on the Honduran national team and trained managers in Antigua. And so he went on for three decades: Schalke, Chile, Offenbach, Cristal Lima, always on the move, home and away, Botswana, Hamburg, Fiji, Hertha. He married his wife, Ute, twice and got divorced from her twice. He burned team shirts in the changing room, made his players run against racing horses, and sold his Mercedes 450 SL, allegedly to raise money for his XI at Tennis Borussia Berlin. When journalists called him, he never failed to satisfy their thirst for a memorable quotation. In 2003, at 77 years of age, and by now decorated with the German National Merit Award (1st class) in recognition of his work in international development, he took up his last post as manager of the Samoan national side. He still has his hour-and-a-half siesta every day: it's what keeps him young, says Rudi Gutendorf, now 86.

'He wasn't a con-man,' says Dettmar Cramer, Gutendorf's fellow-manager, 'it's just that he believed, like so many people, that every good manager has to be a bit of a con-man.'

The remaining two months of the 1964-65 season dragged by for Meiderich in the no-man's-land of mid-table, as far from the top as they were from the bottom. Heinz Höher had to start thinking about the next season. His contract was up on 30 June 1965. He needed a new club.

Has Heinz got money of his own, so he doesn't need to earn it? Horst Gecks asked himself, because Höher seemed to accept his fate as a second-choice player with so little concern.

In the afternoons they often went together to one of the new establishments which had opened in the centre of Duisburg, neither restaurants nor bars but a mix of both. They call themselves bistros. They had alcoves with black leather stools and smooth, flat tables. Heinz Höher and Horst Gecks played cards there. Heinz Höher divided card-players into two groups: winners and losers. There was no middle ground. He certainly put himself into the first category. He had no trouble keeping note of the cards which had been played already and working out in seconds which were still in play and who must have what still in their hand.

We've got to go, training's in fifteen minutes, Gecks hassled.

I've got to finish this hand, said Höher.

Gecks was getting nervous, they still had to drive over the bridge to Meiderich and he didn't want to be late.

Look, sorry I'm off.

No worries, said Heinz Höher, and hardly looked up. He said he'd follow him.

As Gecks raced to Meiderich, he said to himself: ladies and gentlemen, that is one ice-cool guy.

Right on time, Höher was there at the training ground. And he'd won 6 marks at that last round of cards, too.

It wasn't about the money, he didn't care if there were 50 pfennigs or 50 marks on the table, it was all about the winning. When he knitted his brow in concentration, when he was afraid that he was risking too much, yet certain that he was going to win, that was the most beautiful feeling of uncertainty that this life could offer.

He was going to go back to Bayer 04. No question about it. In the feverish atmosphere at the start of the Bundesliga, it had seemed as though from now on, perfectly normal club players would move to other cities to play their football, and indeed every year at least two dozen players criss-crossed Germany, players such as Meiderich defender Dieter Danzberg, who was signed up by the newly promoted Bayern Munich for the 1965-66 season. But this kind of move remained an exception. Most footballers stayed where they belonged.

He'd have to do a try-out at a training session, said Bayer's manager, Theo Kirschberg.

Him, do a try-out? In Leverkusen?

It had been a long time since people had seen him play, said Kirchberg, in the second half of the season he'd only played a single match for Meiderich.

Heinz Höher never debated things when there didn't seem to be any point, instead he tried to make the best of things. All alone on the training ground, he went through what Kirchberg called a try-out. The manager got him sprinting, and threw him the ball a few times so he could pass it back.

A few days later, Kirchberg had word sent to him that Bayer 04 was not prepared to enter into a contract.

Leverkusen? They didn't want him?

He learned the reasons why in the city's pubs: or at least, he learned what comes out when something is gossiped about for days in bars and restaurants.

He'd demanded too much money. But Bayer 04 wouldn't have wanted him anyway. He was too lazy, he drank too much and he didn't even turn up to college any more.

Heinz Höher calmly drank a couple of beers and a shot as he listened to people talking about it, no one would see any sign that it worried him. At home, he got his anger down on paper. As happened so often when his thoughts raged inside him, he wrote a letter. In biro, he asked Kirchberg why Bayer 04 didn't just take the final little step and decide that they would no longer pay any wages at all. Then they could play in the amateur league, with a team where no one smoked, drank, or laughed, and they could get relegated again. It was nobody's business, he wrote, if he had a glass of beer, or grew a beard, or if he could afford to break off his studies for two years or 20 years! All the time he had played at Leverkusen, no one had trained longer and harder than him. He had done his bit in getting the club up into the first division, and in raising its income from 200,000 marks per season to half a million, so he was surely entitled to feel proud of it.

He never sent the letter.

Doris didn't ask, where will we be next year? She didn't want to trouble him, the rejections from Meiderich and Bayer 04 must be really hard for him to take. If she didn't ask about it, if he didn't say anything about plans to move house, it would mean that she could still hope that they would stay in Leverkusen.

Heinz Höher turned to the footballers' agents. By now, there were at least four of them in Germany. The most established was Mr Dr Ratz, a Hungarian based in Munich. Ratz told him to come up the stairs to his office on the fourth floor.

You're breathing heavily, said Ratz, who was waiting at the door to greet him, that's rather unusual for a footballer. Had Ratz wanted to test his fitness by getting him to climb those stairs? At any rate, Ratz couldn't do anything for him.

His old agent, Raymond Schwab, was having what people in footballing circles called a few little difficulties. At the end of the first Bundesliga season, Schwab had tried to bribe Preußen Münster striker Manfred Rummel. If Rummel would fake an injury against Hertha, and hobble off the pitch with ten minutes to go, Schwab would pay him 5000 marks. The game was going to be a decider between two clubs both threatened with relegation. Rummel went to his manager and told him of Schwab's offer.

When the story got about, several club presidents allegedly began avoiding Schwab. But he didn't have to worry himself that much, it wasn't the first time someone had tried to fix matches in German football, a little thing like that would be quickly swept under the carpet and forgotten. A little thing like that would never create difficulties. Heinz Höher had no hesitation in entrusting his future to Raymond Schwab once again.

He was 27, getting old for a top-flight footballer. Since December 1964, he'd only been given one game at Meiderich. He didn't have a Bundesliga team for him, said Schwab, but what about Holland?

Heinz Höher said yes to FC Twente Enschede without too much difficulty. He was curious to see the world. Doris didn't see how she could seriously argue against the move. After all, he was the one who earned the money.

In the autumn of 1965 the removal van was standing outside 110 Hauptstraße. His brothers and friends came to help out. The only person nowhere to be seen was Heinz Höher. He was lying in bed. He'd spent the evening before trying to work out how he could get out of the house-moving, and he'd drunk so much beer and schnapps that he couldn't get up even if he'd wanted to.

If you've got it, flaunt it. Doris Höher in the mid-1960s, in the land of the Economic Miracle.

1966:

THE MEN AND THE WOMEN

At the stroke of 12 midday, every day, Doris Höher burst into tears. The house had been dusted, the nappies had been washed, and the shopping had been done. Now, there was nothing left to distract her from the thought that she was spending too much time alone with her 18-month-old son in a foreign country.

When her husband came back from his morning training session at about 12.30, she smiled, she asked how it had gone, and brought lunch to the table, loin of pork with mashed potatoes or steak with roast potatoes and mixed vegetables. A sportsman had to eat lots of meat, to keep him strong.

The couple of professionals at FC Twente Enschede trained twice a day. When her husband drove off to the ground again after lunch, Doris went for a walk with the pram. In their street, Nierstraat, where they lived at no. 15, new brick-built apartment blocks stood lined up as if on parade. The freshly planted trees, which were supposed to give the street a comfortable feel, had yet to grow. Markus was just learning to walk, now and then a woman passing by would lean down to the child and say something. Doris would answer with a smile. She was trying to master enough Dutch to make herself understood. But the feeling of loneliness remained, even with other people about her. Heinz Höher considered that things were going pretty well for him and his wife, in Holland.

He liked to feel that he was discovering new countries, and liked being an observer. Right back at the start of the 1950s, as a youth, he and two friends had hitch-hiked through England and Scandinavia. In a bar in Finland, a man had opened a bottle of beer for him with his last remaining teeth and had handed it over with the greeting 'Cheers, Heil Hitler'. Heinz Höher was untroubled by the fear that, as a German, he might be unwelcome because of memories of the Second World War. He was used to the idea that everybody liked him, and he unconsciously assumed that this would be the same abroad too.

Theoretically, it was now perfectly common for a footballer to move abroad. There were reports about it all the time in the newspapers, offers of millions for Uwe Seeler from Italy, or 'Cologne is secretly chasing a mysterious Brazilian, could it be Pelé?' In practice, there were fewer than a dozen German professionals playing abroad in 1965 and fewer still foreigners playing in the Bundesliga. No one thought about offering them special help in integrating. They were earning good money, often more than home-grown players, it was up to them to integrate for themselves.

Heinz Höher was of the opinion that he was getting on just fine with his team-mates at Twente. In the Netherlands, they had beautiful, lush, smooth pitches, and the defenders weren't as bloody-minded as in the Bundesliga. He felt good here. His team-mates at Twente didn't tell him what they were thinking: that Höher is a strange one, thought outside-left Issy ten Donkelhaar, he doesn't even try to fit in.

In the mornings, the professionals worked with the assistant trainer, Mr Robinson from England, and had to do a long-distance run, 5 or 6km on a country road. The smooth asphalt was supposed to be good for their running style and for keeping the speed up. After a few weeks, they all had inflamed Achilles tendons, Ned Bulatovic, Antoine Kohn, who they all called Spitz, and Heinz Höher. The team doctor prepared Cortisone injections for them. When he saw the doctor's long needle, Spitz Kohn, their centre-forward, their star, said only the toughest of us are going to survive this. As the needle stabbed into his sinews, Kohn fell unconscious to the floor.

Cortisone was a great invention. The way the pain disappeared so fast, just a quarter of an hour after the injection, Heinz Höher couldn't feel a thing, it was incredible. After a few days, the pain came back. But that was no problem, because you got another Cortisone injection. Manfred Manglitz, their keeper at Meiderich, had always had his pain injected away with Cortisone, too, Manglitz had made a hard-as-nails vow never to miss a game, and he kept to it.

When Heinz Höher was spending a few free days in Leverkusen, someone told him that Manglitz was driving to training with Carl-Heinz Rühl these days. They liked to take an imitation pistol with them. On the autobahn, Rühl sat in the passenger seat and tried to make eye-contact with drivers in the other lane. If one of them caught his eye, Rühl would put the pistol to his head, pull the trigger, and sink back in his seat.

Manglitz couldn't remember playing that joke, but what did that matter: a good anecdote lives for ever among footballers, whether it's true or not. It was stories like these that made life worth living.

But generally, Heinz Höher didn't hear much from his German colleagues. There was no phone at no. 15, Nierstraat. Doris's parents in Leverkusen didn't have a line, either. If there was something urgent to discuss, they sent a telegram home.

Their second child was on the way.

Doris should bring it into the world in their home in Nierstraat, said the Dutch midwife. It was much healthier than at the hospital, she said.

The TV was their connection to home, their connection to the Bundesliga. Enschede lay right on the border, and with a bit of luck you could get German programmes. On Saturday evenings at 9.30, Heinz Höher watched *Das aktuelle Sportstudio*. That Wim Thoelke was lively and witty. Lately, he'd taken to getting the guests on the programme to kick a ball at a goal painted on a wooden wall, even swimmers or track athletes in their elegant street-shoes. This was something new: at 40, like Thoelke, or at almost 30, like Höher, you could still be young. Heinz Höher was the only player at Enschede who wore his fringe deep down over his forehead, right down to his eyebrows, like the Beatles.

Twente trundled towards the end of the 1965-66 season in the lower mid-table of the Dutch first division, without a care in the world. Heinz Höher considered that he was having a very good time in the world of Dutch sport.

On 15 May 1966, Twente lost 2-0 to Ajax Amsterdam. Were Ajax playing with 14 men? No matter where the Twente players passed the ball, they found themselves immediately outnumbered. The Ajax players raced forwards and backwards, creating a new kind of footballing geometry: when Twente had the ball, Ajax narrowed play right down by converging on the opposing ball-carriers. When Ajax had the ball they widened things out by rushing players far out to the touchlines. This, said Ajax's manager, Rinus Michels, was 'total football'.

As part of this new way of playing, a wiry 19-year-old winger really shook Twente up. He was in his first professional season, he didn't look an ounce over ten stone and he wore his sleeves right down over his wrists. Heinz Höher wasn't going to forget that name, later he would tell his colleagues in the Bundesliga about this Johan Cruyff. With his mazy dribbling and his sudden changes of direction, Cruyff was the sort of footballer Heinz Höher dreamed about, a footballer – you couldn't say it out loud, of course – of his own stamp. Was there anyone as talented as this in Germany? This new lad from Bavaria was supposed to be good, he played with no apparent effort, with a mysterious elegance, and he could hit a pass. Beckenbauer, he was called.

Heinz Höher didn't claim that he'd played at the same level as Cruyff in the game against Ajax, but he'd been satisfied with his own performance. Two days later, Twente's president, Henk Olivje, sent him a recorded letter. Heinz Höher guessed what news it contained. He refused to accept it.

If a player underperformed, the president would send him a disciplinary warning for behaviour damaging to the club. Heinz Höher felt rage burn inside him. If things went wrong, they always turned on Bulatovic and him, the professionals, the foreigners.

Four days later, his anger carried Heinz Höher passed the Maastricht defenders again and again. Twenty minutes from the whistle, Twente were 2-0 up when their keeper was sent off for a stupid offence and his place was taken by defender Job Hoomans. Heinz Höher couldn't talk about what happened next, he didn't even want to think about it. He just felt: no one should ever hear about it.

When Heinz Höher left the stadium after an unbelievable 2-3 defeat against Maastricht, he thought he must be as white as chalk, his own movements felt like slow motion; when he turned his head, he seemed to be caught in a time-loop. At his thigh, in his trouser pocket, he felt those few banknotes even without putting his hand to them.

At the end of the season, an offer came in for Heinz Höher from Bochum. He would go back to Germany, that had always been obvious, he told himself. Twente Enschede were happy to end his contract. Höher hadn't been a disappointment. But a foreign player had to really enthuse people. And Doris certainly would have no objections to returning home, he thought.

Before going home, the Höhers planned to take a holiday on the North Sea island of Texel. If you wanted to be able to hold your head up at home come September, you had to take a foreign holiday. The newspapers carried whole pages of adverts from travel companies. Cheaper than you think: Lloret de Mar/Spain from 262 marks full board. Relax in genuine tranquillity: flight and accommodation in Ireland, 11 days from Düsseldorf from 730 marks.

His parents had gone on holiday five times in their lives, and never together. Someone had to keep the business going. They never got any further than Austria.

In May, in Enschede, the Höhers' daughter, Susanne, came into the world in the modern way, at home. We'll leave Susanne with your parents, said Heinz Höher to Doris, before their holiday. Their daughter was five weeks old. Doris could hardly breathe. She wanted to shout, are you crazy? She called Heinz's sister, Hilla.

It was the same with me, Hilla told her. When her son Bernd was born two years before, her mother-in-law had demanded that she should leave the six-week-old child with her for the summer holidays. Hilla's husband, Heinz Wachtmeister, needed the summer holiday to recover from all his hard work, she said. A screaming child would disturb him. Hilla got through that holiday wrapped in her own silent despair.

On the island of Texel, Doris looked back over her shoulder whenever a Dutch woman passed by with a pram. Heinz Höher was taken aback when she openly asked if he thought Susanne was all right. Their daughter was surely in the best possible hands at her mother-in-law's place.

At second division Bochum, Heinz Höher signed an official contract – and a simple sheet of thin paper which had no letterhead, nor embossed with the club's insignia. The contract, for 320 marks pay per month, was sent off to the German Football Union. On the bare sheet of paper, which was intended to be seen by nobody apart from Höher, the vital matter of his secret backhander was set out, two typographical mistakes and all. He would get 5000 marks cash in hand and the same again as a bonus if they got to the play-offs for the Bundesliga. The typos he could ignore. Bochum's office was manned only by a single secretary who worked half-days, sometimes aided by the chief executive, who came in after his day job in the city transport office was done.

When Ottokar Wüst was elected chairman of Bochum, he had told a young reporter from the local paper that he would live to see him lead the club into the Bundesliga. The reporter, Heinz Formann, sat down on the stool of a nearby bistro and smiled to himself, with this bold prophecy still in his ear, as he hurried to finish his hand-written report on Bochum's Annual General Meeting before the paper's deadline. Formann knew which of the town's bistros had a telephone he could use to file his copy verbally to the office.

The signing of Heinz Höher just weeks after Wüst's election as chairman was to be a signal. It was the first time that Bochum had ever brought in a player from another professional club. Until now, their ranks had always been filled either from their own youth side or from teams in lower leagues.

To bring Heinz Höher's income up to his usual level, Bochum not only signed him as a footballer, but arranged a job for him in the advertising department of one of their sponsors, Schlegel's brewery. Maybe Höher could go round the pubs talking about Schlegel-Pils, they thought. Plans for his work hadn't got any further than that.

For the first time in his life, Heinz Höher had the feeling that things were going badly. Seen purely in terms of his earnings, there was no massive difference from his days at Meiderich or Leverkusen. But at 28 years of age, he was actually having to go to work for the first time. He took this not just as a personal relegation, but also as a sign of just how bad things were all around him. When his Volkswagen, left parked in front of his own house door in Bochum, was smashed into and written off, the picture of his own misery was complete.

In 1966 the public's idea of modern professional footballers was very different from Heinz Höher's reality: they earned crazy money and were mobbed everywhere by adoring crowds. 'A member of the national team can command upwards of 70,000 marks a year,' revealed Hamburg's vice-president, Mr Dr Barrelet, to *Der Spiegel*. The publishers Bergmann brought out their first collector's album for postcards of Bundesliga teams; thanks to that new, sophisticated TV programme, *Das aktuelle Sportstudio*, the players sat in the living rooms of millions of viewers, and a goalie could be a popstar too: 'Me is Radi, me is King,' sang Petar Radenkovic of 1860 Munich. The founding of the Bundesliga had meant that for the first time a parallel reality had developed alongside the actual lives of the players: a media reality. In that reality, the Bundesliga seemed to be a world of big money and new, cosmopolitan life, of sporting glory and cute financial trickery.

In reality, most footballers of the late 1960s never gave a single interview in their whole careers. Sometimes, the local policeman would turn a blind eye if they were caught speeding, sometimes the team might be bought a round of schnapps that they didn't want anyway by someone in a pub. That was about as much as most professionals could hope for in the way of public marks of appreciation, especially at smaller clubs like Bochum. If the master butcher Antico donated a round of schnapps after a victory, the Bochum players had to raise their glasses and sing 'for he's a jolly good fellow, for he's a jolly good fellow'.

The Höhers found a two-bedroom flat to rent at 26 Kaulbachstraße, where even before they moved in, the landlady explained to Doris in great detail how the flat was to be cleaned. At the corner of the apartment block there was a bar called the Kaulbach Corner. One time, Heinz Höher met the landlady of the pub in the stairwell. The landlady was taking a pee right in front of the door of their flat. Heinz Höher elected not to say hello, nor to wonder if this was some kind of crazy left-over wartime behaviour. The Höhers had to be grateful that they could live at 26 Kaulbachstraße.

Flats were hard to come by in Bochum, like in every city, they said. Since the war, there had never been so many young families about as now. At 26 Kaulbachstraße, in the ground-floor flat of a bare apartment block with a flat roof, Susanne slept in her pram in her parents' room. There wasn't enough space to fit a cot in. She would be able to share Markus's room later.

Visitors could see no sign of financial woes at Heinz and Doris Höher's place. The Höhers had a carpet, the absolute latest thing, with a gigantic bright pattern, and when Heinz Höher's fellow forward Gustav Eversberg brought his wife along, she screamed out in delight: Mrs Höher had built-in cupboards! Made out of teak and reaching right up to the ceiling, the fitted cupboards in the living room, with their innumerable drawers and shelves, stretched more than 2½ metres along the wall.

Sunday was a day for the family. It was when Hilla and Heinz Wachtmeister with their two children, or Doris's sister and her husband, came from Leverkusen for Sunday lunch. The assembled company spent the afternoon sitting in the living room. The women talked to each other, and the men talked to each other. If everyone was in a good mood, after coffee and cake they had a couple of beers and a shot.

At last life was normal again, said Doris to Hilla, though with a footballer it could obviously never really be completely normal; after all, what did they know would come their way after his time in Bochum?

Part of the reason you chose him was because he was a footballer, too, said Hilla. You chose him, and you chose everything that goes with it.

But what kind of choices could they make, really, as women? Hilla knew that her husband was extremely progressive; he'd often said to her, don't chuck your studies in, stick to them, we'll find a nanny for the little one. But the idea of leaving her son with a strange woman was so appalling to Hilla, there was no question of it. Ever since she'd rejected that suggestion, she'd often thought sadly about why she'd broken off her studies. She helped out in her parents-in-law's patisserie. That hadn't been a decision, it was something that had just been arranged, all unspoken. At first she had cleaned in the patisserie. Having done this under the eye of her parents-in-law to their satisfaction, she started delivering the cakes to the clients.

The men talked about money and football, on Sundays, in the Höhers' living room.

Heinz Höher told the story of how, not long ago, after that bloody miserable 2-1 defeat against his first love, Bayer 04 Leverkusen, he went up to his team-mate Hansi Grieger in the changing room. Grieger was the only one in the Bochum team who had played half decently that day. Listen, Hansi, said Höher to him in the changing room, didn't anyone tell you that the game was fixed? Erwin Höffken's got a thousand mark note waiting for you.

Really? Hansi Grieger went straight to Höffken, the club secretary. Erwin, where's my grand?

Höffken, who was already galled by their awful defeat anyway, exploded. How the hell did Grieger dare make stupid jokes after such a performance!

The more often you told the anecdotes, the better they got.

Every day at eight, Heinz Höher appeared for work in the Schlegel brewery and wondered when the day's work would end at last. Sometimes the head of advertising gave him a few documents to work over. Mostly, he sat about.

They don't give me any real work, complained Heinz Höher.

He doesn't pull his weight, complained the boss.

Though Heinz Höher felt that he was being forced to work for the first time in his life, his team-mates saw him as the only man at Bochum who didn't really have to work. The others had jobs at the Westphalia Bank or slaved away in the steelworks and mines of the Bochum Union Works, though it was a good question how long the blast furnaces would still be going. Bochum now only had five collieries working, where once there had been 70. The Prince Regent mine had been closed right after having been modernised. Oil and gas were clean forms of energy, coal didn't have a chance against them. When people at the Schlegel brewery told stories of how the southerly wind used to blacken the freshly washed linen hung up on poles between the apartment blocks, it was as if they were talking about some other planet. That was just four, five years ago.

Gerd Wiesemes, one of the Bochum full-backs, still worked in the steelworks. From 6am till 2pm his job as a quality controller meant that he took flywheels from a stack – they were making them for VW axles – then put them onto the test-bed, then carried them back, 15kg, lift, carry, lift out again, carry back, a few hundred times a day. Though he didn't realise it, it was the finest training. He was naturally a gangly man, with an elegant nose and thick eyebrows, but with his well-defined upper arm muscles and strong legs he became an athlete among players. When he got steam up in a sprint, you didn't want to be in his way.

Wiesemes never wanted to make money out of football. In 1961, when he was 18 and had just made the leap from the youth side into Bochum's first XI, the club secretary said to him several times in passing, Pop in to see me after training. Wiesemes knew exactly what the club secretary wanted. He wanted him to sign a professional contract. Wiesemes ducked out each time. He was ashamed at the idea of getting paid for playing football. He had only ever had one dream: to play for Bochum's first XI. He didn't want to sully this dream with the money.

One day, the club secretary waited in front of the changing room till Wiesemes came out and ushered him personally to the club office to sign the contract.

The card-players met at Wiesemes' place. After the evening training session, Charly Böttcher and Gustav Eversberg went round to see him, Heinz Höher came with them, just for a little while he said, it wasn't far from Wiesemes' flat to Kaulbachstraße. They always intended to put the cards to bed at 10pm. The problem was that, logically, someone was always down. Whoever it was believed that he could, that he must, win his money back, and so he insisted that they should play another hand, it was always just one more hand, until midnight or 1am. One time, Wiesemes' little daughter came into her mum's bedroom at four or five in the morning: Mama, there are strange men sitting in the kitchen.

At the beginning of the evening they would play for 20 or 30 marks. Later that turned into 100 marks ante. If Heinz Höher was losing, there might be 1000 marks on the table by midnight, that was two or three weeks' wages. When the team went for an end-of-season journey to Bulgaria, Wiesemes, Höher and Böttcher even played cards while they strolled around.

They regularly played friendlies abroad, such as against the Bulgarian national team, or else foreign teams visited them in Bochum. German sports teams, theatre troops or orchestras were supposed to be showing the world that the country had changed, that this new Germany was never going to start a war again, although the card-playing sportsmen were at best only dimly aware of this mission.

In the summer holidays, the Höhers went back to Texel. They knew what to expect there. Holidays were about relaxing, not making some kind of discoveries. Heinz's sister Hilla joined them, with her family.

At breakfast, Hilla asked her three-year-old son what he wanted on his bread. Why are you asking him, said Heinz Höher, kids should get what they're given on their bread, end of story. Hilla kept her astonishment to herself: her pampered little brother was preaching about strict upbringing, now? Later that morning, they met on the beach, Hilla saw the Höhers from far off, coming over the dunes. Doris had the two kids, the pram and the beach-bag, Heinz Höher was trotting along with a book in his hand.

The public breathing down your neck: Bochum manager Hermann Eppenhoff and thousands of fans, together on the touchline during the German Cup semi-final.

1968:

HEROES FOR A DAY

Heinz Höher brought two things to every game: his football boots and his magic potion. The professionals at Bochum were allowed to choose two pairs of boots free each year at Koch's House of Sports, one pair for training, one pair for matches. They didn't actually need that many pairs. If you looked after your boots, a pair would easily last two seasons.

On 15 May 1968, Heinz Höher packed boots with moulded studs. He wanted to stroke the ball with his foot. In these lightweight boots with moulded studs, he had a better touch than in the clumpy versions with screw-ins, although those did give you better grip in return. He also packed a towel, his tracksuit, and his shinpads into his kit bag. At FC Cologne, it was said, the players didn't even have to pack their own kit any more, everything they needed for the game was laid out for them at the club-house. That must feel weird: to go to a game without your kit bag, without the ritual of packing it. It would feel as though something was missing.

He brewed his magic potion at the last minute. He filled a glass bottle two-thirds with orange juice, dissolved dextrose in it, topped it up with cava and rounded the whole thing off with a good shot of cognac. Before every game he took a good, strong pull. He could feel the fine, shivery warmth surging though his body, lending him a tingling of decisiveness, a new fearlessness. Once, he took too much of his magic potion and, with a power he had never known before, smashed the ball against the upright in the first minutes of the game. He was shocked at himself. Could he be drunk?

The team met in the morning at the Hotel Lottental. Almost all of them had had to take a day off work for the game. 15 May was a Wednesday. In the Lottental valley, sheep and horses grazed, if you were lucky you might see a deer step out from the woods onto the sunlit meadow. On the other side of the valley, only a few hundred metres away, the orange-coloured cubes housing the faculties of the new Ruhr University reared up against the steep hillside, as gigantic and futuristic as a space-station. There was a lot of talk in the air about change, about progress, about the new age. The collieries were dying out in Bochum and, in their place, Opels were now being built, a Kadett every minute.

Entire new districts were springing up straight off the drawing-board: Hustadt, the Rosenberg quarter, with high-rise apartment blocks that reached for the heavens. But what remained, what gave Bochum its special character, was the impossible harmony of brute industry and unspoiled nature. In Bochum-Rienke, the nature reserve of Zillertal lay right beneath the pillars of the autobahn flyover. Behind the working-class enclave of the Dahlhauser Heide stood fields of vegetables, chicken-coops, rabbit-runs and dove-cotes.

When the manager sent them for their siesta in the Hotel Lottental, Heinz Höher did actually go and lie down. When they were at the training camp, 'siesta' was usually a euphemism for playing cards. But the game on 15 May impressed even him. For the second year in a row, Bochum had been one of the leading lights in the second division, but had missed promotion to the Bundesliga again – and now they were playing Bayern Munich in the semi-final of the German Cup.

The knockout competition had been invented just for evenings like this. There was something in the air; the intimation, the dream that against all logic, the small fry might knock out the favourites in a one-off game. There was something in the air; perhaps it was simply the illusion that everything was possible – if not in real life, then at least in football.

In England, the FA Cup – the mother of all knockout competitions – had a mythical status, it was a celebration of the Little Man, who saw, again and again, how 11 second-class footballers could become heroes for a day. Wembley, where the FA Cup final had been played out every year since 1923, was not a stadium but a field of yearnings.

But then, everything was naturally better in England, the Germans thought. The German footballing community looked across the Channel with burning admiration. German football journalists, their ears red with passion, wrote about the Anfield Roar, the fanatical scream which fired up the Liverpool stadium, without ever having heard it. And then there was the fearless physicality of the English game, and the etiquette: shaking hands with your opponents, the cap presented for every international appearance, the fair play. The way Heinz Höher thought about English footballers was something beyond admiration. He was scared of them. He felt essentially inferior to them. Even though he hadn't lost to them when playing for the National Amateur XI.

Compared to the FA Cup, the German Football Union version, the DFB Trophy, lacked charm. The National Socialists had founded it in 1935 because they were fascinated by the English idea that amateur clubs might once in a lifetime play against the giants. During the Nazi years it was known as the Tschammer Trophy after its founder, Reich Sport Leader Hans von Tschammer und Osten.

After the war, the swastika was scratched off the trophy and replaced with a DFB plaque. But since, pre-Bundesliga, the German championship itself was decided by a knockout game, a winner-takes-all in one evening between the regional champions, the DFB Cup remained second rate. Its games were lovelessly squashed into the match calendar; often, all the stages were played one after another in the summer holidays, as if they were just a preparation for the season proper. At the 1961 cup final in Gelsenkirchen between Werder Bremen and Kaiserslautern, the ground was half empty even though the Kaiserslautern line-up included Werner Liebrich, the last of their players to have figured in the 1954 World Cup winning team.

It was only the founding of the Bundesliga which gave the German Cup a new lease of life. The Bundesliga, combined with TV, gave football a new importance. And the DFB Cup became a sort of replacement for the knockout system of the old German Championship: here, on Wednesday evenings, as the darkness was falling, all that mattered was what happened right now; there were no league tables, no comfort zone of points garnered from previous games, no second chance for the losers to wipe out their shame. On this single evening there was only final victory or utter defeat.

In the 1967-68 season, Bochum had already knocked out one

Bundesliga team after the other in the early rounds: Karlsruhe, Stuttgart, Borussia Mönchengladbach. It was the season when Bochum really showed what a competition the DFB Cup could be.

Bayern Munich were staying at a hotel called the Krummer Weg – the Crooked Path – in Ratingen. Their general manager, Robert Schwan, was worried. If the game went into extra time, they probably wouldn't catch the evening flight from Düsseldorf home, on which they had reserved seats, he told the four Munich journalists who had come with them. The journalists shared his concern. They were staying with the team in the hotel and after the game they were coming along in the team bus directly from the stadium to the airport.

For Bayern, this was the last chance for a trophy in 1968. The week before, AC Milan had beaten them in the semi-final of the European Cup Winners' Cup and in the Bundesliga they were only fifth. Three years before, Bayern had been playing in the second division, but now, already, to end the season only as semi-finalists in the Cup Winners' Cup and fifth in the Bundesliga counted as a disappointment. They had become one of the top teams in an incredibly short time, winning the DFB Cup in 1966 and 1967, and the European Cup Winners' Cup in 1967. By finding a few extraordinarily talented players in their own back yard, they'd started a new era in German football. Almost simultaneously, Bayern discovered Franz Beckenbauer and Georg Schwarzenbeck in Munich, Sepp Maier in the Munich suburb of Haar, Gerd Müller and Bulle Roth in provincial Bavarian towns. Heinz Höher had already forgotten that five years before, he had left an offer from Bayern Munich unanswered.

At his team-talk, Bayern's manager, the Yugoslav Tschik Cajkovski, told them: 'Tonight for us no crooked path, we look for take route one into final.' If Cajkovski could actually speak decent German, he was never going to admit to it: his self-taught German, with its minimal use of the definite article, was an inseparable part of his image.

Heinz Höher could hear the game even from inside the dressing-room. The ancient stands creaked and groaned, and then the teams went out onto the pitch. The old stadium on the Castroper Straße could hold 32,000. Forty-one thousand tickets had been sold. At least 45,000 fans were packed into the stadium. The children sat right at the front, 50 cm beyond the touchline. Someone had made hundreds of white cardboard baseball caps stamped VfL Bochum and given them out, thin rubber bands held the caps to the children's foreheads.

A small group of youths were still on the pitch. They were celebrating Mass: they spread blue and white flags out onto the grass, threw
themselves on their knees and bowed again and again to the colours of
their club. The ground filled with rejoicing. One of the youths burned
a Bayern flag. It was still broad daylight. The game was to begin at 5.30.
The stadium had no floodlights.

Heinz Höher was wearing number nine, the proud badge of the centre-
forward, the man for the big moment, the man who scored the goals. That
was their trick. With the opposition treating him as the centre-forward, he
would keep on drifting back away from their penalty area, tempting his
opposite numbers out, so that Charly Böttcher or Werner Ballte could
storm up into the gaps and he could feed them with cross-passes.

Bayern's team doctor, Erich Spannbauer, looked round the stadium
and said to Hans Schiefele, football correspondent of the *Süddeutsche
Zeitung*, 'I think I'm in for a busy day.'

The referee blew his whistle, and Eversberg played the ball from
the kick-off out onto the right wing, where Gerd Wiesemes picked it
up on the run – it was his great year, 1968; when he steamed up, there
was no stopping him – Wiesemes crossed and Böttcher's header hit the
post. The smack of ball on wood was like an electric shock to the
crowd, the excitement flung their bodies forwards, it took several seconds to clear them all off the pitch again. Not a single Bayern Munich
player had yet touched the ball. Six minutes into play, Hans-Jürgen
Jansen made it 1-0 to Bochum. Franz Beckenbauer just stood there, in
that wonderfully elegant way he had, and silently shook his head. It
was as if you could hear his thoughts.

Half an hour later, the second unconscious spectator was carried out.
One fan fell off the roof of the stands.

Bayern couldn't find their way out of the maze of Bochum's passing
game. Heinz Höher's blond hair could be seen lighting up the place.
He was the only one in the team who wore it down over his ears, even
just by a couple of millimetres. Top-flight sportsmen were not just
pushing things into new dimensions with their muscles, but also with
their eyes. Heinz Höher was playing with laser-sharp vision.
Sometimes he passed the ball first touch into the open space behind
Beckenbauer, sometimes he held the ball for a second and shimmied
in front of Beckenbauer, turning the tempo of the game up or down, as
he saw fit. He was back.

In the first two rounds of the cup, as Bochum were on their way to making a sensation of themselves with victories over Karlsruhe and Stuttgart, Heinz Höher had sat things out on the substitutes' bench. He was unable to take it in. Wasn't he good enough even for a second division side, now?

One of Sepp Herberger's comments plagued him: you've got a lot to do, and even more to give up. What did Herberger know about what he couldn't give up?

He knew very well that alcohol and late nights weren't particularly healthy. But he salved his guilty conscience with the thought that he did more training than all the rest. So maybe he didn't have to give up so much as them, either.

He got up at 5.30 and went running in the woods at Weitmar before beginning his servitude in the Schlegel brewery. When the others finished team training sessions he stayed behind and ran up the grass hill that served as a spectator stand, ten times at a full-on sprint, then did five more 30-second sprints with a half-minute pause in between them.

His team-mates made fun of him. You and your training, you must be crazy. They loved him precisely because he was an oddball. But it would never have occurred to anyone other than him to do extra training like that. Instead, you could use that time to get started playing cards right there in the dressing-room, after showering, dressed only in your towel, and enjoy your well-earned exhaustion after training.

Heinz Höher felt superior to the others. He, the former sports student, the training partner of Holdorf the Olympic champion decathlete, was the only one of them who really understood the principles of training. Or, if he was honest with himself, did he do all that running just so that in the evening, at peace with his own conscience, he could have a couple of beers and a shot?

He wiped those thoughts from his mind, thinking about things brought you nothing but disquiet.

Right, you just put a stop to all that crap for once, manager Hermann Eppenhoff ordered him. The manager forbade him to do any more extra training.

The principle of supercompensation was still not known in the Bundesliga. Heinz Höher and Hermann Eppenhoff had simply employed it, without knowing: a sportsman exhausts himself for a time by training to a level beyond his normal physiological capability. Afterwards, he only undertakes very mild training, but this combination of extreme training/extreme recovery allows the body to reach a higher level of achievement than before. Forty-five years later in the Bundesliga, Bayer 04 Leverkusen manager Robin Dutt wanted to train using the concept of supercompensation. The team rebelled against him: what was he on about, training long and hard in the first days of the week, right after a match, and then, after the middle of the week hardly training at all? Did their manager have no idea at all about training techniques?

In the spring of 1968, Heinz Höher had already been back in the team for the DFB Cup quarter-final against Borussia Mönchengladbach. In the weeks leading up to the game, Mönchengladbach manager Hennes Weisweiler had replaced the Monday sauna session with training, to make the importance of the match clear to his team. The police asked spectators to go on foot to the stadium, because the car park was being used for the Easter fair. Bochum won 2-0. The third-placed team in the Bundesliga was out.

When Heinz Höher turned the radio on next day he heard what had really happened on the evening they were beating Mönchengladbach. In Berlin, someone had tried to assassinate Rudi Dutschke.

Heinz Höher followed the story of the student demonstrations in the media. The extra-parliamentary opposition, led by Dutschke, was demanding that the old Nazis, who still had jobs in government administration and the judiciary, must be got rid of, and that fresh air must blow away the ultra-conservative fug of the country, which meant that the police appeared as soon as someone played a bit of music, and that the Movement for a Moral Screen went into action at the first sight of a little naked flesh in the cinema. Looked at objectively, Heinz Höher could agree with some of this desire for change, he certainly had nothing against an actress with fine, bare legs. But at the same time these wild students were so different from him, they scared him, and seemed to want a different kind of country than he did, maybe even communism? But the main thing he felt was that all of that was incredibly far off from his own life.

The half-time interval of the DFB Cup semi-final against Bayern Munich was reduced from 15 to ten minutes so that even if the game went to extra time it could still finish in daylight. The stadium tannoy read out a telegram from the minesweeper MS *Bochum* to VfL Bochum: 'Go sink that fat torpedo!'

Each time Jürgen Jansen went to take a corner for Bochum, he had to clear a path between the spectators for his run-up. The Bavarians had to take their corners with almost no run-up at all. The Bochum supporters refused to get out of the way. Right on the 60-minute mark, Werner Balte let fly a sizzling shot at goal either from the edge of the box or from 20 or 25 metres out. These differing opinions of the range were given out next day in the newspaper reports of the match. The football writers had to trust their naked eyes, which evidently saw things in various ways. But they all realised one thing: that the ball hit the back of the net. It was 2-0.

The Bavarians snarled back into action. Beckenbauer switched to the attack, his waist-high, side-footed, angled passes were poetry. They had to find a new word for his style of play. The existing names for his position, second centre-half, double-stopper, sweeper – they were all too banal, they got nowhere near to describing what he did. Beckenbauer, who had started out with the Bavarians, at 18 years of age, as a left-winger was now a playmaker who'd come out of nowhere, a free agent, a free-spirited man in a game dominated by systems. Breaking from defence, he charged around over the entire pitch. They called him a *libero*, because that foreign word seemed to express the longing for space and freedom which filled his play.

Bochum manager Eppenhoff did something new, something unheard of, something of deepest cunning, to break up Bayern's waves of attacks. He made a substitution. Since the beginning of this season, one substitution per team had been allowed. With three minutes left, Eppenhoff replaced Jablonski with Moritz simply to break the rhythm of Bayern's attacking game.

In the 90th minute, Ohlhauser scored for Bayern, bringing it to 2-1. From now on, the children in the front row of the spectators ran onto the pitch at every blow of the referee's whistle because they expected it to be the final blast and so the referee did indeed soon blow up for time because he couldn't see any way to drive all the spectators off the pitch again.

Franz Beckenbauer disappeared into the dressing-room, walking next to Heinz Höher. Last night they were playing cards until half-past three in the morning, he muttered: you can't win like that.

The newspaper reporters fought their way through the spectators who were trying to get home. The reporters wanted to get into the dressing-room so as to get to work in the latest journalistic fashion. They needed the actual voices of the people who had taken part. 'Is wonderful team Bochum,' said Cajkovski, 'Bayern was tired. Why, I not know.'

Thanks to their defeat in normal time, Bayern Munich managed to catch the evening flight from Düsseldorf to Munich. VfL Bochum celebrated until late at night in the Gasthaus Frein, 100 metres from the stadium down the Castroper Straße. As ever, all-comers were welcome, the players, the board, reporters, spectators.

Next morning at 6 o'clock sharp Gerd Wiesemes, the flying outside-back, was back at work at the steelworks; he wasn't just proud about getting to the final, but also about a little personal observation: his thighs were even thicker than those of Bayern's legendary striker, Gerd Müller.

'One more win and our next opponents will be called Milan or Madrid,' wrote the *Westdeutsche Allgemeine*'s Ralf Schrage, who was really a legal reporter. With cup final fever in Bochum, everyone was suddenly a sports journalist. VfL Bochum president Ottokar Wüst ordered that club suits be made – they would, of course, be made by his own gentlemen's outfitting business – for the final in Ludwigshafen against Cologne. Heinz Höher and Gerd Wiesemes were pretty astonished when they saw the colour of the suits: as brown as shit.

Not everybody was over the moon that a Bundesliga 2 side should be in the DFB Cup final. At the headquarters of the DFB, the German Football Union, in Frankfurt, some people feared that the stadium wouldn't be full. The DFB wanted to refuse to allow TV 1 to show the final live. A TV transmission would really make sure no spectators came at all.

Doris Höher and Erika Wiesemes got themselves platform-tickets so that they could see their men off on the express-train the day before the final. Erika Wiesemes had bought one of these brand-new film-cameras especially for the occasion. It could shoot in colour. The men wore their shit-brown suits, complete with handkerchiefs in their breast pockets. The *Westdeutsche Allgemeine*'s Knud Beukert interviewed Helmut Oberländer, who was to drive the express train D370 via Cologne to Ludwigshafen. 'I'm keeping my fingers crossed for Bochum,' said the train driver. Doris Höher told the newspaper reporter that Heinz Höher had to put four-year-old Markus across his lap just before they left because the little boy had wet his bed. 'If we win in Ludwigshafen, he can do it for once and get away with it,' she told the reporter, who added for the benefit of his readers that she was joking. In the papers the women were just called: the players' wives.

The wives would travel direct to the final on Saturday. Having them there beforehand would simply disturb the men's concentration.

In the first-class train compartment, even before they got to Wattenscheid, Gerd Wiesemes, Gustav Eversberg, Charly Böttcher and Heinz Höher started dealing the cards out.

Cologne had already been preparing for the final all week at their training camp. The place where they were staying was called Maikammer. There were woods all around, and beyond the woods the vineyards of the Pfalz stretched away. The Cologne players took up residence in a guest-house called Waldhaus Wilhelm. Comfort just made players lazy, was what managers thought. What a team needed at a training camp was to be cut off. On the breakfast tables at the Waldhaus Wilhelm there stood little vases holding wild flowers which the staff had picked themselves outside. The Cologne team doctor injected players Wolfgang Weber and Heinz Hornig against hay-fever.

The Bochum players had had to work during the week. The night before the final they moved into the Gartenhotel Heuser in Bad Dürkheim. The *Westdeutsche Allgemeine* reporter had got out of the express at Cologne. Going on with the team to Bad Dürkheim wasn't worth the pricey ticket.

In the evening, manager Eppenhoff sent the team to the cinema. They watched *Guns of Violence*. On the way back, Gerd Wiesemes plucked a couple of cherries from a branch overhanging the garden fence and ate them, more just to pass the time than from hunger. In the hotel bar he had another beer with Heinz Höher to calm his nerves.

Wiesemes lay awake all night. It must have been the cherries, or maybe the cherries mixed with the beer. He threw up again and again, the sweat poured from him. Next day he played, of course.

The stands were loud with the all-pervading roar of anticipation. Over 60,000 of the 70,000 capacity at the South West Stadium was filled. In one block, where blue and white specks were particularly common, a man held a banner up on two bamboo poles: 'Who's afraid of the big bad goat?'

Bochum had overcome four Bundesliga teams, one after the other. Now it was just Cologne, with that famous goat on their coat of arms, who stood in their way: after that it was Europe here we come, Bochum vs Madrid, Milan, or, yes, well, Banik Ostrava.

Cologne's usual strip was all white, the colours of Real Madrid, the colours of the best teams, or at least, of the teams which considered themselves the best. Cologne's full title was 1. FC Cologne – they even had the word *first* in their name itself. They were the first champions of the Bundesliga, they had a proper training ground like an English club and strips by Pierre Cardin. Their team for the cup final in 1968 included players like Wolfgang Rausch or Jürgen Jendrossek who were already wearing sideburns. Just play your own game, said Bochum's manager, Hermann Eppenhoff to his team.

On the pitch immediately before the whistle blew, Bochum captain Horst Christopeit introduced a visitor to his team. German Chancellor Kurt Georg Kiesinger had come. He welcomed every member of the opposing teams with a handshake. For a moment, Ludwigshafen was part of England. This statesmanlike greeting-ceremony had been copied from the FA Cup final over there; at Wembley, the Queen said hello to the teams before the kick-off.

Bochum's passes were hit with the haste that comes when you try to do something especially well. Most footballers get infected, when over-eager nervousness breaks out in their team. Heinz Höher became suddenly quite calm in the midst of his team's excitement in Ludwigshafen. He drifted deeper into the no-man's-land between the opposition defence and their midfield, where the Cologne players were usually a fraction late in picking him up. 'Clever play from Höher, who took up a good position,' wrote Dieter Überjahn, the man from *Kicker*, and 'Again and again Bochum attacked on a broad front, with Höher usually standing out among them.' Back home in Bochum, there was already a 20-metre long banner in front of the City Hall. 'Bochum welcomes the Cup,' it said.

After 22 minutes a cross came in and Werner Jablonski just got his head to it, the ball slid across his temple and flew unstoppably between the posts – his own posts.

Football pundits often put a victory into one of two categories: 'deserved' or 'undeserved'. But what you deserve is nothing to do with football. There are just goals and victories which come from dominance on the pitch, or victories and goals like Cologne's that day, born from a moment of genius or folly, completely unconnected to the run of play.

Bochum kept trying. Up in the stands, Chancellor Kiesinger thought to himself that he could see no difference between the Bundesliga and the Bundesliga 2. The whole of Bochum City Council was at the stadium. They had voted unanimously to come to Ludwigshafen.

Höher struck another pass from deep. Jablonski, cursed with that own goal, had been driven forward by the desire to make up for his *faux pas*. He latched straight onto Höher's through ball, Cologne keeper Milutin Soskic couldn't hold onto his vehement shot, the ball trundled aimlessly across the box. Charly Böttcher, the card-player, forced it into the net.

The dream was still alive.

There was barely enough time to think that thought. And then Carl-Heinz Rühl put Cologne back into the lead: 2-1.

At half-time, no one thought that the game was decided. 'Respect to Bochum, they've got cup blood in their veins,' said Sepp Herberger, who stood surrounded by Dieter Überjahn and the other reporters as though it was still 1954. Herberger was just another spectator amid the 60,000 now, with his dark hunter's hat and the inevitable trenchcoat, a biro between his fingers. In 1964 he handed over the job of Germany's manager to Helmut Schön. This change of managers had not taken place at exactly the same time as the founding of the new league, but it felt like it, as if an epochal change had been completed with the introduction of the Bundesliga: football before/after Herberger. Heinz Höher had 45 minutes left to prove that he was at home in both eras.

The banner was still being flown aloft: 'Who's afraid of the big bad goat?' Bochum's outside-halves still made ground, Wiesemes charged, though all he could feel was pain where his legs should be. Just inside his own half, Cologne's Rühl broke down Bochum's passing game and simply dribbled forward. It was over 60 metres to the goal, but there were only three opponents before him, since all the rest of the Bochum side had gone forward. Rühl twisted and slalomed, a dummy and keeper Christopeit was beaten too. 3-1. Suddenly – everything in football happens suddenly – Bochum's defenders Wiesemes, Versen and Schiller, who had all come into the game sick or carrying injuries, felt the weight of their wounds. Suddenly Heinz Höher, who had run like crazy, was just standing there. There were still 33 minutes left and he knew: the game was finished.

Gerd Wiesemes was nowhere to be seen when the cup was presented. He was lying on the floor in the dressing-room, thinking that he was dead. His circulation had taken the final whistle as an order to give in. The Cologne players came into the dressing-room. They invited the Bochum team to be their guests at their first European Cup match. Heinz Höher took their invitation in with eyes lowered. He would read the generous reports of his performance in the final, and he too would think: playing for Bochum in the cup final, that was the biggest day. But that didn't stop either him or Gerd Wiesemes from feeling that they'd let themselves down.

What is it about football, that turns you like that? That makes you always feel most deeply about the things you *haven't* achieved?

Erika Wiesemes put on a short black skirt for the post-match banquet at the Garden Hotel in Bad Dürkheim. Skirts were mini, these days. Elegantly dressed like this, she spent most of the evening at her husband's bedside. Heinz Höher sat silently in the banqueting hall, drinking a couple of beers and a shot. Doris, who was troubled with angina, wasn't in much of a mood for celebrating, either.

Gerhard Wendland, his thick hair combed back with pomade, as it had been in his great days, tried as hard as he could to bring joy to the banqueting hall with his band. Wendland, the big recording star, was friends with manager Hermann Eppenhoff, which was why Bochum had been able to get him. He sang his hits: 'Only Dolores Can Do That With Her Legs', or 'No No No Valentina'. And so bit by bit the mood improved. 'Mary-Rose, Mary-Rose!' shouted the players' wives from their places, sat before the fine white tablecloths. Wendland smiled, nodded to his band, and then sang, to round the day off: 'Mary-Rose, Mary-Rose, it's your tears, I suppose . . .'

Bochum invented a job for Heinz Höher: manager Eppenhoff greets his new assistant manager.

ON THE OTHER SIDE OF THE TOUCHLINE

Heinz Höher was less and less happy in his work at Schlegel's. It came as a surprise to him that the brewery might no longer wish to keep him on either. Perplexed, he let the words of their personnel manager sink in: we have thus decided to terminate your employment.

He had thought that no longer having to go to that office would feel like liberation. Now, it came as a shock. He'd always defined himself as a professional footballer, even at a time when that job officially still didn't even exist in Germany. The 1000 marks monthly which Schlegel paid him had allowed him to live on in the illusion that all he really did was play football, it was just that in addition to training, he had to while away a couple of hours in the office beneath the malting-silos. He was the playmaker of Bochum, who were pushing for promotion to the Bundesliga, a cup finalist with 'the most astonishing team of the year', as *Kicker* called them. But the fact was that, all the same, he was out of work.

He had never had to worry about money. Now, he started counting. He got 320 marks a month from Bochum plus, if he was lucky, 500 marks more through bonuses for matches won, and then that 5000 marks cash in hand per season. But no one knew when the club's president was going to pay their bonuses. On the debit side of the ledger stood 392 marks per month for rent alone, bills not included. Car, food, clothes, card games. He didn't have to count for long to know that things were going to be tight.

Those useless idiots at Schlegel's, if they'd actually let him work, he would have thought up the most incredible advertising campaigns, all they'd have had to do was ask him for his ideas. Instead, they had him doing rubbish jobs, like writing personal letters to pub landlords, Bochum's star player writes to you, crap like that. Bunch of useless idiots.

He joined the queue at the dole office in Universitätsstraße and signed on as unemployed. He refused to talk about what it looked like in that office, or what it felt like to report there.

Not long after Heinz Höher was made redundant, his team-mate Gerd Wiesemes opened an agency for Allianz Insurance in the Alleestraße. If you played your cards right as a professional footballer, you saved up the money that you'd earned from playing football on top of your actual day-job, so that by 30 you had some decent start-up capital for a new career when your playing days were done.

Heinz Höher came to Wiesemes's insurance office on a regular basis. The back room was great for playing cards. But he couldn't see himself in an office like that. Back as a 16-year-old, he had broken off as an apprentice salesman at Humboldt Deutz after three months. He didn't want to spend his days at work that didn't interest him. The only thing for which he had a really burning interest was sport. Maybe writing, too, but that was a non-starter, for sure. He'd blown it with his teaching qualification; in 1968, people were saying that everything was possible, but there was certainly no way that he could go back to university at 30. There was only one way out. He would have to become a manager.

From among his old letters, Heinz Höher dug out the address in Hohensachsen. He held onto the vague hope that Sepp Herberger still liked him. He wrote to the retired Germany manager asking if he could put a word in for him so that he would be accepted as a trainee manager at the German Sports University.

At the Sports University in Cologne, Borussia Mönchengladbach manager Hennes Weisweiler taught the future elite managers of German football side by side with ordinary sports students. Football was a special subject within the normal programme of sports study; after an intensive one-year course, aspiring managers were awarded the Diploma of the Union of German Football Coaches. During his teaching,

Weisweiler now and then set unexpected tasks: if one of the normal sports students got above himself in the theory class, when it came to the training match later on, he took great pleasure in telling one of the Bundesliga players: give that one a good kicking. Willi Holldorf, the Olympic decathlon gold medallist from Leverkusen, took the football managers' diploma as part of his sporting studies. Gyula Lóránt, praised by many Bundesliga players as the best manager of their careers, had to do the course twice. The Examinations Committee who worked with Weisweiler found that the Hungarian's lecture had been impossible to understand – just from a linguistic point of view, naturally.

The Germans maintained that their way of training managers was unique in all the world. No other country, they said, prepared its managers so systematically. As well as running its course of study, the Union of German Football Coaches also often published double-page essays in *Kicker* on Mondays, by sports scientists from all over the world, such as that by Dr Miroslav Choutka, lecturer at the Sports University of Prague concerning 'The analysis of movements in kicking with the instep'. These two pages in *Kicker* also gave out the addresses and telephone numbers of the top managers so that every interested aspirant trainer could turn to them for advice. Paul Oswald, the great manager of Eintracht Frankfurt, place of residence 10 Letzter Hasenpfad, could be reached on 06102/5515.

Hennes Weisweiler let Heinz Höher know exactly what he thought about people who elbowed their way onto the managers' course by going over his head and getting recommended by Herberger. When Höher said something in class, Weisweiler stared out of the window of the lecture theatre. When Höher turned up one Monday with a torn muscle in his thigh, Weisweiler didn't exempt him from practical training.

Mr Weisweiler, please, I need my thighs so that I can feed my family by playing football, said Heinz Höher. Imagine it was one of your own players that was injured.

Mönchengladbach's Berti Vogts, Hartwig Bleidick and Rudolf Pöggeler were on the course with him. It was common for current players to start training as managers towards the end of their careers; the lectures took place only in the mornings out of consideration for those in Bundesliga teams. But Vogts was only 21, Bleidick 23.

Whoa, did you hear that: he thinks I'd give you preferential treatment, said Weisweiler to the Mönchengladbach trio, so loudly that everyone could hear it.

Heinz Höher buckled to and, with his torn thigh muscles, carried out the training exercises on the football pitch without complaint. From that day on, Weisweiler treated him in a friendly manner. Heinz, you have a go, said Weisweiler sometimes at 8 o'clock in the first theory class, when his head was still heavy from a few schnappses the previous evening. Heinz Höher stood before the class and gave a spontaneous talk about how playing four against four on a miniature pitch was the ideal way to improve passing, or whatever else was on the timetable. Weisweiler sat next to him, arms crossed and eyes open, sleeping off his hangover.

Forty years before, Ernest Hemingway had shown everybody what a real man was: someone who could hold his drink at the bar and go his own way, as hard as nails. Neither Weisweiler nor Heinz Höher, nor anyone else with any sense, doubted this ideal of manliness.

At night, Heinz Höher lay awake and thought about the snow falling outside the window. In the morning, at the Sports University, he had the practical component of his managerial exam, and the theme was a warm-up game played five against two. How was he supposed to demonstrate this to the commission, in all that snow?

He often woke up at night, and then he couldn't stop thinking. Yesterday in training, why didn't you make that sidestep a tenth of a second earlier? If you had, you'd have got past Dieter Versen; if Wüst never actually pays the cash in hand, at least I'll get a couple of suits from his gentleman's outfitters; those bastards at Schlegel's, those bastards.

If he could only tame his thoughts, and order them, it wouldn't be so unbearable to lie here awake.

And then Heinz Höher had an idea. He invented Mr Winzlinger.

He imagined that there was a man with him in his bedroom, to discuss all his night thoughts with. Then the problems wouldn't circle round him any more, he'd be able to deal with them, structure them as a fictional dialogue.

Hello there, Winzling, he greeted his imaginary person.

I'm no Winzling, I want a real surname and would prefer the title Dr. After all, I am the boss of your ideas.

What about Mr Winzlinger?

Pah.

Now just you listen, Winzlinger, tomorrow it's the final exam for my managers' course. If I'm going to pass, I've got to put something original into a game of five against two. But with all this snow, there's no way to get the exercise going properly.

I just might have an idea there, said Winzlinger.

Next morning, the examining committee was there, standing on the Sports University's football pitch, five men, their hands in their jacket pockets, their chins tucked down into their collars. Heinz Höher laid out a circle of little orange plastic cones. Seven of his fellow-students were there as his laboratory rabbits. All over the world, five against two was a favourite game among all footballers, five stand in a circle and kick the ball about, the two in the middle have to try to get it.

Right, since there's snow today we're going to change the rules, said Heinz Höher: the two in the middle can go for the ball with their hands too.

What the hell's this? grunted Weisweiler.

Gentlemen, said Heinz Höher. Let's go.

The ball zipped across the smooth, round the circle, from foot to foot, and then one of the two in the middle tried for the first time to dive for the ball like a goalie. Everybody laughed.

This is supposed to be football training! shouted Weisweiler.

This is a playful warm-up, said Höher.

The players taking part in the exam laughed and made the ball zip about; they wanted to watch the two in the middle dive and fly. Even they themselves didn't notice that while they were doing so they were practising a fast, precise passing-game.

You just graduated, said Weisweiler, and held his hand out to Heinz Höher.

He was still playing for Bochum and was already being treated as a manager. Ottokar Wüst was keen to seek his advice in sporting matters, and in the early summer of 1969, Heinz Höher noticed during a conversation with his president that he was acting as a future manager, though he was a player. Just sign Walitza, he hassled Wüst. Hans Walitza of Schwarz-Weiss Essen was seen as an immensely talented centre-forward. That was the position Heinz Höher usually played at Bochum. He had just recommended his own demotion to the subs' bench.

In the summer of 1970, after a season in which Bochum, with a revelation of a centre-forward in Hans Walitza, reached the play-offs for the Bundesliga and once again missed promotion, football player Heinz

Höher officially became a manager. He was 32. Not many players had been able to keep their playing careers going so long. He wasn't looking back on unfulfilled dreams any more, now he was looking to the future.

Footballers became managers at the end of their careers either because they loved football so much that they wanted to stay in the game whatever, or because they had actually always seen themselves as some kind of teacher figure, or because being a manager was at least better than being landlord of a pub. It was only rarely that specialists like Hennes Weisweiler or Dettmar Cramer made their way in the Bundesliga, men for whom being a manager was not just the second best job after being a footballer, but the great fulfilment, their true goal.

Anyone who hadn't been a good player themselves, couldn't work with good players, that was what everyone thought. Apart from two managers whose time as players have been lost to the war, only one out of the 18 Bundesliga managers in July 1970, Klaus-Dieter Ochs of Hamburg, hadn't played in the first or second division himself.

Bochum invented a job for Heinz Höher. He became assistant manager. In the last few years, several clubs in the Bundesliga had got themselves an assistant manager, it was seen as modern. Not to mention chic, a sign of real attention to detail. The only problem was that Bochum manager Hermann Eppenhoff had no use for an assistant.

Eppenhoff had the taciturn ways of a man who'd lost too many feelings in the war. It was four years after the end of the war before Eppenhoff came back from captivity in Russia. Part of his formal elegance was the minimalism of his gestures, the stiff smile that was his only indication of joy after a sensational cup victory. With his suit he wore a rollneck sweater instead of a tie. He had learned his football in the 1930s.

The training timetable at Bochum sounded extremely scientific: on Mondays, swimming and water exercises at Bergmannsheil; on Tuesdays, endurance training; on Wednesdays, power training; on Thursdays a game between two teams; on Fridays, individual training and tactical practice. In reality what they did almost every day was to have a free-for-all game over the full pitch.

Heinz Höher had ideas, in the nights, he had talked it all through with Winzlinger, he could bring the team on with a completely new kind of training. He needed to sit down with Eppenhoff just once and talk it all through.

At the training sessions Eppenhoff and Höher stood silently next to each other, day after day.

Well go on then, you coward, you just don't dare talk to him, said Winzlinger at night.

You just stay out of it, I'll do it, I just need to wait for the right moment.

You'd been saying that for days.

Shut up, I want to get some sleep!

Two days later, just after the start of the season, Hermann Eppenhoff found a letter in the manager's room. Heinz Höher, with whom he had just been exchanging meaningless pleasantries, had left it there before rushing home.

Bochum, 21.8.1970

Dear Mr Eppenhoff,

You will be doubtless surprised, to say the least, to receive a letter from me, since we, after all, see each other almost every day, and I have certainly had the opportunity to say to you what I herewith put down to you in writing. I have been moved to do this not by fear of an open discussion, but rather by the fact that every time I have sought to have such a discussion, you have cut yourself off and made yourself unapproachable, for reasons I quite understand since this subject is one of the few in footballing matters about which you and I – as I understand it – are of different opinions.

I would like to begin by saying that I, who as a player have indeed got to know a few managers, and have conversed with a few, consider you one of the best managers in Germany. What follows therefore merely concerns a few small aspects of what it takes to be a good manager.

The immediate catalyst for this letter was the night of Wednesday to Thursday, more specifically the television report of the Cup game between Aachen and Cologne. What Cologne showed in terms of speed, movement and endurance, against an opponent of approximately our own present playing strength was, in my opinion, the stuff of dreams.

Compared to these footballing jet-planes, our players seem at best like two-engined propeller machines.

This morning, I carried out a lengthy telephone conversation with Cologne player Werner Biskup (call charge: c. 15 marks) during the course of which it became clear that Cologne's weekly training programme consists 70% of work under conditioning trainer Rolf Herings and 30% of work more focused on play and tactics under Mr Ocwirk.

You, like me, are of the opinion that the kind of performances we produced last season will attract 3 to 4000 fewer spectators per game this season, and our first three home games against Gütersloh, Hamborn and Gelsenkirchen have fitted all too well into the pattern of last season.

My immodest proposal is this: let me have charge of the conditioning and athletic development of our players for eight weeks. If, in that time, we do not have a thoroughly trained-up team, on my head be it.

I remain, with hearty greetings, yours sincerely
Heinz Höher

No manager likes to be told that he's got no idea, however politely the words are chosen. Hermann Eppenhoff agreed to a compromise: Heinz Höher was to be allowed to give extra training to the second XI. But he would leave the first team in peace with his fanatical training ideas.

Every day after training, the old hands like Gerd Wiesemes went into the changing room and laughed at the young players. They were still being flogged round the training ground by that nutter Höher. Up the hill behind the goal and down again, long steps on the way up, small steps on the way down, and keep your rhythm, faster, hup hup hup.

Any self-respecting professional hated hard training. This mind-set was part of a player's self-image. A good footballer didn't need to train, he had talent. But secretly, just to themselves, some of the young Bochum players, like Jürgen Köper, the most talented of them all, were thinking that Heini Höher was making them better with his modern training methods; that he was the manager for them, for a new generation.

When second division side Schwarz-Weiss Essen went looking for a manager in the autumn of 1970, their choice was Heinz Höher. Many at Bochum – players like Gerd Wiesemes or the director of the youth academy Erwin Steden – had the feeling that Höher was only leaving so that he could come back. Essen was the neighbouring city, he was simply going to finish his apprenticeship there before taking over at Bochum.

On 6 June 1971, Heinz Höher was feeling pretty well pleased with the way his first year as manager at Essen had gone. Then he turned on the TV and his first thought was: Oh sweet Jesus.

He was sure he'd land on his feet, whatever: Heinz Höher's friend Manfred Manglitz after the Bundesliga Scandal.

6 June 1971:

REAL FRIENDS

He recognised the voice straight away. The tape-recording was a bit fuzzy, but Heinz Höher could immediately put a face to that Cologne sing-song. He was sitting at home in his living room on 6 June 1971, a date that he wasn't going to forget, and he'd turned on the TV to watch the evening news. The screen showed the tape-recorder from which that voice was coming.

'It's nearly all set up,' said the voice. 'But listen, Mr Konrad said something to me about Jupp Kappelmann.'

'Yeah, he called Kremer. I don't know what he wanted,' replied another voice on the end of the telephone line, a voice croaking huskily, short of breath from stress.

'Yeah, yeah, yeah. He's too green for this business.'

'Too green.'

'He's twenty, I'm not keen on having green kids like him in on a deal like this, they're too gabby.'

'Absolutely.'

'You think so too?'

'Absolutely.'

'You've got to know who you're doing this thing with and what you're doing and all that. No twenty-year-old's any good for that, they're all over the place, mouthing off.'

Heinz Höher didn't need the TV presenter to explain things. He could hear between the lines. The voice with the Cologne accent was

that of Manfred Manglitz, his old team-mate at Leverkusen and
Meiderich, who had risen to be national keeper and was presently
keeping goal at 1. FC Cologne – and who had tried to sell Cologne's
last game of the season, against Kickers Offenbach, to Offenbach president Hans-Georg Canellas. It'll all come out now, thought Heinz
Höher, hopefully it won't all come out now.

Five-year-old images came back into his mind. He'd hoped to have
forgotten them long since: with a surging run, he breaks through the
Maastricht cover, it's May 1966, the penultimate matchday in the Dutch
first division, he crosses low into the box . . . and not one of the Twente
Enschede forwards even attempts to reach his perfect ball. Heinz
Höher looks up in consternation. Heinz, shouts one of his team-mates
and gives him a sign, a quick cut through the air with his hand flat. End
of. Heinz Höher can't understand, and at the same time he suddenly
understands everything: why Twente Enschede's keeper just smacked
an opponent as if he was positively begging to be sent off, why a com-
prehensive 2-0 lead has suddenly turned into 2-2, why his team-mates
lose the ball every time they touch it. For Twente, there's nothing at
stake in this game, Maastricht need a win to escape relegation.

Heinz Höher won't have it. He dribbles like a man possessed. But
no one wants his crosses. Heinz Höher doesn't complain, he doesn't
accuse anyone, he keeps on running, he feels as if he's being driven by
panic. Just before the final whistle, one of Twente's defenders stumbles
inside his own box, leaving Maastricht forward Michel Thal a clear run
at goal. Heinz Höher thinks he saw how come his team-mate stumbled:
he tripped himself up. Thal scores and Maastricht win 3-2.

Heinz Höher is already showered when one of the Maastricht players appears in Twente's dressing-room, holding a plastic bag. He goes
around, from man to man. Everyone gets something from the bag, it's
like he's dishing out sweets. The banknotes feel hot in Heinz Höher's
hand.

Saying no is not an option. In any group, few people have the guts
to break step, and it's doubly so in a football team, where the most
important thing is to belong, to be loyal, to create a group mentality
where you prove to each other that you are all cool, that you are never
uncertain of yourselves.

Heinz Höher hastily shoves the notes into his trouser pocket. He
doesn't count them properly till he gets home. It's 320 guilders. He'd
have got 250 as his normal bonus if they'd have won. For a profit of 70

pathetic guilders, that's all of 77 marks, he's bought shame upon himself. He's done something he was sure he would never do, and he doesn't even know why.

In that game at Maastricht he went along with things silently, rather than actually doing them, but he shows himself no mercy: alone with himself, he calls himself a cheat, a criminal.

In June 1971, he had no real reason to fear that the investigation into match-fixing in the Bundesliga would lead to the discovery of a thrown game five years before in the Netherlands. But he didn't need to be summoned before any commission or media investigation; it was enough to be summoned by himself, enough that being confronted with Manglitz's dealings reminded him of his own repressed shame. As the revelations broadened out, in the months following 6 June, into what became forever known as the 'Bundesliga Scandal', Heinz Höher kept his head down, quietly longing for it all to be over and done with at last.

Almost 20 games from the final weeks of the 1970-71 Bundesliga season came under suspicion of having been fixed. Three teams threatened with relegation, Bielefeld, Offenbach and Oberhausen, had got into an insane bidding-war in the attempt to buy their way out of the drop. A fourth club facing relegation, Eintracht Frankfurt, had at least thought about improving their luck through a dose of cash. Corruption was no longer the exception, but a generally accepted means to an end, and the introduction of the Bundesliga had probably played its part in this development. Eight years after the foundation of the national league, playing in the Bundesliga had taken on such social and financial importance that many a powerful figure in a club would do anything, just to stay up. Demotion to Bundesliga 2 meant the threat of your turnover going down from 3,000,000 to 300,000 marks, and to many club bosses, given the level of debt which 16 of the 18 Bundesliga clubs had heaped up, that seemed to spell ruin. If they lost their place in the Bundesliga, a club was faced with losing all their decent players, because under the rules of the German Football Union, professional contracts applied exclusively to the Bundesliga; relegation rendered those contracts null and void. And what kind of prestige would be left to a city, to a club, to the club bosses themselves, if they were now playing not against Mönchengladbach and Bayern Munich, but against Lünen and Neuss?

Corruption was also nourished by the arcane laws governing professional players. The official maximum wage was unrealistically low, so black-market cash payments had become the norm. Taking illegal payments was just part of everyday life for the players. That chipped away at their sense of right and wrong.

Gradually, Heinz Höher found more and more names of his friends and colleagues cropping up in the Bundesliga Scandal. But much of it he learned only 40 years later, while researching this book. He wasn't sure if he really wanted to know.

Manfred Manglitz had always liked to treat ideas which other people thought of as crazy as golden opportunities. When, in the middle of the 1960s, the sports equipment firm Hummel published the first autograph card collection of the Meiderich team, his team-mates kept the cards as the proud sign of their new-found fame. Manglitz, the keeper, had the cards copied by the thousand at a printer's. At the next home game, he sent his 17-year-old nephew and a friend out with them, the nephew took care of the main stand and his friend took over on the opposite side of the ground. They demanded 25 pfennings a card. Within three or four home games they'd sold all 10,000.

From his parents, bookbinders who had never employed more than four or five people, Manfred Manglitz had come to see that every penny counted, and he'd learned that one deal can generally be tied in with another. When, at 21, his talent as a goalkeeper with SC West in Cologne could no longer be ignored, his father advised him to switch to Bayer 04 Leverkusen. When it came to signing the contract, the son was also to secure contracts from the Bayer works for his parents' bookbinding business.

'Never say no to a mark,' was Manfred Manglitz's motto. He was Meiderich's keeper and at the same time, together with forward Heinz van Haarem, he published the match programmes. They personally knocked on the doors of potential advertising customers. Manfred Manglitz appeared in adverts for Handelsgold cigarillos at a time when hardly any players did ads and he himself didn't know how you held cigarillos. In Meiderich, he took over a petrol station: in the mornings, he stood there in the winter's cold at 6.30am, waiting for the tanker with its 400 litres of diesel. His fingers still frozen stiff from filling cars, he went to the training ground at 9am, although training didn't begin till half-past. Then lunch, more training, back to the petrol station till 8pm and then, said Manfred Manglitz, 'then it was time for my sweet little mouse, she still had to be satisfied as well. And somehow, it got to be three am.'

He had met his mouse during his years at Meiderich, in the Discotheque Number One. She worked behind the bar. Manglitz rushed out into the street, found a woman selling flowers, and asked her to take a bouquet of lilies of the valley to the beautiful woman behind the bar at the Number One, with all best wishes from a man who was no bad looker, tall, his hair neatly cut, and who was a some-body in Duisburg. How about that, a woman gets lilies of the valley in a disco, Manglitz thought to himself: cute move, or what?

The thing was, he could never sleep at night. Ever since he was a boy, Manfred Manglitz woke up at night, sometimes at one, sometimes at four, and that was that, after that he lay there awake and thought about things. It was then that all his cute ideas came to him.

In the spring of 1971, when Manfred Manglitz was keeping goal for 1. FC Cologne, the team of his childhood dreams, they played four of the five teams threatened with relegation in their last five fixtures. Cologne, stranded mid-table, had no particular ambitions left. On 1 May, Bielefeld were the first of Cologne's opponents from the group of endangered clubs.

'Raymond Schwab was batting for Bielefeld,' says Manglitz. Schwab, the footballing agent, who had got Heinz Höher his contract at Meiderich and Enschede, was like Manglitz in one respect: he also thought it was cute to make money. How, well, that wasn't so impor-tant. In the meantime, Schwab had been putting himself about as an artiste, as he called it. Department stores could hire him for their open-ing ceremonies. As the crowd stood there, open-mouthed, Schwab would burst asunder the iron chains which been placed around his chest.

Schwab was not named in the investigations surrounding the Bundesliga Scandal. To this day, Cologne's game against Bielefeld is officially regarded as unsullied. Bielefeld were surprise 1-0 winners.

Manfred Manglitz doesn't actually say that the game was thrown, he says: 'It was bad luck for me that we played against all four of the clubs threatened with relegation': Bielefeld, Essen, Oberhausen, Offenbach. 'I got offers from various clubs for all four of those games.' Some clubs offered to pay if Manglitz and Cologne won against their rivals at the bottom of the table. Other go-betweens offered cash if Manglitz and Cologne lost.

120 | MATCHDAYS

Or did Manglitz himself suggest these bonuses, if no one offered them to him?

Four days after their 1-0 defeat to Bielefeld, 1. FC Cologne were once again playing God in the relegation battle. Essen were the visitors to the Müngersdorf stadium. At nine in the morning on the day of the match, Manglitz phoned Offenbach's president, Horst-Gregorio Canellas. Somebody had offered him 25,000 marks to let a couple in against Essen, declared Manglitz, but if Offenbach would match that for Cologne to win, he would naturally play a decent game.

Cute move, thought Manfred Manglitz to himself, that way he could keep himself clean and still earn money.

Canellas got the impression that Manglitz was speaking not just for himself, but for several of the Cologne players. At this point in time, the Offenbach president had never paid bonuses or fixer's fees, but he had certainly heard rumours that money was being deployed in the relegation battle. Canellas told how his own manager had said to him: 'That Raymond Schwab offered us eighty thousand marks to throw a game.' Offenbach's manager was Rudi Gutendorf. 'Boss,' Canellas reported him as saying, 'if we don't buy ourselves some wins, we're going down.'

Canellas lived in Hausen, a suburb of Offenbach where the streets were named after flowers and the hedges were neatly kept. He was boss of a tropical fruit importers in Offenbach. The bigwigs from the German Football Union in Frankfurt liked to go shopping at his place. Canellas gave them a decent discount on bananas and pineapples. Who knew when it might be useful to have friends in the German Football Union? But buying games? Canellas had resisted Gutendorf's pressure up till now. But what if he didn't pay Manglitz? With two points from victory over Cologne, Essen would pull even further away from Offenbach. Canellas called the German FA's general secretary, Horst Schmidt.

Was it forbidden to pay winners' bonuses to members of other teams? asked Canellas. Schmidt promised to have a look at the regulations. Soon afterwards, he called back.

From a purely ethical viewpoint, bonuses like that would naturally not be very sporting, said Schmidt. But they weren't illegal.

Cologne defeated Essen 3-2 in a hard-fought game. On that very evening, Offenbach's chief executive, Willi Konrad, appeared outside Schmitz's hairdressers, 609 Aachenerstraße, right on the outskirts of

Cologne, almost in Junkersdorf. Manfred Manglitz had arranged this meeting-place. Konrad handed Manglitz's bride an envelope containing 25,000 marks. He'd need a receipt for that please, said Konrad.

No one said anything about a receipt, snapped Manfred Manglitz's bride, but signed it nevertheless.

The thing that surprised Manfred Manglitz was this: Bielefeld, Oberhausen and Offenbach always seemed to know about each other's plans for bribery.

In the Bundesliga, bribery was gossiped about like in a game of Chinese whispers. Few people knew what was really going on, but lots of people talked about it among themselves. There were even jokes about it. 'If you take your foot off the gas a bit today, you can earn yourself five grand,' said Eintracht Frankfurt's international Jürgen Grabowski before the kick-off, to his Offenbach opposite number, Walter Bechthold.

In their fear of relegation, the clubs concerned had gone so off the wall that they just couldn't see how insanely they were behaving. Once you started buying victories and defeats, it swiftly came to feel completely normal.

In Bielefeld, president Wilhelm Stute called the club's board to an emergency meeting in the spring of 1971. Anyone who was in Bielefeld and wanted to read Goethe or Heinrich Böll, went to Stute. His bookshop, Gehner & Stute, in the old town centre, was where friends of literature met up. And among the other commercial middle classes who worked in the city centre, Stute was highly respected as well, so active in the community, so honourable. Stute ran Arminia Bielefeld because he wanted to do something for his town. But now, having played a bare year in the Bundesliga, they were threatened with going straight back down. The city had renovated the stadium especially, at a cost of 2.5 million marks, and had slipped Arminia Bielefeld a couple of hundred thousand more, disguised as advertising expenses, so that their football club could put the small town from Eastwestphalia up there on the map of Germany. 'Just don't get relegated again straight away,' Oberbürgermeister Herbert Hinnendahl had said. 'Having a team in the Bundesliga is important for Bielefeld. It improves the image of our town.'

So what are we going to do? asked Stute the bookseller at the emergency board meeting in the spring of 1971. Their manager, Egon

Piechaczek, was ready with advice. They had to do what everyone else was doing, he said: buy matches.

That became the mantra of the season: but everyone was doing it.

Schwab, the players' agent, having evidently been informed by manager Piachaczek about Bielefeld's new tactics, raced from service station to service station across West Germany. He summoned Horst Gecks to the Medenbach autobahn services on the A3 between Frankfurt and Cologne.

Gecks, who eight years previously had battled his friend Heinz Höher for a place on the wing in Meiderich's Bundesliga XI, had at last brought himself to leave his homeland. He now played for Offenbach.

Gecks had received offers from other clubs almost every year, Hanover offered him 40,000 marks before tax per year, in Nuremberg he actually agreed to take on rented accommodation so that he could play for the club there. Every time, he backed off at the last moment. He came from Meiderich, his wife came from next door, in Hamborn. In 1965 they moved into one of the flats which had just been built for the workers at the Phoenix steelworks, the rent was 150 marks. To them, the world beyond Meiderich seemed far off and unknown.

It was only after six years in the Bundesliga that the Geckses could bring themselves to leave. The Meiderich fans had booed too often. When a pass came in and Horst Gecks could feel the opposing thug right behind him, aiming right for his Achilles heel again, not for the ball, he jumped high in the air or turned away, never mind if he lost the ball.

The fans didn't understand it, it had been just the same for Heinz Höher, the spectators didn't understand that while he was certainly brave, he wasn't tired of life. If people in Meiderich liked booing so much, well, they could see how the team did without him, decided Horst Gecks. And so he went to Offenbach.

Schwab was already waiting for him at the autobahn services. So: they were playing Bielefeld on Saturday. Horst Gecks could earn himself 15,000 marks if he hit a few loose passes to make sure that Bielefeld won.

Horst Gecks drove a second-hand VW beetle, for 500 marks a month he worked every morning from nine till 12.30 as a salesman of sporting goods at the superstore in Offenbach. The other, younger Bundesliga players considered themselves to be above such things, as professional footballers, but to Horst Gecks, having a job on the side could only be a good thing: the Kickers didn't train in the mornings anyway and by working in the superstore the rent was already covered and he could get a discount in the fashion department on the one new jacket that he put on each winter. He told Raymond Schwab he wouldn't do something like that.

Schwab accepted this and seemed unperturbed by it. He said that when Gecks went, he'd be staying here at the services. Any minute now he was meeting two other Offenbach players.

The game between Offenbach and Bielefeld is considered not to have been fixed, to this day.

Offenbach won 5-0, with a standout display by Horst Gecks.

At Bielefeld, they realised that they couldn't rely on Schwab. They sent out their own emissaries – their own players. Jürgen Neumann took 45,000 marks to three Stuttgart players, Waldemar Slomiany delivered 40,000 marks to the Schalke team. Bielefeld won both games 1-0. A new problem arose for Bielefeld's president, Stute: winning this way didn't exactly come cheap. Where was he supposed to get all the money from?

He remembered about a man who bought books from him. Rupert Schreiner was a property developer who had amassed considerable wealth from contracts in the Eastern Bloc. He wasn't interested in football. Stute visited him at his own party-cellar at his house.

Schreiner thought to himself, if I help Arminia Bielefeld out, then surely it'll deliver building contracts for me later, in the stadium, at the training ground. At any rate, that was the kind of thing that Schreiner said later, to justify himself in his own eyes.

But really, it could only be explained by the very human tendency to act against your own convictions and your own reasoning when you feel under pressure from outside. That pressure could make a zealous bookshop-owner turn off his business brain and throw away more and more money on bribes to help a football club. It could make a property developer with no interest in football, Rupert Schreiner, not only give Arminia Bielefeld over 100,000 marks, but even jump into action himself as courier for the money.

Bielefeld spent 500,000 marks on bribes. And it didn't seem to occur to anyone that with money like that – if they'd used it legally, to sign new players – they could have stayed up anyway.

'Fixers, fixers!' cried the fans, as Schalke 04 graced their home game against Bielefeld with some lethargic defending and lost 0-1. But could the spectators really smell something rotten? Or was 'fixers' simply the worst word they could think of to shout, when faced with their team performing so feebly?

The show went on, unstoppably. A Cologne hairdresser's salon became the branch office of the scandal.

At 609 Aachenerstraße, coiffeur Wolfgang Schmitz tended to the hair of those in Cologne who counted as prominent figures, or wished they did. The more famous the client, the keener Schmitz was to call him a friend. He called Manfred Manglitz and Eintracht Frankfurt manager Erich Ribbeck really good friends.

When he found out that Manfred Manglitz's wife had pocketed an envelope with a cool 25,000 marks inside, from the chief executive of Offenbach, at the very door of his salon, Schmitz thought to himself that there must be something in it for him.

His really good friend Erich's team, Eintracht Frankfurt, were also stuck in the relegation battle. And his really good friend Manfred was playing against Frankfurt's competitors, Oberhausen, on the third last matchday of the season. What if good old Manfred could help good old Erich out by beating them? Good old Erich would surely be happy to pay a bit for that.

They could talk about it, said Manglitz.

For 22,000 marks, Manfred guarantees you that Cologne will blow Oberhausen away, said the friseur to Ribbeck on the phone. Ribbeck promised he'd get hold of the money.

Twenty thousand for Manglitz, 2000 for me as my percentage, Schmitz calculated. The hairdresser was really excited. He had to share this knowledge with someone. He let his good friend Peter Georg Friesdorf from Opladen in on the secret. Friesdorf was trying to keep his head above water somehow or other in the property business. Well now, if you ask me, Manglitz thought to himself, that Friesdorf was a cock-sucker.

The day before the game between Cologne and Oberhausen on 25 May 1971, the hairdresser asked his friend Friesdorf to come with him to an autobahn service station, where Erich was to hand over the money. To confirm the meeting, Schmitz phoned Erich Ribbeck again from his salon.

Erich told him it wasn't going to work after all. The guy who was providing the money had got cold feet.

What, had he gone crazy? raged the hairdresser, it was all arranged with Manfred Manglitz, what was he going to say now? At this point, Friesdorf elbowed the hairdresser in the ribs. 'Oberhausen,' whispered Friesdorf. Schmitz immediately understood.

'Erich, if you can't do it, it'll happen the other way around,' the hairdresser threatened.

When Schmitz hung up, Friesdorf called directory enquiries and got the number of the Rot-Weiss Oberhausen club office. Oberhausen president Peter Maassen could not be got hold of. The hairdresser took the receiver from Friesdorf's hand. It was very urgent and very personal, said Schmitz, when could he speak to the president?

If you were able to appear in person at the office in about an hour, Mr Maassen would no doubt be around.

They used that hour to actually talk it through with Manfred.

Manfred Manglitz didn't mind it at all that the tabloids called him 'Cassius' these days. Big sports personality, big mouth, he was happy with that image of himself. In the 1960s, when he was still playing for Meiderich, the Schalke fans had heckled him while he was warming up: 'Manglitz is a mor-on, Manglitz is a mor-on.' At Schalke, the fans stood so close behind the goalposts that they could take the keeper's legs from under him with an umbrella handle. Schalke's ground, the Glückauf-Kampfbahn, was the only place in the Bundesliga apart from the Grünwalder Strasse stadium shared by München 1860 and Bayern Munich where the players had to be protected from the fans by fencing. Hold on a sec, said Manglitz to the assistant coach who was warming him up, then he turned round and, with his index finger in the air, began to conduct the Schalke fans in their singing. After three repetitions, the refrain of 'Manglitz is a mor-on' turned into laughter. During the match, the Schalke fans applauded Manglitz whenever he did well.

He worked with journalists the same way he worked with people: if they needed a story, Manfred Manglitz gave them one; and if the stories weren't always true, that was no harm to anybody. His hearty, open manner worked very much to his advantage, thought Manfred Manglitz.

At Cologne's training ground at Müngersdorf, on the Friday before the third last matchday, the hairdresser explained to him that Erich had dropped out. But why didn't they try to just sell the game to Oberhausen?

Yeah, we can sort that out too, answered Manglitz, you pair just keep working away at it.

The hairdresser and Friesdorf drove to Oberhausen, where they were told that Mr Maassen was already with the team in Cologne, at the Hotel Jungbluth. They turned around and drove off again.

In the garden of the hotel, the Oberhausen team were playing cards. Manager Günter Brocker told them that Mr Maassen wasn't there, but that he would certainly be phoning in again. At that moment, Brocker was called to the telephone at the hotel reception.

After a few minutes, Brocker handed the phone over to the hairdresser.

Good evening, Mr Maassen, said the hairdresser. It would have been good to meet up. I may be able to do something for you about the game against Cologne.

Come over right now to the Fritz pub in the Old Marketplace in Oberhausen, answered Maassen.

The following day, Cologne lost 4-2 at home to bottom-of-the-table Oberhausen. 'Manglitz had a truly awful game as well,' wrote *Kicker*, 'he was out of position for the second and fourth Oberhausen goals and made several other mistakes of the kind we're not used to seeing from him.'

Oberhausen's assistant manager, Alfred Preissler, wasn't on the subs' bench as he might usually have been, but was up in the stands, sat next to the celebrity hairdresser from Cologne, Wolfgang Schmitz. At the final whistle, Preissler left a folded-up newspaper behind for the hairdresser.

Eintracht Frankfurt manager Erich Ribbeck was livid when he was told the result at Cologne. He couldn't contain himself, even in front of sports journalists: 'You slave away, week after week you drag the last ounce of performance out of your team, and then you can only watch while other people get gifted away wins like that. Don't try telling me there was nothing funny going on in Cologne.'

The sports journalists came to the conclusion that the relegation battle was stressing Ribbeck out right to the limits.

'Just like that!' cried the hairdresser, when he met Friesdorf at the Derby Gentleman's Club in Cologne that evening. He reached into his wallet and gave Friesdorf 1000 marks.

'What, only a thousand?' asked Friesdorf, offended.

Yeah, well, Maassen had given him only 25,000 instead of the 30,000 they'd agreed on, the hairdresser claimed. He'd had to take the 1000 for Friesdorf out of Manglitz's cut of 21,200 to keep everyone happy.

But Friesdorf needn't get upset. Next Saturday, Oberhausen were playing Werder Bremen. The game had already been sold.

'The most dramatic day ever' was the headline with which *Kicker* chose to announce the final matchday of the 1970-71 Bundesliga season. Essen were already relegated. One more club was for it today. Four teams were still endangered, Eintracht Frankfurt, Offenbach, Bielefeld and Oberhausen, who had surprisingly won their last three games in the row, most recently with a 3-0 victory over Werder Bremen.

Horst-Gregorio Canellas was troubled by stubborn angina. On Whit Monday, five days before the final game, the Offenbach president's voice was no more than a croak when it came to a phone conversation with Manfred Manglitz. On Saturday, Cologne were playing Offenbach. Later, Canellas said Manglitz had called him. Manglitz said it was Canellas who made the call.

Manglitz declared that for 100,000 marks, Cologne would throw the game. He had five players in the palm of his hand, ready to do their bit.

Canellas croaked that he'd need time to think about it. He'd call back.

Meanwhile, the warm-up for the final matchday of the season was in full swing. Bielefeld sent player Jürgen Neumann to Berlin. He mission was to buy victory for Bielefeld against Hertha for 150,000 marks. Neumann swore. All the flights to Berlin were full. He'd have to take the car. On behalf of the Bielefeld board, property developer Rupert Schreiner flew to Braunschweig in his private jet. He had 120,000 marks with him to ensure that Eintracht Braunschweig beat Oberhausen, Bielefeld's rivals for the drop.

All of a sudden, a multiple auction was taking place over the phone lines.

The hairdresser phoned Oberhausen president Peter Maassen: Cologne were ready to throw the game against Offenbach; what would Maassen stump up to make sure Cologne won instead? The hairdresser told his pal Friesdorf that Maassen had 15,000 marks at the ready.

Speaking for the Hertha team, defender Tasso Wild explained to Bielefeld's messenger, Neumann, that 150,000 was not enough for them to promise they'd lose to Bielefeld. He'd have to be looking at a good 100,000 on top of that. Then Wild called Canellas: what would Offenbach pay to make sure that Hertha *didn't* lose to Bielefeld?

'Right, just listen, I can make you a very good offer,' said Wild to Canellas. 'Because we like Offenbach, let's cut all the horse-trading crap and say: one hundred and forty grand, and it's in the bag for you.'

The boys at Braunschweig were cutting up rough, too. A hundred and twenty thousand marks wasn't enough, they wanted 170,000 from Bielefeld to make sure they won against Oberhausen. If not, they could always sell the game to Oberhausen instead.

We can get that together, Bielefeld board member Wilhelm Pieper told Schreiner, the property developer, so as to calm him down. Bielefeld president Wilhelm Stute parcelled the money up for Schreiner using Gehner & Stute Bookshop wrapping-paper.

Horst Gecks, Offenbach's little winger, trained all week with absolute focus. If they played at the top of their game on Saturday in Cologne, they'd stay up, all they had to do was play at the top of their game.

On the Tuesday, four days before the final matchday, Cologne team captain Wolfgang Overath came up to Manfred Manglitz.

He'd just better not try any funny business on Saturday, said Overath.

What was he on about?

Just what he said. No funny business.

Manglitz was nervy. Did Overath know something?

On the Wednesday, three days before the final matchday, Canellas phoned Manglitz back, as promised.

'How's it going?' Manglitz's voice had the sweet sing-song tones of the Cologne dialect.

'Thanks, Mr Manglitz, in terms of my health, somewhat better.' Canellas's voice was still horribly croaky. Muffled by his shortness of breath, his words sounded brusque and snappy.

'Listen,' said Manglitz suddenly, after a few minutes. 'Have you met up with Wolfgang Overath?'

'No.'

'You haven't?'

'No.'

'Because he's saying some weird stuff.'

'What did he say?'

'He wanted to know what's going on, he said a player-agent had phoned him up, a guy who knew figures and this and that and he was really pissed off and all, he asked how come he never knew anything about it. So I thought maybe you'd been with him and said something.'

'I haven't set foot out of Offenbach, I'm not in any fit state to go any-where.'

Without lying, Canellas hadn't told Manglitz the truth. He really hadn't been to see Overath. But he had phoned Cologne's captain on Monday and told him of Manglitz's plans.

From the moment when, back on that Monday morning, Manglitz had offered to assure him victory for 100,000 marks, Offenbach's pres-ident had been playing a double game. He had kept on negotiating with Manglitz and the match-fixers from Berlin. And at the same time he had been taking measures to reveal this corruption.

What Canellas hadn't told Manglitz was that he'd recorded their telephone conversation that Wednesday on a Telefunken tape-recorder borrowed especially for this purpose.

On that Wednesday evening, with two-and-a-half days still to go before the final matchday, Kuno Klötzer, who had taken over as man-ager of Offenbach after the sacking of Rudi Gutendorf, visited Canellas in his bungalow on the Rosenweg in Hausen to find his president 'worked up, all over the place, exhausted'.

Canellas was taking two steps in one direction – to blow everything open – and one step back in the other – to cheat their way into staying up. Was Canellas plagued by some vestige of decency, was he at heart too honest to play happily along in all this bribery? Or did he feel that if he was up against the boys from Oberhausen and Bielefeld on a pitch made of money, he was going to lose anyway? Was he torn by con-science, or a beaten man? Or both?

No matter what he did, Canellas felt that there was no one who could help him, no way to know the right path; he was alone.

He had already called Germany's manager, Helmut Schön, on the pre-text of asking for Overath's number. During the call, he told the national manager about what Manglitz and the Hertha team were planning.

Jesus wept! cried Schön, and promised to put Hertha's manager Helmut Kronsbein in the picture about what his team were up to.

Later that day, Schön called Canellas again. He was just to leave him out of all this, please, said Schön, he had a reputation to lose.

Canellas called Wilfried Straub, officer responsible for the Bundesliga at the German FA. Straub was taken aback. But – according to Canellas – he asked him to wait till after the last matchday. Straub denies having given Canellas this advice.

On Thursday, two days before the final matchday, Manfred Manglitz didn't want to play along any more. It'd all got too hot for him, there were too many different interests in play, too many people pitching in and talking crap, and he was troubled that Overath had blown the whistle on him. Even though Manfred Manglitz hated admitting that anything ever troubled him.

Overath held quiet sway at Cologne. His power rested on the fact that he was the best player there. Almost every club had a player like that, Beckenbauer at Bayern, Seeler at Hamburg, Grabowski at Eintracht Frankfurt, Heinz Höher around 1960 at Bayer 04 Leverkusen. The best player didn't make loud demands, at face value he didn't seem to make many decisions; he raised his voice in a corner of the dressing-room, if something felt wrong to him. And then, the matter was sorted out to his satisfaction, whether that meant that for once, the team didn't want to stay in a hotel before a game – or that the best player felt the manager had to go.

In 1971, Overath was already sporting long hair and sideboards, the badges of the student protest movement. People often interpreted long hair in a footballer, like Günter Netzer of Mönchengladbach, as a sign of rebellion, though in fact Bundesliga players wore their hair long simply to be fashionable. But in the case of Overath, the international, the captain of Cologne, that haircut strengthened the impression of the real man: when he ran, and passed, and his hair flew in the wind, there was something majestic about it. Manfred Manglitz didn't want to cross him.

He wouldn't play against Offenbach, he said. At the same time, he kept up his dealings with Canellas.

On the Friday at about 6pm, one day before the final matchday, Horst-Gregorio Canellas and Offenbach's chief executive, Willi Konrad, met Manfred Manglitz at an autobahn service station at the Bonn interchange.

They'd exchanged descriptions of their cars so as to recognise one another:

F-CA 70 was his number-plate, said Canellas.

He'd be sitting in a mid-blue Mercedes 250 SE with a Grevenbroich plate, said Manfred Manglitz.

Canellas and Konrad didn't get out. The keeper hurried over and got into their car.

Manfred Manglitz wanted to see and feel the 100,000 marks.

So much money, yet such a small bundle, the thought flitted through his mind.

He'd have to take the money with him to show the others, said Manglitz.

That's not on, said Canellas.

Manfred Manglitz, who didn't want to play himself, because the thing was too hot for him, and Horst-Gegorio Canellas, who had made all sorts of preparations to blow the whole of this grand corruption sky-high, vehemently discussed how the money was to be handed over if Offenbach won.

Manglitz's bride would sit in the stadium next to Konrad, they agreed. Canellas gave the Cologne keeper a ticket to the game at Cologne's stadium, so that his bride could sit with the VIP guests from Offenbach.

That evening a certain Mr Hagen called the Hotel Schloss Auel and demanded to speak with Mr Canellas, who was spending the night there as one of the Offenbach party before their match in Cologne.

Mr Canellas, I can sort things so that Offenbach win tomorrow, said Hagen.

Peter Georg Friesdorf had thought up the code-name Hagen for himself. Evidently, Manfred Manglitz had not told the hairdresser and Friesdorf that he had long been negotiating with Canellas. As the final matchday approached, the old thieves' motto was the order of the day: every man for himself, and grab what you can.

On the final matchday, there was almost nobody left in Cologne who wanted to watch football. Only 7000 spectators had come to the Müngersdorf stadium. Horst Gecks noted in passing that his old team-mate from Meiderich, Manfred Manglitz, was missing from the Cologne goal for the first time in the season.

Herbert Windecker, the Offenbach correspondent for *Kicker*, did what journalists did and stood right on the edge of the pitch itself to watch the team warming up. Windecker was hoping he'd still get the chance for a few words with the manager and the players, to snap up a few last snippets. Offenbach midfielder Walter Bechthold shook the journalist by the hand: 'You'll see,' said Bechthold. 'Today we're going to be cheated good and proper.'

Bechthold himself didn't really believe what he was saying. The whole week leading up to the final matchday, the Offenbach players had hardly spoken among themselves about the rumours of match-fixing. Our fate's in our own hands, they said.

They played like European Cup winners Ajax Amsterdam – indeed, like almost all teams – with three forwards, two on the wings and one in the centre. Horst Gecks was always breaking from inside his own half, in the German Cup final of 1970, against this very Cologne team, he had dribbled over 60 metres to make it 2-0, that was the signature move of a supreme winger, to take the ball right down the length of the touchline. At half-time, Offenbach, playing with passion and as fast as you could wish, were 2-1 up in Cologne.

Braunschweig were leading Oberhausen 1-0, while in Berlin it stood at 0-0 between Hertha and Bielefeld. As things stood, Oberhausen were going down. Up in the stand, Offenbach chief executive Willi Konrad turned to Manfred Manglitz's bride.

Looks like I might as well give you that 100,000 right now.

Manglitz's bride laughed along with him.

In Berlin, the newspaper reporters were puzzled. Hertha forward Zoltan Varga had appeared among them in the press box, in his studs and his match-strip, demanding to use one of their telephones.

Varga called home.

Is the money there, he asked his wife.

Varga had demanded that a school friend from Budapest, at present studying in Bielefeld, should deposit his share of Bielefeld's donation with his wife, when the whistle blew for the start of play.

No, no one had come, his wife reported.

A poor performance first, then you get paid, that was what Bielefeld had insisted. But Varga didn't trust anyone any more. He had started thinking that his German team-mates at Hertha were going to do this thing without him, that they wanted to keep back his share. Well, they'd see. He'd blow the whole deal for them.

As the second half began, Zoltan Varga began to play his shirt off. His team-mates tried to keep the ball away from him.

It was over an hour in to play when Cologne made it 2-2 against Offenbach. In Braunschweig too, the scores were evened out at almost exactly the same time. Oberhausen forward Lothar Kobluhn was given a free header at goal when Braunschweig keeper Horst Wolter, going for a cross, leaped smack into his own defender, Wolfgang Gryzb, bringing them both to ground.

But Oberhausen were still going down, a point behind both Offenbach and Bielefeld.

Bielefeld manager Egon Piechaczek played his best forward, Gerd

Roggensack, on the left wing instead of his usual place on the right. This meant that his direct opponent was Bernd Patzke, who had negotiated the match-fixing with Bielefeld. Twenty minutes from the end of the season, a low pass rolled from the right into Hertha's box. Patzke ran directly away from Roggensack, leaving him to make it 1-0 unchallenged.

'It's a fix!' yelled the spectators in Berlin's Olympic Stadium.

In Cologne, the men from Offenbach were overcome with the terror of failure. For an hour they had run the tempo of the game. The 2-2 equaliser, coming from a mis-hit back pass from their tough defender, Roland Weida, reminded them of all the things that could go wrong; of how much they had to lose. Suddenly, their passes were all going adrift, rather than forwards. Horst Gecks ran, but hardly ever with the ball now, just after it. Eleven minutes before the end of the final matchday, Offenbach let one in to make it 3-2 to Cologne, and then, in the twinkling of an eye, it was 4-2.

There were three minutes left to play in Berlin and Hertha's Zoltan Varga, who was being kept out of play by his own team-mates, won the ball for himself. He burst through the Bielefeld defence and smacked the ball with all the power he had. The ball slammed against the wood-work. You stupid bastard, thought Varga's team-mate Jürgen Rumor, and waited for the final whistle.

People equipped with transistor radios spread the news of the final scores from all the grounds. Hertha 0, Bielefeld 1; Braunschweig 1, Oberhausen 1; Cologne 4, Offenbach 2.

Horst Gecks dragged himself to the dressing-room but couldn't make it inside. He slid down the wall to the ground and stayed sitting there for an eternity. Offenbach were relegated.

In his capacity as head of state of Cologne, Wolfgang Overath came into the Offenbach changing room to express his condolences.

Horst Gecks found the strength to think: just leave us in peace or I'll give you a kick up the arse.

In Berlin's Olympic Stadium the journalists crowded around Hertha manager Helmut Kronsbein.

Helmut, the fans are shouting 'It's a fix!'

'That is utter rubbish.' Kronsbein played it down. 'Favourites getting beaten is just part of the game.'

In Frankfurt, where Eintracht had escaped relegation, Erich Ribbeck couldn't stop hinting at the truth. 'When I look at a few of the results today, it feels all wrong. I really can't say how sorry I am for the boys at Offenbach.'

In Braunschweig, Bielefeld's bagman, Rupert Schreiner, set off on his journey back to Waggum airport. Could it have gone any better? Bielefeld were staying in the Bundesliga – and he still wouldn't have to pay the 170,000 marks to Braunschweig. He'd agreed to make the payment for a Braunschweig victory against Oberhausen, but not for a draw.

A man with thick hair and an imposing chest ran up to him.

Lucky I caught you, said the man, and introduced himself as Max Lorenz, the German international who played for Braunschweig. He was there to pick up their bonus.

We agreed to pay for a victory, Schreiner objected. Soon afterwards, Lorenz having in the meantime hoisted him into the air by his jacket collar, Schreiner handed over 40,000 marks in return for a receipt.

Schreiner was flown to Travemünde in his privately chartered aircraft. There, in a hotel on the beach, Bielefeld were celebrating their escape from relegation. The party had been going on for some hours when manager Egon Piechaczek jumped into the hotel pool, complete with suit and cigar. Bursting to the surface again, he roared: chuck that Canellas in here too, and some girls.

But Horst-Gregorio Canellas was preparing his own celebration. On Sunday 6 June 1971, the day after the final matchday, he was celebrating his 50th birthday. In his garden in the Rosenstraße, he set up small round tables with white tablecloths, the guests appeared in light summer suits and colourful, striped ties. Canellas wore a black suit. His dark fringe, which had originally been combed back with water in the old style, was standing up crazily from having his hands run so often through it. Germany's manager, Helmut Schön, deigned to appear. 'If the fickle gods of luck are not around for once, it's good to have your friends about,' he declared, standing on the lawn, to the local sports journalists whom Canellas had invited along, as was only right and proper for the private birthday celebration of the president of a club in the Bundesliga. Canellas waited until his guests all had glass in hand. Helmut Schön went for orange juice rather than champagne: after all, he was the national manager. Canellas asked to say a few words. His guests waited to see if he would be able find a few positive things to say, despite Offenbach having just been relegated. I'd like to show you something, said Canellas.

He sat down at one of the little round tables where, on the white tablecloth, there stood a wood-veneered Telefunken tape-recorder. Canellas pressed 'play'.

Fifty-five football players and two managers were found guilty by the disciplinary committee of the German Football Union as having fixed Bundesliga matches for a total of 1.1 million marks. Nine teams, that is, exactly half of all the clubs in the Bundesliga, were involved. Offenbach and Bielefeld had their Bundesliga licences revoked.

It was an affair of state. The Germans' self-image had taken a knock: they had always considered that corruption on the grand scale was a problem for others. Football, Germany's favourite sport, was especially dependent on the illusion that the world was exactly as you saw it on Saturdays in the stadium: a world divided unambiguously, by means of goals and non-goals, into winners and losers, without double meanings, without secret machinations behind the scenes. In the end, it had been naive to imagine that professional sportsmen were highly developed moral beings. But without these naive demands, sport couldn't function: professional sportsmen were obliged to try to win with all the means at their disposal, but at the same time to stay within the bounds of fairness. Without fairness, football was dead. And that's just what it was, right then, for hundreds of thousands if not millions of German football fans.

Canellas and reporters from *Der Spiegel* and *Bild* acted like private detectives, carrying out their own investigations to provide ever more evidence. But to some of the actors in this drama, the German FA's inquiry was merely an extension of the Bundesliga Scandal: they kept right on bribing or cashing in, now in order to steer the truth on their own behalf.

Peter Georg Friesdorf, who felt himself to have been underpaid by his friend the hairdresser, got in touch with Canellas. He hoped to be able to sell him the whole truth for a stack of cash. Canellas persuaded him that he was not in a position to pay, but offered to put him in touch with *Bild*. They paid Friesdorf 25,000 marks for his stories. At the same time, Friesdorf, confirming his identity with his personal ID card no. F3216827 as a citizen of the Bundesrepublik Deutschland, deposited a statement notarised by notary Elmer Winter, in which he set out every detail of Manfred Manglitz's and Oberhausen's involvement. When Friesdorf was supposed to give evidence in front of the German

FA's national disciplinary committee, in the trial of Oberhausen and their president Peter Maassen, he did not appear and took back his notarised declaration. *Bild* and *Der Spiegel* reported that 'a person unknown' had offered over 150,000 marks to Friesdorf if he kept quiet. Maassen was acquitted due to lack of evidence. Unlike Bielefeld and Offenbach, Oberhausen did not have their league status revoked, but were punished merely with a five-point penalty, to be applied the following season.

Because this was a sporting disciplinary hearing, not a true, civil court, the German FA had no powers to subpoena people who, like Friesdorf, were not members of any of its clubs.

Manfred Manglitz received a lifetime ban from the German FA and was also issued a 25,000 mark fine. But there was still some money to be made. 'The clubs I didn't finger showed me their appreciation,' he said.

Manfred Manglitz was only one of probably almost 100 Bundesliga players who in one way or another were involved in the match-fixing scandal. There's no doubt that he wasn't the worst of them. It's just that he was the only one of Heinz Höher's friends in football who took part in it; that's the only reason that his tale is told here, as an example of what was going on.

By 1971, Manglitz already had a firm picture in his own head of the kind of man he wanted to be. He was one of those people who always land on their feet, come what may. When they banned him from professional football, he opened a disco in Cologne, the Old London. On Sundays, when all the other clubs were dead, he turned his establishment into a steak-house. The ideas never stopped coming.

Four years after having been banned for life, he was playing professional football again. Second-tier FC Mülheim paid off the 15,000 marks of his fine that he still owed the German Football Union, and the federation pardoned him, not least because they'd known for some time that his lifetime ban would be quashed by a civil court as being a *de facto* disbarment from work.

Sometimes, an opposing player would call him a fixer or worse, and occasionally, when he kept goal for a pub team for fun and a free dinner, the opponents announced that they'd refuse to play if that match-fixer was on the pitch. Manfred Manglitz, who, after all, could cope with anything, accepted these insults stoically. It's only 40 years later, in Villajoyosa Bay that he says: 'Did it hurt? What do you think?'

In the 1970s, when Manfred Manglitz was on holiday at the Costa Blanca and saw the mighty blue light that flowed straight from the heavens into the sea, he knew: this was where he wanted to live.

There are only a couple of tennis courts and a fine, sandy beach between his home and the sea. By now, he's spent almost half his life in Villajoyosa. Of all the many things that Manfred Manglitz has done in his life, because he's always taken things easy, always been a real Cologne connoisseur of the art of living, the only thing he wishes he could make undone is the match-fixing of 1971. And because he can't make it so, he tries, 40 years later to ward off accusations with his own version of the truth.

'Take the one-nil defeat in Bielefeld, for example, I had exactly the same offers on the table whether we won or lost. So I played my normal game, in fact, I was the best man on the field. I just stopped everything as well as I could and I knew, afterwards you'll get twenty-five thousand marks in the car park from one side or the other.'

The swimming pool at his home at Villajoyosa Beach lies quietly beneath the palm trees.

'I swear to you, if that banana-dealer had won the last game, the whole thing would never have come out. Canellas just went crazy because he'd got relegated and he thought: I'll crap on the lot of them!'

Manfred Manglitz has laid a towel ready for his guest on the sunbed beside the swimming pool. He's proud of himself for thinking of such little details. 'I never thought such a complete and utter shit as that Canellas could ever exist. If I start a scam like that, or if I get involved in it, I don't go leaving fifty other blokes in the shit. There's a thing called honour among thieves and that's where Canellas went wrong.'

Honour's an important thing; doing a thing the right way, even if that thing is one gigantic scam.

'Every time they report about that scandal today, they write that Manglitz got his twenty-five thousand from Offenbach or he demanded this or that. But who's saying it was always just me who got that twenty-five thousand? What do you think, why was no one at Cologne apart from me fingered in the scandal? Because I kept my trap shut. Honour among thieves. I could have named a few names, of course I could: whatsisface and whatsisname were in on it too, they each got their five thousand marks.'

He names a few names.

'But what good would it've done me to name names?'

Right, says Manfred Manglitz, now he feels like taking a dip in the pool.

Horst-Gregorio Canellas who, like Manglitz, was banned for life from holding any office in German professional football, noticed that his tropical fruit business increased its turnover after the Bundesliga Scandal. Later, worn out by the frustrations of the scandal and damaged in his health, he emigrated to Majorca. Wilhelm Stute, president of Bielefeld, was praised for being so active in the restoration of Bielefeld's old city centre. Peter Maassen, their opponent at Oberhausen, was awarded Germany's equivalent of the OBE as well as the German FA's official tie-pin for, it was said, his efforts to build up sport and the economy in Oberhausen after the war. Horst Gecks, who had said no to all attempts to bribe him, stayed playing with Offenbach in the second division after their relegation.

When his professional career ended, Gecks worked as a salesman for Hummel's sporting goods in Kevelaer. He opened his own sports shop, and because they asked him, Horst Gecks was still playing for Kevelaer in their regional league at 50 years of age; and because they asked him, he kept on running his sports shop even after he could have retired at 65.

Without fail, on the first Wednesday of every month, Gecks meets up with the old gang from Meiderich. Many of the team who were runners-up in the 1963-64 Bundesliga still get together. If it works out, if he's back in the country, Manfred Manglitz gets himself a rented car and calls by as well. His left knee is made of steel, in his right knee and his shoulder, arthritis has taken hold. All those Cortisone injections. He still feels at home with the boys from Meiderich, those were the great days, the unsullied days.

When they sit down together, Horst Gecks never brings up the Bundesliga Scandal. Loyalty is stronger than any curiosity, never mind any outrage. The feeling is still there: as Bundesliga professionals they belong together, come what may.

'Manglitz was one of the real greats,' says Horst Gecks, 'he had a big mouth, but that wasn't all that was big about him.'

Heinz Höher recognises the voice right away. 'Guess who's on the line?' says the chatty voice on the phone, in that Cologne sing-song, almost before Höher has a chance to say hello. These days, he only talks to Manglitz now and again, what with the distance between Germany and Spain. Last time, they talked about artificial knees.

Manfred Manglitz highly recommended his Spanish doctor, he'll set your knees up like new.

Heinz Höher feels the same loyalty to Manglitz as Horst Gecks does. 'Whatever might have happened, sooner or later you have to draw a line under it.'

In the many weeks of conversation that went into this book, Heinz Höher only once asked that he be allowed to stay silent. That was when the question came up: what part did he himself play in the Bundesliga Scandal?

'I can't say anything about that.'

Why not?

For a few seconds, all that could be heard was his breathing.

'In the years leading up to 1971, we were still fighting for promotion into the Bundesliga ourselves, at Bochum,' he says at last. 'And wherever we went, to see if something couldn't be done about it, the answer was always: sorry, lads, you're too late. The other lot were here before you.'

You can recognise some of the faces right away: Heinz Höher (standing, far left) at the annual meeting of Bundesliga managers, 1973. Seated at the centre is Germany's manager Helmut Schön; second from left sits Udo Lattek; standing fourth from the right is Hennes Weisweiler.

After 1971:

AFTER THE SCANDAL

Before Karl Hagen went to bed, he switched on all the lights in the hotel room and turned on all the taps. Heinz Höher, who was sharing the room with the vice-president of Bochum, waited for a moment to see what was going to happen next. But nothing did. It seemed that Hagen was determined to sleep with the lights full on and the taps running.

They'd gone to Denmark in May 1972 to check out a potential new signing, sweeper Morten Olsen, during a match between the Danish national team and an English amateur invitation XI. Heinz Höher was still manager of Schwarz-Weiss Essen and was already working for Bochum. In July, he was to take over as their manager. For years, club president Wüst had regarded Höher as the natural successor when Hermann Eppenhoff's time was up. Now, that day had come.

Hesitantly, Heinz Höher asked club vice-president Hagen, if he couldn't maybe turn off the lights and the taps?

No, snapped Hagen. We're paying the hotel so much for this room, I'm going to use everything they've got.

Heinz Höher recalled why his room-mate's nickname was 'Smack' Hagen. Because in earlier days, as an amateur boxer – smack! smack! – he had packed a real punch. Heinz Höher elected not to pursue the isssue. When he awoke next morning, unable to work out how he had ever been able to get to sleep, all the lights were still on. The water was still running in the washbasin and the shower. They didn't sign Morten Olsen.

Heinz Höher faced his first game as a Bundesliga manager on 16 September 1972, away to Eintracht Braunschweig.

The start of the season had been put off by a month so as not to clash with the Munich Olympics. The Bundesliga clubs feared that few fans would go to football matches during the Games. They were already suffering financially because of the cold shower the public had taken in shape of the Bundesliga Scandal. In the first year after the scandal, a total of 800,000 tickets fewer had been sold. Top-flight football in Germany had never had so bad a reputation as in 1972. Yet that very summer, the victory of the national side in the European Championship meant that it stood at its zenith.

It was the best of times, it was the worst of times. On the one hand it was suddenly chic to consider football as primitive. The Bundesliga Scandal had surely just demonstrated what a shameless, sickly business professional sport was. Furthermore, by virtue of a decree in the early summer of 1971, every Bundesliga stadium now had to erect protective fences because the pitches had been invaded ever more frequently by fanatical supporters.

Bayern Munich keeper Sepp Maier had actually been knocked to the ground in Duisburg by out-of-control fans. Football was the sport for proles in a society in which hardly anyone wanted to be known as working class any more. The Germans, who for 20 years had come to see progress as the natural state of things, and who had raised the motto 'our kids will have it better' to the status of a holy commandment, dreamed of a world with office jobs and white collars for everyone. In Bochum, the last collieries were closing.

And while many people looked down on their own favourite sport, Germany's footballers, the alleged street-kids of the nation, were playing with an elegance which grabbed the attention. The national side's victory over England in the European Championship quarter-final in April 1972, at Wembley, became the stuff of myth: Germany's players, who, in the eyes of the Germans themselves, had always won by playing in such a German fashion, so forceful and determined, won at Wembley, the home of football, in fresh and spring-heeled style. At Wembley, Franz Beckenbauer broke out of defence again and again with his exquisite passes and dribbles. But it was the long-haired Günther Netzer rather than Beckenbauer who embodied the yearning for a new Germany, its cobwebs blown away and really enjoying life: and so West Germany's mightiest organ of high-flown ideas, the cultural supplement of the *Frankfurter Allgemeine Zeitung*, decided that it was in fact Netzer who had burst from deep into space at Wembley to give birth to a new kind of German football.

The best and the worst of times: how many Germans spent Friday night at their neighbours' house-parties, bad-mouthing the proletarian sport of football and then, on Saturday at 6.10pm, sat happily down to watch *Sportschau*? How many Germans sat in their offices cursing these moneygrubbing professional footballers, and then, back home, glowing with admiration, christened their pet cats Grabowski or Heynckes?

It was during this paradoxical footballing era that Bochum attempted to cement their place in the Bundesliga. In their first season among the big boys – still with Eppenhoff as manager – they'd come ninth. But Bochum president Ottokar Wüst was not unhappy when Stuttgart made an offer for Eppenhoff's services. It would seem like a natural handing-over. Wüst wanted a manager with fresh ideas. He only had one name in mind.

Heinz Höher's reception at Bochum was standard issue for a new manager. He was already being criticised before he'd even started work. 'Does the team respect him enough? Has Höher got enough distance between himself and them?' asked Heinz Formann, the new sports editor of Bochum's biggest paper, the *Westdeutsche Allgemeine Zeitung* when, in March 1972, Höher was introduced to the press as the new manager for the following season. Heinz Höher was only 33, the youngest manager in the Bundesliga. For some of the Bochum players, he'd still been a team-mate, a card-playing pal, just two years before. But the truth was that Formann wasn't really that worried by objective questions like this. He was simply personally offended that his friend Hermann Eppenhoff was no longer wanted as Bochum's manager.

There goes Formann again, thought Heinz Höher to himself when he read the *Westdeutsche Allgemeine* over breakfast in Kaulbachstraße at the start of May. The Höhers had subscribed to the paper, as was only right and proper. Every morning, when they got up, there it was waiting for them at their door. For weeks now, as if he himself was the one charged with making sporting decisions for VfL Bochum, Formann had been urging them to sign Lothar Emmerich, one of the 1966 World Cup finalists, who now, at 30 years of age, was playing out the autumn of his career in Belgium, with KV Beerschot. 'Those who are against signing Emmerich hardly make a very convincing case,' wrote Formann, 'they say "we don't know what condition Emmerich is in."

Really? Don't they? Well, that's a pity. They could read about it in any newspaper. Anyone who's ready to fly to Denmark twice to look at some player called Olson can take a trip to Belgium just as well.'

The fact that Olson was actually called Olsen was hard to establish at this distance. Even the Bochum talent scouts, who had been watching him after a second-hand tip-off, weren't quite sure about it.

Heinz Höher laid the paper aside. He needed to talk to Wüst about how they could calm Formann down. He couldn't have the most important paper in town against him. And there was no way he was going to sign Emmerich. Heinz Höher was afraid of having aged, one-time star players in his team. As far as he was concerned, they were just potential troublemakers. They demanded to start every game, but only delivered if they actually felt like it: they knew everything better than the manager and only obeyed him if they happened to be a one-time star player in a good mood. He of all people was in a position to know all about that, since until recently he himself had been an aged, one-time star player.

At Bochum, he already had two of them lying in wait for him, the 32-year-old Eia Krämer, who he'd played alongside at Meiderich when they stormed into the Bundesliga, and the 34-year-old Reinhold Wosab, who'd won the European Cup Winners' Cup in 1966 with Borussia Dortmund. He knew how to deal with Krämer: you just had to let him smoke his fags and drink his beer in the dressing-room, and old Eia would be as good as gold. But Wosab? Somehow, Heinz Höher had a bad feeling about him.

Leave it to me, I'll talk to Formann, club president Wüst reassured Heinz Höher.

Heinz Formann didn't just think that it was perfectly normal for the Bochum president to call him regularly, he positively expected it. After all, the *Westdeutsche Allgemeine*, with its 80,000 copies sold daily in Bochum, was a power in the town. He didn't want to sound arrogant but really, you could just ignore whatever Franz Borner wrote about VfL Bochum in the *Ruhr Nachrichten* with its pathetic 10,000 daily sales.

At home, in his wardrobe, Heinz Formann still had a few ties hanging up, colourful, but from the days when ties were not yet wide. They were all that remained of his old life. In his mid-20s, he had been one of the youngest senior officials in the Bochum city administration. At the occupational insurance office for the mining industry, he decided upon the sick pay, compensation, or disability benefits due to miners after accidents. In his spare time, and purely out of his own enthusiasm, he wrote freelance reports for the local sports columns of the *Westdeutsche Allgemeine*. When, in 1972, he admitted to his mother that he was leaving the occupational insurance office in order to become sports editor, he might as well have told her he was going off to join the circus. How could he give up being a senior city administrator to become a newspaper worker! Why had he bothered studying administration and economic science, why had she bothered doing all she'd done so that her son could have a better life, if he was now going to become ... a sports editor!

Heinz Formann could never explain it to his mother: when he worked on some document in the office, he'd never met the miner in question, never seen his face, he was just a grey name on his desk in this grey office. But journalists, they didn't wear ties. They grabbed hold of life with their sleeves rolled up, they were always on the spot, they knew everything, they helped to make the decisions; and there was the heady rush of hurry when he was racing against a deadline, the deep satisfaction when, next morning, he could hold what he had created in his own hands, in black and white.

Heinz Formann thought that his mother wept over his crazy decision, at night, in the dark of her bedroom. But he also felt that it was about time to follow his own wishes. He was 38.

In the editorial office, the typewriters beat out the time. The legal reporter, Schrage, already had five or six different pages of manuscript lying on his desk. Schrage was never completely satisfied with his texts, he always wanted to change just one sentence, and then maybe another. He fed another sheet of paper into the typewriter and typed his new sentences, until finally, he cut the best sentences out of each version and, with his UHU-stick, glued them together to create his definitive manuscript. Bugger it, yelled Schrage. He'd stuck his sentences together in the wrong order. On his desk there stood a bottle of schnapps.

A good journalist could take his drink. The whole editorial office even took lunch in the Panzergrotte bar or the Gasthaus Dingel. They didn't serve mineral water. Formann had never done any drinking with his fellow officials at the insurance office. Journalists now, they were real men, Hemingway himself hadn't just been a writer, after all, but a journalist as well.

In the evening the big shadow of Wolf, the typesetter, appeared in the editorial office. Right then, time's up, cried Wolf, I need your copy! At about 9.30pm, Formann brought his article about VfL Bochum to the typesetting machine, Wolf entered the text via his keyboard, so that it could be cast in lead. If the column came out a bit too short, Wolf the typesetter added some little news at the end. Thus it was that on the 'Sport in Bochum' page, you might find information such as that at the World Cup in Mexico, the balls had been of plastic rather than leather for the first time.

Heinz Formann worked from 10am till 10pm, he never missed a day, a real journalist was never sick. When he got back at about 9.30pm one time, his wife Hanne, the love of his life, asked: What are you doing home so early?

'And now we come to a question which is going to put someone or other on the spot,' read Heinz Höher in Heinz Formann's column on a day in May 1972. 'What's really going on with Lothar Emmerich? Yes, what's really going on?'

No one had taught Formann to write. Journalism wasn't a thing you could learn, never mind study. You had to have it in your blood. And Formann didn't care about standards which someone or other had maybe laid down at some time or another, such as the strict divide between fact and opinion in newspaper-reporting. He wrote as a self-taught man, completely convinced of his own opinion, with a new beauty and sharpness in his sentences that was all his own. On Mondays he started up his very own column, on the left of the page, in which he gave free rein to his cultural observations. Many people in Bochum opened up the *Westdeutsche Allgemeine* on Monday mornings and went straight to the left-hand column of the local sports page.

Whereas in the 1960s, articles about VfL Bochum had largely been limited to the game previews on Friday and the match reports on Monday, Heinz Formann now often devoted four articles a week to the club. The most important things were still the reports about the obvious issues – discussing injuries and the line-up, telling the story of the last match – but Formann also shed light on the background to these things, reported about the indebtedness of the club or its efforts to find an outside-left; he also reported his own activities: Heinz Formann travelled with club president Ottokar Wüst to check out Lothar Emmerich.

If he had no social commitments on a Saturday evening, Formann watched *Das aktuelle Sportstudio*. He liked the lively informal way they did things, but it would never have occurred to him that the rise of TV should alter his own style of writing in any way. Newspapers were the leading players in the media. If you wanted to really know about football, and especially about VfL Bochum, you had to read the papers – you had to read his column.

If he wanted to do an interview, Heinz Formann called the club's president or its manager into the editorial office. He never interviewed the players. He met them now and again in the Panzergrotte bar, or exchanged a few words with them after the matches, but what would a journalist from a respectable daily newspaper be doing, interviewing football players as part of his job? Maybe his colleagues at the tabloids would do such a thing, but a journalist who worked for a proper newspaper with proper subscribers was distinguished by the very fact that he could describe and analyse a match in words better than any footballer, so why on earth would he put quotations from players into his reports? And in any case, a good journalist was the social equal not of the players, but of the club's board and its manager.

A journalist didn't go to training sessions, either. Why would he?

The few pensioners who came to the training sessions every day at the Castroper Straße in order to escape the loneliness of their flats, experienced football as a new kind of sport in the summer of 1972. The new manager arranged matches on reduced space, two players against two, three against three, or – where on earth did he get his ideas? – he had them play with four sets of goalposts. Every Wednesday, he had his team run through the sand at Die Haard nature reserve.

Heinz Höher thought it only natural that he should think up training exercises for himself, that he should invent new methods. There was no point trying to copy anyone, and where could he have done so anyway? You couldn't just fly to Munich, Amsterdam or even Italy to look at other people's training methods.

In the nights, he went through his training plans with his friend Winzlinger.

If we set up practice matches between mini-teams playing on 25-metre pitches instead of just having 11 against 11 over the whole pitch, every player will get ten times as much time on the ball per training session. That's bound to have a significant effect on the rate of learning.

Hark at him! Now Mr Manager's coming at me with mathematical equations, is he?

Try and come with me for once instead of just taking the piss, Winzlinger!

Was he imagining things, or could Heinz Höher no longer sleep since he'd become the manager?

There was always something to get him thinking, as soon as he lay down in bed. How often should he programme training sessions, now that, right from the beginning of the Bundesliga, they were playing in the English rhythm of Saturday-Wednesday-Saturday? Could he build young Köper into their midfield already? What would Formann be moaning about again tomorrow in the paper?

He got the team doctor to prescribe sleeping pills for him. He took them every evening. He kept waking up at night, even so. But that didn't matter much, at 4am he could call for Winzlinger and think things through with him, so long as he could get to sleep in the evenings.

In the training sessions some of the Bundesliga players of VfL Bochum wore dark-blue tracksuits, others wore light-blue cotton sweaters; some had tracksuit tops with two stripes, others with three. At the ninth best football team in Germany, there was still much room for improvement: for example, the tracksuits might have been washed and laid out in a uniform style by the club. At Bochum, the players washed their training-gear at home and brought it back with them. There was no room to leave training-gear in the tiny washroom at the stadium.

Only the team was in the top division, the stadium had stayed third class.

We haven't even got 2000 seats, it's a catastrophe, wailed Ottokar Wüst to Heinz Höher, those Bavarians are going to have 40,000 seats in their new Olympic Stadium, they're going to bring in five times as much money as us every Saturday.

And as for signing Lothar Emmerich, said Wüst to his manager, he could forget that right away, far too expensive. It was just a question of how to break the news to Formann without the sports editor taking the refusal of his own obsession as a personal rebuff.

Instead of Emmerich, the World Cup runner-up, Heinz Höher brought along two players from second-tier Schwarz-Weiss Essen,

Reinhard Majgl and Michael Lameck, to strengthen his squad. As well as them, there was a new goalkeeper and an 18-year-old from Bochum's own youth team who had driven everyone there nuts with his ambition, because the rest of his team-mates weren't good enough for him. He was called Hermann Gerland, or something like that.

Heinz Formann could not believe that Bochum's new outside-left was going to be called Majgl and not Emmerich. 'Reinhard Majgl cannot be called a real alternative,' he wrote in the *Westdeutsche Allgemeine*, 'at least not seriously. Do you, dear reader, even know who he is? I have questioned my colleagues in Essen about him. Their impression is: "Good technique, but far too soft."'

That Formann was getting on Heinz Höher's nerves. The only good thing about it was that Borner from the *Ruhr Nachrichten* was automatically on his side, just because Formann was against him. It seemed that this was the ultimate law of press competition: if one paper was in favour of something, the other one must be against it, never mind what it was all about.

The nearer the first day of the season came, the more Heinz Höher had his team play, that's to say, he got them running without them being aware of it. He kept the pitches artificially small so that without noticing it, the players were permanently sprinting at high pace with extremely short pauses. In one such game, it seemed that Reinhard Majgl had somehow provoked Eia Krämer, either by saying something or by fouling him, Heinz Höher hadn't seen what had happened, but whatever it was, Eia was furious. He blatantly brought Majgl down. Heinz Höher had decided not to interrupt training games, he wanted play to flow and his players to get used to a rough time. Eia Krämer got Majgl from behind again, right in the Achilles tendon. As Majgl ran at full tilt, Eia Krämer slashed his weight-bearing leg from under him. Heinz Höher felt powerless. He knew that he should step in, but at the same time he felt that he couldn't step in now, because he had let the game go on like that for so long, to step in now would seem inconsistent. Krämer hunted Majgl down. He fouled him five times, ten times. Heinz Höher pretended not to have noticed anything, and broke off the training session ten minutes earlier than planned.

He'd never thought much about how a manager creates authority for himself. He'd always assumed that he just had authority.

In secret, the young players like Hermann Gerland were longing for a few inspirational words from their manager, for a few personal tips.

But Heinz Höher liked to keep silent. He preferred thinking about football on his own to talking about it with his players.

For the first game of the Bundesliga season 1972-73, Heinz Höher travelled to Braunschweig with the same basic idea used by two-thirds of the clubs in the league: home games you absolutely had to win, away games were something to survive and maybe manage a draw. They were going to defend in depth, throw themselves into every contested ball, run run run and then at sometime or other, if luck broke their way, they might find a counter-attack landing them in front of the opposing goal.

Heinz Höher had a vision of a clear, pure footballing style in mind. Simple passes, quick passes, clean passes. That way, simplicity would turn into beauty. What he didn't need were players who sometimes managed brilliant solo runs, who could sometimes split the opposing defence with a brilliant pass, but who might, next time, blow their runs and genius passes, creating conditions for a dangerous counter-attack. Most managers forgot what kind of players they had been themselves, as soon as they took on the job.

With the eye of the young manager who believed that every detail might be decisive, Heinz Höher took in everything about their experience in Braunschweig. Their hotel was on the Lange Straße, one of the town's arterial roads, he'd have to keep an eye on that in the future, it was too noisy. As it should be for sportsmen, the salad had been ordered by fax to the hotel and served without gherkins. But there was too little meat. Sportsmen needed meat. The Braunschweig keeper warmed up a whole 40 minutes before the start of the match, ten minutes before the rest of the team, very interesting, he'd have to have a think about that.

Obviously, he didn't have any real knowledge of the Braunschweig side. He knew something of the rivals around Bochum, but a far-off team like Braunschweig was always an unknown quantity. You might get to watch them two or three times a year in the ten-minute match reports on *Sportschau* or *Sportstudio*, if they were playing Bayern, Mönchengladbach or Cologne, but that was hardly enough to get a picture of them.

Heinz Höher had an idea. Dieter Fern, who had played with him at Bochum, now lived near Braunschweig, in Salzgitter. Perhaps he would know their opponents.

Heinz Höher was toying with the idea of playing Michael Lameck, his youngster fresh out of the second division, against Braunschweig's great goalscorer, Bernd Gersdorf. But after Fern assured him that Gersdorf was not particularly fast, Höher decided against marking him so closely. Lameck would play in the midfield.

Michael Lameck had played under him at Essen as an outside-forward who hardly ever scored. What had fascinated Höher was the way Lameck broke down so many opposition attacks by the way in which he immediately went for the man carrying the ball out of defence, and robbed him. This forward would be a good defender.

Lameck's left leg was 1.5cm shorter than his right. So that this didn't affect his play, he developed a special style of running. When his right foot was to strike the ground, he never stretched that longer right leg completely through the stride. That kept both his legs at roughly the same level.

Lameck had only started playing football at a club at 17. His mother had forbidden it on religious grounds. She was a Jehovah's Witness. His friends at home in Essen called him 'Vim' in their kickabouts after school; because he always slid so wildly across the black coal slag that made up their football pitch, he always went home so black from head to foot that it looked like only a scouring powder like Vim could ever get him clean again. When Heinz Höher offered to take him with him to Bochum, and into the Bundesliga, Vim Lameck threw in his job as a communications technician and went away, all alone, for a two-week holiday at Lake Königssee. He treated this as his personal training camp. He ran every day, he did sprint training, and played alone on a deserted football pitch at Berchtesgaden. He dribbled around dozens of invisible opponents, and hit crosses that he chased after himself, sprinting to get the ball back. After his first Bundesliga game at Braunschweig, Vim Lameck asked his team-mates: Is that it? You don't have to do any more than that in the Bundesliga? Bochum had won 2-0.

After the match, Heinz Höher called the 18-year-old Hermann Gerland over to him. He'd put Gerland on as sub in the 72nd minute.

You're going to give half your winner's bonus to Günter Etterich, said Höher. Because he's got a kid and you haven't.

There was 800 marks in it for everyone who'd played. Etterich had sat the game out on the bench.

No problem, guvnor, said Gerland, the money's no big deal, I've played in the Bundesliga, that's all I want.

Often, they played in stadiums where the fans were just specks scattered here and there across the cold grey of the cement-built stands.

Only 6,500 spectators came to the game in Braunschweig, at Kaiserslautern in November it was even worse, only 5,000, while in Wuppertal and Duisburg, 8,000 came. The public's disenchantment with football, this game for fixers and proletarians, was always most keenly felt on a lousy, freezing winter day when the opposition was only called Bochum or Oberhausen. On the other hand, if it was against Bayern or Mönchengladbach with their glittering line-ups of European medal-winners, over 25,000 of them always turned up.

We've got to do something to bind the spectators more closely to VfL Bochum, thought Wolfgang Hellmich to himself. His title at the club was press spokesman, which meant that he dealt with everything from selling adverts for the match programme to publishing the club's annual souvenir book – in fact, anything that was remotely to do with the media and official statements. Meanwhile, he worked at his actual job, as an engineer in the city construction office. Being a press spokesman for a Bundesliga team was something you did in your spare time, for fun.

Hellmich had an idea: what if they organised a club for the young fans, a club where they could meet up regularly outside the stadium as well, a club where VfL Bochum became the central thing in their whole free time? At Tuesday's weekly sitting of the VfL Bochum board at the Haus Frein pub, Hellmich explained his thoughts out loud. When he had finished, the reaction was a murmuring which could only be interpreted as agreement.

And so, in 1972, in the press office of VfL Bochum, Hellmich and 20 young fans founded Germany's first football fan club. He called it, simply: *der Fanklub*. Members would get free match-tickets from the club. So that these meetings outside the stadium would also give the fans something to do, Hellmich decided that every other week, Bochum players would visit the fan club. Heinz Höher and his captain, Hannes Walitza, kicked things off in November 1972. They could hardly get in through the doors at the fan club's chosen pub, Die Beckporte: almost overnight, the fan club had grown to have 300 members. And soon it was behaving with all the formality typical of any German club for anything: the entire board had to stand for re-election every two weeks. Heinz Höher and Hannes Walitza stayed for over three hours. They thought they should answer every question, they really couldn't go before they'd done so, this was about their spectators, after all.

Over the following months, VfL Bochum received enquiries from fans from all over Germany, and even some Bundesliga teams such as Borussia Dortmund asked to be informed what Bochum were doing with their fans – what was this thing, this 'Fanklub'?

Spectators scored goals. That was obvious, you only had to look at the figures for a moment, especially for the teams in the bottom third of the table, to see what proportion of their points were garnered at home, with their own fans behind them: it was at least two-thirds.

Did you know, Heinz Höher informed his players, that small fish will actually attack bigger fish, when they're in their own territory?

Their 4-1 defeat at Eintracht Frankfurt one Tuesday evening in October was, wrote Heinz Höher in his manager's notebook, 'exactly the sort of game which the home team will win, given an equality of team formation and playing form'. At about 1 o'clock in the morning, the team bus was back from Frankfurt, and at the Haus Frein. The lights were still on in the pub. The landlady and landlord, Hertha and Walter Czech, always waited for the team, never mind how late they arrived back. Heinz Höher only meant to just quickly take his two beers and a shot in the pub, to help him get to sleep. He played cards till 5 o'clock in the morning.

'Big mistake,' he wrote in his manager's diary. 'Alcohol. Allowed the substitute (Dewinski) to join in the card game, and robbed him of sleep. Bad conscience all week.'

Doris Höher was certainly not happy if her man lost the match. It was just that she found him more bearable then. Defeat made him modest, meek; human. After victory he always thought he had to act modestly and meekly. But in effect, he seemed unapproachable. He meant it in the best way, he didn't want to seem puffed-up. That was the way he hid his pleasure. But by doing so he hurt other people, without noticing it, by waving away their congratulations.

For home games, Doris Höher went to the stadium. She handed out bottles of Bommerlunder schnapps to the players' wives, to help their nerves. Away games were hard to bear. She turned the radio off, knitted and smoked. At 5.15 she waited for the telephone to ring. Someone always called to share their happiness when Bochum achieved a decent result away. If the phone still hadn't rung by 5.25, Doris Höher didn't have to ask.

Sometimes, the thought came to her that it really would be nice to go out to work again. The children were at primary school, now. But obviously, she knew, it was impossible for her to go out to work. Everyone in town would come to the wrong conclusion: the manager's wife has gone back to work; what does he do with all his money, if he can't provide her with a decent life as a housewife?

Heinz Höher earned 5200 marks per month as a Bundesliga manager. That was 3000 more than just two years ago as a novice manager at Essen and double what, for example, Heinz Formann got as sports editor. As a consequence of the Bundesliga scandal, the German FA had abolished the hypocritical maximum wage for players, which had only encouraged under-the-counter payments. Bundesliga players and managers were now true professionals. They all still trained for a job such as locksmiths or bank workers, or did their A-levels before they became professionals, but hardly any of them still worked as well as playing in the Bundesliga. A typical Bundesliga player – not a member of the national team, but someone who appeared each Saturday on his club's team-sheet – earned between 5000 and 12,000 marks per month, putting him somewhere between a bank manager and a hospital consultant. For the first time, there was a whole class of professional footballers who could feel themselves to be prosperous. And if they treated their money carefully, they could even become genuinely prosperous.

In newspaper articles, journalists began to mention it as a curiosity that the manager of a Bundesliga team still lived in a simple, small, rented apartment in Kaulbachstraße, for 392 marks a month. They had no idea that Heinz Höher abhorred few things as much as the idea of wasting money on moving house.

This business with the card games had to stop, said Heinz Höher. He didn't mean his own gambling, but the team's poker-school on matchdays. As far as he was concerned they could pass the time with cards a day before the match in the training camp, but on the day of the match there had to be an end to it. They used up too much of their powers of concentration, Heinz Höher feared.

It was the old problem. Someone was always down in a card game, on the evening before the match just as at any other time, and insisted on carrying on. Sometimes it was a question of 200 marks, sometimes 1000. On the morning of the game against Stuttgart in the autumn of 1972, yesterday's loser insisted on a chance for revenge. Erwin Galeski, Jürgen Köper and Hans Walitza went searching for some place where they could hide away from the manager and start gambling. They played poker from 10am till 1pm in the sauna of their hotel on the

Killesberg. In theory, the sauna was turned off. In practice there was still a residual temperature of 40 or 50°C.

Christ, Hennes, do you feel knackered too? Jürgen Köper asked Walitza later on, as they were warming up in Stuttgart's Neckar Stadium, where a hot, dry wind was blowing.

It's unbelievable, gasped Walitza. What kind of weather do they have here?

Bochum lost 4-0 in Stuttgart. Heinz Höher couldn't understand why on earth his team was so wrecked. 'Their bodies were not in the best of condition,' he wrote in his manager's diary; 'Walitza failed in his role as captain, no movement forwards. Galeski unrecognisable, no sense of shape, no playmaker, no rock.'

Bochum wended their way through the season, winning nine home games, losing eleven away games and hovering around the safe mid-table of the Bundesliga. The young players were a revelation. Vim Lameck was always swarming all over the left wing, usually an instant quicker to the ball than the opposition, he seemed to read the shape of the game before it even developed. The 18-year-old Gerland was a thoroughbred, and at 22, Jürgen Köper could dominate the midfield on a good day. In footballing circles people were saying that Heinz Höher must be a talented manager with lots of new ideas. Heinz Höher himself felt that he was somehow being watched with mistrustful eyes in Bochum. He had yet to learn that a manager is never without his critics.

He had to get the Bochum public on his side. Heinz Höher signed himself up for the Bochum International People's Marathon. It was the sort of advertising coup that was always in his mind, the kind he would have proposed by the dozen to those useless idiots at Schlegel's brewery, if only they'd let him carry them out: he would show himself as a man of the people and, at the same time, as a mighty athlete. The People's Marathon was run over 50km.

Since starting work as a Bundesliga manager, Heinz Höher ran every day: from the training sessions straight through the city and back to his home; at 6.30 in the morning on matchdays in the training camp, while the players were still asleep; in the evenings on matchdays, after the press conference, in the empty stadium – there was nothing like the feeling of peace in an empty stadium after the battle. On Sunday mornings, it was the turn of the subs who hadn't been given a game on the Saturday. They served Heinz Höher as running partners, an hour through the woods at Weitmar.

He set off in the People's Marathon at a stiff tempo. He passed the 25km mark in just over two hours. Running was healthy. 'After work, don't just kill your free time,' declared the National Centre for Healthy Living in a joint campaign with the *Neue Ruhr Zeitung*: 'Germany's citizens only spend a third of their free time outdoors. There's more to life after the working day is done.' Out into the fresh air with you all! prescribed the National Centre for Healthy Living. But the fine art of using their free time so that it really increased their well-being was something that few people understood without help and direction. And so the People's Marathon movement was born.

Heinz Höher has got the right idea, thought some people at the club, he's reducing his stress through relaxed running. Actually, Heinz Höher was running so that in the evening he could have another two beers and a shot without a guilty conscience.

After 30km of the People's Marathon, his legs started to weaken. He slowed to a jog, and then to a walk. Three kilometres before the finish line was an uphill stretch. To his right, Heinz Höher saw a bar named Auf der Prinz. It was run by a former team-mate of his at Bochum, Hansi Grieger. Grieger's father had died three times. At least, Grieger had three times explained his absence from training by claiming that his father had died. Heinz Höher set himself down on the window-ledge at the front of Grieger's bar and drank a couple of beers and a shot. Then he ran on. He took four hours to cover the second half of the route. Whether that was going to improve his public image in the way he had hoped, he couldn't really say.

But naturally, that wasn't the only idea he had to buttress his reputation in Bochum, and to finally quell Formann's niggling in the *Westdeutsche Allgemeine*. He would act as though he was going to move to SV Hamburg. Hamburg were interested in him, that fact had already leaked out. He had no interest in moving to Hamburg. But he'd fly to talks there. Confronted with his threatened abdication, Bochum president Ottokar Wüst would do everything to keep him: his kudos at the club and in the city would rise at last. So as to make the whole thing look real, he gave his notice to VfL Bochum in writing.

A few days later, as the spring was nearing, the 1972-73 season was going into its decisive phase, and clubs were already planning for next season, Ottokar Wüst, president of VfL Bochum, phoned through to the editorial office of the *Westdeutsche Allgemeine*.

Mr Formann, Heinz Höher wants to leave Bochum. He has handed in his notice in writing. I have spent an eternity to dissuade him – but in vain. He has told me that he's going to Hamburg, because he can no longer stand your criticism. Please, just meet him for once. I am not demanding that you simply change your highly respected opinion, but I do believe that it would be helpful all round if you were to get to know Mr Höher personally.

If you think so, Mr Wüst, said Heinz Formann.

Meanwhile, Heinz Höher flew to Hamburg. He met club preident Mr Dr Barrelet in a hotel. Uwe Seeler, the heart and soul of SV Hamburg, whose playing career had ended the year before, appeared along with him in order to impress Höher.

At SV Hamburg, rich in tradition, economically strong and properly run, he would be able to build up a team with better players and earn more money. Was there something wrong with him, for him not to want to go to Hamburg despite all this?

Heinz Höher certainly strove to achieve great things. It was just that in his first year in the Bundesliga, he had created a distinct vision of what, for him, would be the greatest thing: to take Bochum, against all the odds, into a European cup competition.

He told Uwe Seeler and Mr Doktor Barrelet that he would have to think about their offer. Back in Bochum, he received the offer that he'd really been hoping for: Heinz Formann and his wife invited him and Doris to a tennis club dance in May.

Well, why don't we share a taxi home, said Heinz Formann at the end of the evening. The Formanns lived in the Hugo-Schultz-Straße in Ehrenfeld. That was on their way home to Kaulbachstraße.

That was a good evening, said Formann, as he got out.

She'd really enjoyed it, said Doris.

It was really very nice, said Frau Formann.

Heinz Höher said to Heinz Formann that he wouldn't mind coming in with them for a bit.

Heinz Höher really loved the green corduroy sofa in the living-room, where Formann invited him to sit. Frau Formann disappeared swiftly to the bedroom. Her husband put Daliah Lavi's new LP on.

'If I were a book you could read,' sang Daliah, 'tell me what sort of book would I be? The kind that has never been written before – and would that make you want to read me?'

When the record was finished, Heinz Höher said: please, Mr Formann, play it again.

In the course of the next few hours he said at least five times: please, put it on again, Mr Formann. By the time the sun was rising, they had talked of VfL Bochum, of the old stadium, of Majgl, who had come to them instead of Lothar Emmerich. And after that, as far as Heinz Formann could see, there was no longer any question of Heinz Höher going to Hamburg.

Heinz Höher found that afterwards, Heinz Formann's articles didn't become less critical, but that they were more evenhanded and showed more understanding. He hadn't bargained for one thing, however: from the moment that he at last had Formann on his side, he automatically had Franz Bonner of the *Ruhr Nachrichten* against him.

'If there's one thing we can do,' said Doris Höher, 'it's party.' At the VfL Bochum Christmas Dinner, 1973.

THOSE WERE THE DAYS,
MY FRIEND

Drink was bad for you, explained Heinz Höher to his players. He wasn't talking about alcohol, but about water, juice, any kind of drink. At the beginning of the 1970s, a cutting-edge discovery in sports medicine was spreading through the Bundesliga: the fewer fluids a footballer took in, the better his muscles would grow and function. No one in the Bundesliga could actually say who precisely had made this great discovery, but most managers stuck strictly to the programme. At their training camp, the Bochum players were only allowed a single glass of water with their lunch after a hard morning's training. It was no different for their colleagues at Eintracht Frankfurt: there, the players were so dehydrated that in their desperation they secretly drank water from the showers until their manager, Erich Ribbeck, walked in on them and immediately had the showers turned off. Helmuth Johannsen, manager of Hanover among other teams, followed his players to the toilets at half-time, to keep an eye on them in there and make sure sure that nobody took a drink. Heinz Höher didn't go as far as that. He was more interested in developing his own ideas.

Thus it was that on 19 May 1973, five hours before their Bundesliga match against Kickers Offenbach, the players of VfL Bochum were running around the training ground at the Wedau Sports School. Heinz Höher had established the habit of getting their muscles working and their spirits fresh with a light introductory gallop on the mornings of Bundesliga matches. The only trouble was that on this gorgeous Saturday it was already 20°C at 10.30 in the morning. On a hot day, Heinz Höher explained to his team, it was particularly important to get your body used to the temperature before the game; and then, just don't drink any more water! He looked at his players' faces, and didn't see much enthusiasm for his latest idea. Modern sports medicine confirms it! he added for good measure.

Franz Beckenbauer, who was also at the Wedau Sports School with Bayern Munich before their away game at Düsseldorf, was chatting happily away with a couple of companions on the half-shaded terrace. Every now and then he let his gaze pass in astonishment over the Bochum players, as they ran by. At the end of the session, Heinz Höher went on coaching the keepers. He didn't have an assistant manager. He himself didn't believe that anyone would be able to work alongside him.

The Bochum outfielders left the pitch. Sweat-stains had gathered on their training-shirts.

Hey, said Jürgen Köper to Hannes Walitza as they walked together: I'm tooled up.

You're what?

I'm tooled up. Wait here, I'll fetch it.

At one time, Jürgen Köper thought he might turn out like Heinz Höher. At the end of the 1960s, when Heinz Höher was the man for the elegant moment of play at Vfl Bochum, Köper, then in the youth first XI, seemed to be his natural successor. Köper knew how to dictate the pace of a game by speeding up or slowing down his passes. With him as their star player, Bochum became German youth champions in 1969. Germany's manager, Helmut Schön, had a word with him. Go to Eintracht Frankfurt, Schön advised him. Köper took him to mean: If you go there you could get into the national side, if you stay at Bochum, you won't. He stayed. Like so many people, like most people, he really only had one aim: to be a fixture in his very own club's first XI.

In the Bundesliga, Heinz Höher played Köper in the heart of the midfield, but kept him locked up – the word was his own invention – in a 'mission cage'. Köper's primary task was to keep the opposing playmakers out of the game, but only to act like one himself if he had energy to spare and the chance offered itself.

At 22, Köper had a decisive insight into play in the Bundesliga: it was the dummy runs that really mattered. If he made those short sprints again and again, even though he had no hope of actually receiving the ball, the opposing playmaker would simply have to go with him. Absolute man-for-man marking was the rule. His sprints exhausted the playmakers, his senseless running about tired out their nerves.

Just stay still for once, will you, Cologne's Overath shouted at Köper: we don't even want to win.

There were already grey streaks in Jürgen Köper's hair, he was a trained tax-advisor. Heinz Höher didn't want it to show when he particularly liked a player, but Jürgen Köper was a favourite of his. 'Köper is achieving things even I had not expected,' he wrote in his manager's logbook, 'but when he has freedom of movement, when he breaks out of the mission cage, things become critical. Is he mentally mature? What of his private life?'

Jürgen Köper loved pistols and cars. He had a weapons permit. He had brought a Bentley Air White with him to the training camp at the Wedau Sports School.

The usual card-school gang, Hannes Walitza, Erwin Galeski and Jürgen Köper, went looking for a quiet place in the grounds of the sports school. Behind the countless football pitches, set apart by a thicket of trees, there lay two basketball courts.

I'll show you now.

Jürgen Köper flicked the safety-catch off on the revolver, took aim even as he raised the weapon, and blew the basketball hoop away.

C'mon, let me have a go too, cried Walitza, I did my National Service too.

In four hours' time they were playing against Offenbach in the Bundesliga. They went to the other basketball hoop. Walitza fired. There was a loud bang, Jörgen Köper was surprised, he hadn't thought that firing it would create such a thunderclap despite the long barrel. They looked up. The basketball hoop was undamaged. Walitza fired again, from closer range. Still no dice.

Hey, and you call yourself a goalscorer, Galetski mocked him.

On the other side of the thicket, Heinz Höher and his keepers were at their special training session when they heard a sort of hissing in the air.

Guvnor, that's wasps, shouted Werner Scholze, the first-choice keeper, panic-stricken. If I get stung, I won't be able to play, I'm allergic!

Heinz Höher listened to the noise in the air. But then – what on earth was that bang on the basketball court, those were no wasps. Something hissed through the air again, directly over their heads. He was just going to take a quick look, said Heinz Höher.

What are you lot up to here?

Walitza, Galeski and Köper tried to avoid eye contact with their manager. He had already seen the object which Walitza had hastily put down on the ground.

Guvnor, you better use the towel to pick up the shooter, shouted Köper, as Heinz Höher reached for the Bentley.

What? On top of all this, you're trying to take the piss?

At this point Heinz Höher let out a short cry of pain, almost no more than a hiss. He'd burnt his hand on the hot barrel of the revolver. In the end, he wrapped the weapon up in the towel Jürgen Köper had used to smuggle it out of his room, and marched off before them, gun in hand.

Goalkeeping training was at an end, he told Scholz. The three poker-playing footballers slunk off in his wake. To Jürgen Köper, it felt as though everyone was staring at them on their way back to their room.

Heinz Höher didn't say a single word about the event, before the match. Bochum lost 3-2 to Offenbach, who had returned to the top flight stronger than ever just a year after the Bundesliga Scandal. Jürgen Köper's play was somehow less together than usual.

Three days afterwards, Jürgen Köper was called before the club's board in the back room of the Haus Frein pub. At VfL Bochum, the week's business was done in an orderly fashion: the board met every Tuesday, on Thursday it was the playing committee.

It appears that there has been some kind of incident, said Ottokar Wüst by way of opening the session. I call upon our manager, Mr Höher, to make his report.

On Friday, at 15.10 hours, said Heinz Höher, there's the team bus standing ready outside the Haus Frein, and a loaded shooter is lying on the rear seat. Jürgen Köper deserves to be fined 5000 marks.

The members of the board looked at one another. For a moment, everything was silent. Would it be quite possible for Heinz Höher to explain his mysterious words, club president Wüst enquired. I just explained it all, answered Heinz Höher.

He loved speaking in riddles. He thought that his hints and word-games were a refined way of putting other people to the test, an example of the high art of human speech. The people who he tried it on thought that the actual riddle was Heinz Höher himself.

Jürgen Köper, having contritely explained the details of the incident, was indeed hit with a fine of 5000 marks. It was agreed that this be kept quiet. When Köper's contract came up for renewal, he received, just as quietly, an extra payment of 5000 marks. And so the matter was closed.

VfL Bochum was not going to allow a mere bagatelle like bringing a pistol to the Sports School to damage their spirit of solidarity. Other Bundesliga teams had their own mythologies: they might have their legendary past, like Schalke, or their money, like Hamburg – or maybe they had floodlights, like Kaiserslautern. Bochum had the feeling: 'Us, together.' On Saturdays, just before 3.30pm, the battle-cry in their dressing-room was: 'Now they're for it!'

At the Castroper Straße ground, the only space with a welcoming feel, a place where the players could hang around together a bit after training, was the 30-foot square room they called the club office. As a Bundesliga team, Bochum could now afford two female office employees, the two Christas, Frau Jewers and Frau Ternow. You sort it out, club president Wüst told them. And so the two Christas dealt with the club's correspondence with the German FA and held therapeutic telephone conversations with callers who moaned first about VfL Bochum and then, after a few minutes, about life itself. The two Christas were the club's travel agents, press officers, and advanced box office – and now they offered souvenirs too: posters of the team could be ordered by mail. In the evenings, Christa Jewers sometimes answered her own telephone as 'VfL Bochum', before realising, Oh yes, I'm already back at home.

Before she started working at Bochum in 1966, as a young lady, Christa Jewers had not been interested in football. Now, once a year, Christa Ternow and she took a weekend trip without their husbands and children. These trips were to Munich, Nuremberg or Berlin – whichever city Bochum were playing in right then.

If one of the Christas was typing a letter to the German FA and made a mistake on the last line, she had to type the entire thing out again. If she wanted to copy a very important letter, or a contract, for safety's sake, she had to go into town to see the chairman of the trustees, Heinz Brämer, at the Westphalia Bank. He had a Xerox machine.

After morning training finished at about 12 o'clock, the footballers hung around the office with them. The two Christas had a bag of sweets in the drawer.

Sometimes, when the players noticed that the Christas were having a stressful time of it, Vim Lameck or Hermann Gerland would take over the phone. 'VfL Bochum,' Lameck answered: Yes, of course, there were still tickets for the game against Hamburg, you could get them here at the office, or in town, at Koch's sports shop, or Hutmacher's cigarette shop.

Sometimes Heinz Höher hung around in there too. When he did, he would lean for what seemed an eternity against the office wall, in silence.

It seemed impossible to really talk to him, even if he actually said anything. When Christa Jewers asked him for the list of players' names for their away game, so that she could fax the names to their hotel, he just grunted: the same as last time. Is he actually here with us at all? Christa Jewers asked herself.

Heinz Höher took great pleasure in leaning on the office wall, listening to the footballers and the two Christas chatting away. He just didn't see any reason to chip in. As the minutes passed, he disappeared the way into his own thoughts.

Great men – and Bundesliga managers had to be larger-than-life characters – were allowed to be eccentric. People called it mysterious. Just at the time Heinz Höher was about to become a manager, men like Branko Zebec, who, in 1969, had led Bayern Munich to their first German Championship for 37 years, or Ernst Happel, who, in the early 1970s, had made Feyenoord into European and World Club champions, had given the impression that great managers should be men of great silence. Fascinated, sports journalists tried to make out the secret of Zebec's or Happel's silences. Surely, it must be a sign that they were permanently thinking things through, always tweaking their ideas. And then, wasn't keeping silent a well-known way of leading a team? If a manager kept the players in the dark about what he was thinking, that meant they were permanently standing to attention, it kept things in a high state of suspense and concentration.

Heinz Höher convinced himself again and again that it was better for a manager to talk too little than too much. That way, he didn't wear himself out. In the evenings, in their hotel rooms, on the days before Bundesliga matches, some of his younger players felt a rising panic, because they didn't feel properly prepped by him. Hans-Joachim Pochstein, who had come to Bochum from amateurs Brambauer, opened his heart to his room-mate Jürgen Köper: Jesus, I'm supposed to be playing outside-left tomorrow, but I've got no idea who I'm playing against or how he plays, or if I'm supposed to get right down to the line, or hit the cross as soon as I'm into the channel.

But Heinz Höher didn't hear any of that. In his opinion, you could safely assume that any player who wanted to make it in the Bundesliga could work things out for himself, without needing much in the way of individual teaching about tactics. He handed the number 11 jersey to Pochstein with a smile, saying: Have a go.

The players, especially the younger ones, would never have dared to go to the manager themselves and ask for advice. At the start, they were even uncertain if they should call their older team-mates 'Mr Walitzka' or 'Hannes'. They thought that asking the manager for some tactical advice would've seemed like impertinence, or tactical stupidity. So instead, they tried to learn for themselves through their mistakes. When Frankfurt's Bernd Nickel played a short pass, Hermann Gerland chased off after the ball, giving Nickel space to get the ball straight back from a one-two and score from 35 metres out. That'll never happen to you again, next time you'll stick to your man, Gerland vowed to himself. If only the manager had explained that to him before. But maybe Bundesliga managers didn't explain stuff like that? How was he to know, he'd only ever had one manager, and that was at Bochum.

Ottokar Wüst got the feeling that behind Heinz Höher's silence, his manager had something to say. While most people saw Höher's taciturnity as coldness or a personal mystique, throughout his life he always met someone, now and then, who was fascinated by him, who looked at his training ideas – playing with four goals, short games played as interval training – and wanted to understand them. On Sundays, after their matches, club president Wüst used to invite Heinz Höher to his weekend home in Haltern.

Having a weekend home by the lake in Haltern, not far from the Marl-Hüls chemical works, where the Ruhr area seemed green and lovely, was a status symbol among the prosperous citizenry of Germany's industrial heartland. Wüst's wife, Ingrid, served them lunch. Then the men went for a stroll by the lake.

Mr Wüst, we've got to release Eia Krämer and Reinhold Wosab.

Do you really think that Wosab cut such a bad figure last season, Wüst asked, carefully.

He's almost thirty-five, he won't be able to keep it up at this level for much longer.

Has anything particular happened?

No, no.

It was Ottokar Wüst, and not his manager, who gave the half-time pep talks at Bochum, although this was just beginning to change under Heinz Höher. The club president checked out potential new signings together with the manager. Unlike most presidents of Bundesliga clubs, Ottokar Wüst had a good understanding of football. This made him sure enough of his own position to normally allow his manager the last word on professional matters.

Right then, if Heinz Höher was of the opinion that Wosab had to go, go he must, said Wüst, even if he himself didn't think he'd done so badly last season.

Reinhard Wosab couldn't understand the world any more. He had a European Cup Winners' Cup medal, as he liked to remind his team-mates at Bochum. And at 34, in Höher's first season at Bochum, he'd played in 25 Bundesliga games, usually doing pretty well, he'd shaken hands with the president on an extension to his contract, and now the manager was kicking him out without any explanation or a word of thanks.

We're letting you go, was all Heinz Höher said.

As far as he was concerned, there was nothing else he could say to Wosab. How could he tell him that the mere presence of Wosab had him feel under threat?

It was simply this feeling that Wosab was a disturbing influence. He just couldn't shut up about how fantastic everything, including him, had been at Borussia Dortmund when they won the European Cup Winners' Cup. Heinz Höher felt that players like that always thought that they were better than the manager and would cause trouble at some time or other, even though others, such as Ottokar Wüst or Heinz Formann, saw Wosab as the perfect sportsman.

When someone makes a drastic decision and can only explain it by saying that they went with their feelings, it always sounds somehow weak, or false. But it's precisely that feeling that sets really good managers apart from just good ones. Wosab went, Franz-Josef Tenhagen was signed from Oberhausen in the summer of 1973 and the VfL

Bochum known to history was born. In the Bundesliga, they became a byword for the outsiders who were always snapping at the heels of the big boys.

In the 1970s, every Bundesliga club was personified by a nexus of players: Maier, Beckenbauer and Müller at Bayern; Vogts, Heynckes and Wimmer at Borussia Mönchengladbach; Grabowski, Hölzenbein and Nickel at Frankfurt. Bochum were Lameck, Gerland and Tenhagen, who ran and ran and never stopped running.

These players were like the fans: they belonged to the club. There was an unwritten law which forbade them to change clubs and it really was only a few free spirits among those emblematic players, such as Günter Netzer or Paul Breitner, who ever thought about leaving *their* club. It was simply the greatest thing you could be: the symbol of a club, the local hero.

And thus the 1970s became a real epoque in the Bundesliga. Every season it came round again: Lameck vs Hölzenbein, Gerland vs Heynckes, the sweepers' duel Tenhagen vs Beckenbauer. Every time I see you again, said Schalke outside-right Rüdiger Abramcik to left-half Vim Lameck in the tunnel at Bochum, before their nth duel, it really spoils my day.

In West Germany in the 1970s the greatest thing was to have a secure job, where you could say: this'll see me through to my pension. Of course, Bundesliga players did really know that unlike people on the production line at Opel in Bochum, or chemical engineers at Bayer in Leverkusen, they'd have to start all over again at about 30, but in principle a Bundesliga club was run on the same ideas: if you had a steady job, you stayed. Teams in the 1970s not only played with the same core team, the personnel behind the team stayed the same, too. The spirit that made up Bochum's sense of *us* wasn't just made up of Lameck, Gerland, Tenhagen, but also included the two Christas, Wüst, the club president, Brämer, chairman of the board of trustees, and Liese, the official in charge of looking after the players. And unlike at other clubs, at Bochum even the manager always stayed the same.

Being a football manager was the one great exception in West Germany, the land of secure jobs. At other clubs, Bundesliga managers had been fired at the double since the inception of the league; 62 of them were sacked in the first ten years. Ottokar Wüst said quite early on to Heinz Höher: you can stay as long as you want to.

In the back of Heinz Höher's mind there certainly flitted the idea that he might one day manage a mightier club. But that was a purely theoretical idea, as if he felt it was his duty to think about it; no more. He set three goals for himself: never get relegated; never get sacked; never be unemployed. He felt that at Bochum, he could fulfil all three.

With their chins sunk down onto their necks, and their hands at their backs, because you could think about things better that way, Heinz Höher and Ottokar Wüst strolled beside the lake at Haltern.

We just need to stick fast to one principle: we'll never let ourselves be bounced into selling a player against our wishes, said Höher.

Ottokar Wüst nodded.

Continuity was the essence of success. It wasn't particularly difficult to keep the most important players at Bochum. Most of them didn't want to leave anyway. Apart from forward Hannes Walitza, none of them had an agent, either. And if offers from other Bundesliga clubs came in for Jürgen Köper, well, Wüst just stonewalled until they gave up. He thought it best not to even inform Köper about them.

In the autumn of 1973, after the tenth match of Heinz Höher's second season at Bochum, they lay third in the Bundesliga.

Walter Czech, landlord of the Haus Frein, brought out his signature drink, the Pulimo. At least, that was what Jürgen Köper always heard when Czech brought the gigantic bowl to the table in the back room where the Bochum team always ate together after home games: 'Here comes the Pulimo!' Walter Czech was not in possession of an exact recipe for Pulimo. He poured in all the alcoholic drinks that happened to be standing about. I've got something new today, said the landlord, and served them apple schnapps in wine-glasses.

Excellent wine, this, said club president Wüst, having tasted it, and nobody could tell if Wüst actually thought that the schnapps was wine, or was just going along with the joke.

When it came to away games, Herr and Frau Czech prepared packed lunches for the Bochum players. After home games, not only the fans but even the referee came back to the Haus Frein with the team. If your players just refuse to ever go down, I can never award you a penalty, said Walter Eschweiler to Heinz Höher on their way to the Haus Frein. Another referee, Wolf-Dieter Ahlenfelder, stood on the bar to conduct the fans as they sung 'We're going to win the league!'

It never occurred to anyone that Ahlenfelder might be biased. He probably gave the same performance in Dortmund or Braunschweig.

Why not come back to our place? said Doris to some of the officials and players and their wives after dinner at the Haus Frein.

Without her really noticing how it happened, her fun-loving personality had made her into the manager of the players' wives. She regularly organised get-togethers. They went bowling, or knitted together. The spirit of Bochum, that exuberance, that feeling of being all in it together, could be felt here as well.

On Saturday evenings, the Höhers were fond of having a spontaneous party at home.

Having your own party-cellar with its very own bar was the absolute latest thing, any Bundesliga professional who was building a house simply had to include a party-cellar in the plans. Obviously, the Höhers couldn't claim to have one of those in their two-bed apartment in Kaulbachstraße. But if there's one thing we know how to do, said Doris, it's party. There were always ice-cold champagne glasses ready in the fridge. On Saturday evenings, Doris or Heinz stood at the door, to greet each guest with a chilled glass of Bommerlunder schnapps. A Bommi, they said.

On the turntable the latest hits were playing, 'It Never Rains in Southern California', 'Saturday Afternoon in our Street', 'Ginny Come Lately'. When it got to 'Crocodile Rock', Doris and her sister Helga threw their fists into the air, now even Heinz Formann had to dance, whether he wanted to or not, he was grabbed and dragged onto the dance-floor, which appeared spontaneously, sometimes in the hallway, sometimes in the living room between the table and the TV. No one dared to grab Heinz Höher and pull him onto the dance-floor.

One time, Ingrid, the wife of Jürgen Köper, came too early to see Doris. Heinz Höher opened the door to her. Doris wasn't back yet. Ingrid waited with Heinz Höher in the living room. He wasn't impolite in any way, but between his few words an uncomfortable stillness kept spreading out. Ingrid was relieved when Doris finally appeared.

But on Saturdays, at their house parties, when Elton John was singing 'Crocodile Rock', Heinz Höher was happy. Those two beers and a shot cleared the block in his throat. To the other people there, he still seemed reserved. Heinz Höher himself felt relaxed and relieved, at last.

After a couple of beers and a shot he said to a fan who'd been begging and begging for a Bochum pennant at their training ground in the Black Forest: only if you can get it out of the plastic bag using only your mouth. Müller, the VfL Bochum bus-driver, was there to see it. Every time the fan started to get hold of the pennant with his teeth, Heinz Höher pulled the plastic bag down over his head and tightened it at his neck. Müller the bus-driver almost died laughing.

No one voiced the thought, but everyone felt that same thought in their own way, Doris and Heinz Höher just as much as Heinz Formann and Ottokar Wüst or the two Christas: Bochum in the 1970s, those were the days, my friend.

On Monday mornings, when there was no training, Heinz Höher went to one of the more exclusive inns in Bochum, like the Lottental, to have a couple of whiskies with his best friend. He and Heinz Formann discussed the situation at VfL Bochum.

He also took his holidays in Gran Canaria together with the sports editor. Formann went on about it so much, I had no choice, said Heinz Höher. Höher could be a pain sometimes, said Heinz Formann. It was as if, somehow, they had to play down this friendship between manager and journalist.

After a game like that, we should really crack open a special bottle, said Heinz Formann after they had watched the 1973 cup final in Düsseldorf together. Cologne against Borussia Mönchengladbach, a mighty duel with an unbelievable cast. Mönchengladbach manager, Hennes Weisweiler, had left Günter Netzer fuming on the substitutes' bench because he was so angry about Netzer's imminent move to Real Madrid; didn't Netzer know that he belonged to Borussia like the fans belonged, that an emblematic player never left? And then, when it came to extra time, Netzer simply got ready himself to go on, catching Weisweiler completely off guard: he couldn't countermand it, because the whole stadium could already see Netzer waiting there on the touchline. With his second touch of the ball, Netzer scored the goal that won it for them, 2-1. Today it's time you tasted Chivas Regal for once, said Heinz Formann to Heinz Höher in the house on the Hugo-Schultz-Straße. Their wives, and the Höhers' children, were there too. The children used to just go to sleep in the Formanns' bed when they got tired.

In the living room, the lights stayed on until late into the evening. Netzer'll come good in Spain too, he's got chutzpah. Those Spaniards would love to buy up every star in the Bundesliga all in one go, now Franco's lifted the ban on foreign players. Five million for five years, that's what Barcelona have offered Gerd Müller.

No one's going to go apart from Netzer. People like Müller or Beckenbauer will stay at Bayern, they know where they belong. And why should they leave? The Bundesliga is the strongest league in the world.

That's some whisky, eh?

It's like a drug.

It's over two hundred marks the bottle. C'mon, here, have another.

When Heinz Höher said that he was just going to the toilet, and didn't come back, Heinz Formann thought that his friend had lain down in bed.

Heinz Höher liked doing that. He would say at about 11 o'clock, at his own house parties, but also when he was at the Formanns', that he was just popping to the bathroom, and he just lay down and slept, even if it was in the Formanns' marital bed, until his wife woke him up and said it was time they were off. Heinz Formann liked it. That way, his nights with Heinz Höher always ended early, and he could get out of bed next morning with no trouble.

A few minutes later there was a knock on the door to the balcony. Heinz Höher was standing outside.

He had either fallen out of the bathroom window, or he had jumped, he couldn't remember any more. He could hardly turn his head. He must have sprained his neck when he landed on the floor of the balcony, hopefully he hadn't broken a vertebra. Whatever, now it was about time to have another glass of this fiendishly good whisky.

For a manager, Heinz Höher led an exemplary life. He went to play chess in the park, he went for runs, with friends he drank a little more than was necessary to quench his thirst, now and again. He did everything to switch off from the stresses of a manager's life. He didn't tell anyone about the sleeping tablets. And in any case, tablets were there to be taken, to make a person's life a bit easier.

Heinz Höher was hot. As always happens when a young manager makes good, many people in the media and in club boardrooms unthinkingly take him as the representative of a new age and new methods. The time when managers were like field marshals was over, explained Otto Rehhagel, another young Bundesliga manager: he said the new generation of managers worked with more professional understanding and more empathy. The new managers of the 1950s and the young managers of the 1960s had said exactly the same thing.

Heinz Höher, the face of a new generation of managers, was wooed every spring by clubs like Eintracht Frankfurt, Borussia Dortmund or Stuttgart. He said no to all of them. It was enough for him to know that he was in demand. If he ever did ever want to leave Bochum, he'd be able to freely choose where to go.

The papers who carried pictures of him liked to show him with his family. A good manager seemed even better if he was a decent family man.

The '68 movement had, among other things, given rise to new ideas about bringing children up. Kids should be allowed to do just as they wanted, or if this wasn't actually possible, they should at least be brought up with understanding, rather than strictness. Heinz Höher did not feel obliged to take on any of these anti-authoritarian ideas about bringing up his children. The 68-ers were left wing. You were either on the left or the right, there was no bridge, no grey area. And he, having worshipped Adenauer since childhood, assumed that he was on the right, without thinking much about it.

His way of helping Markus with his maths homework was to sit next to his son and wait until he'd solved the problem. If Markus was finding it hard, well then, he'd sit for three hours next to his son. There was no question of helping him, of explaining things to him. His son had to solve it himself, if he was going to actually learn anything from it.

Heinz Höher enrolled Markus in Ju-Jitsu classes. He thought it was important that Markus should learn how to defend himself. He didn't ask his son if he wanted to do Ju-Jitsu.

In the afternoons, if there was no training session, Heinz Höher did sometimes take the kids out into the woods at Weitmar to play, come on, let's catch a deer. If he drove to see the club president at his gentlemen's outfitters on the Brückstraße, he took the kids along, now and then. He left them in the car. They could play better there.

One time, the meeting went on too long for the children. Susanne and Markus ran all the way home from the Brückstraße. It was over four kilometres. Heinz Höher was a little bit proud. Because the little ones had found their way home all alone.

Ottokar Wüst used to call Heinz Höher to meetings in the clothes-room. That was what the Bochum manager and players called the room at the back of the gentlemen's outfittters, which contained not only a desk but also surplus items of clothing. In practice, this was the presidential hall of Bundesliga members, VfL Bochum.

If you weren't always and forever an optimist, never mind how

things were, you would and could never be a leader of men, said Wüst
to Höher – before proceeding every time, without further ado, to a
topic which was enough to turn anyone into a pessimist: the precarious
finances of VfL Bochum. After their first year in the Bundesliga, the
club had already taken on obligations to the tune of 500,000 marks. It
wasn't going to get much better.

Bochum was the headquarters of firms like Opel and Aral, but the
big sponsors of the club were Schweinsberg's bakery and Antico the
butcher, where you could get fresh pig's liver, rich in vitamins and easy
to digest, for only DM 1.98 the pound. The baker and the butcher
couldn't contribute more than a few thousand marks a year. That was
enough to get them seats on the board. Why would international businesses like Opel and Aral get involved with a Bundesliga team who
really only mattered in their own region?

When a player at Bochum wanted to get paid the backhanders he'd
secretly been promised, Wüst would send him along to Brämer, chairman of the board of trustees, at the Westphalia Bank.

With his grey hair and thick, horn-rimmed glasses, Brämer always
looked the very picture of an elegant, elderly man: but when a player
appeared, he would hysterically fling open the drawers of his directo-
rial desk.

You see any money in here? he would roar at the player. Or maybe
here? All empty!

Brämer's agression was really aimed at himself. What was he doing,
lending Wüst the bank's money again and again, against his own better
judgement? When he knew it in his bones that a large chunk of that
money would never be seen again by the bank?

Look, okay, come with me, he would eventually say to the player,
and get the money from the safe.

Was it Vim Lameck, Jürgen Köper or Franz-Josef Tenhagen who
actually had the following scene with Brämer happen to them? The
Bochum players didn't know any more. They each told the story as if
it had happened to them personally:

So there I am, I go to the Westphalia Bank to get my money, and
from way off I can already hear Brämer, inside his office, with the door
closed, yelling away.

'I have had enough of it, Mr Wüst! That's it, you're not getting
another penny out of me!'

I'm stunned, and I turn to look at Helga, his secretary.

'Oh, never mind him, just go on in,' she says. 'Mr Brämer's only putting on a little show, just for himself, to get it out of his system.'

The money that was never there made VfL Bochum into elegant fibbers and noble scammers. At their training camp on the island of Sylt, Heinz Höher persuaded several restaurant owners to make him out bills for several thousand marks. He'd only had a pot of coffee in those restaurants. When they submitted their accounts to the taxman, the club put these through as expenses, for team dinners. That way, they could set those figures against their tax bill.

No one asked Heinz Höher to do it. He had subconsciously taken on board Wüst's lamentations about their lack of money.

You had a high old time at your training camp, said the German FA's book-keepers admiringly to Bochum club secretary Willi Hecker, when he presented them with the club's annual accounts: You spent more in restaurants than Bayern Munich did.

Jesus, aren't you the likely lads.

Who could have anything against a smile like that? Carmen Thomas, new on *Das aktuelle Sportstudio*.

30 November 1974:

HERE COME THE WOMEN

In a TV studio on the Lerchenberg in Mainz, a railway station clock was ticking inexorably forward. On the dot of the third beat of the accompanying jingle, the TV cameras swung away from the station clock and onto the banks of seats in studio; the studio audience wore beards and hornrimmed glasses, yellow shirts with brown jackets or white blouses with enormous collars and all of them, men and women, wearing their hair the same way: straight down and over the ears, and a side-parting made with a few gentle strokes of a comb. Heinz Höher, dressed in a grey-beige jacket with broad lapels, was sitting in one of the dressing rooms at the back of the studio. For the first time, he was a guest on Channel 2's *Das aktuelle Sportstudio*. It was like being knighted.

Anyone who had achieved anything in sport was invited onto *Sportstudio*, Franz Beckenbauer, Muhammad Ali, Pelé. And anyone who was anybody in Germany could get on as well, provided only that he was a true sports fan, or at least declared himself to be one. Germany's president Gustav Heinemann and the actress Heidi Brühl had been guests on the show. Following Germany's World Cup victory in 1974, people were happy to watch the Bundesliga again and happy to be seen linked to football; the match-fixing scandal was three years gone, it was history, wasn't it? The stadiums were filling up again, and *Das aktuelle Sportstudio* was even being watched by many people who would never have gone to a stadium.

Watching *Sportstudio* was one of the great Saturday evening leisure-

time rituals of the 1970s: on 30 November 1974 at 9.15p, 12 per cent
of all German households were tuned in to it. They regularly had more
female than male viewers, to the surprise of the producers themselves.
It was easy for them to imagine a scenario in which the man of the
house decided what they were going to watch on Saturday evening,
and the woman simply had to watch it as well – but in that case, how
come the majority of viewers were women? Could it be that they liked
the programme because here, sport wasn't about statistics and records,
but about real people?

Or did many Germans watch because on a Saturday evening there
was nothing else going on? The average German living room was used
for parties considerably less often than the Höher's, families rarely went
to restaurants, and when they did, it was for Sunday lunch. Discos were
reserved for the youth, theatres catered exclusively to the educated
middle classes, and cinemas were dying out. Of the 7000 cinemas in
Germany in 1959, only about a third were still in business. The cinema
owners partitioned their splendid theatres into thirds and quarters, so
as to be able to screen several films at once, and somehow survive. In
a single decade, TV had come from almost nowhere to be the domi-
nant evening leisure-time activity.

God, do you remember the way we produced the first edition of
Sportstudio back then, the Rhein-Ruhr Mafia in Channel 2's sports team
asked one another after the show, in the Adlerstübchen bar in
Wiesbaden. It was just 11 years ago.

That first show in 1963 was four hours long, said one of them. No,
it was more than four hours, said someone else. Every time they told
it, it got a bit longer.

Remember the way we used to eat in the village pub in Eschborn,
in Telesiberia?

We used to stick toothpicks into the middle of the chips we didn't
eat, because we wanted to test the theory that they really did serve left-
over food again the next day.

Remember the equipment we had back then. I can still see Kurt
Lavall, trying to get his round-up of the Bundesliga ready and shouting: I need another goal! Has no one got another goal for me?

As the theme song of *Das aktuelle Sportstudio* died away on 30
November 1974, here came Carmen Thomas, descending the steps
down through the audience. Her dark-grey flannel trousers were skin-
tight on her hips and thighs, then spread out at her calves into

enormous flares. With them she wore a shirt with horizontal stripes of blue-white-red, and two black & bright green vertical stripes, which were supposed to look like braces, but were in fact printed on the fabric. Her hair gleamed with the latest sensation from the hairdressing salons: blonde highlights. She was 28. She, a woman, had moved out of her parents' home and lived with her boyfriend in Cologne in a maisonette – without having married.

Some of the men in the audience found her charming. Some of the women secretly regarded her as one of them. Many men were of the opinion that she'd do better cooking a decent dinner for her fiancé for once, after all, she was engaged, right?

She had been chosen as presenter by Channel 2 sports chief Hanns Joachim Friderichs explicitly because she was a woman.

Women's liberation had been turning Germany upside down since 1971. In June 1971, 374 women had declared, on the cover of *Stern* magazine: We have had abortions! Abortion was illegal according both to the Word of God and to paragraph 218 of the German Basic Law. Alice Schwarzer published her polemic, *Work for Women – Freedom for Women*, in which she demonstrated that equality could only be reached if women fought to take their places in careers outside the home, thus also becoming financially independent from men.

To large sections of the German population, this was a frontal assault on their way of life, on Adenauer's vision of the German idyll: the woman hanging out the washing in the garden with a happy smile as she waits for her husband to get back from work so that she can cook him dinner. At a time when life was lived in terms of polar opposites – east or west, left or right, student or worker, Bayern or Mönchengladbach – the clash between the women's liberation movement and those who wished to maintain the old relationship between men and women bid fair to become the most disruptive conflict in West Germany.

In this climate, Channel 2's sports boss Friedrichs wanted to send out a message. In February 1973 Carmen Thomas made her debut on *Sportstudio*. It was the first time that a woman had played anchor on a sports show on German TV.

At Channel 2, they realised that the decision wouldn't please everybody. The channel released a pre-emptive announcement to the press: Carmen Thomas, who had until then worked on Channel 3's *Daily Magazine*, had, they pointed out, been a sportswoman herself, a gymnast who 'in her youth had won a championship in the Düsseldorf region' and that 'in order to prevent viewers of *Sportstudio* from react-ing with "well, she's a woman", she intends to gather specialist knowledge of the subject.'

Carmen Thomas would actually have liked to work as a political editor. On the *Daily Magazine*, she had contributed reports about abor-tion or suicide, leading to cries of horror even from her colleagues, you couldn't report stuff like that, you couldn't talk about it! That only spurred her on; she fought to get her reports broadcast, for a dedicated journalist had to reckon with resistance. The offer to take over at *Das Sportstudio* came out of the blue. You're going to have to do this, she thought to herself: it's a cutting-edge format with live interviews, with the public there in the studio, with cameras filming other cameramen, and if you make a name for yourself there, you'll be able to get ahead on political programmes later. For a year, Friedrichs had sent her the sports reports from news agencies to her desk at the *Daily Magazine* office, and then she was supposed to just have a go.

There was no form of training, what would be the point, either you could present a programme, or you couldn't. Instead there was the edi-torial conference on Monday mornings. That's where the criticisms were made. There was no need to talk about the things that worked. She was too full-on in interviews, cried her male colleagues, she didn't seem to understand that here in *Das Sportstudio*, her job wasn't to be some investigating journalist, squeezing stories out of people, but to be a hostess of the show. She didn't treat the sportspeople as guests enough. She just gets parachuted in and now she's allowed to present our *Sportstudio*, thought some of her male colleagues, angrily. Carmen Thomas constructed a wall of apparent indifference to defend herself against such criticism, she rejected it all: she knew very well herself that she could seem bossy, and she hated it, but that wasn't the point, what was important was not to show any vulnerability, any weakness. You just didn't talk about your real feelings.

Carmen Thomas sometimes felt like a fraudster. She constantly felt that she was having to play the expert on sport, which she really wasn't. She longed for someone who would help her become that expert. But to ask for help would have been an admission of weakness.

And – strictly between ourselves, murmured her male colleagues in the corridor after the conference – have you seen the way she dresses?

Meanwhile, Carmen Thomas opened her post-bag. A viewer of *Das Sportstudio* had sent her a sheet of used toilet paper.

In only her second appearance on *Das Sportstudio*, Carmen Thomas broke a taboo. She gave the public at least an indication of how she must be feeling. 'You don't need to bother watching tonight because a major German paper already knows what I'm going to be like,' she said, then held up next morning's *Bild am Sonntag* to the camera and read what their TV critic, Michael Bernhard, had written on page 32 about her performance: 'Charm is not enough, Frau Thomas! Actually, I trembled along with you out of sympathy, but you couldn't convince me. In my opinion, *Das Sportstudio* should remain men's business. Because in the end, sport is basically a game for the stronger sex.' Since the deadline for copy at *Bild am Sonntag* was before the time *Sportstudio* came on air, Bernhard had rubbished Thomas without waiting to watch her performance. What he hadn't reckoned with was that early editions of the Sunday papers could already be bought at main railway stations on Saturday evenings.

Some outraged viewers called Channel 2 as well as the editors of *Bild*, complaining at such impossible, disgusting behaviour at a news-paper. You would have done better not to go public with this, a few male colleagues told Carmen Thomas. You're declaring war on that lot. You can only lose, they doubtless thought.

Because it was not a woman's place to have any notion of football. The people who clove to Adenauer's world were not going to change their ideas about that. *Bild* believed it was talking for these people, for this endangered vision of Germany.

In July 1973, Carmen Thomas was already an established and sym-bolic figure for friend and foe alike, making her fifth appearance on *Sportstudio*. The Bundesliga was on its summer break, and in its place the European Inter-Toto Cup was being played, with five German teams taking part. On her sheet of presenting-notes, which she held in her hand, she wrote down: 'Inter-Toto' and 'five German teams'. But she simply couldn't get the name of Schalke 04's opponents, Standard Lüttich, to stick in her mind. As she introduced the item about the game all she could think about was that blasted name, Standard Lüttich, and somehow or other the number five from that sentence 'five German teams', unconsciously swam up into her mind, and she added a year to the age of Schalke 04: Now, said she, they were going to show a clip from the game between 'Schalke 05 and – er, now, I've forgotten – Standard Lüttich.' Schalke 05!

It was only a slip of the tongue. It was treated as the great proof: you couldn't let a woman present *Sportstudio*. *Bild Zeitung*, however, made no mention of Schalke 05 for 18 days. The paper was usually only six pages long, so every now and then a piece of news might well get left on the shelf. Then, suddenly, on 8 August, it stood on the front page: 'Carmen Thomas blows it on Channel 2's *Sportstudio*', directly beneath the main headline: 'The Queen's doctor poisons himself'. One of the male members of Channel 2's sports team had informed *Bild*'s editors that there were impassioned discussions going on about the presenter within the channel. 'Frau Thomas has been caught in a critical crossfire,' Channel 2 sports chief Friedrichs told the paper: 'When things calm down, she'll get another chance.' Giving her a second chance hardly sounded as if she had 'blown it'. But no one would care about little details like that. *Bild Zeitung* was only being playful. On page 2 they published a comment article on the business: 'What would happen to a man who went on television and talked about a perfume called Chanel No. 4? People would smile about it – what a charming mistake. But what happens to a young charming woman who, like Carmen Thomas, goes on *Sportstudio* and talks about Schalke 05? She gets the sack. Oh come on, guys! Can't you have a little more understanding for just a whiff of femininity in sport?'

At their editorial meetings, Channel 2 sports chief Friedrichs told Carmen Thomas her interviews were really very interesting and so multi-faceted. He wanted her to carry on just the same after the summer break. Friedrichs never mentioned the *Bild* business; it was as if it had never happened.

It felt to her as though she was presenting in the teeth of the whole nation. Even the feminists ignored her, or wrote letters to her in which they claimed she was just a figleaf for males. Meanwhile she was producing items for *Sportstudio* which gave her great satisfaction – for example, about sports in prison – and she felt that she was getting better in the interviews. Carmen Thomas remained the first woman who talked about football on television, the woman who some people thought had to fail and some people thought couldn't be allowed to fail. As such, all unabashed, she continued to present *Sportstudio* 15 months after *Bild Zeitung* thought she'd been sacked.

'And now it's a fitting moment,' said Carmen Thomas on 30 November 1974, in her naturally sympathetic, gentle way, and indicated the man next to her, who was sitting dressed in a black shirt with fine brown zigzag stripes beneath his grey-beige jacket: 'Heinz Höher, manager of VfL Bochum.'

The audience clapped. In the backs of their minds, many people no doubt thought that her sentence had been somehow incomplete. But everyone could work out what Carmen Thomas meant. On television, it didn't matter much what you said. What mattered was the effect. The sentences, the statements, the content all rushed past: what stayed with the public was the impression.

Bochum's 3-0 victory over German champions and European Cup winners Bayern Munich that Friday had earned Heinz Höher the honour of this invitation. For the first time since the semi-final victory in the German Cup in 1968, when he himself had played, Bochum's stadium had seen a full house of 34,000 once again.

'It's a carnival atmosphere at the Castroper Straße,' reported *Sportstudio*'s match commentator. 'Even before the whistle blew for kick-off, a nine-year-old boy had to be taken to hospital with alcohol poisoning.'

Every Saturday, *Sportstudio* invited three guests along. Two of them were decided upon in advance, the third – in this case, Heinz Höher – was chosen at the last minute on the basis of what had happened in sport over the weekend, often only four hours before the programme was broadcast. If they weren't able to get hold of any outstanding third guest, producer Karl Senne had to call Germany's manager Helmut Schön again.

Schön lived in Wiesbaden. From there he could quickly get to the studio in Mainz. That – and the fact that he'd managed the World Cup champions of 1974 – made him *Sportstudio*'s go-to man in case of need.

Often, Annelies Schön answered the phone and told Senne: 'Helmut's gone for a walk with Dickie.' Dickie was their dog.

Who's let you down again today then, Helmut Schön would say later, when Senne finally got hold of him. Okay, okay, I'll be there now.

'Did your chest swell with pride?' Carmen Thomas asked Heinz Höher, 24 hours after their 3-0 victory over the mighty Bavarians.

'I think that in football that feeling only lasts for six or seven days and then you have to get your feet back on the ground. So a good piece of advice is to always keep normal.'

Cautiously, Carmen Thomas sought to establish eye contact with her guest. Most of the time, Heinz Höher was staring, shyly but not impolitely, at the floor. He'd been to the hairdressers just before the programme. No doubt his wife had reminded him to do that.

'Mr Höher, you've resorted to very unusual methods to support your club. Perhaps you could tell the viewers about that?'

For a moment, Heinz Höher raised his head up from his hunched shoulders so as to look her carefully in the eye. 'Well, if you mean that I don't draw part of my salary? I don't know, it's not meant to set an example to anybody, it's just a way to show my belief in the team.'

'And that's why, I think we should say it quite clearly: You allow a thousand marks a month of your salary to be withheld so that the money can be used to strengthen the team. Obviously I ask myself: What does your wife think of that?'

Laughter in the audience.

'Actually, my wife only found out about it in the papers and she really only said one single sentence: so you've gone and done it again.'

The camera found Doris Höher in the front row of the audience, she was wearing a brightly coloured shirt over a black rollneck pullover, she smiled softly and pulled a face when she realised that she was in the picture.

At the end of the interview, Carmen Thomas got it out of Heinz Höher that the Höhers were awaiting their third child, and then, with an inviting wave of her hand, she led him to that compulsory part of the programme where he was to shoot at a painted goal.

For six weeks in 1974, *Sportstudio* had been broadcast without showing that famous goal. Every Saturday they were having to drop excellent items because of a lack of running-time, they had to make cuts somewhere and the producer, Karl Senne, decided it was better to leave out the entertainment element than the content element: he had abolished the painted goal. 'It was an incredible mistake,' Senne realised after a few days. They had never received so many complaints. Objectively speaking, it was just a question of six shots taken with a football at a painted fairground goal with two holes in it, six shots which every guest on the programme had to take, for fun, in their ordinary street shoes, whether they were a female jockey or a football star. But emotionally speaking, it was a ritual for the viewers, it was *the* comfortable, ever-recognisable part of the programme which confirmed for millions, every Saturday evening: that's my *Sportstudio*. After six weeks, Senne brought that painted goal back without any explanation, as though nothing had ever happened.

Next to the goal there hung a scoreboard, using Otl Aicher's famous design for the Olympic Games of 1972, on which the highest scorers were recorded. Günter Netzer held the top spot on his own with five.

The viewers shouted 'oh' and 'ah' as Heinz Höher took his six shots. The balls flew wildly all around. He only got one shot through the hole. 'That really doesn't matter when you had such success yesterday,' said Carmen Thomas, wished him all the best, and then, having already invented 'Schalke 05', she made her second wonderful, though less widely known, slip of the tongue: she meant to say 'I hope you have a healthy child.' What she said was: 'I hope you have a beautiful child.'

Everybody laughed, most of all the presenter herself.

Sitting there on a white gym-bench in front of the cameras, Carmen Thomas as the gentle host and Heinz Höher as her shy guest had been more than pleasant company, they'd been quite charming. But it had already been decided that this was to be Carmen Thomas's last show.

Her two-year contract was up in a few weeks. Shall we call it a day? sports boss Hanns Joachim Friderichs had asked producer Karl Senne.

Carmen Thomas had bravely got over all the hysteria about 'the woman who said Schalke 05', and her experience of those two years had made her into a charming presenter, as the interview with Heinz Höher showed, but her bosses had already formed their opinions. She had only too rarely showed the sensitivity to create an atmosphere like she'd done with Heinz Höher, in which her studio guests opened up to her. Her ironic tone had too often been catty instead of light, as it had been with Heinz Höher. And so what was perhaps the best interview she did for *Sportstudio* was also her last. WDR, her old employers, offered Carmen Thomas a job presenting their new radio entertainment show *Hallo Ü-Wagen*. At the end of 1974, after two years, the first visible woman in the German Bundesliga quietly left the scene. She became a much-loved, supremely professional radio journalist. But as happens to so many footballers, whose careers end up being reduced to one goal, one great mistake, or one phrase, Carmen Thomas, no matter what she achieved as a journalist, always remained 'the woman who said Schalke 05'.

The only people who always remembered her other, wonderful slip of the tongue were the Höher family. Four months after the show, when Doris and Heinz Höher's third child was born, they sent cards announcing: 'The beautiful child is here.' They had agreed on the child's name on the way back home from *Das aktuelle Sportstudio*. They called the newborn boy Thomas. If it had been a girl, they would have christened her Carmen.

The important thing was having your hands behind your back and your jersey tucked into your shorts. Bochum players (l to r): Dieter Bast, Matthias Herget, Michael Lameck and Jupp Tenhagen, with Heinz Höher far right, pose for a classic image of 1970s heroism.

The Later 1970s:

UNRELEGATIONABLE

His players liked to say of Heinz Höher: 'There's nothing else left he could surprise you with,' but then he astonished them yet again. In July 1976, with three weeks still to go before the beginning of the new Bundesliga season, Heinz Höher got his team together on a Sunday evening at the training camp to prepare them for a friendly against second division side Wuppertal on Monday.

But Heinz, you're going to the training camp before a friendly? President Wüst, who was by now on first-name terms with his manager, tried to sound as factual as possible.

Yes, from the point of view of scientific training it was important to get the team really exhausted from training and then, immediately afterwards, have them play a test game, replied Heinz Höher: that way, their bodies would learn to call up the inner reserves which they reserved for emergencies. Heinz Höher knew that his words weren't really convincing Wüst; his arguments weren't even convincing him himself. But there was no way that he could tell the truth: that Heinz Höher was dragging his team to their training camp before a friendly so that he could bunk off from his own house move.

After living in the Kaulbachstraße for eight years he had had to admit that with the best will in the world, the flat was too small for a family with three children. The Höhers were moving into a detached house, 42 Bonhoefferstraße, built of white bricks, with a patch of lawn in front of the door. The worst was over, the trunks dragged in, the furniture set up, by the time Heinz Höher came back on Monday night from the training camp in Wuppertal and moved into their new home.

Most other managers were always having to move from city to city. Heinz Höher set himself up in Bochum, as if he were going to stay for ever. Because there was exciting news.

VfL Bochum were getting a new stadium. In 1975 the North Rhine Westphalia region had suddenly made millions available for the construction of a new stadium, as part of a programme to stimulate the economy. In four stages, the stands at the Castroper Straße where to be rebuilt one after the other. If everything went according to plan, in three years' time, 1979, Bochum would be playing in a completely renovated stadium. They would be a whole new, stronger club, dreamed Höher and Wüst. At their tottering old stadium, Bochum only made about five marks on every ticket; their competitors, like Dortmund or Schalke, who played in modern arenas built for the 1974 World Cup, were making twice that on every spectator.

The future was Bochum, thought Heinz Höher, especially after their late run in the Bundesliga season 1975-76, which had not just been an event, but a revelation.

In March 1976, they had to get out of the stadium. During the first phase of building, the demolition and rebuilding of the south stand, the whole ground was locked up. In fact, Heinz Höher helped out a little in making the stadium unusable a little earlier even than that. Their home game against Schalke at the end of February could not be played in Bochum anyway, after heavy snow had fallen, and was transferred to Dortmund, but the part which Höher had played in getting the game abandoned was to remain a secret.

Apart from that match against Schalke, Bochum played their remaining six home games at the Schloss Strünkende ground in Herne. Heinz Höher's team had no home any more and had not won an away game for 18 months. The manager shoved his players around at will through every position on the field, without explaining much to them – Hermann Gerland played at outside-right one day and centre-half the next, their sweeper was called Hartmut Fromm, then Klaus Franke, then Jupp Tenhagen – but this method, which a few months ago was still being thought of as brilliant experimentation, was now cursed by Bochum's fans as chaotic interference. In early May 1976, with five matches left in the season, Bochum were in the relegation zone.

Two days before their home game against Eintracht Frankfurt,

Heinz Höher went and stood at the gates of the Opel works at Bochum to ask for help. The Opel workers must have looked at him from afar and thought: another one of those activists with his leaflets, probably a Communist or some other nutter. Even when they got close, not everyone recognised Bochum's manager, and many was the man who took the flyer quickly, with his head down, and stuffed it unread in his jacket pocket, as if he was ashamed to be seen near this zealot.

On the flyer stood a report about the serious plight of VfL Bochum, who, it said, truly expressed the values of the Ruhr area in their style of play: power, passion and indefatigable will. Robbed of their home thanks to the rebuilding of the stadium, in their dramatic battle against relegation they needed, now more than ever, the help of their fans, of the people of Bochum. It was simply unthinkable that the fine new stadium would be ready after so many years of waiting – but that VfL Bochum would no longer be playing in the Bundesliga. Come to Herne on Saturday! Help us!

Höher himself had single-handedly produced and financed the flyer. The print workers at every German newspaper had been on strike for days, demanding a rise, none of the papers was appearing. Heinz Höher decided that he would have to get the fans by some other means. Later, Heinz Formann wrote that a friend had written the text for Höher. He himself was that friend.

No way was he going to stand in front of the Opel factory like some agitator, Formann declared, horrified. So Heinz Höher went on his own.

At the Schloss Strünkede ground, the changing rooms were not, as they usually were in the Bundesliga, below the main stand, but in a barracks-room under the stand behind one of the goals. The players had to run onto the pitch along an uncovered, earth path between two of the stands. This path was scarcely more than five metres wide and to their right and the left, the spectators were standing directly above them. It semed to Jürgen Köper that they had to run straight through the fans. For the match against Eintracht Frankfurt there was a good crowd of 20,000. As the Eintracht team ran onto the pitch between the ranks of howling and threatening Bochum fans, Köper thought that he could see the Frankfurt guys shrinking in size, even world champions like Bernd Hölzenbein and Jürgen Grabowski.

Bochum's fan club, which had been invented by Hellmich, their press spokesman, had taken on a life of its own. Because every fan had his own ideas about what being a fan meant, the original *Fanklub* had split into 12 different fan clubs. Newspaper photographs from England revealed that real fans dressed in their club's colours. So the fans got their mothers to knit them blue and white scarves. They bought the club's coat of arms – it was one of the few bits of insignia that could be purchased – and got their grandmothers to sew them on to their denim jackets. They had got that idea from the rockers. In the stadium, they clapped their hands above their heads to the rhythm of their chants – they were so closely packed together that there was no room to clap with their hands in front of them. Anyone who felt that these proofs of loyalty weren't enough could join the Blue-White Fanklub. The Blue-Whites beat up opposing fans into the bargain.

Nine minutes into the game, centre-forward Jupp Kaczor put Bochum 1-0 up against a cowed Frankfurt side.

A number of the Bochum players found that their chests were itching. This was caused by stray pieces of thread from the pictures of black bulls which had been hastily sewn onto their polyester jumpers; when these got mixed in with the sweat from their exertions in the game, it irritated their skin. During short pauses in play, the men from Bochum all scratched their chests like apes, it was the same every game. The idea of putting adverts on strips was a new one, and one which had obviously not been properly thought through yet.

The 'Osborne Brandy' Spanish bull on the Bochum team-strip was also a more powerful beast than the German FA guidelines permitted. Advertisements were allowed to be 14cm high, whereas the bull was almost 20cm tall. But that was only changed during the summer break when new strips were delivered in any case. The idea of throwing jerseys away just because the advertising logo was too big seemed absurd.

In 1973, Eintracht Braunschweig president Ernst Fricke and his pal Günter Mast, the maker of Jägermeister, had ambushed the German FA. Instead of a lion, the symbol of their club, the Braunschweig shirts were now decorated with a stag, the logo of Jägermeister. The German FA did not take kindly to having the rules of the game dictated to it by anyone else, but their lawyers established that they had no recourse against sponsorship. On 24 March 1973, before the match between Braunschweig and Schalke, referee Franz Wengenmayer produced a ruler to measure the stags on the chests of the Braunschweig players, to ensure that they did not exceed the regulation 14cm. Germany once again began one of its beloved moral debates. Was advertising on soccer strips the modern way, or would it mean the end of the sport if football players were abused as advertising hoardings?

Even three years later, fewer than half of all teams in the Bundesliga wore advertising. Most firms believed that such advertising had little effect. Wouldn't opposing fans buy VWs if Schalke wore the Opel logo? In any case, the adverts would only have a regional reach. The *Frankfurter Allgemeine Zeitung*, a serious broadsheet which was indeed read all over Germany, edited out the adverts on the strips in their photographs of soccer matches, using a black felt pen. Their paper was not going to give free advertising space to Osborne or Jägermeister! As for the clubs, the sums on offer were not enough to send them out aggressively looking for sponsors.

Osborne paid Bochum 100,000 marks per season, and out of an annual budget of 3.5 million marks, that didn't make much difference. On top of this, Bochum were sent a couple of cartons of Osborne brandy gratis – which wasn't to be despised.

Bochum lay in wait at their temporary home ground in Herne. They often allowed Frankfurt to come well up into the midfield without much opposition, and then they sprang the feared Bochum Ambush. Like lightning, two Bochum players would race towards Frankfurt's man on the ball. Following the World Cup of 1974, Heinz Höher had refined their method of play. He'd studied the Dutch national team. Their manager, Rinus Michels, the prophet of total football with its attack who defended and its defence who attacked, had created an offside trap. Heinz Höher watched the way that the Dutch suddenly sprang forwards, as if following an order, and often left an opponent standing offside. But Heinz Höher saw the offside trap less as a means of defence and more as the perfect way to begin a counterattack: the word 'Out!' was not just the command for the defence to rush forwards, but also for two men to always charge straight at the opposing man on the ball. That meant that there was a very high probability they would win the ball and could then, by passing forward as quickly as possible, ambush their opponents before they could regroup to defend.

The first season that Bochum tried to use the offside-counter-trap, it often failed thanks to the linesmen. They weren't used to having to react as quickly as they had to when Bochum stormed downfield, and on more than one occasion they missed the offside. As time went on, the ambush became the trademark of Bochum. They developed their own secret codes: if they get a throw-in in their own half, we go. Or: whenever they play a back-pass, up and at them.

In Eintracht Frankfurt, however, they met an opponent who hit back just as quickly, and with superior technique. By half-time, they had turned Bochum's 1-0 lead into a 2-1 deficit.

Heinz Höher didn't say anything in the changing room; or at any rate, nothing the players found to be a tactical help or a boost to morale. For once, his silence carried no mystique. It seemed their manager was simply crushed by the situation: if they lost this game, they were certainly going down.

Come on lads, cried Vim Lameck: we're not going down like this, we're going to go out there and kick anything that moves off the field!

Frankfurt are a bunch of softies!

We always win against them!

Now they're for it!

In football, there are legendary games where everyone in the world believes, afterwards, that the manager turned things round with his half-time pep talk. Whereas in fact, he did nothing at all.

Frankfurt were never again given a moment to get the ball in midfield. Jürgen Grabowski or Wolfgang Kraus stretched for it – and were straight away charged bodily by Jupp Tenhagen or Jürgen Köper. This was Köper's great season, he was chosen six times for the 'XI of The Day' by *Kicker* magazine. Chase, pass, chase, pass, and then here came Lameck again, charging from deep. Bochum won it 5-3 in the end. Their president, Wüst, appeared in the changing room and said one single word: Thanks!

His colleague, Will Nauheim, president of their Bundesliga rival and neighbour, Rot-Weiss Essen, was furious when he was told that before Bochum's game against Frankfurt, flyers had been given out at the gates of the Opel factory, in which it was stated that he, Nauheim, would be happy to see Bochum relegated. That was a dirty lie, raged Nauheim. Who could be responsible for spreading it?

The victory over Frankfurt felt like salvation. Over the next four games they needed at least two or three acts of salvation like that, if they were really going to be safe. They lost their next game against Bayern Munich 4-0. Two days later, Heinz Höher flew with his team to the beach.

The year before, he'd timetabled in a week's holiday with training in Majorca, mid-season. This time, their destination was Gran Canaria.

He believed that the sunshine and the feeling of togetherness would release new energy. No one else in the Bundesliga had ever believed it, or tried it.

If you think you've got to do it, said club president Wüst to his manager, then do it. He would say the same thing two months later to Heinz Höher's idea of going to training camp before a friendly.

Only Vim Lameck and Klaus Franke didn't fly out with them. Lameck was getting married. Franke had caught a fever last year in Majorca. He was scared of those Spanish bacteria.

When the Bochum players arrived at the hotel on Gran Canaria at Monday lunchtime, their rooms weren't yet ready. So they sat themselves down at the hotel bar. After a while, they forgot what time it was and where they were. After six hours' worth of beer and liqueurs, they also forgot their hunger. They went off to another bar.

On the way back – what time was it, anyway? – centre-forward Jupp Kaczor ran along a row of parked cars. Ranging over the car roofs of Gran Canaria, he informed everyone, at the appropriate volume, why exactly VfL Bochum were never going to get relegated. To further stress his point, he annihilated a neon advertising-sign by throwing a vodka-glass through it.

Next morning, Heinz Höher ordered them up for a run on the beach.

You've got to tell the manager, his team-mates crowded around winger Heinz-Werner Eggeling.

Nope, no way am I telling him that.

Eggeling was Kaczor's room-mate.

During the run, the team finally agreed that it should be Dieter Versen who took the news to the manager. Versen and Heinz Höher had even played together for Bochum in the 1960s.

What? Heinz Höher stopped the beach-run in its tracks.

Jupp Kaczor's in prison, Versen had told him.

Allegedly, it seemed, no one really knew for sure any more, their centre-forward had also tried to hit the hotel's owner with a sign from a building site, because he hadn't opened the door for him quickly enough in the middle of the night.

After a day filled with negotiations, Kaczor was released on bail.

If this gets out, we're relegated for sure, thought Heinz Höher to himself. The team would be blown away by all the public excitement. They fly off to the beach in the middle of the relegation battle and have a skinful. It wasn't difficult to imagine the headlines for yourself – and it wasn't difficult for Manfred Jüttner, *Bild Zeitung*'s man at Bochum, either. He had flown with the team to Gran Canaria and had been right there to see it all.

Manni, if you write about this, you'll never again get a single piece of info from us as long as you live.

All due respect, but I've got to write this.

If you write this, we're dead and so are you.

They don't pay me to keep quiet, they pay me to write stuff, you've got to understand that.

We'll do you a deal: if we lose against Hertha, you can write about it. Deal?

On 29 May 1976, the third last game of the season, Jupp Kaczor lost his balance in the 24th minute inside Hertha's box. The ball was still rolling about in front of him. In the twinkling of an eye, he jumped up, spun around, and before the fans could think 'Wow! Just like Gerd Müller!' he shot to make it 1-0. His team-mates raced to Kaczor, some of them sprinting 60 metres, and buried him in their jubilation. The Berlin men glared at the Bochum men: fair play, but why were they screaming like cavemen because they'd taken an early lead?

Bochum ran out easy 2-0 winners. In the two remaining games, Kaczor's two further goals made sure that Bochum would stay in the Bundesliga. Manfred Jüttner had any number of heroic tales to tell. His reports spoke, without going into any further details, about a team spirit which had been born in Gran Canaria.

Many years after the legendary escape of spring 1976, a grammatically incorrect word was created to describe Bochum's ongoing show of sheer bloody-mindedness: they were called unrelegationable. The years under Höher were the keystone in the myth of their unrelegationableness. The 1975-76 season saw the peak of this feeling.

The following summer, Heinz Höher thought that he was going to have to start another special advertising campaign – rather like the way he had taken part in the People's Marathon or handed out flyers in front of the Opel factory – but it went nowhere. He announced in the *Westdeutsche Allgemeine* that he was putting the money saved up for his children's futures on the table. He said that he'd saved 12,000 marks for their education – anyone take a bet that Bochum would avoid relegation next season too? But no one took him up on it. No one believed that this Bochum side would ever be relegated.

Heady from their own show of strength, carried away by the prospect of the new stadium, the club's dreams were now going way beyond simply avoiding relegation year after year. 'Next year at the latest, we'll be contending for the Championship,' said their president, Wüst, to *Der Spiegel* in March 1977.

Instead of frowning or laughing at this, the news magazine wrote in its lead article: 'The procession of triumphs at the grand clubs, Bayern Munich and Borussia Mönchengladbach, has ended. Duisburg and Bochum are upgrading their stadia and staking their claims to the succession.'

Since 1969 the German champions had been called either Bayern Munich or Borussia Mönchengladbach, and on top of that, Bayern, with their three European Cup victories from 1974 to '76 had given the impression that an era had been founded. But in the late 1970s, Mönchengladbach's victories under manager Udo Lattek had been won in a far more conservative style than under his predecessor Weisweiler, and the Bayern team built around Meier, Beckenbauer and Müller had slid into the footballing equivalent of a midlife crisis after their European Cup victories. It was Franz Beckenbauer who put the quasi-official seal on the end of Bayern's victorious era, when he went to New York Cosmos in 1977. Soccer was going to be a really big deal in America. Beckenbauer's abdication at 32 was not just the end to a sporting tale, but also a question of love. Though still married, he was living with another woman, which was just not on in West Germany, for a member of the national team with three sons.

Meanwhile the Bundesliga waited with bated breath for the successor. It was fondly believed that any team could be the next Bayern Munich or Borussia Mönchengladbach: if a club in the Bundesliga discovered an exceptional generation of players in its home region, had a decent manager and posessed a stadium that provided enough income to buy in a couple of stars, there was nothing to hold that club back, never mind whether it was called Bayern or Bochum. When the *Spiegel* article appeared in May 1977, Eintracht Braunschweig were top of the Bundesliga and MSV Duisburg lay fourth. 'German football is heading for a changing of the guard,' declared Heinz Neuhaus, chair of the playing committee at Duisburg, who had newly taken to calling himself general manager, 'the great clubs of Grandad's day are finished. Now it's our turn.'

Bochum, however were still battling against relegation. In away games, above all, they too often played an honest but in the end defensive game. Still, it wasn't only Ottokar Wüst and Heinz Höher who dreamed of better things, their competitors certainly thought that Bochum had the potential to pose a challenge.

'We didn't worry about Schalke or Duisburg, it was Bochum,' said Bayern Munich manager Dettmar Cramer, 'no one liked going there. We were really scared of them.'

Every year before they went to the Castroper Straße, Cramer spent an entire week trying out countermeasures against the Bochum Ambush.

When Bochum charged out of defence, Cramer's players were supposed to delay trying a through-ball, which is no easy thing. They tried passing across field or making a side-step and then dribbling for a couple of yards, so as to give their own forwards time to run back onside. Then, they were supposed to hit long passes behind the advancing Bochum defence, to make use of the space which they had left empty. That was the theory, at least. In autumn 1976, Dettmar Cramer's Bayern were 4-0 down against Bochum after 53 minutes. In the penultimate minute, Uli Hoeneß scored to scrape a 6-5 win for the men from Munich. The changing of the guard was put off. But surely, that game had showed that it was possible?

On the days when Heinz Höher's vision became reality, Bochum were tremendously fast in attack and irritatingly systematic in defence. If you ran past, or took the ball past, a Bochum player, he didn't run with you, but instead, a few metres further on, the next Bochum player appeared in your path: Heinz Höher was the second Bundesliga manager after the Hungarian Gyula Lóránt to introduce an element of zonal marking.

To Bochum's opponents, this mixture of man-to-man marking and zonal marking often felt like a labyrinth; whenever they went round one man and saw space ahead, the next opponent had already appeared as a wall in front of them. However, this experiment with zonal marking didn't always succeed, as Hermann Gerland explained to his manager Heinz Höher after they lost 4-2 to Borussia Mönchengladbach in 1976-77: Guvnor, you said if Jupp Heynckes went past me I should let him go – so I did, and he scored three times.

The pros and cons had been debated in German football ever since the World Cup final of 1954, when the Hungarians demonstrated the idea of zonal marking, and the Germans had responded vehemently with man-to-man marking. But somehow it seemed to have become set in stone: Germans marked man-to-man. Chasing an opponent and never giving up, keeping close guard on him, seemed to be second nature to hard-working, conscientious, tenacious Germans – that's what he had long believed, said the most successful manager of the 1970s, Udo Lattek. In the mid 70s, a mixture of both systems spread out from Frankfurt, under Gyula Lóránt, and from Bochum: the opposing play-makers were still marked strictly man-to-man, as the German obsession with a duel demanded, but more and more often, players were no longer supposed to cover a particular opponent, but rather a certain area of the pitch. They didn't go looking for duels the whole time, but only in predetermined zones, at particularly favourable moments. Düsseldorf manager Dietrich Weise believed that the Germans needed re-educating by the hundreds of thousands: 'If the fans are going to understand the finer points of tactics, we are going to have to gradually re-educate them.' Because wouldn't the public stay away, if it felt that too many demands were being made of it?

The day had come, Ottokar Wüst and Heinz Höher said to themselves in the summer of 1977. The new stadium wouldn't be open for two years yet, but with those bigger box office takings clearly in sight, they'd surely be able to squeeze a loan out of Heinz Brämer at the Westphalia Bank. The day had come to take the great leap. Bochum signed Dieter Bast from Essen for a transfer fee of 800,000 marks.

What, we're getting Dieter Bast? cried the Bochum players. They were used to newcomers arriving, as Jupp Kaczor had done, from lower-tier clubs like Eintracht Hamm-Heesen, for 25,000 marks.

Dieter Bast was considered one of the best attacking players in Germany, he could operate on the wings or lurking behind the centre-forward. He created goals. With one move, one touch of the ball, one pass, he could get a game moving. Heinz Höher believed that here was the one player Bochum still needed, a player whose passes and runs could turn a consistent team into a really good one.

To the outside eye, Bochum were still the poor relations among the Bundesliga teams. One time, Heinz Höher was sitting in the Haus Juliana Hotel, where the team regularly spent the nights before their home games, when the owner, Wilzbach, came up to him, beaming with joy. Mr Wüst had promised him, said Wilzbach, that he'd get his money at last on Saturday. Heinz Höher replied: And did Mr Wüst tell you which Saturday?

But on Saturday, 6 August 1977, at 3.30pm, those stories of the money that was never there were now just old anecdotes. The day had come. It was the first day of the new Bundesliga season, and Bochum were at home to the German champions, Borussia Mönchengladbach: it was a game just made for a game-changer. The building site that was the Castroper Straße was sold out, 22,000 spectators packed the brand-new south stand as well as the old terraces, while behind one of the goals a gigantic hole still loomed. There, the standing terraces had been torn down, but not yet rebuilt.

Some months before, the two Christas from the club office had gone into town to lodge a protest with the city council concerning the plans for the stadium. Yet again, there were no ladies' toilets included in the plans!

Christa Jewers asked the vice-chairman of the Bochum Social Democrats, Heinz Hossiep, if he could imagine what it was like to spend two hours at a football match without going to the toilet.

What do you mean? Hossiep replied, in a rage. Women didn't go to football matches anyway.

But the two Christas got their toilets into the plans. Now they just had to wait another two years.

Bochum and the champions, Borussia Mönchengladbach, played the way so many clubs play on the first day of the season, like two teams neither of whom actually wanted to win, and both of whom just didn't want to lose. Every time they passed the ball they were really think-ing about what might happen if they lost it. So there was no forward movement. Dieter Bast tried to lose his man-to-man marker, Horst Wohlers, in the no-man's-land between midfield and attack, which was always going to be a tough job. But Heinz Höher was irritated by the way his new man paused to take a rest for a change now and then. Didn't Bast know that you never just stood about when you were wear-ing a Bochum shirt? The other new players had a better idea of Bochum's style: Matthias Herget, who'd come from an amateur side in Gelsenkirchen, and Lothar Woelk, who Heinz Höher had discovered playing for the Opel works XI in the local league. A Bochum counter-attack suddenly woke the 22,000 spectators from the lethargy of all this just-don't-lose-it play, it was the 32nd minute, their goal-hunter, Jupp Kaczor, bore down to one-to-one on Mönchengladbach keeper Wolfgang Kneib and for a second it flashed before him: 'It's going in.' Then there was a sickening crunch. Kaczor, sliding across the turf in an attempt to get his toe to the ball before the keeper, collided with Kneib. Kaczor had heard exactly that noise months before, in the game at Duisburg, when Jürgen Köper smashed both his fibula and his tibia. He knew right away what had happened to him.

Heinz Höher, wearing a simple blue T-shirt with a round collar, clapped his hands in front of his eyes. Substitute Hartmut Fromm addressed him imploringly, with hands spread wide; a player was trying to remind the manager that it was he who now had to keep them fighting, give them the will to go on. But Heinz Höher had forgotten his lines. Jupp Kaczor had scored 21 goals last season – the season after his climb across the cars in Gran Canaria – and he was Bochum's only class goalscorer.

No Bundesliga side possessed a genuine replacement for their outstanding goalscorer, sweeper or playmaker. If Gerd Müller had been injured at Bayern, all their goalscoring would've depended on a substitute whose name most people weren't even sure of – was he called Janzon or Janson? (His name was Norbert Janzon.) True, the days were gone when manager Branko Zebec had won the 1968-69 title for Bayern using only 13 players in the entire season, and managers these days made good use of the two substitutes per game they were now permitted, but there was still a high wall between the regular team and the substitutes. The idea was that you fielded the strongest possible first team and made as few substitutions as you could.

Bochum fought holders Borussia Mönchengladbach to a 0-0 draw on that first day of the 1977-78 season, but Heinz Höher felt that Kaczor's broken leg was the end for them. That evening, he knocked back a couple of beers and a shot with Heinz Formann in the Haus Frein and started to sing: Where are we going? Down! Where are we going? Down!

Are you nuts? asked Formann.

Where are we going? Down!

Have you lost your marbles, you've just got a nil-nil draw against the holders. You're never going down. You've got Dieter Bast!

You watch, in a few months everyone's going to forget that we've lost our main goalscorer, they'll soon be shouting Höher Out! I can see it right here in front of me.

Look, just have another shot.

On top of Kaczor's injury, they were already missing their left-winger, their rocket, Heinz-Werner Eggeling, after a cartilage operation; Bochum's whole first-choice attack was a hospital case: and they were still waiting desperately for the return of Jürgen Köper after *his* broken leg.

Sporting medicine had made vast strides: thanks to ultrasound, it was now clear that what have been called 'pulled muscles' for decades were in fact torn muscle fibres. But still, recovering from a severe sporting injury took months, maybe whole half-years, there was nothing to be done about that. Once, when Jürgen Köper was diagnosed with torn muscle fibres, he was operated on by a doctor at the Hellersen Sports Clinic, where they used a brand-new method: Köper lay in bed for seven weeks with his leg up high, suspended from the ceiling, to avoid putting any weight at all on it. By bribing the night porter with 10 marks and complimentary tickets for Bochum, he at least got himself shoved to the toilet in a wheelchair. The doctor had forbidden it. No movement at all. Köper was supposed to relieve himself in a bedpan. After he broke his leg, the first stage in Köper's convalescence was a course to build up his strength in the power-gym at the Castroper Straße stadium. This power-gym consisted of a single stationary bicycle which had been stuck in a corner of the box-room.

It's time you took some advice from your pillow, were Heinz Formann's words of farewell to his friend Höher, on the evening after Kaczor broke his leg.

The next morning, Heinz Höher reported that he had thought everything through carefully. He was going to resign as manager of Bochum.

What next?

The End of the 1970s:

IS IT REALLY TIME TO GO?

Later on, when newspaper commentators all over Germany began to speculate about how easily his feelings were hurt, Heinz Höher realised that he'd done something beyond belief. There had by now been over 70 sackings of Bundesliga managers, but 7 August 1977 was the first time a manager had said, I don't want the job any more. The excitement among football journalists was off the scale. Having informed club president Wüst of his resignation, Heinz Höher took his daily afternoon nap.

That afternoon, too, he just let the telephone ring and ring. Doris had to persuade him that he should at least take the call from Heinz Formann.

Formann's call to Heinz Höher was the strangest conversation of his life. He had to ask tough questions of this manager who'd resigned, to secure an exclusive story about this spectacular event, but at the same time he wanted to persuade his friend to take that resignation back. Höher's answers saddened Formann as his friend, and put him on his mettle as a journalist. His readers would have to study the quotations twice, to understand them. Heinz Höher, whose mind worked on a different level from most people, spoke – when he spoke at all – on a different level too, or rather, a more complicated one. It was as though the synapses in the speech centre of his brain meandered out along finer paths. Formann knew shorthand, thanks to his earlier incarnation as a bureaucrat, and so he was able to write it all down, as Heinz Höher constricted his meandering sentences: 'I refuse to carry a shield upon which is written: I am not guilty of Eggeling's meniscus operation, I am not guilty that Jürgen Köper broke his leg, I am not guilty that Jupp Kaczor suffered the same fate, I am not guilty that the club has had to live for so many years on so little money. I've tried everything, really everything, to make this work, because I feel more for this club than just as an employee. And now I can't do any more. I'm hollowed out, I'm tired.'

As Heinz Formann sat at his Truimph Adler to type out his story about the first manager to leave a Bundesliga club of his own free will, the feelings ran high. Journalists were always claiming that a report had to be rational, even-handed and objective, but that was, of course, nonsense. The best newspaper reports were those that were written most passionately. Formann's typing fingers were guided by his pain about Heinz Höher's resignation, and rage about the loss of his friend, the manager: 'He's had enough of the bad atmosphere that's been created,' his fingers flew, typing all by themselves. Hah! Borner of the *Ruhr Nachrichten* was really going to see that his sneaky campaign against Heinz Höher was one of the main reasons for his resignation. The emotions churning within him meant that Formann's anger was overlaid with melancholy. His other column, his personal piece on Monday, ended with the following sentences: 'Many things are weighty. A football, for example. And life, too. The only things that are truly light are the artificial things, the plastic things, the cheap mottos.'

Bochum's president, Ottokar Wüst, didn't take long to choose a strategy for dealing with Heinz Höher's resignation. He was going to simply refuse to accept it. On Sunday evening, a day after the match against Borussia Mönchengladbach, he rang at the door of 42 Bonhoefferstraße.

Heinz Höher offered Wüst a beer, and had a beer and a shot himself.

Heinz, you can't give up now. We are just at the beginning. Try to summon up the energy to see things clearly: Dieter Bast's wearing our strip. And in two years, we two are going to be standing together on the touchline of a fabulous stadium, surrounded by 40,000 cheering fans.

I can't stand it any more, because I can see everything as if it's through a telescope: we play the best football, we make incredible efforts, fabulous young players like Tenhagen and Lameck push themselves beyond their own limits, and we get the points too – but in the end, it's not working.

You're in shock, I understand that. But you mustn't let your feelings lead you astray to a hasty decision which you, and certainly we, would rue for many years to come.

Sure, if we really push ourselves, we have a couple of good games in us, but you can't go on for long without an attack.

Heinz, we can talk about strengthening our attack. I'll get the money together somehow, I swear that to you on my three sons' lives.

Strengthening our attack ... If someone tells me we could replace Kaczor, I say: I know we could. With Klaus Fischer or Dieter Müller – there's no one else up to it.

You're bitter. I understand that. We'll talk again tomorrow.

Heinz Höher drank another beer.

On Monday, Wüst shifted his strategy a bit. He still refused to accept the resignation, and at the same time he installed long-time Bochum player Dieter Versen as the new manager: temporarily, Wüst told himself. Then he started searching around for forwards. Bundesliga clubs always tried to keep it secret that they were looking for players, but Wüst told Formann quite openly that Bochum were going after Dieter Schwemmle of AC Bellinzona and Hans-Günther Plücken of second division Solingen. Wüst had nothing against this appearing in the papers. He wanted Heinz Höher to know just how hard the club was seeking replacements.

Michael Lameck, Klaus Franke, Heinz-Werner Eggeling and – from hospital – Jupp Kaczor all called Heinz Höher.

Kaczor reported to him that he was going to have to spend three weeks in hospital, and then 13 weeks in plaster. Christ, guvnor, the forward suddenly broke off his own medical report: shit happens, but we can't lose you. That'd be much worse than me breaking my leg.

Klaus Franke, the defender, said much the same thing in different words. Look, Franke added, he'd heard Höher on WDR radio, he said, any chance that you had a drink before the interview, guvnor? Höher's thoughts had seemed that meandering, that cryptic to Franke.

A drink. No, said Heinz Höher, and tried to sound offended.

'WDR already knew who would be the successor,' Heinz Formann wrote the next morning in the *Westdeutsche Allgemeine*: 'Mr Schwärmer was said to be standing in for Heinz Höher. Actually, Schwärmer is called Dieter Versen, and was already taking charge of training on Monday.' Who did these radio people from Cologne think they were: they reported on VfL Bochum once every couple of years, and here they were, acting as if they knew what was going on!

In addition, Formann dedicated almost half a page to readers' letters. He chose the letters carefully, so that Heinz Höher, who subscribed to the *Westdeutsche Allgemeine*, would come away with the impression that the whole of Bochum was urging him to stay

'In my 20 years of teaching at the Goethe School in Bochum, I have principally dedicated myself to teaching swimming. That is obviously no comparison with the tough work of a manager in the Bundesliga, but I do understand that sort of thing. Does Heinz Höher know how much sympathy there is for him right now in Bochum?'
Werner Günther, Witzlebenstraße 1, 4630 Bochum 1.
'Dear Mr Höher, actually, we were going to send birthday greetings to you today, but now we decided to write this letter to the newspaper: stay in Bochum – our entire holiday will be ruined.'
Markus und Jürgen Hoppe, at present in Wyk.
'It's true that I own a season ticket for the main stand, but at heart I'm a real man on the terraces. After Kaczor's injury, I was on the verge of throwing my season ticket into the fire. But I didn't do it, because the team hasn't given up. For Christ's sake, Mr Höher, do you think managers like Cajkovski can do something that you can't? I ask you straight out: if the man on the terraces means anything to you, then stay!'
Name and address supplied.

On Wednesday morning, three days after his resignation, Heinz Höher climbed into his silver Mercedes 190 and drove past the grave-yard, in a northerly direction. At 10 o'clock precisely, he was standing on the training field to prepare the Bochum team for their away match against Cologne.

Wüst's assurances that the problems with their attack would be given whatever help was possible, as well as the overwhelming vote of confidence from his team and the fans had, said Heinz Höher, moved him to withdraw his resignation. 'Only one person shouted "bastard" at me down the phone, but I suppose he was just telling me his name.'

The next day, the readers' letters in the *Westdeutsche Allgemeine* went back to discussing the subject of the Red Army Faction terrorists and particularly the question of what women were doing in the underground movement. On this point, a reader named Hartmut Strucksberg from Essen stated that it seemed to him that many women erroneously believed that taking part in acts of violence was emancipation.

Might VfL Bochum just get back to being part of normality now? The manager was back, but the basic problem remained: they had no goal-getter. Schwemmle, who had often caused problems for Bochum as a young player wearing the colours of Stuttgart, was indeed signed for 400,000 marks, and had trouble fitting in. They had some change left for a second new forward from a lower-tier club, but they couldn't come to a snap decision, they'd have to stick with whoever they went for.

Meanwhile, Heinz Höher had a go with a solution which was at the same time the most obvious and the most impossible: in the first few matches after Kaczor's broken leg, he left the vital position of centre-forward unfilled. Whenever Bochum were on the attack, one or other of the midfielders or wingers was to push forward into position in front of the opposing goal, explained Höher. That would require colossal presence of mind and physical ability. It couldn't work, said the experts.

In their first home game after Kaczor's broken leg, Bochum recorded the greatest Bundesliga victory in their history, 5-0 against Hertha. The Bochum players swarmed goalwards from all over the pitch, sometimes it was defenders like Hermann Gerland, sometimes it was midfielders like Lothar Woelk, always it was Dieter Bast, who scored twice. The Berliners lost all sense of shape and orientation in the face of Bochum's incessant changing of positions. 'I've never seen Bochum play so well,' said Hertha's manager Kuno Klötzer in the smoke-filled press room. 'They were so full of dynamism, aggression and spirit, and with a fantastic understanding of the game as well.'

Heinz Höher said that he'd prophesied as much: his team would, at first, play out of their skins. But in the long term, no one could keep things at a level beyond their own limits.

At night, Winzlinger, the boss of his ideas, called to see him again.

So, you can't sleep again?

Well spotted, Winzlinger.

What's eating you?

The journalists are after me. The *Frankfurter Allgemeine Zeitung* called me a delicate flower because of my three days' resignation and the *Westdeutsche Allgemeine* mocked me, they said that Heinz Höher, the sensitive little soul of the Bundesliga, always has a fit of the vapours at the start of the season.

It almost sounds as if they're on to you.

They can never know the truth, Winzlinger, or it's all up with me.

The truth?

That my resignation was a bluff, right from day one. I wanted to put pressure on Ottokar Wüst so he'd find the money for some new forwards.

In Herne, the neighbouring town, Heinz Höher found Boombangabang. 'Boombangabang boombangabang, Jochen Abel's here,' sang the Westphalia Herne fans, and Abel, who was 25, quick thinking and cunning, put them away in the Bundesliga 2 as if it really was as simple as in the pop song – he averaged a goal every other game. Was this the man Bochum were waiting for?

Every Bundesliga team went off into the draughty stadiums of the Bundesliga 2, and out to the local council sports pitches of the amateur leagues, trawling for treasures. If a talented player didn't happen to live in a city with a Bundesliga club, or in one of its suburbs, at 20 he was probably still kicking a ball about in an amateur or regional league. In 1974, Bayern Munich found Karl-Heinz Rummenigge at fourth-division Borussia Lippstadt. What a Bundesliga team needed was a talent spotter like Bochum's August Liese, who got calls from old colleagues and opponents because he was good old Auli: Hey, I've just seen a real centre-forward right here in the local league! Liese paid the tab for the beers and the shot when they bumped into each other next time in the regional league club-house.

Heinz Höher loved the way his heart beat faster when he followed up a tip from Auli Liese and saw something in a player that few people had noticed. And, unconsciously at any rate, Heinz Höher realised that there was another reason that he liked working with newcomers from the lower divisions so much. They felt respect and a natural gratitude towards him; it was he who had got them out of there. He had no need to worry, the way he had to worry with time-served Bundesliga professionals, that they might rebel against his tight-lipped, eccentric ways.

The boombangabang song drifted over from Herne to Bochum. After his transfer to Bochum in October 1977, Jochen Abel just kept right on scoring, 15 goals in the 20 remaining matches of the 1977-78 season. And so, even with Kaczor out, Bochum were able to save themselves from relegation for another year. The sports-reporters fell back on their well-worn clichés, and praised Bochum's unbelievable effort. It was forgotten that Wüst and Höher had had higher ambitions, and bigger dreams.

For the first time in ten years, the German champions of 1978 were called neither Borussia Mönchengladbach nor Bayern Munich; their successors weren't Duisburg or Bochum, as predicted by *Der Spiegel*, but one of the old-established top-flight clubs, 1. FC Cologne.

Wüst and Höher had hoped that they needed only one or two top-class players to make their team into a special one. In 1978, they saw what happened to a team if only one or two players were injured or didn't deliver dream performances.

What do you think about Dieter Bast? Heinz Höher suddenly asked, breaking the silence which, as usual, held sway when Jürgen Köper gave his manager a lift to the training session. It was taboo for a player to drive to work with the manager. But Jürgen Köper hadn't been able to say no. Heinz Höher had ordered him to give him a lift. Höher wanted to run home after the training session, so he couldn't bring his own car to work. And apart from that, he rather liked being chauffeured about.

What did he say on the way over? Köper's team-mates asked him inquisitively during the training session.

Nothing, said Köper, and his team-mates naturally didn't believe him, they thought he was keeping the manager's information and views to himself. But Heinz Höher really did say nothing on those drives to the training ground. Sometimes he even forgot to say good morning to Köper when he got into the car.

Now, suddenly, that question floated in the space between them: what do you think about Dieter Bast?

Jürgen Köper hesitated. What was he supposed to say? He had to give his manager an honest opinion, he had to show his manager that he understood something of football. But on the other hand, he couldn't bad-mouth a fellow-player to the manager. Jürgen Köper decided to say a careful version of the truth.

Actually, I'm a little bit disappointed in Dieter Bast.

Heinz Höher made no reply. They drove on in their accustomed silence, as if the conversation had never happened.

Dieter Bast had done for Bochum all the things they'd valued him for at Essen: the through-balls, the dribbling, the goals. But he did it only in small doses. Heinz Höher asked himself despairingly how he could have missed seeing that in between his standout moments, Bast needed longer and longer pauses. Bast's muscles were those of a sprinter. After a single surge, they were done. Heinz Höher changed him to sweeper. There, he could have his breaks, and pull his weight. But actually, Höher already had a few decent alternatives for the sweeper's position, Tenhagen, Franke, Fromm, there'd been no need to pay 800,000 marks for yet another. They'd had one free shot at making Bochum into something more than the eternal survivors, and they'd missed it.

Heinz Höher was entering his seventh year as manager at Bochum. Some people thought he'd been there too long. He was doing no fewer things right, and no more things wrong, than in his first year – it was just that after seven years, some people now had difficulty putting up with him. Time doesn't just heal wounds, it also wears out human relationships. For the Bochum fans, it had become an unthinking ritual to start shouting 'Höher out!' after every 15 minutes of weary play. Karlheinz Antico, the master butcher who sat on the board of trustees, was more and more open about his growing dissatisfaction with the manager. Höher drank so much, and talked so weirdly. One evening, before an away game at Bremen, Heinz Höher sneaked secretly out of their hotel with board member Paul Kortmann, to have a couple of beers and a shot, and for a brief moment Höher asked himself: my God, what are we doing, a man of over 70 and a man of 40, so scared of Antico that we're sneaking out of our hotel like schoolboys bunking off?

Borner of the *Ruhr Nachrichten* was another one who had trouble hiding how much he longed simply to see a new face as manager. His reports more and more often read like this: 'So, is there actually anything like a Bochum system? One thing that has always been there: almost perfect crossfield passes and back-passes. But when it comes to going forward, the phrase "head over heels" springs to mind.' And that was his verdict on a Bochum victory.

Heinz Höher said to himself that he couldn't care less what Borner wrote – but with all due respect, Borner took things too far, for Christ's sake! On 27 October 1977 the editor-in-chief of the *Ruhr Nachrichten* received a reader's letter from Günther Traube at 49 Alter Bahnhofstraße, Bochum.

Dear Mr Dr Jungermann!

I do not know to what extent you feel responsible for the activities of your local editors; I believe however, that as a long-time reader of your paper, I have duty to write you these lines.

The manner in which Franz Borner has for months, indeed I should say, for over a year, treated the manager of VfL Bochum, is monstrous, and verges on character assassination; one cannot avoid the feeling that personal elements are involved here.

Football lives on surprises and sensations, great teams lose, and VfL Bochum, as a mid-ranking team, naturally loses more often. What Franz Borner heaps upon the Bochum manager's head in cases of defeat is dirt and filth, not fact, and goes miles beyond any constructive criticism. Even self-declared opponents of Höher – I know this from my own circle of friends – are embarrassed at it. I will not withdraw from readership of your newspaper even in the future, but I have looked for the last time at the section on sport in Bochum.

Yours sincerely
Günther Traube

Heinz Höher wrote a further three readers' letters to the *Ruhr Nachrichten* using fictional names and addresses. As with all his correspondence, Doris typed the letters out for him. He rounded off Günther Traube's letter with a postscript:

PS: I am not acquainted personally with Mr Borner. However, the sudden change in many of his articles between skilfully written passages and incomprehensible drivel makes one suspect that these pronunciations were written in a condition of the most advanced drunkenness.

You can stay here as long as you like, repeated Ottokar Wüst, when the critics attacked Heinz Höher. But was Heinz Höher deceiving himself, or was it not a long time now since he last heard these reassurances from Wüst?

Just get on with it, Heinz Höher said to himself, next year the new stadium would be ready. And so he just got on with it: before one home game against Bayern Munich, he ordered the team to the usual tactical talk on Saturday morning in the meeting room of the hotel.

Everyone came, but Heinz Höher didn't. The team waited, five minutes, ten minutes. Then August Liese was summoned to the hotel reception, there was a phone call.

Just turn the tactics whiteboard around, said Heinz Höher to Liese, and hung up.

Liese turned the board around.

Upon it stood just five words: Go! Have them for breakfast!

Another time, before a Bundesliga match, Heinz Höher heard a noise in their hotel, the Haus Juliana. He went out into the corridor. The voices of card-players were coming from Paul Holz's room.

Well what about that, they went and chose the room at the end of the corridor, so I wouldn't hear them, thought Heinz Höher to himself, not without admiration, and sat himself on a chair in the dark corridor. And he waited, he couldn't say exactly for how long, until 1 o'clock, until 1.30am, silently, on his chair in the corridor. The next day, they were playing Eintracht Frankfurt. At last, the door of Paul Holz's room opened. Jürgen Köper, Jochen Abel and Heinz Werner-Eggeling sneaked past Höher. They looked at the manager, the manager looked at them. Nobody said a word.

Heinz Höher thought that this was the most effective way of making the players feel guilty and of drawing a reaction out of them on the pitch the next day. They beat Eintracht.

In their seventh season under Heinz Höher, Bochum again awoke short-lived hopes of making the great leap, before shortly afterwards looking very commonplace and then spending the entire season respectably enough mid-table in the Bundesliga. At the end of the 1970s, it wasn't Bochum who were surreptitiously changing, but the Bundesliga itself: the football in Germany's premier division resembled no longer the formerly glorious attacking style of the national side, of Bayern or Mönchengladbach, but every team looked more and more like Bochum. Gradually, Bochum's playing style, based on strength, endurance and willpower, possessing enormously tactical cunning but in the end based on defence, with only two forwards at most, was insidiously gaining the upper hand.

Heinz Höher had constructed this style of play specifically as a way of defending a club which had few resources. In the late 1970s, had the smaller teams like Bochum imposed their style on the big clubs?

Desperately, the national side tried to rediscover their lost elegance. But couldn't Germany's manager see the things Heinz Höher saw?

Didn't Helmut Schön understand that you can't administrate your way to glory? On the eve of the 1978 World Cup, Heinz Höher wrote the national manager an unsolicited letter three sides long.

'Dear Mr Schön,' he began. 'I stood in awe of your dead predecessor, Sepp Herberger. I have never truly been enthusiastic about you as a manager.'

Heinz Höher was not always capable of telling when directness was honourable, and when it was insulting.

He wrote on: after Germany's victories in the European Championship of 1972 and the World Cup of 1974, Schön, like the English after 1966, had looked down upon the other nations for too long. But Schön had ignored the fact that world-class players like Beckenbauer, Gerd Müller and Grabowski were getting older. The national manager had to realise that he no longer possessed outstanding players with whom his team could dominate every match. The national side had to play – to put it in a simple image – more like Bochum, and stop trying to be the romantic ideal of the early 1970s. 'So I am surprised that in the last preparatory match before the World Cup, against Sweden, you are playing a team which is split 50/50 between players who are strong in defending, and players who are weak in those situations.' Instead of playing an ultra-offensive midfield, consisting of Hölzenbein, Hansi Müller and Rummenigge, Schön would do better to use one playmaker and two forwards, whose backs were covered by three hard-tackling athletic players in midfield – players like Bernard Dietz, Erich Beer and Rolf Rüssmann. 'And now we come to the forwards, Abramczik and Fischer. I was surprised to see how long you have watched the cheaply crowd-pleasing style of the Schalke players without passing comment. When I read or hear that players have been practising overhead kicks thousands of times, although these situations only come about once every second or third game, I ask myself where you find the time to train for things which come up 30 or 50 times in every game.'

Helmut Schön, who had in the past often addressed letters to Höher as 'Dear Heinz', didn't answer at all this time. Heinz Höher watched the 1978 World Cup in Argentina with the feeling that he'd seen it all coming. Germany went out to Austria 3-2 in the intermediate stage.

Every Sunday, Heinz Höher bought his copy of *Welt am Sonntag* at Paul Kortmann's bar on the Freigrafendamm. Kortmann was one of the first in Bochum to realise, in the 1970s, that a bar could also be a shop. He sold everything: liquor, sweets, newspapers, gardening gloves. One Sunday in February 1979, Heinz Höher learned from *Welt am Sonntag* that Bochum were about to sign a new manager.

If it was in the *Welt*, there must be something in it, thought Heinz Höher to himself.

The report claimed that Helmut Johannsen, who in 1967 had taken Eintracht Braunschweig to the most unexpected title in the history of the Bundesliga, was the chosen one.

Many managers, probably most managers, would have tried to find out what was going on in their next talk with their club president. Heinz Höher drove to see Ottokar Wüst and told him that after seven years, he wanted to leave Bochum at the end of the season.

If he really had to go, he thought, then at least he'd go of his own free will and not be fired. He was completely serious about leaving, he felt that all his work had been in vain, people were talking about him too much, although Bochum were in a perfectly decent position. Even so, didn't he also hope that Wüst would, for the third time, hold him back from resigning?

Ottokar Wüst invited him into the clothes-room. At Wüst's gentlemen's outfitters, they still made hats with fine silk bands, hats of the sort which hardly anyone apart from Wüst still wore. They spoke for over an hour. Then Ottokar Wüst said: 'You can be married to the most beautiful and charming wife – but after seven years there's always going to be something you don't like about her. So let's go our ways without any fussing and fighting.'

Only one manager in the Bundesliga had been in post for longer, and that was Hennes Weisweiler at Mönchengladbach, from 1964 until 1975. And now it was all over, without excitement, without passion, without a wasted word. Manni Jüttner from *Bild Zeitung* phoned the players. 'Something just had to change,' said Dieter Bast. 'Höher discovered me. But you can't be thankful for year after year,' said Michael Eggert. Heinz Höher kept on smiling, as if nothing had happened.

For one last time, he and his friend Winzlinger had one of their night-time brainstorming sessions. The home game against Hamburg on 3 March 1979 looked like being postponed, snow covered the pitch, there had never been so many Bundesliga games called off as in that endless winter of 1978-79. Because every home game for three months had been struck off, Bochum were bringing in no money at all. Wüst still hadn't paid their salaries for January and February. They simply had to play again, thought Heinz Höher at 4am, wide awake as in almost every night of his managerial career.

Other stadiums have under-pitch heating, to melt the snow.

If you can't get at the snow from underneath, why don't you thaw it out from above, said Winzlinger.

Over-pitch heating? Winzlinger, you're not as stupid as you look.

Heinz Höher thought about it for awhile. The next day he revealed his plan to club president Wüst. They tried out Höher's idea in the garden belonging to the mayor, Heinz Eichelbeck, who was a keen member of the volunteer fire brigade. It seemed to work!

With the help of ten firemen, among them Bochum reserve team player Thomas Duschanski, city engineer Ottokar Dörr laid hundreds of metres of fire-hoses all over the pitch. Then they pumped warm water through the hoses. Gradually, the snow melted. Thirty-five thousand litres of water from the melted snow was then pumped away. Bochum won 2-1 against a Hamburg side which included Kaltz, Keegan and Hrubesch, and which was on the way to winning the championship. Thirty-three thousand spectators poured desperately longed-for money into the tills. Heinz Höher told nobody that it had all been his idea. He was no good at pushing himself forward; and why bother, he told himself, now that he was in any case almost gone from Bochum.

He didn't turn up for the final home game against Darmstadt. Ottokar Wüst had given him three days off for Whitsun. Heinz Höher wanted to take a look at a potential new club. 'Will it be Duisburg?' asked Franz Borner in the *Ruhr Nachrichten*. 'It is believed that he was at Twente Enschede,' wrote Manni Jüttner in *Bild*. Heinz Höher watched a training session and a match at 1860 Munich, who were certain of promotion to the Bundesliga. He had disguised himself with a beard and glasses and a hat, so that no one would recognise him.

At the lacklustre game against Darmstadt on 2 June 1979, the fans shouted 'Höher out!' once more, even though he wasn't even there, and was already out. Rudi Mayer, the team doctor in his black leather coat, sought out Heinz Formann. For seven years, whenever a player was injured, Mayer had informed only two people: Höher, the manager, and Formann, the journalist. 'Seven years,' said Mayer. 'There must be something more to show for that than just ashes that you blow out of your hands, into the wind.'

After two months of searching and checking, Heinz Höher was down to two concrete offers, one from 1860 Munich and one from his first Bundesliga club, Meiderich SV, who had been called MSV Duisburg since 1967. The city of Duisburg had written off debts to the tune of at least half a million marks, thereby winning the right to rename the club.

Four or five years before, Heinz Höher had felt that he could've chosen his next club from half of the Bundesliga. He was still young, 40. But a manager was only ever hot for one short moment.

Heinz Formann, unusually for him, turned up at one of the final training sessions. They said their goodbyes, in a way, although they would certainly see each other again.

They went to the stadium on the Castroper Straße and sat on some steps in the mild June sunshine. From summer, it would be called the Ruhr Stadium.

'The stadium's finished now, and I have to go,' said Heinz Höher. They let their gazes drift across the steep new terraces, and for a long while said nothing.

At home with the Höhers: Heinz Höher liked to invite his entire team back to his place, now and then. MSV Duisburg are the visitors here, second from left their captain Bernard Dietz.

The Fabulous 1970s No More:

NOTES ON THE
POSSIBILITIES OF FAILURE

Heinz Höher got special cards printed to give out to the sports journalists in Duisburg: prayer-cards, done on thick, yellow paper the
size of paperback books, the way notes asking for intercessions from
the saints always are. These cards pointed out the critical situation at
MSV Duisburg: having been robbed, by financial necessity, of three of
their most distinguished players, in the coming Bundesliga season they
were going to have to find new talent from the amateur leagues and
stay injury-free, 'otherwise,' the epistle concluded, 'only your prayers
can help us.'

Heinz Höher planned to give out his prayer-cards by way of introducing himself to the local press. It would, he thought, be a charming
gag as well as giving the journalists something to write about.

Duisburg club president Paul Merzhäuser had called him at an
unexpectedly early hour on 6 June 1979, the day after his presentation
to the club, to tell him that he was the chosen candidate, but that he
must sign the contract immediately: Heinz Höher said yes without hesitation, and without even talking to 1860 Munich any more. He liked
taking big decisions with no messing about. That was the way he'd
gone off spontaneously to Twente Enschede and a foreign country
back in 1965, with a simple 'Fine, we'll do it.' And the Duisburg team
must, he thought, surely have a somewhat better foundation to it than

the newly promoted boys from Munich. On top of that, he'd save himself a house-move, Heinz Höher justified his decision to himself retrospectively. He hadn't noticed that in reality, it wasn't him at all who had made the decision, but the club. Duisburg had been in negotiations with two other qualified managers, Horst Franz and Eckhard Krautzun. In his Bochum years, Heinz Höher had always had the notion that a talented manager like him could carefully choose his next team, but now he found that the reality of the manager's life was very different: a manager in the Bundesliga couldn't choose, but had to grab his chance quickly. There were always more applicants who could do the job than there were jobs to fill.

In his own mind, Heinz Höher still saw his career developing according to a grand plan. He would show what he was worth with one good season at Duisburg, then parachute in next summer as the successor of Hennes Weisweiler at Cologne. Weisweiler's forthcoming move to New York Cosmos in July 1980 was an open secret. What Heinz Höher didn't know was that in June 1979, at Duisburg, he was at the start of many years in the Bundesliga in which there were no plans, just improvising and getting by.

'I'll be in the loony bin by fifty. But at least I want to earn enough money by then so I can have a first-class cell,' said Otto Rehhagel, who was two days older than Heinz Höher and had begun his managerial career at the same time. During Höher's seven years at Bochum, Rehhagel had already been sacked three times and changed clubs himself twice. Heinz Höher smiled when he heard what Rehhagel said about the loony bin.

In one respect, the position of manager was more comfortable in 1979 at Duisburg than it had been for Rudi Gutendorf during their first Bundesliga season back in 1963. The manager's natural stomping-ground, the running track around the pitch, was nowadays made of artificial turf. You had to look carefully to see, in such details, what had changed here since Heinz Höher had made his first steps as a player in the Bundesliga, 16 years before. And yet, your heart said that here at Duisburg, and in the entire Bundesliga, everything had changed radically since then. In 1963, this had been a team of Meiderich boys from the Phoenix steelworks. By 1979, players from the Duisburg region, like Rudi Seliger, Norbert Dronia or Gregor Grillemeyer, were in the minority on the team-sheet almost every Saturday.

A market had developed where solid professional players were sold from Schalke to Duisburg, from Duisburg to Hamburg, and came into the Bundesliga from Norway or Belgium. At Bochum, Heinz Höher had lived in blissful ignorance of this reality, too: in seven years there, they'd brought a player from Oberhausen now and then – and never once brought in a player from abroad. A Bundesliga club needed to have a local heart; Duisburg held on to its changeless icons, Bernard Dietz and Rudi Seliger, at all costs and Bayern obviously were always going to have some Bavarians in the team, but if you wanted to succeed, you had to go out shopping. And if you didn't succeed straightaway, you had to go back out and go selling. For at least a third of the teams in the Bundesliga, the annual transfer market wasn't about strengthening the side, but simply about getting hold of money when they were in a financial hole. The Bundesliga clubs together were in debt to knocking on 40 million marks.

At the end of the 1970s, Duisburg wanted to become one of the top clubs and had, indeed, reached the semi-finals of the UEFA Cup two months before Heinz Höher signed his contract with them. They had to pay for this success by return of post: three pillars of the team, Kees Bregmann, Ditmar Jakobs and Ronnie Worm, had to be sold to fend off the debts that had piled up in their attempt to buy themselves into the top flight. Eintracht Braunschweig paid them a million marks for Ronnie Worm. In 1976, Cologne had been the first Bundesliga team to do the unbelievable and pay a million for a player, the Belgian Rofer van Gool. A million stood for grand dreams, for absolute wealth. By 1979 the words had lost a lot of their magic: transfer fees of a million, debts of a million had become everyday expressions in the Bundesliga. And that was in spite of the fact that many Bundesliga clubs couldn't realistically expect more than five million marks' annual income.

Ronnie Worm's parents stayed in Meiderich, and when you looked at them it gave you the feeling, deep inside, that something wasn't right any more, if even *their* son was off playing in any old North German city. Since 1969, his parents had been landlords of the Duisburg club-house.

Heinz Höher tried to hold back the years with the demolished team that he inherited at Duisburg. He went back to the methods which had so often helped him in the 1970s in the relegation battles at Bochum: since the sale of Ronnie Worm had left him without a goal-scorer, he played without a centre-forward; he made a young man by the name of Thomas Kempe, straight from the local league, into the keystone of his game; he pulled his best player, Bernard Dietz, back to play sweeper, as a final redoubt; and he spoke little. For the first ten matches, Duisburg made a fist of it. Then they lost three in a row, including a 6-0 defeat at Frankfurt. Now they were only two points clear of the relegation zone.

Heinz Höher believed that when he had his back to the wall, his greatest strengths came to the fore. He became ice-cool. He saw things, and decided things, hard and clear. To his players, it came over as iciness.

On 24 November 1979, they were playing Bayer 05 Uerdingen at home, and they simply had to stop the downward slide. The penultimate training session before the encounter took place without Bernard Dietz being there. He had played for the national side against the Soviet Union in Tbilisi on Wednesday and was only going to land in Stuttgart at 9pm on Thursday. Duisburg's two Austrian internationals, Kurt Jara and Hans-Dieter Mirnegg, landed at 1.30pm after their Euro qualification game against Portugal. They, too, were not there for training at 3pm.

Austria had beaten Portugal 2-1. Their banquet after the game had gone on until 3am. The Thursday morning training session in Duisburg had been running for half an hour when Jara and Mirnegg appeared.

When did you land? asked Heinz Höher, without greeting them.

At half past one.

It's half past three now! Get off, into the dressing-room, you can go straight home.

The sour, stinking miasma which had always hung over the training ground on the Westender Straße back in 1963, was long gone. By 1979, the fumes from the steel being made in the Phoenix works, which was nowadays called the Mannesmann Works, were filtered and rose almost odourlessly into the air.

They'd only nipped back home quickly after arriving, to get something for lunch, Mirnegg defended himself. Surely the manager wouldn't deny them a warm meal.

Next day, Heinz Höher announced that Jara and Mirnegg would not be playing against Uerdingen. At Duisburg, all roads to an opponent's goal went via Jara.

Under Heinz Höher's predecessor Rolf Schafstall, international players had indeed been allowed to miss training the day after playing for their countries, but Heinz Höher was giving no special favours to divas, he had explicitly told the Austrians that they should be back immediately on their return, it was about time that he disciplined Jara, he couldn't be doing with players who took liberties, he was sick of hearing about 'players you need to take warts and all'. If he heard a player saying 'you've got to take me warts and all', well, Heinz Höher knew straightaway what kind of player that was: an arsehole.

Horst Leroi, who reported on Duisburg for the *Neue Ruhr Zeitung*, wrote: 'You can see where the manager's coming from, because the team really isn't in good shape,' and no one could be permitted to break discipline.

After 18 minutes, Duisburg were leading Uerdingen 2-0. The team compensated for the loss of Jara's silky passes with work-rate and aggression. After 34 minutes, Uerdingen had got it back to 2-2. The spectators in the roofed main stand, who were paying 25 marks a ticket, started throwing their matchday programmes onto the pitch. One of them began, and many joined in: 'Höher out!' On the standing terraces, where blue-and-white knitted scarves were tied to the rails, you could hear, piping and shrill, the voices of children: 'We want Jara!' Doris Höher went to the ladies' toilet and locked herself away from the shouting. Her nerves couldn't stand it any more. In Bochum, they'd shouted like this about her husband now and then, too. But in Bochum she'd been sitting between the players' wives, her friends. In Duisburg, she was alone, even if she was sitting beside the players' wives. Here, she was an outsider come among them, the wife of their disciplinarian manager, someone you'd better keep at arm's length.

She spent the whole of the second half locked into the toilet. Why did she go to matches any more, anyway? She should never come to the stadium again she told herself, and knew that she'd be there for the next home game, and hate it again.

It was already dark – Germany, in November – when the game ended at 5.20pm, 2-2, amid the whistles of the 10,000 spectators. On top of it all, Bernard Dietz had missed a penalty. The reporter on *Das aktuelle Sportstudio*, Rolf Kramer, fetched Jara and Mirnegg from the main stand and sat them on the substitutes' bench to film his interview. Kurt Jara had pulled the belt of his trenchcoat tight, and even when sitting, he stuck his hands deep into the pockets of his trenchcoat to shield them from the biting evening cold. Mirnegg looked on, a silent witness, as Jara, his head towards the ground in concentration, spoke: 'I've already let it out in the newspapers, and I stand by what I said: I can't work with Heinz Höher any more. Either he goes, or I go.'

The basic problem, Jara continued, was this: 'Heinz Höher thinks too much, and talks too little.'

In the Duisburg papers, the spat was given more space, and more prominently, than the report on the game. The sports editor of the *Neue Ruhr Zeitung*, Horst Leroi, who had shown some understanding for the manager's disciplinary proceedings on the Friday, wrote on the Monday: 'Can a manager really go so far as to leave such an excellent player as Kurt Jara out? Is it really such a big deal as Heinz Höher makes it out to be?'

Club president Paul Merzhäuser summoned his two fighting cocks to sit down together for lunch at the Hotel Duisburg.

Merzhäuser was a lawyer. He set out the incident as he saw things, invited the players and the manager each to put themselves into the other's shoes, and all of a sudden, Jara and Mirnegg took back everything they'd said; all of a sudden, Heinz Höher found that he could understand how outraged his players had been at his ruling; he didn't hold grudges, he said, they should have sat down together even before the Uerdingen game.

'Stay here and have yourselves a drink!' cried Duisburg's business manager, Heinz Neuhaus, to the manager and his two players, when they stood up from the table at around 3pm. The sports reporters from the Duisburg dailies were already waiting in the hotel foyer to be given the result of the peace summit.

Heinz Höher was thinking about how he himself had once threatened to walk out, in his days as a winger at Leverkusen, when a manager had punished him by leaving him on the bench – just like Jara now. But in those days, he remembered, the manager and he had dealt with it as a young man's natural act of rebellion, all by themselves, without thousands of spectators demanding someone's head, and without a single line about it in the papers.

His conflict with Jara – the clash, as it was called in the media – won Heinz Höher the honour of being invited onto *Das aktuelle Sportstudio* the following Saturday. Bayern Munich's World Cup medal-winner Paul Breitner was also on. He was wearing Bavarian costume, complete with lederhosen. Bayern had taken to appearing dressed like this at away games. Their opposing fans shouted 'we'll catch Bayern with their lederhosen down!', so they wanted to show that they had their lederhosen on. This was one of Bayern's new general manager's first ideas. He was called Uli Hoeneß. He'd had to give up playing in February 1979 after a knee injury. But really, said Paul Breitner on *Das Aktuelle Sportstudio*, it was terrible that Uli now had to play the general manager at a football club. Leaning broadly back into his leather chair, Breitner explained: 'It's a shame for Uli to go into a crap job like that, he's got a real business brain, he knows so much, he's good enough for something much better than that.' The fate of a Bundesliga club was determined by the star-players, the president, and the manager. The general manager was just the man who dealt with everyday business matters. He had to do stuff like find new sources of money, but the fact was that 85 per cent of their income came from ticket sales, transfer fees and those not-to-be-despised club memberships. In the 1979-80 season, the public television channels paid 3.5 million marks for the rights to broadcast the Bundesliga. That meant a bare 200,000 marks for each club – enough for the wages and bonuses of a single above-average player.

Anchorman Harry Valerien accompanied Breitner's words with repeated nods of his head. Beneath his wide-open collar he was wearing a silk neck-scarf. The sideboards of the 1970s were gone, his hair was cropped short. Heinz Höher had even given up the peroxide. A decent grey streak shimmered in his hair.

'You managed Bochum for seven years, and now you're at Duisburg,' said Valerien, gesticulating heavily. 'How has the landscape changed in the Bundesliga, what's got tougher?'

'Think about the cost of living. If that goes up by eight per cent a year, there are ructions. But in the last eight years the pressure in the Bundesliga hasn't gone up by eight or ten per cent year on year, it's been twenty-five or thirty per cent.'

'Really! Can you explain what you mean a bit?'

'The fans are getting more and more impatient, the media reports more and more, sensational stories get created, and it all lands on us players and managers.'

Valerien thanked him for his openness and went on to the next game, Bremen vs Frankfurt: the most important moments – that is, the decisive errors – were shown from two different camera-angles, then repeated in slow-motion.

*

In the winter break, Duisburg set up their training camp in Berlin. The winter was normally worse there than in Duisburg, but going there meant they could include taking part in an indoor tournament at the Deutschlandhalle; it was a way of bringing money in. One evening in Berlin, Heinz Höher was wandering about a bit in the streets near their hotel and – why not? – popped into a bar for a couple of beers and a shot. After a while, he saw two men he knew coming in. Kurt Jara and Hans-Dieter Mirnegg.

Well, what a coincidence.

Right, let's have one together, then.

It was after 1am when Heinz Höher said he was off now, and he'd advise them to do the same. They had training first thing in the morning.

Hey, guvnor, come on, let's go on somewhere else together.

In West Berlin there were really hot joints, they just had to try them out. West Berlin, surrounded by the Wall, was wild, West Berlin only coped with being shut up like this by being one big party, West Berlin was out there tonight, waiting for them.

Goodnight, lads. You're old enough to do what you want, or not. But we've got training first thing in the morning.

But the very first thing in the morning was breakfast. Kurt Jara's and Hans-Dieter Mirnegg's seats were empty. Their captain's, Bernard Dietz, first thought was: They cannot be doing this. Having a night out for once, fine, but how can they be so thick and not turn up to breakfast? They're actually forcing the manager to punish them.

Heinz Höher was sitting at another table with general manager Heinz Neuhaus. A manager didn't eat with his players. Buy two tickets home, right now, said Höher to Neuhaus.

Look, let's just think about it quietly for a bit, Heinz, we've only just got over the fuss about the Uerdingen game, we don't want to kick things off again by going straight to the maximum punishment.

I told you to buy two plane tickets. Jara and Mirnegg are flying home today.

Just calm down, will you!

Heinz Höher wasn't furious any more. He was offended. If Neuhaus didn't want to do what he told him to do, then he didn't want to do any more either, and by any more he meant *any* more. The manager didn't appear at the training sessions that day, morning or evening. Bernard Dietz had to take them.

Heinz Höher didn't say a word until he was in bed at night with his imaginary friend Winzlinger.

You see, you see, you can't stand it, can you, when other people act the way you often did when you were a player.

Obviously, I went out on the town now and then. I can still remember when I was playing for the West German Olympic team in Berlin. I was out all night, and I only got back to the hotel just in time for breakfast. I went and bought a paper especially so I could say to our manager, Dettmar Cramer: I just went out to get the paper. But that's the whole point, I was always ready for action the next day as if nothing had happened at night, that's the difference, Winzlinger!

But why punish Jara and Mirnegg so harshly? You often got away scot-free yourself.

And, in his memory, Heinz Höher travelled back to a different Berlin; 21 years ago, there were already two separate German states but there was no wall yet and no order to open fire on people trying to cross. It was 1958, the upper sixth form of the Carl-Duisberg-Gymnasium were on a class trip to Berlin – and he was going to be sent home early because he'd slipped out at night. His teacher had even bought the train ticket already. But then one of his fellow pupils fell ill with appendicitis, and had to go home. The teacher gave this boy the ticket which had been intended for Heinz Höher. He was allowed to stay. That had been in Berlin. Shouldn't he take it as a sign?

Next morning, Heinz Höher said: right then. Jara and Mirnegg could stay. But they had to give him a written assurance that there would be no more breaches of discipline, or they would face a fine of 5000 marks. For weeks, Heinz Höher carried around with him this piece of paper with their word of honour on it. He had the feeling that he'd have a use for this note some day, he just didn't yet know what it would be.

But it felt more like the time for a different kind of notes – those yellow prayer-notes of his. As the 1979-80 season went into its second half, in January, Duisburg were mired fast in the bottom quarter of the Bundesliga table. Given the makeshift nature of their team this was not really surprising. But the first casualty in the heat of a relegation battle is usually the sense of reality. Heinz Höher was tense because the team kept on making such stupid mistakes, the players were irritated because the manager acted more and more distanced, the board were nervous because the papers were asking questions, the fans were getting aggressive because they saw Heinz Höher's defensive tactics as football driven by fear. And they all dreamed that somehow, everything would turn out all right.

On 2 February 1980, a goal six minutes from time gave Duisburg a hard-won 2-2 draw at Heinz Höher's childhood team, Bayer 04 Leverkusen, who were lying tenth in the table. The sense of relief overwhelmed him. He gave Kurt Jara back the note with his word of honour written on it.

He thought that his playmaker would understand this gesture, and that Kurt Jara would pay back his generosity in the relegation battles of the coming weeks.

The following Saturday's match was at home against Schalke, and Jara just never got into the game. The whole Duisburg team played without any rhythm, Thomas Kempe couldn't do anything right in midfield either, but it was Jara that Heinz Höher noticed again and again, as he hesitated with his passing or failed to break away from his marker. When Schalke went 2-1 up on the hour, Heinz Höher thought for a moment, if you take him off now, the whole thing will kick off again, the boos and the whistles, so just leave it out. But then he thought: if you stop making decisions you're convinced are right because you're scared of the spectators, then you're already finished and you just haven't noticed yet. In the 69th minute the stadium's tannoy announced: 'Duisburg substitution. Gregor Grillemeier replaces number ten, Kurt Jara.'

It was funny, at Bochum, he had never noticed the whistles and shouts of 'Höher out!' He'd read about them in the newspaper on the following Monday, but he had no memory of them. He must have been so involved in the game. On 9 February 1980, with Grillemeier on for Jara, Heinz Höher could hardly hear anything else: 'Höher out! Höher out! Höher out! Höher out!'

In the press box, they were whispering: how can he do that? 2-1 down, sliding into the relegation zone, and he takes off the only man who can hold out any hope of one moment of genius that could save them? He's digging his own grave.

Doris Höher fled to her car. The toilet walls weren't enough any more. From her make-up case she took cotton wool balls and stuffed them into her ears and then, to distract herself, she started making a list of all the things she needed to buy for the traditional ladies' night back home in the Bonhoefferstraße in Bochum. All the Bochum players' wives would be coming.

When the whistle went, 2-1, Heinz Höher was immediately on his way to the dressing-room, into the cover of darkness. Duisburg's general manager, Heinz Neuhaus, stayed sitting on the subs' bench, his arms folded. 'We've got to talk to the president,' said the team medic, Dr Raab, to Neuhaus. Raab was a member of the board as well as being the doctor. Neuhaus didn't react.

Club president Paul Merzhäuser was already at the door to the dressing-room, talking to Heinz Höher: we're not done yet, we're going to fight on. Heinz Höher registered the consoling tone, rather than the exact words. In the dressing-room stood the chief of the board of trustees, Wolfram Weber, the man who had paved the way for Kurt Jara to come from FC Valencia to Duisburg. Heinz Höher had insisted, just as he had done at Bochum, that no member of the board apart from the president should enter the dressing-room before the game or at half-time. Before this deal, they often had as many as ten club functionaries shoving amid the team in the dressing-room, more than one of them with a cigarette in his mouth. But now here was Weber back in the sanctuary and visibly worked up, saying exactly the opposite of their president, Merzhäuser: didn't Höher think he should resign? It hadn't even crossed his mind, replied Heinz Höher.

At the exit of the stadium there were more fans waiting for him than usual. After every home game, the players and the manager walked right through the fans to get to their cars or to the team bus. In 1963, they'd had a beer here with the fans. Now, they signed autographs. Heinz Höher put his head down and his best foot forward. The crowd were indignant.

He drove straight home with Doris, even though the team ate dinner together at the club-house in Meiderich after every home game. He didn't see that way that the club president asked the four most important players, Bernhard Dietz, Gerhard Heinze, Manfred Dubski and Herbert Büssers, about the state of things and about the manager. They said that their manager wasn't giving them any positive signals any more, not even factual help. One time recently, he'd simply given his captain, Dietz, a piece of paper so that he could read out the line-up. On the drive home, silence descended on Heinz

Höher and his wife, and this time she could understand why he was so quiet.

Over dinner, the two parents and their three children imitated normality. Could you pass the bread please, what did you do this afternoon, rote-learned sentences which did not break the icy, threatening silence, but merely underlined how much was not being said.

The phone rang, and Heinz Höher was unsurprised to find Paul Märzheuser at the other end of the line.

Are you sacking me?

Mr Höher, I'm just asking you to come to the club office tomorrow at 12.

So you're sacking me.

Mr Höher! We haven't won in five games, we're in the relegation zone. So everyone's being criticised, you and me alike. Between now and tomorrow midday, think about what you can say in reply to this criticism.

The conversation dragged on, Märzheuser didn't say that Höher was getting sacked, and he also didn't say that he could carry on. He was a lawyer. At some point, Heinz Höher got so irritated that he cried out: Anyway, I've recorded this conversation! and hung up.

Naturally, he hadn't recorded the conversation. And he had no idea what he might have been able to prove with such a recording. He had simply been trying to defend himself out of helplessness. Had it set the seal on his sacking? The phone rang again.

It was Dieter Kürten from *Das aktuelle Sportstudio*. He was wanting to know how Heinz Höher was feeling after this afternoon. The presenters on *Sportstudio* usually invited their guests personally onto the show, and then often stayed in contact with them. Their conversations weren't strictly professional and weren't strictly private either, but at any rate they talked as equals, as one public personality to another.

Heinz Höher told Dieter Kürten that he feared he'd already been sacked. Then he had an idea: couldn't Kürten call Märzheuser and try to find out what was really going on, maybe even – Heinz Höher didn't actually say it out loud – put a word in for him?

Just as Heinz Höher was about to hang up, Doris called from the background that she too wanted a word with Mr Kürten. It was the worst day she'd ever spent at a football stadium, Doris told Mr Kürten, whose soft voice and hesitant smile had made him the darling of many women in the TV audience. But perhaps, said Doris, Mr Kürten would still be able to do something.

Thirty minutes before he was due live on the programme, Dieter Kürten was on the line to the president of Duisburg, trying vainly to get something definitive out of him. But the lawyer's hints were enough for him.

In a TV studio on the Lerchenberg in Mainz, a railway station clock was ticking inexorably forward. On the dot of the third beat of the accompanying jingle, the TV cameras swung away from the station clock and onto a green sign which said *Das aktuelle Sportstudio*. Dieter Kürten, looking youthful at 44 in his dark-blue suit and with his silver hair, wished the viewers 'Good evening' in a notably downbeat manner, and swiftly explained to 6 million people sitting in their living rooms, why 'I was feeling rather depressed minutes ago'. He explained that he'd had pretty detailed phone conversations with Heinz Höher, Duisburg's manager, and with Paul Merzhäuser, their president, and it looked as if Heinz Höher wasn't going to be managing Duisburg much longer. It took Dieter Kürten one minute and 30 seconds of screen time, which in television is an eternity or an impossibility, to tell the story of his telephone calls, and of how Frau Höher had sat outside the stadium in her car and suffered, with cotton wool stuffed into her ears. Kürten ended by saying that he'd be very pleased if, contrary to all the signs, it didn't come to a sacking at Duisburg and that things would soon be better again for Heinz and Doris.

Heinz Höher was not present at his own sacking. On Sunday, 10 February 1980 at 12 o'clock, the club board waited in vain for the manager, and completed the divorce in his absence. Höher, said Märzheuser to the football writers, had been 'a general without luck on his side'. They needed a fresh start.

Heinz Höher went for a walk with the newest member of the family, Clemens, the Old English sheepdog. Really, he said to himself, you had to reckon that something like this might happen. But he had never reckoned with it. He really had believed that he would never be sacked as a manager.

He thought back to the carnival jester he'd been obligerd to greet in the centre circle just before kick-off against Schalke. He'd fought tooth and claw to get out of it, he'd said that in their precarious league situation, he'd just be making an idiot of himself if he appeared in public with a Fool, but the club president and the general manager had yelled at him until he agreed to go along with it. You don't play games with those carnival folk, they said.

The jester had presented him with a carnival medal. Heinz Höher decided to keep this medal, to remind him of his first sacking. On the medal stood the motto: 'Life is a Fool's errand.'

After this World Cup, the image of German footballers was to change for years to come: internationals (l to r) Hans-Peter Briegel, Manfred Kaltz, Uwe Reinders and Bernard Franke prepare themselves for the World Cup of 1982.

NO MORE LONG HAIR
BLOWING IN THE WIND

When he woke up in the mornings, his gaze fell on the ceiling of the bedroom, or the wall, and he saw nothingness. An entire long day lay bare before him. It drove him crazy, when he got up in the morning he needed to know that there was something to be done. Heinz Höher went to the fridge and, at eight in the morning, started off with a glass of champagne. But after it, every morning all over again, he was still out of work.

Some days after his sacking, he went to the unemployment office and had his new status officially confirmed. His unemployment benefit and the child benefit brought them in barely 2000 marks a month. At Duisburg, he'd been on 10,000. He thought about his mother, Maria, who still lived contentedly at almost 90 years of age and who had told them when they were children: anyone who complains, demeans themselves.

He'd devote more time to the children, Heinz Höher said to himself, at last he had time for them. He suggested to them that they could play Monopoly, he asked Markus and Susanne, who were 15 and 13 years old, if he could take a look at their homework with them now and again, but there was always a certain stiffness, the feeling that he wasn't actually any use with the homework, that actually, he couldn't really help his children. It was easier with Thomas, the unselfconsciousness of a five-year-old helped, with him he could simply play with a ball. Doris watched Thomas and thought about the way they'd brought Markus and Susanne up so strictly and casually in the 1960s. Was the more understanding way they treated Thomas at home and in the kindergarten anything to do with the way that he was so lively and self-confident?

Heinz Höher grabbed Clemens for himself and went for a run or walk with the dog every day, those were the best moments. When he could flee from reality.

But then the phone would ring, and his sister Hilla would be on the line and all he could say was: Do you want to talk to Clemens? Without saying another word to his sister, he would pass the phone over to Doris.

It was spring and the decisive phase of the Bundesliga was beginning, the relegation battle becoming more desperate; surely managers would be sacked, as he'd been done, from other clubs, surely there must still be a club president who thought that he was the right man. Heinz Höher waited. Taking the initiative himself, showing himself in the stadiums, making use of an agent, that was out of the question for him. That would be bad form, he said to himself – and by saying that, he protected himself from the question: do you really think that you could take the initiative yourself, could you actually make the call to a president, to a general manager?

In April 1980 he saw a picture of an exhausted manager in the newspapers. Branko Zebec, wearing jeans and a denim jacket, sitting there with arms crossed tight in the manager's dugout. His head was sunk down onto his chest, and the sunglasses behind which he was trying to hide his eyes had slid down to the tip of his nose. In this manner, he watched, or perhaps missed, his Hamburg side playing at Borussia Dortmund. He had drunk himself to the verge of unconsciousness with rum, vodka and cognac. He'd even missed his team's departure for Dortmund, and had tried to follow after them in his own car. The police pulled him over. He'd been driving in S-shapes all over the road. The police found he was more than four times over the limit. They drove him personally to Dortmund. There, Zebec kept on drinking.

Something inside him was still working; as if by Pavlovian reaction, he jumped up now and then during the game and screamed or clapped. Nothing that was happening in the game was any reason for anyone to jump up, shout or clap at those particular moments. At half-time,

Günter Netzer, who was now working as general manager at Hamburg, took him to the team bus and locked him in there for his own protection. It was hard to keep on pretending that the manager just liked a drink now and then; like, say, Hemingway.

All of a sudden, alcohol was a problem. *Der Spiegel* and *Welt am Sonntag* ran long articles about stress among Bundesliga managers. It was said that one in two of them drowned his troubles in alcohol. Readers could stand and wonder at the amazing research the journalists had done – and maybe also wonder how much of it had already been common knowledge before Zebec's blackout at Dortmund, without anyone ever having written a word about it. Eight months earlier, at an away game at Bochum, Zebec had sat in the dugout right in front of the photographers' lenses, with his eyes falling shut again and again. After a victory over 1860 Munich, the press conference had to be broken off when the phrase 'bird's eye view' proved beyond him. The sports writers had decided that these were private problems, even while swapping the best anecdotes about drunken managers among themselves. Now it was a problem of epedemic proportions.

Kuno Klötzer, manager of Hertha, who'd had a fridge installed in his office so that reinforcements would always be on hand, admitted to the reporters from *Der Spiegel*: 'You can only stand my job if you're steaming.' They paraded half a dozen Bundesliga managers who knocked out their nerves with pils and schnapps, and named another half dozen who had had heart attacks brought on by the stress of managerial life, or who'd had to have growths cut from their gallbladders, their intestines or their stomachs. Branko Zebec stayed on as manager of Hamburg after the 'Drink At Dortmund'. He'd taken his team to the championship in 1979, and the year afterwards they were well in the running. He was the maestro of the managers, the players really looked up to him. Even if he sometimes fell down drunk during training. When that happened, the players helped him back onto his feet, and kept right on looking up to him.

Heinz Höher cut out the article in *Welt am Sonntag* about alcohol problems among Bundesliga managers. It named him as a positive example of how to combat stress: 'Heinz Höher, 41, late manager of Duisburg, plays chess with pensioners in the Weitmarer woods in Bochum.'

To cope with the complete lack of Bundesliga managerial stress, Heinz Höher went playing tennis in Hagen with Jürgen Köper, his former Bochum player. Köper arrived in a Ferrari. He said he'd taken it off the hands of someone he knew who was in a fix. On the journey, Köper supplied him with all the latest gossip from Bochum. The team couldn't warm to their new manager, Helmut Johannsen. His training methods were from yesteryear, running with medicine balls under your arms, and then, in a crazy test of strength he'd even tried to sideline the senior players, Lameck and Tenhagen. As usual, Bochum were in danger of relegation. Maybe Ottokar Wüst would bring him back to Bochum?

As Jürgen Köper dropped him off back home in the Bonhoefferstraße, a strong hand grabbed hold of Heinz Höher and threw him against the wall of the house. He felt the barrel of a pistol at the back of his head.

Police. Hands against the wall, slowly.

Doris, who'd heard the car arriving, came to the door and couldn't help laughing out loud. There stood her husband and Jürgen Köper with their hands up, faces to the wall, covered by two policemen with drawn weapons. It must be a great joke, even though she didn't know what kind. Then she noticed that neither her husband nor Jürgen Köper was laughing.

It turned out that the acquaintance who had given Köper the Ferrari was at that very moment being sought by the police. It seemed that he'd just had an oil-tanker hijacked. It took several minutes for Heinz Höher and Jürgen Köper to convince the policemen that they had nothing to do with it.

In the last week of April 1980, Jürgen Köper had more news. He said Vim Lameck and Jupp Tenhagen danced in the corridor of the hotel before the away game at Frankfurt, singing: Ole's got to go! Ole's got to go!

Ole was the team's secret nickname for their manager, Johannsen. Since he had a Nordic surname, the players had stuck a Nordic first name on him too.

Bochum beat Eintracht Frankfurt 1-0, which was giant stride towards staying in the Bundesliga. Wüst was never going to sack Johannsen now, the players could sing and dance as much as they wanted. In any case, it was Wüst's maxim that he never sacked a manager. Just like Heinz Höher himself had once thought that he would never be sacked.

The season came to an end, Bochum avoided relegation, Duisburg, now under his successor, Friedhelm Wenzlaff, saved their necks as well, and nobody was interested in Heinz Höher's services. He thought it must be because he'd shouted *Anyway, I've recorded this conversation!* at Duisburg president Paul Märzheuser. A thing like that would do the rounds of the Bundesliga, the other club presidents would feel that a manager like that was a menace. At moments when he was honest with himself, Heinz Höher also took into consideration that he had, maybe, treated the players at Duisburg too coolly. These days, it was evidently expected that a manager in the Bundesliga should explain things like a teacher at school and not just hold forth. But there was always that barrier inside him, when it came to talking to other people.

He knew how to lay out his ideas to the players analytically. But when he saw that a player really just wanted to hear a friendly word, he couldn't get over that barrier. His throat dried up. And then he told himself abruptly: anyone who wants to play in the Bundesliga has to be able to get by without encouragement, and anyone who's made it in the Bundesliga surely doesn't need things explained to them.

He felt ready for work and went on holiday. They'd chosen Brittany, Doris's sister Helga came too, with her son Lutz. It rained every day. There'd always been a danger of that because they'd come early, it was June, but they had to take their summer holiday so early because in July, Bundesliga teams began their preparation for the new season, and that meant Heinz Höher might get a new job. When the sun finally showed itself, Thomas cut his foot on a shard of glass on the beach. They spent that one fine day in hospital.

On the final Sunday of their holiday the local village wine festival took place under gigantic parasols which in this case were used just to keep the rain off. It was the evening of the 1980 European Championship final in Rome between Germany and Belgium. His captain at Duisburg, Bernhard Dietz, was captaining Germany. Heinz Höher went alone to the Breton wine festival. He wasn't particularly keen on wine. But he started drinking in any case – what else was there to do in this weather?

When he really thought about it, beer and schnapps didn't taste good either. An apple juice was more toothsome than any alcoholic drink. But despite everything that had been written since Zebec's debacle, you still had to say that alcohol really helped. When he drank, it wasn't just that the stress left him, he saw things – well, you couldn't exactly say *more clearly*, but sort of, more consciously, more certainly, more enthusiastically. A Frenchman lifted his glass to him. He poured him a glass of red. The Frenchman replied in kind. They could hardly understand a word each other said but Heinz Höher knew: this was all about seeing who could hold the most. It was the only sport that made sense, in this weather. When the Frenchman couldn't take any more after four or five bottles, he sent in a friend to take his place and keep drinking against Höher. After another four or five bottles, Höher forced him to capitulate as well. Then he walked back through the rain to their holiday home and watched Germany against Belgium.

Germany won 2-1 thanks to two headers from Horst Hrubesch. Hrubesch. Five years ago, in Bochum, he'd had him up for a trial. Back then, Hrubesch was already 24 and still playing in the local league for a club called Westtünnen or something like that. He'd scored 56 goals in a single season. He'd turned up for the trial with his entire clan, family, friends, at least ten of them. One of the clan boasted to Heinz Höher: just chuck our Horst a medicine ball. He'll head that into the back of the net for you, too. He hadn't signed Hrubesch: he thought he already had enough good forwards.

The Bundesliga kicked off on 16 August 1980 and Heinz Höher jogged with Clemens in the woods at Weitmar, three times around the place as a long-distance run. Then, in early September, a man phoned, excusing himself for the disturbance and introducing himself as a clothing wholesaler with Greek roots. Heinz Höher didn't stop to ask where this stranger had got his phone number from, or how serious the offer was. He bought a plane ticket to Athens that very day where, as arranged by the clothing wholesaler, he met the man's acquaintance, who was the president of Ethnikos Piraeus, declared himself immediately available to start managing that Greek first division side, and shook on it. He had received no contract, nor did he know anything at all about the club itself. But that didn't matter. All that mattered was that when he opened his eyes in the morning, he could see something before him.

He went to Piraeus alone. The family was to stay in Bochum. They didn't know how long this Greek adventure would last.

He was already manager at Ethnikos by the time he discovered that they seldom drew crowds of more than 4000, and that nobody seemed very interested in what happened to the club, provided they didn't get relegated. Heinz Höher considered that, by German standards, the team played at the level of a half-decent senior amateur side. That didn't matter much. If he was in charge of training a side, then whichever club it was became his entire universe; he went at it with every ounce of his mental energy, so as to get the best from the team. Never mind how bad they were. The Greek assistant manager he'd been given pestered the translator to say something to Heinz Höher: Guvnor, you've got a face like a man who's got ten cargo ships out there at sea. Piraeus was a port city, and that was their highest praise for a man who was serious about his business.

Before the derby game against mighty Olympiakos, Heinz Höher tried to make everything a bit less irritatingly easy-going by saying: we could take them on with nine men. The translator preferred not to translate this.

Ethnikos proceeded through the season calmly, halfway clear of the relegation zone. The experience that stuck most in Heinz Höher's memory was in Crete, before their match there. As usual, he was taking a pre-match stroll and, on the dusty fields, he came across a herd of sheep. In the grass there lay a sodden lamb. It could only have been minutes old. Heinz Höher watched, fascinated, as the mother licked the lamb clean. He felt an exaltation, and an astonished joy, of which he'd never known the like.

His was the sort of life the English colonial rulers must have led, half a century earlier: splendidly relaxed, lords in a far-off land, and yet somehow aware that this was not the real thing. German managers were the best in the world – Heinz Höher, as a German manager, was convinced of it – so they could always find a corner somewhere in the world as sort of Development Aid workers. Dettmar Cramer had just gone to Saudi Arabia and where was Rudi Gutendorf now, was he still in Australia or had he already gone to the Philippines? It was better than sitting at home and waiting for a new job in the Bundesliga. But at Piraeus it was becoming clear to him that waiting for the next job in the Bundesliga took up a lot of time in the life of almost every Bundesliga manager.

Paul Kortmann, his old official at Bochum, visited him in Greece. They had to phone Kortmann's wife back in Bochum to ask her if you could put potatoes straight into water or if you had to wait until the water was boiling.

When Benno Beiroth, chairman of Fortuna Düsseldorf, called on 3 December 1980 simply to find out if there was any prospect of Höher returning to the Bundesliga after the winter break, Heinz Höher told him he could start at Düsseldorf tomorrow. He had no contract with Ethnikos. Two days later, Otto Rehhagel, whose career was, as ever, running parallel to his own, was sacked from Düsseldorf, meaning that in eight years Rehhagel had been through six clubs. Heinz Höher held his first training session at Düsseldorf in his own Adidas tracksuit, although Düsseldorf were kitted out by Puma. No one cared about such details, they knew things were all moving rather fast. After guiding Düsseldorf's last game before the winter break on 13 December, Heinz Höher was even going back to Piraeus again, to keep on managing Ethnikos briefly during the German Christmas holidays. He wanted to make sure that he got the rest of the money that was still owed to him in Greece, and which had been agreed by word of mouth alone.

In the cellar of Düsseldorf's club office at the Flinger Broich stood a lion. It was life-size, though only made of papier mâché. It had been created by an advertising agency and set up a few times on Saturdays in the stadium, because Düsseldorf needed a new, bolder image. But the marketing experts had quickly established that even with the aid of a dummy lion, only 10,000 spectators came to see them play. People couldn't be bothered with everyday Bundesliga football at Düsseldorf.

Düsseldorf were a special case. Their smaller neighbour, Borussia Mönchengladbach, had stolen much of their support, and many Düsseldorfers felt it was their duty to act according to Düsseldorf's clichéd image of itself: this was said to be a city for fashion, for theatre, maybe for a bit of thrilling ice-hockey even – but not for the vulgar game of football. At a deeper level, though, Düsseldorf was simply an example of what was going on in football all over West Germany after the great days of the 1970s: almost every boy played in some kind of football team, the majority of men watched the Bundesliga on TV. But fewer and fewer of them actually went to games. In 1977, six years after the match-fixing scandal, boosted by the international successes of Beckenbauer's generation, the average Bundesliga gate was 27,600 – back to the level set in the first Bundesliga season of 1963. Since then, gates had been falling, season after season. By 1981, the average was down to 21,800. That meant a total of 1.75 million fewer tickets were bought than four years earlier. In a football-crazy land, the Bundesliga was becoming a virtual competition: something which still interested many people, but which they could no longer grab, feel or smell, because they only experienced it indirectly, via the media.

No doubt the less passionate spectators stayed away because it was more comfortable to watch the highlights on TV rather than because they were fed up. What was the point of freezing in a stadium, when *Sportschau* was bringing football into your own living-room? The feeling began to grow that the stadiums were being taken over by barbarians.

When Düsseldorf played Borussia Dortmund in the Cup in November 1980, the Kaiserswerther Straße had to be closed off for 15 minutes. A tram was burning. It had been set alight by the Borussia Front. Düsseldorf Terror hit back even before the kick-off, because after all, who needed a result as an excuse for a scrap. At least 100 youths were involved in a general riot. In every Bundesliga stadium, a new kind of youth had been born: the hooligans. While their fathers avoided the stadiums out of loathing for the violence on show every Saturday, the 11- or 12-year-old kids, who played in amateur clubs, now came to the Bundesliga stadiums alone, and watched with interest as the hooligans beat each other up with leather belts and shot flare-guns at each other. It seemed just natural that the fathers should stay away and the children should watch: that was just the way it was.

On the playing field, too, the game was getting more physical. A new figure appeared on the scene in the Bundesliga: *der Fitnesscoach*. At Duisburg, Heinz Höher had got the former German steeplechase champion, Claus Brosius, to develop many elements of their training: running, jumping, weight-lifting. Athleticism was becoming the German obsession. It was muscles that won games; just look at who dominated the European Cup, it was the English and the Germans, the big, tough guys. The UEFA Cup semi-finals of 1980 were contested by four German clubs.

These new muscles meant first and foremost that defences were getting stronger. Many Bundesliga clubs now played with five defenders, and almost all of them with only two forwards. They guarded and destroyed their opponents with Prussian efficiency, always going in hard, man to man.

The Ajax ideal of total football, of exhilarating attack with three forwards, disappeared from the Bundesliga. One by one, the great 1970s apostles of style in German football left the scene: Netzer, Grabowski,

Heynckes. Bernd Schuster's long blond hair was already blowing in far-off winds, at Barcelona. The Bundesliga was being taken over by the mini-perm. Was Ugliness the new Beauty?

At Düsseldorf, Heinz Höher was met by a team which included 12 sets of moustachios. His mission was that old, well-known one: avoid relegation. Under Rehhagel's management, Düsseldorf had got off to a flying start with three successive wins, but by 16 games in, they'd slid down into the relegation zone. Things were so bad that when they played Nuremberg, only 5300 spectators turned up – and worse still, only four out of their 21 players came along to eat goose for the traditional Saint Martin's Day dinner at Bert Rudolph's restaurant, the Benrather Hof! Could there be a more telling image of a team on the verge of moral collapse?

To Heinz Höher, a creaky state of things like this was a perfectly good place to start. If a team's in a bad way, any new manager has a good chance of being accepted as a miracle healer simply because he's new, because everything that's new carries within it the hope of betterment. In Heinz Höher's second game in charge, Borussia Mönchengladbach's 18-year-old Bundesliga debutant, Lothar Matthäus, just couldn't keep hold of Düsseldorf forward Klaus Allofs: Düsseldorf were out of the relegation zone, and never dropped back into it for the whole season. Heinz Höher turned holding midfielder Rüdiger Wenzel into a forward, substitute forward Ralf Dusend into a fixture in defence, introduced zonal defending, rejigged the training programme – and though no miracles were achieved, it all breathed life into a team which had been mired in failure.

At Duisburg, the team had complained about his lack of words, but in Düsseldorf they saw him as comfortably quiet. 'Mr Höher sticks to facts, that's the tone he sets,' said keeper Jörg Daniel, 'maybe that suits me better than the others because I'm sure I'd be the same if I were a manager.'

The club's board were relieved to have snapped up the right manager. Benno Beiroth told Heinz Höher how he'd once said to Rehhagel, come on let's open a bottle of red wine for once – and then he had to drink the entire bottle by himself because Rehhagel just sat there sipping at his glass! Sitting down with Heinz Höher was nothing like that. Heinz Höher laughed at the tale of the wine, and didn't ask himself what they might say about him, one day, if he ever had to leave.

But who was saying anything about leaving? Obviously, Heinz

Höher was going to extend his contract after the summer. 'At Düsseldorf,' wrote the *Rheinische Post* after he'd been at the helm for 100 days, 'Heinz Höher has confirmed his reputation as a successful tweaker of teams. He has his own ideas with which to confound the opposition. His record up till now – nine points out of a possible 16 – is pretty impressive.'

But the stadium stayed half empty at best. At the 2-2 draw with Borussia Dortmund, only 18,000 turned up. That was the record gate in Heinz Höher's opening months. Of them, probably 3000-5000 were Borussia fans.

People in Düsseldorf only get out of bed for big names, club secretary Werner Faßbender told him. I should know, Faßbender added, since I am a Düsseldorfer myself.

It was Sunday, and they were standing together, watching the club's first youth XI or their amateur XI. Clemens the Old English sheepdog was rolling in the mud beside them, and Heinz Höher had a hard time of it making sure that the dog's long hair didn't dirty him too.

Those cup finals, Faßbender chatted on in his Rhineland sing-song, that was the kind of thing people wanted in Düsseldorf.

Düsseldorf had been in the German Cup final three times in a row, from 1978 to 1980, winning it twice, and in May 1979, in Basel, they'd had an evening which had etched itself into memory when they lost 4-3 to Barcelona in the final of the European Cup Winners' Cup. Later that night, at the hotel Zum goldenen Knopf in Bad Säckingen, near the Swiss border, the floral decorations disappeared. Werner Faßbender had eaten them all. Lilies, salted and peppered. Well, someone had to do something to cheer everyone up at the formal dinner after the defeat against Barcelona.

So you see, Faßbender concluded the conversation, which, like all their conversations, had consisted mainly of himself talking, things at Düsseldorf were very simple: everyone in town came to a match twice a year – to see Bayern or Borussia Mönchengladbach. If they wanted people to come more often, all they had to do was become as successful as Bayern or Borussia Mönchengladbach.

The weight of expectation, the feeling that he was going to have to deliver something extraordinary, crept into Heinz Höher's mind. He'd led Düsseldorf from the relegation zone into the lower-midtable, at the end of the season they were going to finish 13th, that was absolutely fine – and next season, it wouldn't be enough. He'd never managed such a talented side: the Allofs brothers, Klaus and Thomas, Gerd Zewe, Wolfgang Seel. But it was a team that was past their best, with an unusual number of players who were over 30. They'd had their day in those cup finals. And the way the books were looking, what with the half-empty stadium, it also looked very much as though they were going to have to sell at least one of the Allofs brothers. If he was going to fulfil all those high expectations, he was going to have to make sure, when it came to his new contract, that he would be able to rebuild the team properly despite those merciless financial realities. He would only be able to drive those demands through if he put maximum pressure on the club – but that, thought Heinz Höher, was where he knew how to play it: once again, he would pretend to resign, so that the board would give in to all his demands to persuade him to stay.

On the Wednesday before Easter 1981, he met Benno Beiroth and Werner Faßbender at the club office, to plan the future.

Heinz Höher said that he'd considered everything very carefully and would not be renewing his contract. There had been a few voices raised against him even after the victory over 1860 Munich, and he did not feel that he was going to be able to fulfil expectations here.

It was the perfect moment for Beiroth and Faßbender to say: Hold on! First, let's talk about what we might be able to do for you.

Beiroth said he'd been ready for anything, but not this.

Faßbender said he was flabbergasted.

They called up club president Hans-Georg Noack. Höher wants out. He didn't believe it, said Noack. Has he got another club waiting? He's got nothing, just a feeling that he can't fulfil expectations here.

Well now, if Mr Höher says so. In that case, it looks like there's nothing we can do.

At the *Rheinische Post*, sports editor Friedhelm Körner tried to control his astonishment. Heinz Höher was leaving! That was a bombshell. That was almost impossible to believe. What he'd achieved at Düsseldorf had been pretty impressive, there'd only been a couple of shouts against him at one single match, and that had been just a couple of kids who were looking for trouble. 'Has the manager resigned too quickly?' asked Körner.

Doris Höher couldn't understand the world any more, and she could understand her husband even less. Why did he chuck it all away like that, what did he expect to do now?

He didn't know, Heinz Höher admitted.

But why? Why?

Heinz Höher couldn't bring himself to admit the truth, even to his wife: that his bluff had been called. He felt that he couldn't go back. He had to play the role he'd slipped into, to the bitter end.

He told Doris he'd failed in Duisburg with a team that was hardly capable of Bundesliga football, that the same fate was threatening him in Düsseldorf next season, and that he didn't want to go through it all again. He told the sports writers: 'What Düsseldorf need above all is a manager who's got credit in the bank. In the short time I've had, I've got the feeling that I haven't got that credit at Düsseldorf.'

And it seemed unlikely to hope that someone would say: But that's nonsense. You must stay! Even if everyone was thinking it, including him.

When she was with him, Doris tried to be understanding. At the tennis club in Bochum, she said to her partners: Now let's see how he gets out of this one.

The Greeks hadn't forgotten about him. The clothing wholesaler on the telephone, who he'd never seen, whose name he'd never made a note of, got him a job at PAOK Salonika. His predecessor, Gyula Lóránt, who was, together with Heinz Höher himself, the pioneer of zonal marking in the Bundesliga, had died in the manager's dugout there at Salonika on 31 May 1981. Heart attack, the doctors said. Why didn't he just take over Lóránt's flat too, said the translator. At that moment, Heinz Höher understood all at once, and all too well, what transience really meant.

This time, Markus came with him to Greece. His oldest son wasn't having an easy time of it at school. Bringing him along, having him under under his eye would help the boy to pass his GCSEs, thought Heinz Höher. He didn't stop to think that the daily reality of being alone with his 17-year-old son might be difficult. After all, he knew how to boil potatoes now.

They moved in to the flat on the hills outside Thessaloniki; there were no memories of Gyula Lóránt left in it. Down below, the town was sparkling in the sunlight. Their skin turned bronze.

Lessons at the German school went on into the afternoon. When his son came home, Heinz Höher asked him how's it going, but he didn't really want to know the details. The thing that gave him great satisfaction, the thing that filled him with pride, was watching how Markus was learning windsurfing on the beach. The boy was growing strong, he was learning the skills, he was a king of the sea, the waves, the surf, and Heinz Höher had the feeling that he was becoming independent, growing up.

When PAOK won, as they often did, under him, the market traders ran after him shouting Mr Höher, Mr Höher. Take this. They would shove whole raw legs of lamb or thick, bloody chunks of beef into his hands. Is for you, is for nothing. Heinz Höher knew how to make a steak with salad. The only problem had been the potatoes.

The translator had told him one other little thing about Gyula Lóránt. After four months in the job, his predecessor had driven to training sessions in an armour-plated car. The fans, Mr Höher.

Heinz Höher told himself that he'd stay mentally prepared for the atmosphere to flip over at any time. When they arrived for their away game against Panionios at the stadium in Athens, stones began to fly. Stop the bus, screamed keeper Mlantan Fortuna, and charged off the vehicle. He threw the stones back at the fans. When he was getting out of the bus, Heinz Höher found a chunk of stone still lying on the floor. He took it home with him and placed it on the chest of drawers, as a trophy. It was fine: it had only been the opposing fans. PAOK were doing more than respectably, staying in sight of the leading clubs, Olympiakos and Panathinaikos.

In December 1981 he got a new neighbour. Dettmar Cramer took over at local rivals Aris.

While Heinz Höher told himself that he was in Greece just to pass the time while waiting to return to the Bundesliga, Cramer seemed really to have found himself in exile. He trained managers in Africa or Asia for FIFA, and on his CV, European Cup victories in 1975 and 1976 at Bayern Munich sat between managerial stints in Japan and Saudi Arabia. He wasn't waiting for the call that would bring him home. He had a quite different idea of what it meant, as a German, to be asked by foreigners to teach them football.

Dettmar Cramer had been 14 when Hitler declared war on the world. He was hardly out of school when the Nazis made him a para-trooper. He was an excellent sportsman with a body ideal for flying. He was only 5 foot 3½. His unit was sent straight from Minsk to Tunisia, from 23° below straight into the desert sun, they were the elite troops, they were sent in everywhere, theirs not to reason why. Now they dived out over Sicily, the rushing of the wind as they cut through it on their drop was the only noise, the heavens belonged to them alone, the elite. Then the rat-tat-tat of machine-guns started up.

They had dropped straight into an ambush. They, the elite, were now just fat, helpless, targets sitting in the air. Dettmar Cramer heard his comrades dying to the right and to the left of him in mid-air, shot down like clay pigeons, and dropped on down, towards the ground, towards the bullets. The questions a man asks himself afterwards, in his guilt: why me? Why did I survive it, and not the others?

At the war's end, he became a PoW in Holland. They locked him up in the internment camp at Esterwegen. The sign on the door said: *Arbeit macht frei*. Esterwegen had been built by the Nazis as a concentration camp. The victors had locked the Germans into their own prison. The beds had no mattresses. Each prisoner got one blanket. Dettmar Cramer could choose whether to use it to protect himself from the bedsprings, or from the cold. There was a single wash basin for 75 men. They had tulip-bulb soup in the mornings, and tulip-bulb bread for lunch. After six months, it was by now March 1946, Dettmar Cramer was released from captivity. His fingers were blue. His temperature was 108°F. He weighed 7 stone.

Half unconscious, he flagged down a milk-wagon that picked him up. He made it back to Dortmund, to home. He found the house burned out, no mother, no father, no brothers. Then someone recognised him as Dettmar Cramer, the one-time youth international, and told him that Lippstadt were looking for a manager.

Teutonia Lippstadt were actually looking for a sports teacher, it was 1946 and they were trying, you had to try, to act as though life would go on. Dettmar Cramer got a room in the house of the club's box office lady, and 250 marks a month. A pound of butter cost 40 marks. Four days a week he trained footballers, track and field athletes, boxers, any kind of sport, any team, any age. He could hardly keep his head above water. When his football team won the local derby against Borussia Lippstadt, someone smashed the window of his bedroom. He protected himself against the cold with cardboard.

He had been sent by Hitler into a war of annihilation against other people: how could he say no when those same people now offered him a generous salary to teach them the game of football?

In Thessaloniki, Dettmar Cramer and Heinz Höher met now and then and discussed the new image of German football. In 1981, one particular photograph even made it into foreign sports papers: Bielefeld forward Ewald Lienen was sitting on the pitch of the Weserstadion in Bremen, and his hands were crying out loud. He was holding them high in the air and they were shouting: look! His right thigh was split open from top to bottom. Bremen's Norbert Siegmann had gone into him as they fought for the ball, from dead ahead and with his studs straight out. Lienen claimed that Bremen manager Otto Rehhagel had shouted out to his defender: Make sure you get him good and proper next time!

Brutal fouls intended to deter the opposition had been an everyday tactic in the Bundesliga right from the beginning. Vendettas were paid back by fouls in return, and in the evening it would all be sorted out over a couple of beers and a shot, it was a man's game, said the defenders. But was the new obsession with athleticism and muscles leading to excesses like they'd never seen before? 'If we don't stop the brutal way things have been developing in the last few weeks,' wrote Eintracht Braunschweig president Hans Jäcker in a note to his team after the foul on Lienen, 'the spectators are going to think of you as nothing but primitive kickers who should be put in a camp next to the ancient Roman gladiators.'

Then came the World Cup in 1982. Horst Hrubesch ordered 20 fried eggs in a row at Germany's training camp, just to test the cook; the Germans and the Austrians shoved the ball shamelessly back and forth between them, because that way, they were both going to qualify for the second round, and in the semi-final, goalkeeper Harald Schumacher knocked two of Frenchman Patrick Battiston's teeth out miles off the ball as a cross came in, whereupon he declared: 'There's no such thing as sympathy among professionals, but I'll pay for him to have crowns done.' The leading lights of this new generation of German footballers had been born in the mid-to-late 1950s, when the economic miracle was already under way and the wartime rubble had already been cleared away: they were self-confident, they chased success at all costs, and they were completely uninterested in how foreigners might judge them. The big film of the day was *Rambo*.

In his Greek exile, Heinz Höher only heard dimly of the growing clamour about how the Germans played ugly. Here, he was the honoured master of the sport, here he was the good German. He couldn't talk to Dettmar Cramer about this new aggressive style in German football, because Cramer was already off again. Bayer Leverkusen had summoned him to take over their Bundesliga side. Couldn't Bayer have thought about him, too – their very own former star? Heinz Höher brought his family over to Thessaloniki, his job there seemed secure, they had ended his first season as third in the Greek league. It seemed that he'd be able to stay longer at PAOK – and that he'd have to.

They spent their afternoons on the beach and grilled fish, the family were even closer alone here far away, said Doris on the phone to her relatives, but she quietly asked herself, if this was so, why didn't she feel right in her heart of hearts, so far away from home? Heinz Höher wrote goodnight stories for Thomas. They were about Tommo, who was a highly talented nine-year-old from an orphanage who had grown up amid the animals at the city pound, didn't have to go to school, and was to lead the animals to victory in the European Canine Football Championship. 'Now, about the way Tommo could talk to the animals: you mustn't think that he meowed to the cats or grunted to the pigs. Or that the animals could speak to him in his language. The reason that the animals understood Tommo was because of the tone and the power that he put into his voice.'

The football was okay. Or had Heinz Höher forgotten something, had he missed one of those little troubles which grow so rapidly in football and can tear down a whole successful system? Should he have taken it as a vote of censure when club president Mr Pantelakis ordered him to travel to France to watch PAOK opponents in the UEFA Cup? Mr Pantelakis was a hard-working, serious man, with his lips drawn down by his bushy, carefully shaped moustaches. Asking him to go especially to France was just a sign of Pantelakis's conscientious way of doing things, Heinz Höher told himself. He went to Sochaux, to watch their opponents. After he had done so, he found that the train back to the airport at Paris didn't leave until early in the morning, so Heinz Höher, manager of PAOK, at present competing in the UEFA Cup, laid himself down on a train station bench to sleep. They beat Sochaux. No, there was no sign that trouble was about to break out.

In one of the following home games, PAOK played half-heartedly. At the press conference, Heinz Höher defended himself by saying that nobody could win every time. PAOK were still lying fourth. When he went back into the dressing-room, he found the players showered and washed, sitting on the benches.

What are you still doing here, why don't you go home?

Look out of the window.

Beyond the stadium fence, hundreds of fans were waiting, holding their flag-poles like baseball bats.

The fans, Mr Höher, the translator had said, a year before.

A few days later, after the training session, Heinz Höher found a hulking great man waiting for him. He started having a go at the manager in Greek, Heinz Höher understood hardly a word, but he understood everything. Those great, gesticulating paws and those brows drawn together into one big fold of rage said that he didn't like Höher's kind of football and if things didn't get better, Höher would find him waiting for him in his garage.

The hulk came to training every day and sat in the stand, alone, motionless.

Tell you what, said Heinz Höher to Jürgen Köper, the next time he visited his former player in Bochum, can you lend me one of your pistols?

Jürgen Köper gave him a 7.65mm Beretta.

Heinz Höher had never thought how exciting it would be to fire a pistol. The warm resistance of the trigger against his index finger, and then, eyes narrowed, he slowly pulled, feeling the whole tension of his body concentrated in this single movement of that index finger. He carried the weapon around close to his body the whole day.

It had only been a small detour to Bochum because he was staying with PAOK at a training camp in the Sauerland. After seeing Jürgen Köper, he also popped over to Heinz Formann's. The journalist drove him back to his team in the Sauerland. Stop here a sec, said Heinz Höher suddenly, as they passed the city limits sign.

What?

Stop a sec!

Heinz Höher got out of the car, put five bullets through the Bochum city limits sign, and got in again.

On his flight back, the customs men at the airport didn't disturb the gun. It was stashed securely away in his luggage.

At the next training session, Heinz Höher scanned out of the corners of his eyes, trying to find the hulk in the stands. The hulk stayed sitting there when the training session was done. A couple of athletes had started to train, apart from them the stadium was empty. Heinz Höher looked significantly up at the hulk, drew the Beretta from his pocket, and aimed. Under the stand, there hung a tin sign advertising a margarine made out of sunflower oil. Heinz Höher fired into the picture of the sunflower, twice, three times, four times. The metal sign clattered as the bullets slammed through it, the athletics coach and his pupils ran for it. The hulk didn't move. But Heinz Höher thought that he'd got the point.

In his second season with PAOK, they reached the Greek Cup final. They lost it 2-0 to AEK Athens, but that game was enough to establish Heinz Höher's reputation in Greece. Eighteen hours after the final, right out of the blue, he was offered the managership of Olympiakos. Olympiakos had just won the Greek Championship for the fourth time in a row. You didn't say no to Olympiakos. And you had to be prepared to be sacked on the spot if the president found 15 minutes of a game, or a few quotations in the newspapers, not to his taste. In September 1983, in the first round of the European Cup, Heinz Höher's Olympiakos faced an Ajax Amsterdam team that included Ronald Koeman and Marco van Basten – and knocked them out. Dozens of photographers swarmed onto the pitch in the middle of the game to snap double goalscorer Nikos Anastopoulos in the midst of his celebrations and 10,000 voices were united in the club anthem: 'Fame be to your children, Olympiakos, ten thousand times praised in song, renowned in the world, they tremble, when your name resounds, and they can still remember you, Santos and Pelé.' Two months later, Heinz Höher was sacked. Olympiakos were lying only second in the Greek league, behind Panathinaikos.

This sacking came at exactly the right time for Heinz Höher. FC Nuremberg were looking for a manager again.

Wearing red canvas training shoes which had been designed for the Greek summer, he arrived in the snow of Nuremberg. On 1 January 1984 he held his first training session. People like to believe that the new year can be a new beginning. Mid-way through the season, Nuremberg, who held a record nine German titles, had nine points and were lying bottom of the table.

Heinz Höher told the sportswriters that he taken over at Düsseldorf in a similar situation, at a similar point in the season, and had got them out of it. In fact, he'd already realised that Nuremberg weren't Düsseldorf.

At the end of the training sessions, Heinz Höher would sometimes get a game going, and to break the ice he would leave it up to two of the players to choose the teams themselves, like children on the play-ground. Winger Rüdiger Abramczik was often one of the best players in training. And he was always chosen last.

Why does nobody want me? yelled Abramczik.

By way of answer, the others looked at the ground or looked away.

The growth of cliques and problems with integration were new phrases in the football-speak of the early 1980s, as Buying + Selling became a sport of its own within the Bundesliga. Teams who had grown into shape were broken up every summer by the Buying + Selling of players from all four corners of the earth. What remained was usually an inner circle of established players – and the question of how they would accept the newcomers. For with those newcomers came sneaking suspicions: Do they pay that lot more just because they've brought them here from far away? Do these guys just want to cash in? Are they going to drive us out of the team?

For the 1983-84 season, Nuremberg signed ten new players. One of them, Stefan Lottermann, had studied sociology and sport. On the blackboard in the changing room he hung up an article from *Der Spiegel*: 'How Heading the Ball Damages Your Brain'. Two of the other newcomers, Manfred Burgsmüller and Rüdiger Abramczik, preferred making jokes about sexual organs the size of anacondas.

Oh well, we lost again, said Abramczik, who was called Abi, one Monday: So what, I still get my money.

It was just one of Abi's little sayings. But the old hands in the Nuremberg dressing-room, led by Reinhold Hintermaier, didn't get the joke. Was Abi really getting paid as much as he boasted: was he getting paid more than them? Hintermaier or Herbert Heidenreich were often on the subs' bench these days, while Abi shouted before the game: I'm on fire today, I'm going to chew the posts today – and then screwed up his dribble again.

Heinz Höher saw how some players didn't pass to others in the training sessions, how some kicked others, and others still withdrew into themselves. Maybe, in this age of Buying + Selling, a manager had to be a bit of a social worker too? Didn't he at least have to hold the ring to help integrate the newcomers? Heinz Höher just kept the training sessions going, and hoped that the tensions would disappear all by themselves.

Teams with such widely different characters as Abramczik, Lottermann and Hintermaier could work very well indeed; most teams were groups made up of contrasting types, but something had to hold them together, even if it was just the manager's authority – or hatred of him. At Nuremberg, Heinz Höher was the fourth manager in six months. At least his distanced way of doing things didn't stir up any strong reactions from the team, other than one of Abi's little sayings.

One Thursday evening, Heinz Höher came into the Kontiki to have a couple of beers and a shot, and there was Abi, sitting at the bar with one of the younger players, Roland Grahammer, two days before a game. Easy, easy, said Abi to Grahammer, he can't touch us. He needs us, we don't need him.

They charged full ahead into defeat after defeat. In March 1984, with over two months – over a third of the season – still to play, Roland Grahammer imagined he could read the thought-bubble hanging there in the bus as they drove to away games: why do we even bother going there? Club president Gerd Schmelzer took secret refuge in gallows humour so he could still find something to laugh about: Great, if we lose, we save on paying out winners' bonuses.

They lost the last ten games one after the other, a defeat every Saturday for over two months, 6-0, 6-1 or 4-2. With a wretched 14 points, half as many as the fourth-last team, they trundled towards the drop, propping up the table. Heinz Höher looked at his players, Eder, Burgsmüller, Kargus, and felt ashamed: he was taking such class players into relegation. The newspapers called Nuremberg 'the sleeping giant'. And it was you who couldn't kick the giant out of bed, he told himself.

Every day, he arrived at training, expecting to be sacked. Five years earlier, he'd left Bochum behind, to make his way in the world. Since then, he'd managed six different teams, he'd been sacked, he'd been out of work – and now he'd even been relegated. Every day, he went home after training thinking, okay then, I'll be sacked tomorrow.

But Nuremberg president Gerd Schmelzer had other ideas.

The others are training on their own in the woods. Only five Nuremberg players turn out for training under Heinz Höher: (l to r) Fred Klaus, Frank Nitsche, Reiner Geyer, Dieter Eckstein, Rudi Stenzel.

October 1984:

REBELLION!

The grass was still black in the night as Heinz Höher laid down small, orange, plastic cones to set up a running-course stretching around two football pitches. Now and then the training-ground was swept by light from the headlamps of a passing car driving down the Regensburger Straße. The cool of the morning crept up from the damp grass into your body. The weather forecast had promised a golden autumnal day for 29 October 1984, but at 6.30 in the morning, there was already a hint of winter in the biting cold of the air. Heinz Höher lined up his team in the darkness.

Guvnor, there's a mistake in the training schedule, keeper Rudi Kargus had said the day before: it says here Monday, 7am.

That's no mistake, Heinz Höher had said, and shut his lips tight.

He didn't turn on the floodlights. You didn't need to see the ground to run, your feet could find their way by themselves. The players of FC Nuremberg set off. Heinz Höher stayed motionless at the start point. In his hand he held a calendar. One page per day. Each time his players came past him, he tore a page out. He had chosen a month with 31 days. Each lap of the course was 500 or 600m. The only move Heinz Höher made was to tear out the pages from the calendar.

The workday traffic started out up on the Regensburger Straße. Daylight broke through. And still they ran. An hour, Heinz Höher had said. Amid the pack of runners, Roland Grahammer asked himself, has the manager frozen stiff? It occurred to Grahammer that Heinz Höher frequently didn't make a move during training, he'd just stand there on the spot and nobody knew if he was watching or dreaming until he called the session to an end with a blast of his whistle.

Grahammer had made the best of this early start to the morning's training. To avoid having to get up early, he'd stayed in the Leopardo until five in the morning and then driven straight from the discotheque to the training ground on the Valznerweiher.

With every lap, his thoughts grew darker. What was the point of arranging punishment training for 7am? And after all that, we just jog feebly around, thought keeper Rudi Kargus: if Höher really wanted to do something about our continual lack of success, he'd have to really punish us hard. Kargus had played for Hamburg all through the 1970s, including under manager Branko Zebec. Zebec had got them running interval training for an hour and a half, while he sat on a ball on the centre of the pitch and broke a stick to mark each lap. And that hadn't even been punishment, just everyday training. With every lap of the pitch, their thoughts took flight more swiftly than their feet. They couldn't be doing with Höher any longer. There was no guidance any more, just half-baked activities for the sake of it, like jogging about at seven in the morning. And his silences weren't going to get them going, either. Why hadn't the board sacked him straight away when they were relegated five months ago?

Club president Gerd Schmelzer couldn't exactly say why he hadn't sacked Heinz Höher. Often, he was just absolutely convinced about a decision, and this conviction gave him the energy to carry it through. After he'd watched Heinz Höher for some months, and analysed his work, he was convinced that he had an excellent manager here, even if the results didn't yet confirmed this. Once, Schmelzer had sat in the dressing-room at half-time, Nuremberg were behind yet again, and then Heinz Höher grabbed the ball, held it above his head with both hands and shouted: What's that?

Surprised and speechless, the players looked at him.

That's a ball, roared Höher, and flung it so furiously against the ground that it bounced back up and hit the ceiling. So now go out and get it for once! he yelled.

At that moment, Schmelzer could feel what great managers did: they passed on their qualities. He felt that after Höher's half-time pep-talk, he could've raced out onto the pitch himself, full of nervous energy and wild determination.

He just had to keep on supporting his manager patiently, he mustn't wobble, he had to hold to a clear line, and then success would follow, sooner or later. Gerd Schmelzer tried to believe it.

The club president was 33. With his generously cut jackets and the remains of his balding hair growing luxuriantly down over his temples, there was nothing about him that seemed young any more. At 20 years old, he had opened a bar, which he called Gaudimax, and had become the general manager of a few regulars: the Nuremberg handball team. He led them to the first division and got relegated again. He took over a car dealership and, on the side, studied management, he took over a warehouse from a food cannery, found the cellars full of stinking herrings in tins and sour pickled gherkins in jars, and converted the space into a showroom. He came to FC Nuremberg as a jack-of-all-trades and then, after the spontaneous resignation of Michael A. Roth at the end of 1983, he suddenly became club president. Heinz Höher was the first manager he had hired.

Schmelzer was fascinated by him. One time, he said to Höher: Someone at Duisburg told me that you didn't speak to the players for weeks on end.

If the ball's not talking to someone, he doesn't deserve to have me to talk to him either, answered Höher.

Heinz Höher did talk to Gerd Schmelzer. He liked Schmelzer's gaze, he could look at you so calmly.

On Monday morning at 8 o'clock, the physical part of the punishment – that run in the dawn twilight – was followed by the sermon. The president appeared, to tell his team that enough was enough. After their relegation, they were supposed to be starting anew without Abramczik and Hintermaier, and without all the old conflicts. But after seven games of the 1984-85 season, Nuremberg were lying only seventh, even in the Bundesliga 2. The 1-1 draw at home to Oberhausen on 27 October 1984 had been too much for anyone to bear. Nuremberg had given away the draw in the last minute of a miserable game. The defenders had stormed upfield to play Heinz Höher's signature move, the offside-trap-counter. As they did so, they almost ran straight over their own forward, Stefan Lottermann, giving Oberhausen forward Dieter Allig a free run at goal as he chased a long pass from deep. For weeks, Heinz Höher had been waiting for his team to finally master the offside trap! For weeks, team captain Udo Horsmann had been trying to persuade Heinz Höher to finally give up with the offside trap!

After the president had given his speech on that Monday morning, Horsmann asked, in the name of the team, if for once they could talk about the problem from their point of view.

This wasn't the time for discussions, it was the time for them to take a good look at themselves, cried Schmelzer, who felt that in a serious situation like this he had to stand foursquare behind his manager. Now go home!

Rudi Kargus was seething with rage. The manager and the president were blocking every attempt at change, and meanwhile they were sinking into the mediocrity of the Bundesliga 2 with eyes wide open. At 32, Kargus still immersed himself in every single game. Basically, he didn't come up for air all week. He was able to play with his children, or eat dinner with friends, without anyone noticing that he really wasn't there at all, but he was still thinking about the shots he'd saved a few days before, and of the way he'd had to really throw his body in just right to stop the ball. When he held onto a shot, the feel of the ball between his goalkeeper's gloves gave him a physical kind of happiness that few people experience in their life: he could feel the tension of the hard ball between his fingers, and yet the pure beauty of a smooth round ball; he was truly holding his own deeds, his own life's work, in his own hands. He believed that to deserve such moments, a footballer had to live with utter dedication and searing ambition.

At Hamburg, he'd made himself one of the best keepers in the country for nine years, and had been Sepp Maier's stand-in at the 1978 World Cup in Argentina. In his tenth year at Hamburg, he felt the weight of Branko Zebec's critical gaze upon him. The manager treated him in a tight-lipped way that seemed to suggest he despised him. He doesn't trust me, thought Kargus. The fact that Zebec treated all his players like this didn't make any difference. If you make a mistake, he'll kick you out, Rudi Kargus persuaded himself. He began to tremble inwardly. Please God, no crosses, he thought during matches, and when the crosses did come in, he stayed frozen on the goal-line. He started actually making the mistakes which he'd begun thinking about. In his head, he could hear the words hammering away: we're going to lose because of you, it's your fault, all yours.

He could see the story repeating itself at Nuremberg now, though in a less drastic way. After his move from Hamburg to Nuremberg in 1980, he'd played better than ever; people might talk about his performance in the Cup Winners' Cup final of 1977 with Hamburg, but in his own eyes, the game of his life was Nuremberg's 1-0 win over Schalke in October 1982. And then along came Heinz Höher and once again sowed the seeds of doubt in his mind.

Höher sent him over to the second training pitch with assistant manager Fritz Popp. At first, Kargus was happy. Now, in 1984, he was getting the services of something like a dedicated goalkeeping coach; where else would he get that in the Bundesliga? Under Zebec, he'd had to do runs with the rest of the team for weeks on end. In the national team, at the 1978 World Cup, he'd trained with Sepp Maier himself. But what Popp did, what he'd obviously been told to do by Heinz Höher, was hit hundreds of crosses at him. Did the manager think he couldn't cope with crosses?

Now and again, Rudi Kargus thought about going to Höher and saying, please, talk to me, I need to know if you're worried about something, the uncertainty is undermining me and my performance. He always repressed the thought straight away. A professional sorted things out for himself. A professional mustn't show any weakness.

His conversations with Heinz Höher remained one-liners.

Are you scared? Höher asked him, out of the blue, in that first season.

I'm scared we're going to be relegated, answered Rudi Kargus, snappily.

And the manager went his way, silently.

He was a mystery to Kargus. How could he have had any idea that when his manager had to deal with him, Kargus, his European medal winner, who was naturally so very self-confident, he was just as uncertain as Kargus himself?

They could all come to his girlfriend's place, Kargus suggested to his team-mates, after club president Schmelzer had left them feeling powerless that Monday morning after the punitive training session. They had to do something, it couldn't go on like this. Rudi Kargus's girlfriend had opened a café a few weeks before in the Museum of Toys. It was called Dolce Vita. The walls were painted green and white, and breakfast classics were still served at lunchtime. The tables were shoved together and 15 players from FC Nuremberg sat down together to discuss things; only a few of the younger players were missing – they were doing national service.

When the team split up after an hour and a half, it was clear that it was down to the senior players to do something; and no one knew exactly what. Five of them, Udo Horstmann, Rudi Kargus, Stefan Lottermann, Thomas Brunner amd Horst Weyerich stayed on in the café.

At shortly after 5 o'clock, the sports pages of the *Nürnberger Zeitung* were almost laid out and ready; it was Monday, there was nothing going on in the world of sport and if they were lucky, sports editors Wolfgang Haala and Dieter Bracke could soon be going home.

There was a knock on Dieter Bracke's door. He was the senior sports editor, he had his own private office on the fifth floor of the newspaper's publishing house in the Marienstraße. Udo Horstmann, Rudi Kargus, Stefan Lottermann, Thomas Brunner amd Horst Weyerich were standing outside his door. A thought, or more like an instinct, zipped through Bracke's mind: were we so tough on them after that 1-1 draw against Oberhausen that they've come here to complain?

No Bundesliga player had as yet had the notion of making an unsolicited visit to a newspaper editor. But that was just the start of the surprises in store for Dieter Bracke. The footballers had written a document for the paper.

They didn't know who else to turn to. As their captain, Horsmann had three times tried to talk to Heinz Höher himself about the training sessions and that unspeakable offside trap, by now it was obvious that the manager just thought of him as a troublemaker. The club's president was so completely on Höher's side that he wouldn't listen to a word they said. As for the sports director, Manfred Müller, nobody really knew how much of a say he had at the club, but it probably wasn't much. The Nuremberg sports editors themselves seldom came to training sessions, but simply got their copy through telephone calls during the week to the manager and the club president. The Nuremberg team believed that they'd have to write their own press release, to get a hearing. After going to the *Nürnberger Zeitung*, the five emissaries visited the *Nürnberger Nachrichten*.

Wolfgang Haala, who had a good line to the manager, phoned Heinz Höher. He said there was something he had to read to him.

'We, the professional team of 1. FC Nuremberg, dare to take a step before the public with a short statement of our position. This declaration in no way seeks to deny our shared responsibility for the late catastrophic results, especially in the game against Oberhausen.

We would like to draw attention to deficiencies in the following areas:

In the composition of training sessions

- A lack of endurance-training during preparations for the new season (has caused demonstrable vulnerability to injuries)
- An inconsistent training programme, in which shooting-training only took place once last week, and in which sudden power-exercises are undertaken, leading to muscle problems lasting several days. On one occasion there were six training sessions within three days, but then a period of three days with only one training session.

Regarding tactics:

- The manager gives individual players no clear instructions for the match.
- and despite its failures, and despite insufficient preparation and resistance from the team, Heinz Höher insists on playing his offside trap.

Regarding the breakdown in relations between team and manager: Mr Höher often expresses his criticism of performances in a too cynical manner. His uncommunicative manner has led to the loss of all human contact with the team. There is no possible way in which Mr Höher can psychologically nurture the players. We feel ourselves to have been forced into this action because several attempts to discuss the situation with Mr Höher have failed.'

Mr Höher? Are you still there, Mr Höher?
For a moment, the line was silent.
What do you say to that, Mr Höher?
Heinz Höher told Wolfgang Haala that he'd have to chew it over for a bit. He promised to call back later with a statement.

After hanging up, he went to the fridge. He drank back a beer in a few pulls, and began to think.

There'd never been anything like this in the Bundesliga. Players officially denouncing their manager. It was mutiny.

Doris didn't notice that anything out of the ordinary had happened; it was just another one of the chronic states of emergency that she lived with. She didn't think that her life could get any more stressful than this.

Gerd Schmelzer had locked himself into his office to prepare his speech at the club's Annual General Meeting the following Wednesday, when his telephone rang. Klaus Westermayer, sports editor of the *Nürnberger Nachrichten*, bade him good evening. His newspaper had received a communication from the team, he said, did Schmelzer know anything about it? All Gerd Schmelzer knew right then was 'that's a heap of lying crap, and we're not standing for it'.

He was supposed to be a guest this evening on TV Bavaria's *Blickpunkt Sport*. He had to cancel his appearance. He didn't have the number of the programme's presenter, Fritz von Thurn und Taxis. He phoned the porter at TV Bavaria. Oh yeah, so you're Schmelzer and you're the president of FC Nuremberg, are you? Well, anyone can say that, replied the receptionist. After several convolutions, Schmelzer finally got through to Thurn und Taxis. There was a little something going on in Nuremberg that he had to deal with, said Schmelzer.

Then he immediately rang up some of the players who he knew well. Horst Weyerich wasn't at home. The others didn't know anything about the letter.

One of the first questions which zipped through Schmelzer's mind was: could old Roth be behind all this? Michael A. Roth, wholesale dealer in carpets, had resigned as club president ten months before of his own free will, and had brought Schmelzer in as his successor. But that seemed to have been the start of a rivalry between the two men. Who was the authentic, better, finer president of FC Nuremberg? In two days' time, Gerd Schmelzer had to lay everything out for approval at the AGM. Was Roth planning to topple him?

Heinz Höher phoned Wolfgang Haala of the *Nürnberger Nachrichten* back, as he'd promised. 'I can see the way the wind's blowing. This is a rebellion led by players who've got too comfortable, who want to train less hard and less often,' he said, and added that it was certainly Udo Horsmann's idea: he'd been at odds with him for weeks. Horsmann, said Höher, wanted to play a kind of football fit for old men, to hide his own weaknesses. And as for the accusation of not talking to his players enough, he'd told them before the start of the season: 'I'm making things easy for you by not talking much. But the few things I do say, you've got to get them into your heads and use them on the pitch.' When he'd hung up, Heinz Höher felt that there was nothing more that he could do except wait.

On Tuesday morning, Rudi Kargus was on his way to training when he jumped at the sight of his own face. It was standing right there on the front pages of the tabloids in the newspaper kiosk, beside the faces of the other four men who'd signed the letter, like in some Wanted poster. Rebellion at the club! cried the headlines.

When they'd written that letter, they knew they'd be in trouble. But knowing it in theory was one thing, seeing the actual results was something very different.

Centre-half Roland Grahammer read the paper at breakfast and was taken aback. What was this letter they were talking about? No one had said anything about that at the Dolce Vita.

Rudi Kargus wondered what was going on, when he got to the dressing-room. Where were all the others? Only four of the players turned up. The four who had written the letter. The fifth signatory, Thomas Brunner, had called in sick. He said he'd pulled a muscle avoiding a dog when running in the woods.

Sports director Manfred Müller appeared in the dressing-room. He said the four were to go with him today for a run in the woods. To get their heads clear. He'd brought along rain-proof tops from last season as training-wear for the four of them. These tops still carried the logo of ARO, Michael A. Roth's wholesale carpet business. If a newspaper photographer snapped them running in the woods, the four of them would be branded as running in the name of Roth.

Where were the other players?

Club president Gerd Schmelzer had been sitting in his office with vice-president Sven Oberhof and treasurer Peter Karg since 9am. One by one, all the players were called in to report.

Sitting all in a group in the Dolce Vita, they had been absolutely convinced that they were in the right. Standing alone before the officers of the board, most players suddenly saw things in a more nuanced way. They still believed that it was extremely difficult to work together with their manager, but of course, as players they couldn't have a go at the manager in public, that had been a mistake.

Now it was the turn of the four signatories of the letter, who by now – it was hoped – would be so tired after their run in the woods with Manfred Müller that they wouldn't be so bloody-minded. One by one, they stepped before the board.

When Gerd Schmelzer was taking a walk or riding on his bike, that is, when he was relaxed, he often fell into doubts about his judgement, his thoughts took him prisoner, swinging him this way and that. But when a stressful situation demanded a decision of him, he could see things clearly and strategically. He had no plan about what to do with the men who'd written the letter. He just knew that he couldn't give into them. No club could allow decisions like sacking a manager to be dictated to it by the players – never mind in public.

Horst, said Schmelzer. He was on first name terms with Horst Weyerich, they'd often had a beer together. Surely you can see that we can't go on like this, you lot have got to take your accusations back and ask for an apology in the proper manner, then, somehow, we can brush this under the carpet.

But Weyerich crossed his arms. One after the other, they all said that they couldn't take anything back, because everything in the letter was true. Heinz Höher had to change. Or, better still, he had to go. But none of them said it out loud.

The signatories of the letter were excluded from normal training that afternoon. We can't accept that, cried the other players, the moment they entered the dressing-room: those four were speaking for all of us. A couple of them, like Manfred Walz or Detlef Krella, 23 years young, straightened the backs of the men who were hesitating and they once again felt they were standing all together: nobody's getting changed. We're boycotting training in solidarity with the guys who've been sidelined.

Gerd Schmelzer summoned his supporters to a crisis meeting. The AGM was in 28 hours, he couldn't take individual measures that would be thrown back in his face there. Other members of the board, including the honorary president, appeared at the Valznerweiher. Heinz Höher stood there like an alien presence among them. The president's office was too small to hold them all. They decamped to the back room of the Stuhlfauth-Stube, the club's own pub. The kitchen there became the break-out room where secret conversations were whispered.

Gerd, don't feel that you have to stand by me because of our friendship, said Heinz Höher to Schmelzer in there. They'd only been on first-name terms for a few weeks.

The club president would happily have smacked him one. He was – pardon his French – shitting bricks, and here was Heinz playing his little psychological games again, to make himself feel loved and supported.

Gerd Schmelzer acted as though he had not heard this remark.

Throughout the whole business, Heinz Höher never heard the sentence he was longing for his president to say: Whatever happens, you're staying on as my manager.

Beyond the wall of the back room, out in the pub itself, the journalists had been waiting since midday; already over seven hours.

Gerd Schmelzer phoned some of the players again, he phoned the younger players' parents, he dramatised everything, he made it all theatrical, it lessened the tension inside him, somehow. He shouted down the line at Roland Grahammer's dad, Have you really got any idea what your son is getting into if he boycotts training? That's called withdrawing his labour, there'll be a trial at the German Football Union, and that'll be that as far as football goes for him, he'll be banned for life and all just because a pair of lazy old gits who can't stand the pace in training have turned his head, who was it who put him up to this anyway, was it that bastard Horsmann or what?

But nothing changed.

By now, it was Tuesday evening. If the players are sticking to it, we've got to take harder measures, said Gerd Schmelzer to his emergency cabinet. The others nodded. Gerd Schmelzer phoned a certain two telephone numbers once more. He informed Udo Horsmann and Stefan Lottermann that they were being sacked on the spot.

As team captain, Horsmann had necessarily been the spokesman. Lottermann, who was studying for a PhD in sports science, appeared to the board, and to Heinz Höher, as the ideological brain behind the letter. In fact, no one in the team itself felt that any one player was the leader of the pack. Horsmann was respected by almost everyone in the side, he'd won European medals with Bayern in the 1970s and, at 32 years of age, he had a calming way of stepping back from the stresses of everyday life in professional football. Lottermann, 'the Professor' to his team-mates, had frequently drawn inward groans from them as he lectured yet again in the dressing-room – but the technical accusations against Höher hadn't come from him alone; he'd just put into words what the majority of the team felt.

On Wednesday morning, only five players turned up to training. One of them was Dieter Eckstein. He was the only one of them who had straightaway said that if they were going up against the manager, they could count him out. Dieter Eckstein felt that Heinz Höher was *his* manager. So many people had thought he didn't have what it took to be a professional player. Heinz Höher had made him into one.

Heinz Höher walked the muddy path to the training pitch with the usual dozen footballs – but with only five players. He walked on the right-hand side, at some way from the players: with his shy, almost scared gaze, it looked not so much like he was keeping his players at a distance, more like he was trying not to compromise the five players by being too close to them.

The rest of the players trained pointedly alone in the woods near the stadium.

One problem could not be put off: on Friday, that was, in two days, Nuremberg had to play a second division match against Aachen. But with what team?

Rudi Kargus and Gerd Schmelzer agreed that the team and the board should meet at 4pm in the back room of the Stuhlfauth-Stube.

Gerd Schmelzer was already dressed in the black suit and light-green tie which he intended to wear in three hours' time at the AGM. The players came in jeans and jumpers, some of them didn't take off their jackets. Nobody sat down. The board and the team stood facing one another in the back room of the club's own pub. Never mind whatever had gone on, said Schmelzer, he could not permit the players, who were employees of the club, to go to the papers and indirectly demand the manager's head. He said that he'd given the signatories of the letter a chance to apologise and that Thomas Brunner had been the only one of the five to have shown remorse.

Rudi Kargus's gaze rested on the president's shoes. Schmelzer stood up on his toes to the rhythm of his speech, settled himself back on his heels, and stood up on his toes again.

He was asking Rudi Kargus and Horst Weyerich one more time, do you retract your accusations?

We can't do that.

Very well, then the time has come for action. Gerd Schmelzer now gave the floor to Sven Oberhof, his vice-president. Oberhof was a defence lawyer. This time, he was playing judge.

Rudi Kargus, Oberhof thundered out the judgement in his court-trained voice: Dismissed.

Horst Weyerich: Dismissed.

You can't do that, shouted Detlef Krella from the crowd of players, if you do, you'll have to sack us all.

They were only speaking for all of us, cried Manfred Walz.

And you pair are dismissed as well, thundered Oberhof.

The board had planned Oberhof's set-piece as way of deterring the other players. There was a real fear that they would turn up in Aachen on Friday with no team. The spontaneous dismissal of Krella and Walz showed how easily things could get out of hand.

Tomorrow at 10am, said Gerd Schmelzer, they were leaving for Aachen. Anybody who did not turn up would be reported to the German Football Union and could count on a long ban.

The board had decided on an early departure especially so that the players would have as little time as possible to coordinate any new boycotts. Gerd Schmelzer, though, didn't even know if he'd still be club president on Thursday at 10am. He had yet to survive the AGM. How would club members react to the dismissal of the players?

General meetings of Bundesliga clubs were often enough to make you doubt if democracy was really such a great way of running a state. In smoke-filled halls, alcohol and crowd-pleasing speeches whipped the atmosphere up, and a few months afterwards, it was no rare thing for the members to find themselves wondering exactly who they'd elected back then. The president of a Bundesliga club wasn't elected for what he could do, said Michael A. Roth, but for what he promised.

Gerd Schmelzer didn't consider himself a particularly gifted speaker. He told himself that the most important thing was not to give way, that there was no way he was taking back the dismissals, even if a storm of outrage greeted him.

Almost 500 members of the club turned up. Dozens of them had something they wanted to say, anyone could demand their 15 minutes of fame at the lectern during the AGM of a Bundesliga club. A few of the normal members strengthened Schmelzer's resolve, while others expressed their outrage that a real club man like Horst Weyerich could be just chased off into the wilderness like that. But the seas didn't really get choppy. Not until Lutz Combe took the floor. He'd been a member of the board under Roth, and was seated next to Roth in the hall. Horst Weyerich and Rudi Kargus were waiting outside the door, announced Combe. He asked that the club's members allow them to give their version of events.

Ex-president Roth had had nothing to do with the team's open letter, or with their training boycott. But seeing that his successor, Schmelzer, was already in a difficult position, Roth obviously wanted to blow on the flames a bit.

Sven Oberhof, the lawyer, believed he had blocked the attempt when he declared that it was not in accordance with regulations to have players speak, but emotions were running high.

Let Weyerich have his say! He's a real club man! You can't just chuck a man like him out!

Zapf Gebhardt stood up. As a player, he'd won the German Championship with Nuremberg in 1948; as manager, he'd taken them up into the Bundesliga in 1980. Though he was howled down at other Bundesliga clubs for making his players run with medicine balls under their arms, at Nuremberg he was a figurehead. If players were trying to blackmail the club, cried Gebhardt – silence fell upon the hall – that was something you couldn't put up with, they had to go, never mind who they were.

A shout arose. Exactly! Zapf has said it! They're a bunch of scum and gypsies! The individual words got mixed up with one another, but to Gerd Schmelzer, it sounded like rejoicing.

He was confirmed in his office.

Heinz Höher sat at home. He was not permitted to attend the AGM. He was not a voting member of the club. He was still waiting to see how the story would end for him.

They couldn't start the game at the Tivoli Stadium in Aachen. Thousands of spectators were still standing in front of the gates. They'd have to delay kick-off by ten minutes, said one of the Aachen officials to Heinz Höher, who was standing on the touchline with the collar of his puffa-jacket turned up, watching his team warming up. 'You could have told me before!' yelled Höher. 'What am I supposed to do now? Go out there and fetch the players in one by one?' And then he immediately recovered the relaxed attitude which he'd displayed ever since they'd set off on that Thursday morning. Just for one second, he'd let slip how things really stood in his mind.

Every Nuremberg player who was neither injured nor fired had turned up for the departure to Aachen. A lawyer, Peter von Pierer, had been hastily summoned to the Hotel Daucher on Wednesday evening, in order to advise the rebels, who were having their latest – and for the time being, their last – meeting there, that they should absolutely turn up for the game, or face the threat of a substantial claim for damages. Nine professional players now remained at Heinz Höher's service. He made up his team with players from their reserve and youth teams, and named sports director Manfred Müller substitute keeper. The average age of his team was 20.4.

Aachen were top of the table. The floodlights blazed, the stadium was filled with 22,000 fans. We're going to go for it, said Heinz Höher, we're going to attack, we can do this!

And then they ran out onto the pitch. Aachen pushed forward, Nuremberg attacked, the game crackled with intensity. At their finest moments, footballers get a high from their own play. The pace and vehemence which they themselves created spread from the Nurembergers to the Aacheners and back. In the end they went down 2-1 to a goal five minutes from the end. They lay on the pitch, with their eyes filling up, and felt, even if they didn't want to admit it, even if they didn't understand it, that they'd somehow achieved something great in the act of that memorable performance. The club president, wearing a handknitted red-and-white scarf around his neck over his black leather coat, embraced Heinz Höher on the touchline. 'That was the birth of a new team!' cried vice-president Sven Oberhof.

The team bus started off into the night, it was 384km to Nuremberg. At midnight, it was Roland Grahammer's birthday. They bought beer at a motorway service station and in the bus the players and the board sang together: 'One thing, one thing will always remain, FCN will always be there again!' Two days earlier, the team had refused to train under Heinz Höher, six of their team-mates, men with whom they basically still felt solidarity, had been sacked, and now the players celebrated like mad, without really knowing why. It was just the relief that the extraordinary tension of the last few days was gone.

Soon, the defeat of the rebellion at Nuremberg was to become a classic tale of Bundesliga history: it was the first and only time that in a conflict between manager and team, a club didn't sack the manager, but kicked half the team out instead. Yet it's still not really understood that for club president Schmelzer, it actually wasn't a question of manager versus team. 'To us, it was simply a matter of principle: we couldn't allow players to dictate our decisions to us. Heinz annoyed me, to be honest; I was on the point of saying: Right, that's it. He really could have talked more to the players. He always wanted players to be grown-ups, he expected everyone just to function by themselves. He didn't realise that he was making them unsure of themselves by his silences, and by looking at them out of the corners of his eyes.'

Dettmar Cramer, who was still manager at Bayer Leverkusen, and

Michael Meier, general manager of Cologne, offered Heinz Höher young players on loan, as a sign of their solidarity – one of them, an 18-year-old who'd until now played only 12 Bundesliga minutes at Cologne, was a youth by the name of Thomas Häßler. But even as congratulations and declarations of support were coming in from all sides, Heinz Höher felt that nothing had been got through yet, but that the true test was only just beginning. How was he going to achieve any success with a team so young, that had been cut back to the bone?

On the evening before their next game, against Wattenscheid, Heinz Höher and Gerd Schmelzer were playing cards with Dieter Reiber, of the club's board of trustees. They bid up and up without any thought about how much they might lose. Raise you, said Gerd Schmelzer. See you, said Heinz Höher even though he knew he had a weak hand, still driven by the feverish mood of those days of rebellion, days in which it was possible to experience fear and a crazed euphoria in one selfsame moment.

'Shoot!' screamed the fans, and Thomas Brunner shot: Nuremberg's ground on 9 June 1985 after that goal, Heinz Höher in the foreground.

ONLY ONE DIRECTION: FORWARD

Heinz Höher made out that he was deeply hurt by the rebellion, but after a couple of weeks had passed, he had to admit to the following thought: the uprising was the best thing that could've happened to him. The sacking of those six established players had presented him with the team he'd always dreamed of, without him even knowing it.

They gloried in their own youth: for the remaining months of the 1984-85 season, Nuremberg, with an average age of under 22, played with great spirit and small errors, it was youthful football in the best sense of the word, sometimes daring, sometimes careless, but usually with a heady freshness.

Heinz Höher supplied them with the direction that suited them: Forward! Having survived the rebellion, he felt a limitless trust in his own luck. He made a 19-year-old, Hansi Dorfner, into the fulcrum of their pulsating game, he called upon a 23-year-old, Günter Güttler, to take on the captainship, he gave the 18-year-old schoolboy Stefan Reuter the feeling that he was irreplaceable – and he asked himself: Why did you never dare to do this before? Suddenly he saw as clear as day how irrational it had been to play the offside trap with rather ponderous defenders like Horst Weyerich and Udo Horsmann. It was as if he had woken up.

He didn't need to change his own ways. Heinz Höher still preferred to speak a word too few, than a word too many. What had changed was the make-up of the team and, above all, the atmosphere. The young players, eager to learn and enthused by their own new status, didn't question him. And defeats were forgiven, by the public and by the team themselves, given their youth: now, people didn't react by instinctively asking what mistakes the manager had made.

Shortly before this new, young Nuremberg's first game at Aachen, Günter Güttler came to talk to Heinz Höher. Four days earlier, at the Dolce Vita, Güttler, just like the rest of them, had still thought that the solution to their problems would be to sack their manager. At Aachen, and now suddenly Heinz Höher's captain and sweeper at the age of 23, Güttler asked: Guvnor, what do you want us to do about the offside trap?

Let's leave it out, said Heinz Höher – he wanted to oblige his players.

No, let's play it, said Güttler, and to Heinz Höher it could only sound like a declaration of love.

At the end of the first half of the season in December 1984 they were eighth in the table, one place worse than on 29 October when rebellion broke out. But while to be seventh had seemed dreadful back then, to be eighth now looked like a position with good prospects. A young team needed time to develop, said Heinz Höher in December while visiting a fan club in the Rhön area; this season they'd stay stuck mid-table. Next year though, they would be competing for promotion to the Bundesliga.

Then Nuremberg won their first five matches on the trot after the Christmas break.

Thomas Brunner, his pale, wiry body set off by his white v-necked jersey, charged towards the Hessen Kassel goal in the final minute of play in the 1984-85 season. The sense of expectation in the creaking Nuremberg stadium, which dated to 1928, set the 57,000 fans screaming – and set Heinz Höher shivering. If Brunner put the ball into the net, Nuremberg's season, which had started with the rebellion, would end with them going up into the Bundesliga. Heinz Höher stood there, on the touchline, between players who'd been substituted but who were too excited to put on their tracksuits and spectators who'd scaled the fencing without anybody sending them back. Time went out of joint. To many of the fans, the seconds raced by out of sheer excitement; to managers like Heinz Höher, the seconds ticked more slowly by at such moments. The tension made him see things on a different, higher level, in super-sharp focus he saw each individual movement that Brunner made, and he could also see what was bound to happen next.

Brunner's speed sent his hair flowing back, revealing his receding hairline, Kassel's keeper, Hans Wulf, came out to meet him as Thomas Brunner, with the ball at his right foot on the edge of the box, braked.

Of the 11 players who took the field for the club against Hessen Kassel, nine had still been playing reserve team or youth football, or been sitting things out on the subs' bench, just a year before. But in the spring months of 1985 their inexperience seemed to mean only that they'd had no bad experiences as professional footballers yet, so there was nothing to cramp their style. Everyone – the journalists, the fans, even their opponents – were always praising them as a bold and special team. They themselves seriously began to believe it. And that made them play with extra boldness.

Most of them were only just grown up, they still didn't have steady girlfriends and stayed a team in the evenings too: Hansi Dorfner, Roland Grahammer, Stefan Reuter, Fred Klaus and Rainer Geyer recced the night together. At lunchtime they obviously didn't drink beer, but only apple juice or Coke with lemonade. Nowadays, they weren't as unprofessional as the Bundesliga players of the 1970s.

Immersed in the team's benevolent atmosphere, Heinz Höher could experiment away to his heart's desire. In training games, as soon as one team had won the ball, he went sprinting down the touchline. They had to complete the attacking move before he reached the other goal post, that was his rule, it was a way of practising a speedy attacking game, with he himself as a visible, living stopwatch running up and down the touchline. From the pocket of his tracksuit trousers there hung a yellow T-shirt which the worst player had to wear for the next training match. Heinz Höher had had printed upon it the words: 'I don't like scoring'. Things like that, which had seemed weird until October, now seemed charming.

During indoor training in winter, he got the players sprinting from one wall to the other, five times there and back. Then a short pause, and again. When Dieter Eckstein couldn't hack it any more, he was permitted to stop. Heinz Höher didn't allow any other player to do that. But hey, Dieter was the guvnor's favourite, said his team-mates to themselves – and smiled about it, rather than growing jealous.

When Dieter Eckstein, a man without fear in front of the opposing goal, was afraid of the dentist, Heinz Höher decided to deal with the problem. One Wednesday, Eckstein had an appointment with the dentist because of acute pain. He was coming back to Nuremberg by train, after a couple of days off, from his home town of Kehl. Heinz Höher knew that Eckstein would try to get out of going to the dentist. He placed a Nuremberg official as a guard on every way out of the station and he himself watched the rear exit. When he saw Eckstein leaving the station, he came up behind him, laid a hand on his shoulder and said: Dieter, you've got an appointment. Who said a manager had to do a lot of talking to get his ideas across?

An hour into the game against Kassel on 9 June 1985, Dieter Eckstein at last managed to win a little bit of space from the stubborn Kassel defence to score from just outside the box, making it 1-0. Kassel had been leading the Bundesliga 2 for four months. Nuremberg were lying fourth. The top two teams would automatically go up. There was only one point in it between the top four teams. If Nuremberg beat Kassel, they would go up, and Kassel would drop to fourth. If Kassel could hold them to a draw, they would go up, and Nuremberg would stay an unlucky fourth.

The match so far had been ragged with nerves, but once Eckstein put them ahead, it became more fluid, the young side made chances and they wasted chances. With one minute remaining, a counter-attack led to Kassel's Michael Deuerling appearing unopposed in front of Nuremberg's goal. His run-up was long enough for everyone to think, End Of. But Nuremberg keeper Herbert Heider held onto the shot. In the counter-attack that followed, Thomas Brunner broke through.

'Shoot!' screamed hundreds of voices when Brunner, the ball at his right foot, braked at the edge of the box. When a forward's about to shoot, before the fans know whether the goal that will decide everything has been scored, or if it was just that fatal missed chance, there is always a little moment of silence; an absolute absence of all noise that exists only in the head while outside the stadium screams on. Only Thomas Brunner, wrapped in his own concentration, could already see what was going to happen the next instant. He had braked in order to fake a pass to the right, to Günther Güttler, who was racing in support. Wulf, the keeper, bought the dummy to the right, and Brunner went round him to the left.

Thomas Brunner was the only one of the five rebellious letter-witers who was still with them. He had recanted, and for his pains even the board secretly despised him as a turncoat. It was his shot into an empty goal that made it 2-0, securing promotion for Nuremberg.

Hundreds of fans stormed onto the pitch. The ref blew the final whistle even though actually, there were still one or two minutes of injury time left to play. But the game – the promotion – was decided in any case, there was no need to be too fussy about it.

Eleven days previously, 39 spectators had been crushed to death at the final of the European Cup between Liverpool and Juventus, when English hooligans charged a stand full of neutral supporters, causing panic to break out and a wall to collapse. The world of football, including the Bundesliga, could no longer turn a blind eye to violence in the stadiums. On 9 June, the police in Nuremberg had one sole incident to report: a lost car-key.

The promotion celebrations went on for a week. There was always one more invitation Heinz Höher and the players had to accept, always one more bar they wanted to visit. On the very first evening, Heinz Höher was stopped by the police while driving. Have you had anything to drink, asked the policeman. *Anything*, that was a good one. Oh, the policeman suddenly noticed, it's the manager who's just got us promoted. Drive on please, sir.

Old friends from Bochum, like Jürgen and Ingrid Köper, celebrated along with him. They'd come to visit Heinz Höher, they were, for Doris above all, still the Höhers' real home team. At Nuremberg, she wasn't one of the wives any more but the manager's wife, more than 20 years older than the players' wives. Jürgen Köper had finished his playing career at 30, he'd never really been the same after breaking his leg. He retrained as a tax advisor, and when he saw the profits one of his clients was making out of one-armed bandits, he opened up his very own amusement-arcade firm, Megaplay. Bundesliga players of the 1970s like him had been able to lay aside enough money to start second careers as small businessmen, car dealers, ice-rink owners or estate agents. In the papers, though, the talk was only of the ones who'd lost all their money through dodgy property deals or gambling.

During the promotion celebrations in Nuremberg, centre-half Roland Grahammer thought, for once, Heinz is really letting go. Had he been dreaming, or had the manager even joined in as they sang

'Goodbye-ee, second division, goodbye-ee for evermore!' for the thousandth time?

They all agreed that the club had to stay young. 'Just don't ever buy an old player!' said Dieter Eckstein. Youth had been forced upon Heinz Höher and Gerd Schmelzer by the rebellion, but they too both saw it as their own concept, their way ahead.

Until then, being young in a Bundesliga team had meant taking your place at the back of the queue and waiting. At 20, and that was just a year ago, Roland Grahammer had jumped up from the massage-table in the middle of his treatment when Reinhold Hintermaier, the old-established Austrian international, walked into the room. Grahammer had waited like a good boy until Hintermaier was done with his massage, and had then resumed his own session.

The sensational promotion of this young club was seen by the fans, the sports editors, and the Nuremberg players themselves as a triumph over the old, pampered, egotistical professionals. It fitted with the zeitgeist, because ever since the half-hearted performance of the German national side in the World Cup of 1982, people had been complaining about the alienation of the public from the Bundesliga players, who were allegedly interested only in themselves. 'Wages down, arrogance out!' said one of the placards which German fans held up to the national side at their training camp in Gijon during the World Cup of 1982. This was the first generation of footballers who could expect to earn as much as company directors at 23, and who were put up in hotels, rather than in sports-schools. In Gijon, the German internationals bombarded their fans with water-bombs from their hotel windows.

Contrary to the clichéd myth, though, the rebellion at Nuremberg wasn't the work of shameless, self-seeking professionals. The four sacked players were unusually serious professionals, and all of them were to become interesting people with notable CVs. Stefan Lottermann helped bring the German professional players' union into existence. At 40, Udo Horstmann went to Ludwig-Maximilians-University in Munich, where he studied theology, philosophy and German literature, before discovering that his true passion was for wood. He became a cabinet-maker. Horst Weyerich has made his second career as a mentor for handicapped people in Fürth. And on one of those North German winter days when it's not actually raining but you get soaked through simply by the damp of the air, Rudi Kargus shows the way into a shed in the north of Hamburg. The infra-red heating blazes away, and it's still cold. This is where he works. He's an artist, now.

In the oil paintings in the studio, done in the expressionist style, figures hidden behind hoods or scarves turn away from the watcher. As if they're on the run, as if they have to find themselves some place to exist away from the public gaze.

When Rudi Kargus ended his goalkeeping days at 38, he first spent six weeks in his attic building a model railway. It took a couple of years for him to really think that life must go on, that he could begin something new. He became curious about the world that he'd kept locked out as a professional footballer. He started reading the classics like Dostoevsky, and modern masters like Coetzee, he was fascinated by Hispanic authors, by the magic realism of Garcia Márquez and the light-footed imagination of Chirbes. Soon, books covered three walls in his living room. He tried to discover if he might be able to paint, and at the art school at Blankenese in Hamburg he met the lecturer Jens Hasenberg. Hasenberg said he'd never met anyone like him. A man so thoroughly trained.

Kargus accepted any criticism he made, every suggestion on how to improve his work, as if it were a law, or an order, without any resistance, without defending his own work. Hasenberg said it all very warmly, but it was still clear enough for Rudi Kargus to see that his mentor was not just teaching him about art, but also, retrospectively, about himself, about the goalkeeper. In the 1970s and early 1980s, he had been brought up as a Bundesliga professional to do everything in order to succeed, no questions asked. 'If someone had said to me here, if you take these two pills, you'll let in two goals less, I'd have done it.'

It was this – this striving to do anything to succeed – that made them rebel against Heinz Höher, not spite, a wish for power, or destructiveness. One particular scene sticks in Rudi Kargus's memory: Heinz Höher, standing in the dressing-room before a training session, and bidding the players fall silent by his mere presence.

What's the difference between a forward and an offensive midfielder, asked the manager.

Seconds ticked by and no one wanted to speak, no one wanted to be seen as the manager's pet, for that was the worst insult in any Bundesliga team. And the truth was that none of them knew what answer Heinz Höher expected. The difference between a forward and an offensive midfielder?

There's no difference, one of the players said at last.

Heinz Höher stared at him motionlessly and said: let's go train.

'Nowadays, I think that's a fantastic scene,' says Kargus, 'it's like something in the theatre. Now that I've read X thousand novels, I know: a great writer only hints at his messages. But back then, when I was a professional footballer, a lesson like that just went over my head. The way Heinz Höher did things, that introverted and intellectual way, maybe it would've worked with a team made up of psychology students. But then again, they wouldn't have been so good at football.'

How close was Heinz Höher to being kicked out of the place during the rebellion? Would it just have taken a speech by Horst Weyerich, that real club player, at the AGM? It's quite possible that the public, that easily led creature, would immediately have celebrated the rebels as mature, conscientious players and whistleblowers.

Twenty-nine years after the events, the rebellious players smile gently about their attempted coup. Obviously, if you call for a boycott of training, you're going to be punished, says Detlef Krella. The idea of a press-release against the manager was completely amateurish, says Udo Horsmann. Rudi Kargus says that these days, he can certainly better understand some things about the way Heinz Höher acted.

He's preparing for his next exhibition at the KD Art Gallery in Bremen. The exhibition's entitled: 'All will be well'. Compared to other artists, he produces a lot of pictures, it's driven by the feeling that as a late starter who's 60 years old now, he's got to catch up, but it's also that old footballing discipline that's still in him. When he speaks about art, about football, or about the rebellion, his words have a magically unpretentious sound. Rudi Kargus isn't making any attempt to defend himself, or to present himself in a better light, he investigates his memories as though he's just trying to find out how it was, how he was.

Like the other rebels, he's never met Heinz Höher since. Heinz Höher says brusquely that he wouldn't have the slightest interest in meeting them again. He has no idea what they could possibly have to say to each other now.

He's hidden his real feelings about it for almost three decades. Being relegated at Nuremberg paralysed you, you didn't trust yourself to make tough decisions any more, like taking Horsmann and Weyerich out of the defence, you just let it all run; the rebellion gave you back your strength and your spark. The rebellion saved you.

This young Nuremberg team, with players like Dorfner, Reuter, Grahammer and Eckstein, had the same potential as Borussia Mönchengladbach's 1965 side with the striplings Netzer, Heynckes, Vogts and Rupp, said Heinz Höher after their promotion, and he absolutely believed it. With this side, he was going to storm the Bundesliga, euphorically, gracefully, absolutely free of personality clashes. When club president Schmelzer's daughter, Jasmine, was born, captain Günther Güttler brought flowers over to them, in the name of the team.

Family portrait with tennis-socks: Doris, Markus, Thomas, Clemens the dog, Susanne and Heinz Höher in the 1980s.

PLEASE, ENTERTAIN US

They landed in the Bundesliga from out of a clear sky. Before Nuremberg's first game upon returning to the Bundesliga, in August 1985, a squad of paratroopers sailed down into the city stadium. You had to offer an attractive programme of events before the game itself, these days: now, in 1985, no one was going to put up with being entertained only by the usual pre-match youth team game, or by the Ice Cool Brothers wind band playing a march at half-time. If the Bundesliga teams wanted to survive, declared the advertising agencies to the honorary presidents, they had to be more than just football, they had to be good entertainment. The thing was, people had a completely new set of leisure choices compared with ten years before. Inspired by Boris Becker, they went to play tennis; they went dancing in the gigantic discotheques that had opened up on the edges of business parks, even in provincial cities – or they stayed at home in their living-rooms, where commercial TV stations had multiplied the programmes on offer four-fold. After the paratroopers, a squad of girls dressed in guards' uniforms danced into the stadium at Nuremberg. Cheerleaders, people had started calling them.

Erwin Steden, youth coach at Nuremberg's first Bundesliga opponent, Bochum, wrote an angry letter to Cardinal Karl Lehmann, Archbishop of Mainz, concerning the dropping of the youth team game. If Cardinal Lehmann really wanted to do something for youth, as Steden had read in a newspaper interview, the Archbishop should put his weight behind the restoration of youth games before Bundesliga matches! Did he have any idea what a great motivation it was for 12-year-olds to play in front of 20,000 or 30,000 people for once? The Cardinal didn't answer him. Steden didn't understand it: people went to a stadium to see football – so why on earth would a few paratroopers falling out of the skies entertain them more than a pre-match kids' game?

Nuremberg kept flying high for a little while longer. Heinz Höher's newly promoted side just kept on playing as they'd done in division two, fast and free. After five matches, they were second in the Bundesliga.

After their 4-1 away win at Borussia Dortmund on 31 August 1985, Heinz Höher couldn't drive back home with the team. *Das aktuelle Sportstudio* had spontaneously invited him onto the programme. In a TV studio on the Lerchenberg in Mainz, a railway station clock was ticking inexorably forward. On the dot of the third beat of the accompanying jingle, the TV cameras slowly zoomed out from the station clock, bringing the audience into frame. The men in the audience were wearing polo shirts, the women patterned blouses, there was a lot of blue on show, and more yellow. On over half of the front row of the audience, tennis-socks peeped out between shoes and trouser-legs.

Karl Senne, the presenter, didn't take long to wish viewers a good evening because, he said, a day when Boris Becker was playing was a day with a difference in Germany, and on *Das aktuelle Sportstudio* too. Senne was sporting yellow socks to go with his yellow polo shirt. He had casually shoved up the sleeves of his broad-checked suit-jacket.

That Saturday, Becker was playing in the US Open against some New Zealander, Senne didn't bother with the name of his opponent. When Boris Becker was playing, no one cared about his opponent.

They would naturally be reporting on this tennis match against some New Zealander, in Becker's first Grand Slam tournament since his Wimbledon triumph, and so the programme might run a little longer than was planned.

They never ran over by an hour and two minutes any more, as they had done that first time on 24 August 1963, but they almost always did so by five, seven or 12 minutes. Every Monday, there were angry words about it at the Channel 2 editorial conference, and everyone knew that next Saturday, *Das aktuelle Sportstudio* would over-run again. Who was going to stop them? They were *Das Sportstudio*, they got 7.12 million viewers on a balmy August evening which seemed just made to go out and enjoy yourself in the fresh air.

What, and those beginners from commercial television were trying to compete with them for the right to show Bundesliga matches? That wasn't even grotesque, it was laughable. Whatever RTL plus or Sat 1 did, the best thing for Channel 2 was to simply ignore them.

The question which busied the sports editors was this: was tennis going to overtake football as the most popular sport in Germany, thanks to Boris Becker and Steffi Graf? The Bundesliga was still the central plank of *Das aktuelle Sportstudio*, but it was just as important to have many different sports represented on the programme, after all it was called *Sportstudio*, not *Fußballstudio*. Apart from the Bundesliga, the big items of the day were the World Speedway Championship in Manchester, and Boris Becker. Besides Heinz Höher, the studio guests were the American middle-distance runner Mary Decker and the Olympic 800 metre champion from Brazil, Joachim Cruz.

Anybody who was anybody had already been on *Sportstudio*, the Channel 2 sports editors proudly declared over lunch. Apart from the Pope, replied the political editors. So we'll invite the Pope, said Karl Senne.

A few days later, he received a letter from the Vatican in answer to his invitation. John Paul II thanked him for the invitation but regretted to inform him that it was a firm principle of his not to take part in entertainment programmes.

But first, to the Bundesliga, said Karl Senne on 31 August. Every time they tried to begin the programme with athletics or tennis, there were protests. I get home and want to watch football and what do you show? Athletics! complained the Chancellor, Helmut Kohl, on the phone. He was one of the more regular callers to *Sportstudio*. What especially annoyed him was the way the presenters sometimes gave away the result straight away. Why did the presenter say: 'And so to Dortmund, where Borussia had a happy afternoon'? That did away with all the excitement!

Mr Bundeskanzler, 98 per cent of our viewers already know the results.

Well I don't! I work until late on Saturday evenings. I want to reward myself by watching the Bundesliga after a hard day's work. I want it to be exciting.

So that viewers like the Chancellor could at least feel the emotions of the game, despite a lack of excitement, the match reports now ended with a little interview with a footballer or manager, preferably still on the pitch, hair pouring with sweat.

'Thomas Wolter!' cried the commentator, Rolf Töpperwien, after Werder Bremen's 2-0 victory over Hamburg, and, his microphone in hand, he shoved up so close to the Bremen midfielder that the tip of his nose and the fringe of his hair came into frame next to Wolters's own face. 'Your first goal in the Bundesliga, and for it to come in a game like that – how does it feel?'

'You can't describe it, you really can't describe it.'

In the studio, Heinz Höher, wearing a turquoise polo shirt, was already sitting on a white office chair beside Senne, the presenter. 'Yeah,' said Senne, 'when Rolf Töpperwien's commentating, the matches always look great fun. Heinz Höher, is it really such fun, are you guys really so relaxed?'

Rolf Töpperwien was the subject of much discussion both within and outside the Channel 2 sports team: did a commentator really have to communicate the excitement of the game in such a breathless manner? Wasn't the thing that set reporters and journalists apart was their ability to judge things without being carried away by their emotions? The grand question in the cultural and media circles of the 1980s in Germany had now reached *Sportstudio* too: E or S? – that was the question. E stood for entertainment, S for seriousness. In Anglo-Saxon countries it was taken as read that sports reporting, just like novels or plays, should be entertaining *and* serious, and this symbiosis was exactly the idea they'd had when starting up *Das aktuelle Sportstudio*. In Germany though, literary critics insisted, with Prussian stubbornness, on distinguishing between E and S novels. *Das Sportstudio* was viewed with mistrust, in case it should get too entertaining. Being entertaining meant being superficial and uncritical. Yet at the same time it seemed to be completely in the spirit of the times to have a pop-group now and then on *Sportstudio* too. After all, they had paratroopers landing in stadiums, these days.

'And now we turn to the question of the national team. They looked really old in the last three friendlies but when it really matters they've always performed wonderfully,' said Karl Senne, and indicated Heinz Höher with a wave of his hand: 'How do you explain this contradiction?'

Shortly beforehand, Heinz Höher had leaned back in his white office chair and he now remained in this position, steeply reclined.

'If you lose three friendlies, it doesn't mean anything, and that's why we won't get any decent games there in the future either. But what worries me is that Franz Beckenbauer has so many good forwards at his disposal that he's pulled attacking players like Littbarski back into the midfield. It's their defensive mistakes that give away goals to the opposition.'

None of the papers took note of Heinz Höher's criticisms of the national manager, and why would anyone make a big story out of it, after all, it was simply the private, factual opinion of an expert.

'So we're sadly going to have to get used to friendlies no longer having the meaning they once had,' said Karl Senne, then invited Heinz Höher to *Sportstudio*'s famous mock goal and asked one more question. 'Ten years ago, the last time you were with us, Carmen Thomas hoped that you'd have a beautiful child. What's become of that child?'

'That beautiful child plays football for Nuremberg too, now, in the Under-11s. We did want to call him Thomas Carmen. But that wasn't going to work. You can't give a boy Carmen as his second name.'

'How old is the boy now?'

'Ten.'

'Doh! It's ten years since you were here with Carmen Thomas, so of course the boy's ten.' Karl Senne smacked himself on the forehead. 'No brainer!' The audience laughed in appreciation of a presenter who could combine a capital S with a little bit of E.

From the second-place spot, Nuremberg now went vertically downwards. Fifteen games in, they were second from bottom. After their good start they'd only taken one point from the last 20. Winter had come early.

Is Höher for the chop if they lose today? sports editors from other towns had been asking Nuremberg journalists for weeks before every game. No, he's safe, the guys from Nuremberg had always answered, to the astonishment of their colleagues from elsewhere. Club president Schmelzer was deliberately resisting the usual knee-jerk reaction that when things went wrong the manager got sacked. At the end of November 1985, after that one point out of 20, the journalists from Düsseldorf asked their colleagues from Nuremberg before kick-off between the two cities' Bundesliga sides, is Höher for the chop if he doesn't win today? and the Nuremberg football writers answered: hard to say.

Heinz Höher had asked Gerd Schmelzer the same question a couple of days earlier: when am I for the chop?

The tumultuous days of the rebellion and the promotion had made them into friends who thought they could say anything to one another.

You're not for the chop, said Schmelzer. It's only natural for a team as young as ours to have its ups and downs. I don't just look at the results, I watch the matches: the team isn't playing badly, they're sticking to the basic idea of attacking football. We've chosen our path, and that's for you as manager to build up a young team, so we've got to have the patience to see it through. Sticking to your guns is a great thing, in life and in football.

Heinz Höher believed Gerd Schmelzer. But he also knew that there would come a time when a club president could say what he wanted, the sheer power of the facts would be too strong, it would wash the manager overboard. With only one point out of 20, that time was getting near.

Before the game against Düsseldorf, Heinz Höher fled into the more glorious past. He got his son Thomas to put on the videotape that told the story of their promotion. He told himself and his ten-year-old son that he didn't understand video-recorders, at 47 he was too old for modern technology. Agents sent the club videos of potential new signings, and he watched them with Thomas in the living-room, too. Nuremberg did actually sign one player after having seen him on a videotape: the Norwegian forward Jörn Andersen. His agent had filmed the tape and put it together himself. Besides a few flickering clips of matches you also saw Andersen dribbling through slalom-polls on the training-pitch and shooting into an empty goal.

How often had he already watched the video of their promotion? His children knew that whenever there were guests here in the Elbinger Straße, there'd come a time when the conversation turned to their promotion and their dad said: If you fancy, I can show you the video. If the visitors ever failed to get round to that unbelievable promotion, one of the children would remind them that they had a video of it.

Yet again, Heinz Höher watched Thomas Brunner put them 2-0 up againt Hessen Kassel, and watched the pitch disappearing under a sea of fans. In the dressing-room, Roland Grahammer and Hansi Dorfner soaked him in champagne as he told a TV reporter: 'You know, in all the joy of getting promoted, you're already starting to worry again about next season.' He thought that was the way a manager ought to talk. He hadn't seriously been worrying.

Just a quick word, said club president Schmelzer, appearing suddenly at the team meeting in the Hotel Forsthaus in Fürth before the game against Düsseldorf, with that single point from 20 on everybody's minds. Of course what happens today is important, said Schmelzer, but you're better than it looks from our last few results. And Heinz is staying as manager. Good luck, gentlemen.

Gerd Schmelzer liked coming to the training camp. Under all the pretence of relaxation, under the artificial, sleepy atmosphere of the hotel, you could already feel the tension rising before the game. There was something electrifying about it. Only someone who had felt this rising tension could truly experience the joy of a win. Gerd Schmelzer was a Bundesliga club president who would rather have been a player. So he became a president who could seem self-important and distanced in his official capacity, but who was often very close to the team.

Now in his mid-30s, he knew he ought to concentrate on the future of his own company, Alpha, which specialised in redeveloping derelict industrial sites. Being president of a Bundesliga club was something you did at 50 or 60, as an honorary position, when you were a made man. But somehow, he'd got into it. He could see for himself that what kept him there was the addictive sense of being close to the stars, the yearning for fame. At Christmas, he invited the whole team to his home. He laughed at himself for his own pride. 'I think I'll go and walk around the main square in town for half an hour,' he joked with self-deprecation, 'just to have people greet me.'

Schmelzer bought an old castle in Unterbürg, the part of Nuremberg where the houses were bigger and the garden walls higher. He moved into it. Every Sunday, the day after matchday, he left his castle with his wife, who was of the Indonesian aristocracy, and their three children, and went off for lunch back home in Ketteldorf – a little place in Mid-Franconia with 200 inhabitants. There, beyond those few red-tiled roofs, fields and meadows stretched away to the horizon. His father was a cabinet-maker and sacristan of the church. His mother ran their small farm.

On his Sunday drive to Ketteldorf, taking the B14 westwards, deeper and deeper into the countryside, Schmelzer held phone conversations with the four newspapers of Nuremberg. He was one of the first people in Germany to have a car-phone on the new C-Net. It was his duty as president to speak to each one of the four Nuremberg journalists individually, the day after every game. They insisted on their right to exclusive information and quotations. It was absolutely necessary for them to garner quotes from the protagonists and words from the players. After all, everyone already knew how the game had gone, they'd seen it on *Sportschau* or *Sportstudio*: the newspapers had to provide the background story. Heinz Formann did exactly the same in Bochum, splashing after-shave around his neck at midday before going to the Faghera ice-cream parlour, where the Bochum players held court, in his hunt for quotations. A cup of tea, please, said Formann when he got to the Faghera; Antonio, the master ice-cream maker, brought him a whisky in a tea-cup. Lately, the Nuremberg journalists had taken to going regularly to training sessions, to catch the atmosphere.

In 1983, Bayern Munich had been the first Bundesliga club to open a press office with dedicated personnel, and the first important measure taken by their press-chief, Markus Hörwick, had been to persuade journalists from the Munich papers to attend training sessions on a daily basis. He wanted there to be something about Bayern in the papers every day. 'We've got to stop thinking that sporting achievement is what really matters,' said Bayern general manager Uli Hoeneß. 'Sadly, what really matters is the entertainment we deliver. We're an operation working in the entertainment industry.'

Across Germany, half a dozen TV channels and 100 papers carried reports about the Bundesliga every week, but as far as Heinz Höher was concerned, the media world consisted of four journalists. The only football writers he would meet were the ones who wrote for the Nuremberg dailies. They generated all the news about FC Nuremberg. Their stories were then taken up by the news agencies, and papers all over the country took them from the agencies. At the training camp, Heinz Höher played cards with the four football writers, and for away games they were sometimes allowed to travel on the team bus, to save on taxi fares. But when Paule from *Bild Zeitung* or Klaus from *Abendzeitung* started yelling about his possible sacking after getting only one point from 20, it didn't feel like just the voices of two blokes who were always quick to find fault. When that happened, Heinz Höher looked at the newspapers and felt an unbelievable pressure descend upon him, as if there really was an entire, gigantic media world going after him. Seeing a hostile headline in a newspaper, there in black and white, was incredibly tough. Your brain forgot that it was

just one person who'd written that headline, that this was just one article among the hundreds in that paper. Your brain believed that the
whole world would read this one article and accept its opinion as their
own. Wasn't everyone staring at him strangely, somehow?

Their route from the Hotel Forsthaus to the game against
Düsseldorf took them by way of the Graf Stauffenberg Bridge along
the Main-Danube Canal. Heinz Höher looked down at the water. It
was snowing. In his first season at Nuremberg, back when they were
trundling helplessly towards relegation, he'd once thought, on the way
to a home game: What if I stop the bus and jump into the canal? Was
doing a crazy thing like that the only way left to shake the team awake
at last? Despite that solitary point from the last 20, he was miles away
from thoughts like that today. It was still *his* team, his young club, he
believed in their great future. But he also knew that in the Bundesliga,
there were more unfulfilled hopes than there were flakes of snow
falling on the window of the bus.

The stadium looked grim. The spectators were just scattered islands
on the bare cement. On the parts of the terraces that stood deepest in
shadow, the snow was still lying, snow in November, what kind of a
winter was it going to be? Not even 10,000 turned up, even though this
game was, in the martial language of football, a decisive battle:
Nuremberg, lying second-to-bottom, against Düsseldorf, bottom.

Bundesliga crowds were still sinking unstoppably, by now the average gate wasn't even 20,000. The battle against hooliganism had had
one undeniable result: now, they didn't fight in the stadiums any more.
They fought outside them. But no matter what the clubs did to make
visiting a stadium more comfortable, wasn't it a hopeless battle against
the comfy sofa in the living-room? Every Saturday, 18 million people
watched the Bundesliga on TV – three times as many as visited all the
stadiums in an entire year. If the fantasies of the commercial TV gurus
ever came about, if in some distant future they started showing perfectly ordinary Bundesliga games live on TV, everyone would soon be
sitting at home watching games taking place in empty stadiums,
thought Heinz Höher.

After their promotion, Nuremberg's young, enthusiastic side had
seen themselves as an oasis; everyone loved youth, spectators would
pour in. But people in Nuremberg were no more keen than anyone else
to go to football matches in times of snow and defeat.

Twice, the young team took the lead against Düsseldorf. Twice,

Düsseldorf equalised. There were only 16 minutes left. Heinz Höher had been forced to take off his playmaker, Hansi Dorfner. Dorfner had had an operation on his meniscus just two weeks before. He shouldn't have been playing football at all. But of course he had to play, in this decisive battle.

Fear was playing its part in the game, too. Nuremberg's fear of not winning again, Düsseldorf's fear of losing again. Heinz Höher, who the newspapers called an introvert, a man of silence, raged up and down the touchline through the snow. When his team attacked, he ran forward with them, then ran back to defend. He was standing by the corner-flag, when a hand was placed on his shoulder. A draw would suit us both okay, said Düsseldorf club president Peter Förster to him. What on earth was a club president doing on the touchline? In decisive battles, anything was possible. Forget it! yelled Heinz Höher, shook the hand off and kept on shouting, come on, another corner, it's got to work, the way it did in training.

The corner whipped in, Joachim Philipkowski was able to send a header goalwards – but it was no good, the thought cut right through Heinz Höher, it was straight at the keeper. Düsseldorf keeper Jörg Schmadtke was standing there with his legs instinctively spread apart as the header flew towards him, he wanted to be ready to be able to dive in either direction. The ball sailed clean between his open legs into the goal, four minutes from time, for a 3-2 victory. Heinz Höher sank on his knees in the snow.

Nuremberg had to wait until the final day of the season, in spring 1986, before they knew they had definitely avoided the drop. But after the victory over Düsseldorf they were themselves again, a young, highly promising team which couldn't yet always deliver.

The team never arranged to meet up after home games. They didn't need to, they knew that, they'd almost all meet up later anyway at the Warsteiner Stuben, which was run by their physio, Klaus Majora. It was a basic pub. The players brought their parents and siblings along. Now and then, Heinz Höher and Doris would join them. There was nothing forced about the manager joining the young players. He belonged with them.

Actually, thought forward Rudi Stenzel to hinself, it was all no different from playing for Rapid Vilsheim. Just two years before, he'd still been playing for them, a village team from Lower Bavaria, in the district league. At 24, after a single year at Bavarian league club Landshut as a stepping-stone, he'd become a professional at Nuremberg; he hesitated before taking this step, Nuremberg was a long way from Vilsheim, almost 130km. He didn't go until he'd been assured that he could go back at any time to his work as an aircraft technician at the military air-base in Erding. His body wasn't ready for professional training. Some muscle or other, and his tendons, were always in pain. Then you got an injection to stop the pain. After the next game, your tendons and mus-cles were hurting somewhere else. So then you got another injection.

But the great thing about it all, when Rudi Stenzel thought about it, was no different, whether it was playing for Nuremberg in the Bundesliga or playing in the district league: the camaraderie of the team, and the game. He played against Bremen or Cologne exactly the same way as he'd played against Kronwinkel or Adlkofen: he ran from deep, direct at the opposing defence, a swerve, a dummy, and if he did get past them, then came the decision if the best play was a pass to the centre-forward or a run straight at goal. He was revealed as a solid Bundesliga player. He might well have stayed for ever in the district league if it hadn't been for the fact that the club nearby, Landshut, had been threatened with relegation from the senior amateur Bavarian league in 1982 and had gone out to the villages all around in a panic, recruiting anyone who they'd heard might be some use. Stenzel imme-diately became the top scorer in the Bavarian league.

Rudi Stenzel discovered that the most effective move in the Bundesliga was getting a yellow card for your marker. Once he'd been warned, the fear of being sent off meant he stopped trusting himself to go in so hard against a forward, it meant an end to the sliding tackles from behind, where the tackler hit the ball first and then, following through, made a second hit on the forward's Achilles tendon. German markers, thought the Germans, were the best in the world. No one stayed so close to their man, no one slid in so often, so determinedly, with such a feeling for the correct timing. Only Dettmar Cramer asked himself quietly, how are we supposed to play football when our defend-ers are lying on the floor after sliding tackles the whole time? But Dettmar Cramer was already off again, having moved on from Leverkusen to Japan.

In the 1980s, forwards in the Bundesliga reacted to these repeated sliding tackles from behind by screaming. They began making them-selves fall over with loud cries of pain and bodies doubled up, so the referee would feel the foul and pull out that decisive yellow card.

On 21 March 1987, on the A9 from Nuremberg to Munich, it looked as though Heinz Höher and his young team would never walk alone. Thirty thousand Nuremberg fans were driving in a self-created traffic jam to the Bavarian derby against Bayern. The day before, the team had gone ahead on the same stretch of road. We're forever beating Bayern! shouted one of the players on the bus, the others roared, and centre-half Roland Grahammer yelled: We're forever beating blinding Bayern! They were coming off the back of winning ten points from the last ten.

They lost 4-0 to Bayern.

The inconsistency of youth remained. But looking beyond the ups and downs of their daily form, you could make out a continual development. Promoted in 1985, 12th in 1986, ninth in 1987. For the first time in 20 years, Nuremberg once again provided players for Germany's national team, in Dieter Eckstein and Stefan Reuter. Heinz Höher, who was entirely focused on their own progress, didn't notice that his team, with their full-on attacking style, was becoming the pleasant exception in a German game that was getting more and more clodhopping.

Germany prayed at the altar of man-to-man marking. In the 1986 World Cup final against Argentina, manager Beckenbauer sent out seven man-markers. Lothar Matthäus, who could run a game like very few other players, was turned into an über-marker, made to play as a personal shadow for Diego Armando Maradona. 'You lot can't play football anyway,' Beckenbauer told his team with murderous simplicity, 'so you can at least stop the others from playing.'

Beckenbauer, who, at 40, was young for a manager, fought back against the excessive demands made upon him by hitting out suddenly at anyone in range. He'd already told journalists right at the beginning of the tournament that his team were never going to be world champions because Bundesliga sides were 'nothing but old bangers now'.

The German media, all 140 of them, spent the whole seven weeks of the World Cup in Mexico living with the national team in their training camp at Mansion Galinda in Morelia. The German Football Union thought it was a good idea. This was the age of entertainment, after all, they had to offer the media guys something. And Beckenbauer and his players did indeed offer them something, though perhaps not exactly in the manner which the German Football Union had intended.

Keeper Toni Schumacher and captain Karlheinz Rummenigge seemed to be having a duel to establish who was the fairest in the land.

From the hotel rooms of some of the national team, prostitutes were unceremoniously kicked out after finishing their work, and all of a sudden the journalists were writing about all these things, which were surely private matters.

Heinz Höher slept through most of it. The difference in time-zones meant that many World Cup games in Mexico took place when it was night in Europe. He had no intention of wrecking his night's sleep for the sake of a few football matches, even if those few football matches were at the World Cup. He'd always held that getting enough sleep was one of the most important things in life.

But was there any truth in Beckenbauer's harsh claim that the Bundesliga was about the same quality as a heap of scrap?

There was no doubt that a calculating, physical style of play had taken over. Bayern were the great exponents of a game designed to lull opponents to sleep. Patiently, they passed the ball around the defence and midfield, sideways and backwards, tempting the opponents out and then suddenly hitting them. When Bundesliga teams failed yet again in Europe, as they'd habitually done since 1984, the Germans beat their breasts in short outbursts of self-hatred about their safety-first football. But then, come Saturday it was the Bundesliga again, the Germans were back among themselves, and all their reservations were forgotten. Everyone talked about how they had to deliver grand entertainment. But only a very few of them, like Heinz Höher's Nuremberg, trusted themselves to play an entertaining, attacking style of football.

Bayern won the German Championship three times in a row between 1985 and 1987 with their hyper-controlled football. With ten titles, they now replaced Nuremberg as record-holders. Apart from a single drought in the years immediately after Beckenbauer's retirement, Bayern had been the top club in the country, with no rival, not even Borussia Mönchengladbach or Hamburg, able to compete with them for more than a couple of years. Gerd Schmelzer told Heinz Höher that Bayern owed it all to an epochal lucky break: the ultra-modern Olympic Stadium in Munich, with its 78,000 seats, had fallen into their laps at the same time as they found an extraordinary generation of players in Meier, Beckenbauer and Müller – and right at the time that the giant Italian and Spanish clubs had been prevented from signing foreign players by their own national rules. This had provided the financial and sporting rock on which Bayern had been able to rebuild itself successfully again and again.

If only he could convince the city and the regional goverment to completely rebuild the stadium in Nuremberg, said Schmelzer, they too could make history with this talented team. Especially now that TV was promising a nice increase in their income. RTL plus was offering 20.5 million marks a season for the broadcasting rights to the Bundesliga, more than double what the public television companies had paid up till now, they must be nuts! Every club would get a good million out of it – enough for Nuremberg to pay four decent new players.

On Sundays, after the games, Gerd Schmelzer and Heinz Höher would take a walk in Unterbürg, along the banks of the river Pegnitz, and make plans.

We just need to strengthen ourselves in two or three positions, and we'll be competing for the championship, said Höher.

Back in the 1970s, at a meeting of Bundesliga managers, he'd bet his old colleagues Otto Rehhagel and Erich Ribbeck which of them would take a team to the championship by 50. Now they were all 49. After years going from club to club, Rehhagel had finally managed to settle down as manager at Werder Bremen. He'd been there since 1981. Not that it had done much for his manners. He still liked to act up. When Nuremberg were playing at Bremen in 1986, Rehhagel stood on the touchline and stuck his foot out into the pitch to foul Rudi Stenzel as he dribbled by. He said to Schmelzer: Höher! Why d'you bother with him?

Otto Rehhagel wasn't going to lose his rough edges or stop going over the top, not now, but Otto was okay really, thought Heinz Höher to himself. More or less, anyway.

At Bremen, Rehhagel had been snapping at Bayern's heels for years, he was getting close to that championship by 50. Well, Heinz Höher just had to keep quiet and stick at it with Nuremberg, maybe he'd still be the first of them to win the championship, at 51 or 52.

People often say of footballers: he's at the peak of his career. No one ever says that about managers. But a manager has form, too. He has years when great ideas suddenly come to him and his team accept them as great ideas. Between 1985 and 1988, Heinz Höher was working at a new level. Against weaker teams, he played with the sweeper in front of the defence. He perfected his innovations in training. They played indoor football with a tennis ball, they played three against three with four goals and a score only counted if the attacking team outnumbered the defenders in front of goal. No one yet used the terms *reaction-time* or *switching play* but Heinz Höher was already training them. He put together a coaching team like no other club had, with a conditioning coach, a sprint coach and a coach for gymnastics and power-training. He made sports director Manfred Müller into a goal-keeping coach. They didn't need a sports director anyway, the president and him would make their decisions alone. The one thing Heinz Höher absolutely refused was an assistant manager. He could delegate, but he couldn't work with someone else. The good thing was that he knew it himself.

Gerd Schmelzer thought to himself: Heinz can rely on his genius. But he doesn't make it easy for people.

In 1986 they signed a new keeper from the second division, Andreas Köpke, and after a single game, at Bremen, Heinz Höher was already threatening, I'll chuck him out, that Köpke's driving me crazy: he punches every cross away, instead of catching it!

Heinz, now, hold on a minute, he's just gone through relegation from the second division with Hertha, he just needs to find his feet, Schmelzer told him. Everyone thought that Andreas Köpke did spec-tacularly well in his first Bundesliga year. Heinz Höher thought, he's still fisting every cross! He signed up the talented 20-year-old Bodo Illgner, Cologne's substitute keeper, as a successor. Then Cologne's first-choice keeper, Toni Schumacher, became a writer. In his best-selling book, *Kick Off*, he presented dozens of colleagues and officials as pricks, offered insights into modern ways of doping in the Bundesliga ('I assume that these special mixes included anabolic steroids, amphetamines and various other uppers') and in consequence, he was dropped by Cologne. So now Cologne desperately wanted to hang on to Illgner. But he'd already signed to Nuremberg. Cologne paid Nuremberg 100,000 marks to sign a player who was still actually at Cologne. And Andreas Köpke, freed from the shadow of his sup-posed successor, became a goalkeeping legend to Nurembergers. He could punch crosses 20 metres clear, raved his fans.

The club continued to move forward on its course, both in terms of its play and in terms of its position in the table. The 1987-88 season was Heinz Höher's fifth in charge at Nuremberg, no manager had ever lasted that long there, and in that season they joined the title-chasing group of clubs. They had got too strong for their own good. Bayern Munich began to cast a very careful eye on what made Nuremberg so strong.

Stefan Reuter and Roland Grahammer have had offers from Bayern, reported Nuremberg butcher Werner Weiß to Gerd Schmelzer in January 1988. Weiß ought to know. He was partner in a sausage-factory with Bayern general manager Uli Hoeneß.

All of a sudden, Heinz Höher felt infinitely weary. He saw all his work tumbling down around him. Taking Reuter and Grahammer away would be tearing the backbone out of his team. And over the next two seasons, their stadium was being renovated, they'd be playing for two years on a building site, in a ruin, he'd already been through that at Bochum. He didn't think he had the strength to start from scratch all over again.

It wasn't the first time he'd felt this sudden, physical sense of emptiness when things went badly wrong. As far as he knew, there was no actual scientific or medical term for it, even though psychology was a big thing in German sport ever since Boris Becker declared that he won his games through mental superiority. But mental tiredness was simply weakness, nothing more. And to get over that, Heinz Höher just had to have four beers and a couple of shots, and act as though nothing was the matter.

In the second half of the 1988 season, he managed to act the part well in front of his team. When he was on the training-ground, when the ball was in motion, his professional interest kicked in, and usually his instinctive passion as well. The team was still flying, now as a mature side in fourth or fifth place in the Bundesliga, on their way to a European competition for the first time in 20 years. But when the training session was over, or the next game won, waves of melancholy washed Heinz Höher's mind, and his whole body, empty. Without Reuter and Grahammer it would all make no sense any more. He didn't know how to describe it: an absolute lack of any life or energy hung on him like a lead weight.

Gerd, I want out. Say this is a tower with 100 steps, well, we're on the 90th step. I just can't face going back down to the 20th step and start clawing our way up again right from the start.

Gerd Schmelzer tried to persuade him to carry on. That evening he said, just sleep on it, and by the next morning he'd already found a new argument: Heinz, think what it'll be like if we get into the UEFA Cup, and when the new stadium's finished. Heinz Höher shook his head. Right, thought the president to himself, I'll talk to him again tomorrow.

Meanwhile, other and more powerful clubs were also deciding the future of FC Nuremberg. Which talented players would they rip from the team? Roland Grahammer, who didn't just mark his man, but ground him down, was sought after not only by Bayern but also by Cologne, Bayer Leverkusen and Borussia Dortmund. Cologne's young manager, Christoph Daum, met him three times in the attempt to win him over.

Like very many Bundesliga players, Roland Grahammer didn't have an agent. Almost four decades after Raymond Schwab made Germany aware that there was such a job as a footballer's agent, there were probably no more than two dozen agents who lived exclusively from this work. It wasn't easy to make a steady income as a players' agent. Many clubs simply didn't pay any commission, old-school managers like Horst Heese immediately banished even established agents like Holger Klemme if they didn't play the game absolutely straight, and in any case, how often did you hear of transfers over 25,000 marks?

If a club wanted a player on their books, they phoned him up. Roland Grahammer brought his father, who was an official in the Augsburg city council, along to negotiations. After all, you knew that if Cologne, Leverkusen or Bayern put an offer on the table, it was all going to be above board. What deals needed doing there?

Amid all the tempting proposals, Grahammer had this irritating feeling that one offer was missing. Why weren't Nuremberg, his own club, talking with him about extending his contract? Did they need the money from the sale so badly that they'd be happy to see him go?

It was only in March 1988, by which time Grahammer and Reuter had already decided in principle on Bayern, that Gerd Schmelzer said to Heinz Höher: About Reuter and Grahammer. He said he had an idea about that. Heinz Höher listened, and smiled. The smile slowly spread over his face and stayed there a good while.

As arranged with Schmelzer, one day soon afterwards, he visited Stefan Reuter at his home. At 21, Reuter was already an experienced Bundesliga player, thanks to Heinz Höher's early furthering of his career; in Nuremberg, he lived in a footballers' pad he shared with Martin Schneider, another youngster. Reuter's real home was still his parents' house in Dinkelsbühl. Heinz Höher brought his wife and Thomas along. They were going on a little trip. Dinkelsbühl was supposed to have a wonderful mediaeval town centre.

At the Reuters' dining-table in Dinkelsbühl, Heinz Höher said that he wanted to bring Nuremberg's official offer of an extended contract for Stefan. Stefan Reuter's parents and half Heinz Höher's family were sitting there. Stefan was *the* player for his team, said Heinz Höher, and so Gerd Schmelzer and he had decided to double Stefan's salary to 500,000 marks a year just as his basic pay, and he laid a draft contract on the table in front of Stefan Reuter.

Even Bayern had only offered 400,000.

At 21, Reuter had boyishly rosy cheeks. Even when he was playing with absolute concentration – he was a thrillingly fast player with a velvet-smooth pass, who could fill any one of five or six positions – his face seemed to shine, somehow. He was very flattered by the offer, said Stefan Reuter, but he'd already given his word to Bayern.

That was a blow, said Heinz Höher, yeah if that was the way things were, then he didn't want to stay any longer either, he'd be leaving Nuremberg too.

Thomas started to cry. He didn't want to but he couldn't help himself, he was 13. He didn't want to leave Nuremberg, he didn't want to lose his idol, Reuter.

The Höhers said goodbye to the Reuters in an atmosphere of gloom. They didn't bother with that walk through the old town.

Heinz Höher didn't admit it either to his wife or Thomas, but he'd only been using them as extras in a theatrical scene. Even before setting out for Dinkelsbühl, he'd known that Reuter was going to Bayern. Nuremberg would have had to be mad to actually pay Stefan Reuter half a million a year! Heinz Höher had only put that offer on the table to bump up the transfer fee. The salary that the selling club was offering the player was an important weight in the scales if the clubs themselves couldn't agree on the transfer fee, meaning that the German Football Union stepped in and set it for them.

A few days afterwards, Roland Grahammer received a recorded letter. At first, he didn't even want to open it because he guessed what it would say. He'd signed for Bayern a week earlier. The letter contained a contractual offer from Nuremberg for an annual salary of 500,000 marks.

Nuremberg didn't see the point of really fighting for Reuter and Grahammer and actually offering them genuine contracts months earlier. If Bayern waved to a player, the player went to Bayern: in the 1980s that was accepted as a law of nature in the Bundesliga.

One last time, Gerd Schmelzer asked Heinz Höher in vain, you've got to stay. He'd already got his next question ready. What if we make you general manager next year, Heinz?

'A general manager like Uli Hoeneß' was the exact wording of the job description whenever a Bundesliga club advertised such a post or created it anew. In ten years, Hoeneß had developed Bayern into the Bundesliga's sole real brand. He'd increased their income from 12 million marks in 1979 to almost 30 million, meaning that the team didn't have to play 29 friendlies all over the world, as they still had to do in 1983, to plug the financial holes. Bayern advertised lorries and invited their most free-spending guests to a special room in the Olympic Stadium after matches, to meet the players over a buffet. Bayern also sold bed-linen with the team's coat of arms. Merchandising, Hoeneß taught the Germans, that's what they called it in America.

Bayern Munich had become the only club which interested the whole country. Anyone who doesn't love us, should at least hate us, was Hoeneß's publicity strategy. Hoeneß found the right man in Bayern's great manager of the 1980s, Udo Lattek: Lattek kept the stories coming, without caring whether they were good or bad.

Two days before an away game against their closest rival, Werder Bremen, Lattek summoned his team to the Kreitmar pub in Keferloh, a place where Munich seemed to consist of nothing more than woodland and meadows. He told them to have a decent drink there. And of course, the press-photographers were invited along. Bremen would look at the papers and see that Bayern were so unafraid of them that they even went drinking two days before the match. Next day, Lattek made sure his team were feeling deeply guilty. You all got pissed yesterday, the whole world saw it in the papers, so now you've got to work even harder at Bremen: you've had your fun, now get out and run!

Lattek had a go at Bremen's manager: 'Rehhagel, he's off his rocker!' Uli Hoeneß backed him up, accusing Bremen's general manager Willi Lemke of being a demagogue who had taught him how to hate.

That was how to knock the opposition off balance, thought Hoeneß, that was the way to get your own team fired up. That was the way you offered great entertainment.

Heinz Höher couldn't be like that, and didn't want to be like that. You don't have to, Gerd Schmelzer reassured him. He said that he'd give the sound-bites for him.

Heinz Höher's family were confused by him. What was he going to do, go as manager to another club, stay as general manager in

Nuremberg or maybe just keep on managing the club? What was he going to do to them, was he going to force them to move house or let them keep their home in Nuremberg, where they were happy? He didn't involve Doris and the children in his decisions, he was unable to speak about it, even when Thomas asked him, with the innocent inquisitiveness of a 13-year-old, are you staying at the club? How did people do that, talk about their feelings, express their thoughts? Heinz Höher had always felt that his words sounded false before he'd even spoken them.

In the middle of March 1988, Thomas went with a friend of his sister to the ice-hockey stadium at Nuremberg to watch a game. The tannoy announced that they had some hot-off-the-press news for every football fan: Heinz Höher is to be general manager at FC Nuremberg! The ice-hockey stadium rejoiced. Thomas, like 4000 ice hockey fans, had learnt of his father's plans over the PA.

Heinz Höher told the sports writers: 'I've been toying for a long time with the idea of switching to general manager.' In fact, he was still asking himself if it was the right move for him, even after he'd agreed it with Gerd Schmelzer. He'd been a manager for 18 years, and he'd put his heart and soul into it. A secret thought was growing in his mind: he'd sneak away and hide in the general manager's office for the two or three difficult years ahead, while the stadium was being rebuilt and the team reconstructed, and make his comeback as manager at Nuremberg; at some stage or other there'd always be a change of manager.

Gerd Schmelzer let him choose his own successor. Still as manager at Nuremberg, Heinz Höher led negotiations in 1988 to bring Bochum manager Hermann Gerland smoothly in to take over from him. He'd managed Gerland as a player in the 1970s at Bochum. He was, thought Höher, a manager who was technically competent, and with absolute human integrity.

FC Nuremberg now took on two parallel lives. On the surface, they went into the final phase of the 1987-88 Bundesliga season as a team enthusiastically trying to assure themselves a place in the UEFA Cup. At the same time, much of the team, as well as the manager and the president, were haunted by a growing feeling that their great days were coming to an end before they'd reached their peak. Without Reuter and Grahammer, their stadium overshadowed by the builders' cranes and no longer secure in their long-established manager, everything seemed to suggest that next season could only bring a feeble decline from their high-flying ambitions.

In the evenings, the players still went out in large groups. But suddenly, the papers were making vague suggestions about them being out of condition, and the spectators groaned at every mis-hit pass. Ever since it had become known that Reuter and Grahammer were off, people no longer saw the team as their lads with that famous camaraderie, but as well-paid professionals who spent too much time hanging around in bars like the Kontiki or the Central, and who would jump at the first chance to leg it to bloody Bayern.

Gerd Schmelzer started to worry that neither the team nor he would survive the sale of Reuter and Grahammer. A Bundesliga club couldn't sell its iconic players, but what could he do?

Gerd Schmelzer, and Heinz Höher too, showed that they'd quickly learned a few things from Uli Hoeneß. As a lightning-conductor for the fans' anger, they built up the idea of a great enemy – Uli Hoeneß in person. 'Our dear neighbours really haven't been happy with our success,' said Heinz Höher, 'especially not Uli Hoeneß. He really doesn't seem to like the idea that some day or other, we might have contended for the championship. So Bayern gave me one in the eye in by taking Reuter and Grahammer from us.' Gerd Schmelzer even waxed somewhat poetic about it: 'Hoeneß once said: "Nuremberg is my second favourite club." And what has he done to his second favourite club? Plucked it like a goose. And now he's sleeping safe and sound in its feathers.'

There was a real pain in these words. There was no need for them to mention that the pain had been salved by a fat payment. Bayern paid 5.8 million marks for those two players: and they had to pay it because Schmelzer and Höher had bumped up the transfer fee with those belated contract offers. It was almost as much money as the club took in an entire season.

Confusion crept into minds at FC Nuremberg. The sneaking suspicion that these were the last of their great days, and vertigo when they looked at how high they'd climbed, began to intrude into Nuremberg's play. In their penultimate home game of the 1987-88 season, the club, suddenly looking old, lost to Hannover, and the following Saturday they went down again to Karlsruhe. Were they blowing the chance of European football now, too? Since Christmas, they'd never stood lower than fifth in the table. At Karlsruhe, their international, Dieter Eckstein, added insult to injury in the first half by getting his fourth yellow card, meaning he'd be banned for their final home game against Kaiserslautern. That's the final straw, was Heinz Höher's first thought, without Eckes up front we just can't do it. Then he had an idea.

At half-time, he said to Dieter Eckstein: 'Eckes, in the second half, get yourself a red card for something petty, kick the ball away, but whatever you do, don't insult the ref, just do what I tell you and I'll explain later.'

A good 75 minutes had been played when the whistle blew for a perfectly normal free kick against Nuremberg, and Dieter Eckstein belted the ball away. But referee Werner Föckler gave him only a warning. So, 11 minutes from time, Eckstein had to whack the ball into the stand again in apparent fury over a decision, so that Föckler would give him a red card for unsporting behaviour. Captain Stefan Reuter and keeper Andreas Köpke besieged Föckler, they seemed genuinely horrified at the sending-off. Heinz Höher clapped Eckstein on the shoulder – in consolation, so the journalists thought.

If a Bundesliga player got a fourth yellow card, like Eckstein was shown at Karlsruhe, he was automatically banned for one game. But for a red card, on the other hand, the punishment was decided on an individual basis by the disciplinary committee of the German Football Union. They only handed down a financial penalty to Eckstein for his red card at Karlsruhe. Kicking the ball away was a petty offence, stuff like that happened in the heat of the game. Heinz Höher had seen this loophole in the disciplinary system a few months earlier.

In the decisive game against Kaiserslautern, Dieter Eckstein put them 1-0 up after 12 minutes. It was a good hour and a half before radio commentator Günther Koch shouted 'Nuremberg say hello to Europe!' The club had assured themselves fifth place with a nervy 3-2 win. They were in the UEFA Cup. The pleasure was real. It was just that Heinz Höher's embraces with Reuter and Grahammer went on a bit too long.

Roland Grahammer often asked himself what he'd have done if Nuremberg had really fought to keep him. Of course, it was hard to resist if Bayern were calling you, and he'd have probably gone to Munich anyway. But what if Nuremberg had made him a better offer long before Bayern came on the scene? 'I think I'd have stayed. Nuremberg was my club, my team. As soon as a game started we'd be straight at them, going forward right from the off, we tackled and we played until our opponents could hear it loud and clear: "Hello, this is Nuremberg calling!" And in the evenings, the city belonged to us.' Roland Grahammer lowers his voice: 'There'll never be another team like it.'

To celebrate qualifying for the UEFA Cup, a marquee had been built behind the main stand for the last home game of the season against Kaiserslautern. Anyone of the 20,000 fans who wanted to go in, anyone who could fit in after the win, was allowed in. The oxygen content of the air was approximately zero per cent, but at least that kept the temperature up. It smelled of every kind of bodily exhalation. Here, Stefan Reuter and Roland Grahammer were to receive a send-off complete with flowers. After all, a Bundesliga club was still just a regular sports club, where formalities such as saying farewell to worthy colleagues were done just as they always had been.

Reuter and Grahammer stood there with their flowers at the front of the stage in the marquee. We'll all catch Bayern with their lederhosen down! roared everybody. Reuter and Grahammer managed a sickly smile. Vice-president Sven Oberhof took the microphone in his hand: We wish you every happiness at Bayern – and next year we're going to beat you and Bayern too!

Reuter and Grahammer left the marquee. The fans showered them in beer-mugs and bratwurst with mustard. Heinz Höher strode onto the stage. His shirt, opened to the third button, was sticking to his body. In his hair, he wore a thick red and white drawstring taken from a fan's fancy-dress monk's habit. Later, in the black-and-white press photos, that woven cord looked like a modern-art version of a laurel wreath. 'Thank you Höher!' they all sang. Heinz Höher raised his hand in greeting. He was too happy to think that people who were singing your praises one minute could be throwing beer mugs at you the next.

'I liked the way Gerd Schmelzer looked at you. His gaze was so calm.' Heinz Höher with his president at Nuremberg.

The End of the 1980s:

THE RIGHT MAN IN THE WRONG JOB

So as to be a proper general manager, he bought himself a notebook. With this notebook under his arm, he would walk the golf course, talking to possible sponsors. When the conversation demanded, he would open up the notebook and show the businessmen a list of what the club's players were worth, or note down any ideas or demands the businessmen might have. He showed the notebook to Gerd Schmelzer, he'd chosen a red one, red being the colour of FC Nuremberg, with hardback cardboard covers. Gerd Schmelzer looked at him, calmly as ever. But something in his president's widened pupils told Heinz Höher that when he envisioned the work of a general manager in the Bundesliga as a life of golf-courses, sponsors and notebooks, he might have got it wrong.

The notebook disappeared into his top drawer. A press photographer came along and photographed him at his desk. He asked him to hold the telephone to his ear. The photographer said his goodbyes, and the telephone hardly ever rang.

Gerd Schmelzer and he had discussed the sort of things he was going to do as general manager of the club: he was to set up a network of scouts and start a residential school for the youth team. Why did they need a network of scouts, thought Heinz Höher to himself, they had their own eyes, didn't they, and contacts who could discover new talent.

And before they could start up a residential school, they'd have to finish the renovation of the stadium and the club grounds. Heinz Höher, general manager of FC Nuremberg, read the papers in his office and went to watch the training.

About ten years ago he'd bet Otto Rehhagel and Erich Ribbeck which of them would be German champions first. Well, now Otto had actually gone and done it, smack on 50, at Werder Bremen. And he himself wasn't even a manager any more.

Heinz Höher watched Hermann Gerland training them. All he saw was the things he'd have done differently.

But surely, he must've known what to expect from Gerland, said Gerd Schmelzer, taken aback. He'd chosen Gerland himself, after all. Yeah, of course, said Heinz Höher. The 'but' that should have come next, he kept in his own head. But he hadn't considered that every manager had his own ideas, even one who'd played under him for seven years at Bochum. He hadn't been able to imagine how unbearable it would be, to have to watch someone else taking training.

What he'd like best of all, dreamed Heinz Höher, would be to train a team of kids, to go with them every step of the way, year after year, to protect them, to mould them, to make them into professionals. Instead, his friend Dieter Reiber was sending him recommendations about hotels for the team at their UEFA Cup game in Rome. For the first time in 20 years, the club was playing in a European competition and their very first game was against Roma, what a match, it was he who had taken the team there – and now his job was to worry about their accommodation! He waved Reiber's suggestions through without a second thought.

On matchdays he prowled around the catacombs of the stadium, or stalked along the running track while the manager got the team warmed up. During the game, he sat beside Hermann Gerland on the substitutes' bench. The journalists, those newcomers from RTL plus with their brass cheek, were starting to ask: who's really the manager in Nuremberg's dugout?

Really, he should have retreated into the stand, so as not to undermine Gerland's authority and put a stop to the eternal questioning. He told the journalists: 'I can't sit in the stand, I wouldn't be able to bear it, sitting there surrounded by the crap some people talk there. I need to sit pitchside.' He couldn't tell them the truth. The lens-makers Reflecta were paying him 25,000 marks to be there sitting on the subs' bench during games, with their logo on the collar of his jacket, right in front of the cameras. The questioning went on. Is Höher putting a spanner in Gerland's work?

Heinz Höher called Hermann Gerland 'Hermann'; Hermann Gerland called Heinz Höher 'Mr Höher'. Gerland had been 18 when Heinz Höher took over as manager at Bochum in 1972. Back then, club president Ottokar Wüst wanted to introduce Gerland to professional football by way of their reserve team. Gerland, just 18 years old, refused. He wanted to go straight into the professional team, or he wanted out. With Hermann Gerland, it was hard to tell the difference between iron will and sheer bloody-mindedness. Heinz Höher liked that. In training games, the young Gerland always chose to go up against the best opponent, Vim Lameck. Against Lameck, he hardly ever saw the ball. But it made him feel that he was running the hardest, fighting the hardest, training the hardest. Hermann Gerland was never the most graceful player on the ball, but his own experience told him that work and ambition could make up for many deficiencies. He played on even when he was injured. He expected the same from other people: absolute commitment. At 29, by now an established Bochum first-teamer, he once bumped into Dirk Bremser, a Bochum youth player.

Bremser, they tell me you were playing the piano in the Roland Hall.

Yes, Mr Gerland.

At the piano, Dirk Bremser could reduce an entire hallful of people to a dreamy silence, which was why the head of the youth team had asked him to play something at their Christmas festival. Everyone praised Bremser for it. Hermann Gerland told him: you'd better decide if you want to play the piano, or play football.

Gerland came from Bochum, from the mining district of Weitmar. He became assistant manager of VfL Bochum and finally, at 32, manager. When he signed a player from Poland, Hermann Gerland helped the Bochum club secretaries to set up home for the new player. He lugged furniture, he hung pictures. If a hitcher at a motorway services asked politely, he gave him a lift. At least once a year, he visited Frau Mense in her guest-house on the Castroper Straße. Almost two decades before, he'd once spent a couple of weeks in one of her rooms, when his mother was ill. It was his firm belief that gratitude was something you didn't just show once, but again and again. Hermann Gerland's father had died when he was nine.

In the spring of 1988, Heinz Höher and Hermann Gerland had talked for a long time on the phone after agreeing the handover at Nuremberg. He was having real difficulties at Bochum, getting through to his midfielder Thomas Kempe, Gerland explained. You should just have embraced him in front of everyone right there on the pitch when you beat Hamburg 2-0 in the cup semi-final, said Höher, and everything would've been fine. Heinz Höher thought how easy it was to give someone else advice that he'd never be able to take himself: take a player in your arms, show you trust him.

Back then, they'd been a young Bundesliga manager and an experienced Bundesliga manager having a friendly chat about work on the phone. Six months later, in Nuremberg, Heinz Höher asked himself: How come Gerland thought he could ignore his advice now? And Hermann Gerland thought: How come Höher thought he could still give him orders?

And there was no lack of potential causes of a conflict. Just as they'd feared, the club really found things tough without Stefan Reuter and Roland Grahammer. Hermann Gerland, who understood being honest to include telling it like it was, complained in front of the press that at the moment Dieter Eckstein, their international forward, wasn't playing to a high enough standard for the Bundesliga. Eckes, he shouted in training, you're not moving! And from that moment Dieter Eckstein really stopped moving.

Hermann doesn't understand Eckes, Heinz Höher complained bitterly to Schmelzer. A manager had to show Eckes affection and trust, or he never played well.

In the midst of all this, in September 1988, Nuremberg beat Roma 2-1 away in the first leg of their UEFA Cup tie. The *Nürnberger Nachrichten* called it 'a seemingly impossible, sensational comeback on the international stage'. It could have been the moment that united them. It turned into just the next piece of theatre.

In Rome, the team were staying at a hotel without air-conditioning on a noisy arterial road. Assistant manager Dieter Lieberwirth, six players not on the team sheet, and the reporters from the Nuremberg papers were being put up 30 km outside of Rome, in a holiday hotel. It had to be especially opened for them. The holiday season was already over. There was no food, and no phones. At the end of the day, planning their trips was down to the general manager.

His friend Dieter Reiber, who, among other jobs, edited the match-day programmes at Nuremberg and who had helped to organise the trip, publicly apologised for the inconvenience that had been caused. Heinz Höher, though, said: 'If the assistant manager's complaining that he's got to take a taxi to training, when it comes to future trips abroad he'll be offered the opportunity to stay at home and work with the reserves.'

From that moment on, Heinz Höher, the manager who had taken Nuremberg to such heights, was seen by many players, journalists and fans as a general manager who couldn't cope. In the Bundesliga, where a single goal could make winners or losers out of people, a single episode could lead to verdicts that would never change.

Heinz just doesn't know how to sell himself to the public, thought club president Schmelzer. Unfortunately, a Bundesliga general manager couldn't just hide away from the public. RTL's Saturday Bundesliga programme, *Kick-Off*, ran for three hours; football was talked about more than it was shown. Sometimes, *Kick-Off*'s presenter, Uli Potofski, even interviewed sex-expert Erika Berger about some aspect or other of football, or else the camera led the public to the nudist swimming-pool next door to Dortmund's Westphalia Stadium. Those guys are soon going to disappear from the landscape again, the editors of Channel 2's *Sportstudio* said to themselves. There was no way advertising income was ever going to cover the 23 million marks per season that RTL paid for the broadcasting rights. And in any case, technical difficulties meant that the private channel could only reach a quarter of all German households.

At home, Thomas watched the new programme. His brother Markus had moved to Hamburg, where Dieter Reiber had fixed him up with a job as a photo-salesman. Susanne, who was now 23 already, was studying to be a teacher. When Uli Hoeneß stole Stefan Reuter and Roland Grahammer from her father, she drew a picture showing Heinz Höher pulling the strings of a dancing puppet with the face of Uli Hoeneß, so Heinz Höher could look at the picture when everything got him too worked up.

At 13, this was the first time in Thomas's life he'd watched Bundesliga games on television without one of the teams being his dad's very own. He didn't mind teasing his dad at home; one time, when Dad sat next to him to watch as he did his maths homework, he said, why did he need to do maths, that was why people had calculators.

Dad threatened: Thomas was going to do his homework and he was going to do it right there and then. Thomas stood up, ran to the bathroom, and locked himself in. Dad never again tried to watch over his homework. But Thomas felt something towards his father that none of his friends could feel for their fathers: he was his father's fan. He had unconditionally loved his father, the football manager. General manager wasn't the same thing, somehow. Was that just a childish impression, or did the son unconsciously feel his father's disappointment about his new job?

FC Nuremberg prepared itself for its grand entry onto the world stage. Roma arrived for the second leg. People said that the Romans had brought their own cook with them. The landlord of their hotel, the Höfler in the Reutles district, was only permitted to buy meat and vegetables according to a list they had faxed him in advance. The Italians brought their own pasta with them, too, of course. Italian football, now that was the business. Even the Italian football correspondents looked like stars in those suits, those ties and those incredibly elegant leather shoes. Anyone who was anyone in football wanted to play in Serie A: Lothar Matthäus, Andreas Brehme and Jürgen Klinsmann were permitted to play for Inter Milan, Rudi Völler played up front for Roma. In the Bundesliga, it was murmured that the Italian champions, Milan, played the football of the future. Allegedly, Milan's ten outfield players moved like a single machine, bound together by invisible threads, creating triangles and lines all over the pitch, so that the opposition was always outnumbered near the ball, and never found the space to play. It was impossible to imagine the effect if Nuremberg were to defend their 2-1 lead against an *Italian* team.

Their building-site of a stadium was put in order as far as possible for the big day: in the main stand, there shone 3000 or 4000 of the new green-yellow plastic seats, and temporary stands of steel scaffolding had been inserted into two of the holes left by the building works, so that there would at least be room for 31,000 fans. A ticket for one of the new seats in the main middle stand cost 150 marks instead of the usual 30. It was expected that 70,000 people would want to see the club's return to Europe, and see those Italians. Only 20,000 turned up.

The fans had taken offence. The sale of Reuter and Grahammer, high ticket-prices, and a team who'd managed to take no points at all from the last possible ten in the Bundesliga, meant that thousands stayed sulking at home. It was all someone's fault, in football it's always someone's fault, and for the *Nürnberger Zeitung* that someone was Heinz Höher. 'General manager Heinz Höher, who never objects to a high-stakes game of cards, has raised it too high and ruined FC Nuremberg's reputation among precisely those devotees who have stuck to the club through thick and thin in its darkest hour.'

Heinz Höher had had another one of his marketing ideas. He'd created ticket-bundles. For 50 marks, you could get a bundle of three standing-tickets for the games against Hamburg, Leverkusen and Roma, which came out at 17 marks per game. Normally, standing tickets for a Bundesliga match were 13 marks. He thought that everyone would benefit from his scheme: the club would get a bigger crowd against Hamburg and Leverkusen, while the fans would avoid the higher ticket-prices against Roma, when a single standing-ticket was going to cost 40 marks. But the fans and the papers saw the bundle as blackmail: you would only get into the stadium to see Roma at a fair price if you also came to watch Hamburg and Leverkusen. Heinz Höher didn't defend himself against the attacks in the press. He got the feeling that no one was going to understand him anyway.

He went to the game with Jürgen Köper, who had come down from Bochum for the big day, to see his old comrades-in-arms Höher and Gerland – and of course, to watch an Italian team. Heinz Höher said to him that he was going to have to tell Hermann he couldn't treat Eckes so hard, and Jürgen Köper thought to himself that Hermann Gerland and Heini Höher must be really working closely together. After the game, Heinz Höher asked Gerd Schmelzer how on earth Gerland had thought it right to tell the team *we're going to run them into the ground* when they had a 2-1 lead and should simply have wrestled the rhythm of the game away from the Italians? Roma won 3-1 through Renato's extra-time header. The Brazilian had cost 12 million marks, it was crazy, those Italians, 12 million was enough to run the whole of FC Nuremberg for 18 months.

With professional coolness, the Nuremberg team did a bit of light training on the morning after they went out against Roma. Once again, they were just a normal Bundesliga team. Heinz Höher said to himself that he was going to have to talk to Hermann – but did he ever do anything else than spend the whole time talking inwardly to Hermann Gerland?

Over the past few weeks, the manager had already seen Heinz Höher's grim face once too often. What does he want, anyway, thought

Gerland, is he trying to make me into a second Heinz Höher? He knew damn well already who I am, that I don't let anyone talk me into things, that I don't just have my principles, but follow them with an iron will.

Hermann Gerland covered up just how much he suffered from Höher's cold fury. Gerland talked straight to his players and was quite capable of pointing out their failings briskly, but at the same time he longed to work in a spirit of harmony. There was no contradiction in that, it was simple humanity.

The morning after the game against Roma, Heinz Höher watched his favourite pupil, Dieter Eckstein, amid the pack of players on their gentle run-out. Eckes had his eyes on the ground while he ran, that was the way footballers ran, but Heinz Höher asked himself when would Eckes hold his head high again, when would Eckes smile again: Hermann Gerland had publicly destroyed Eckes by hinting that Eckes wasn't pulling his weight, that Eckes tried to get away with anything! Obviously, Eckes smoked and drank too much, but you had to let him show his strengths, not go carping on about his weaknesses.

At about half past ten, while her husband did his gloomy laps around the Valznerweiher training-ground, Ute Eckstein was getting her third child, Dennis, who was seven weeks old, to sleep. At 12.30, Dieter should be home any time now, she went to check that Dennis really wasn't awake yet, he never slept for two hours. She found him dead in his cot.

Sudden infant death syndrome, said the doctors.

Heinz Höher thought: to lose a child was something that you couldn't get over by believing in God or by hating God. He found himself thinking about Markus, Susanne and Thomas, and he shivered.

In the Bundesliga, news spread fast. Dieter Eckstein can't get on with Hermann Gerland; Dieter Eckstein's just suffered the most terrible personal tragedy, the loss of a child; Dieter Eckstein must be ripe for us to grab him. Eintracht Frankfurt made an offer. They'd pay 3.4 million marks for Eckstein.

Nuremberg had never got more than that for a player.

In Heinz Höher's mind, something went into lockdown, not Eckes as well. But then Eckes said that with an offer like Eintracht were making him, he was off, he'd had enough of it all. Enough *of it all*. There was a dark undertone in what was left unsaid by these words.

The manager, Gerland, said that if he got a quality new forward as a replacement, he wouldn't stand in the way of the transfer. Actually, we can't say no to the money, said Gerd Schmelzer. As general manager, it's your job to think about the money too, Heinz Höher told himself. And so each of them persuaded the others to make a sale that none of them was truly convinced was right.

Within five months, Nuremberg had made 9.4 million marks through selling Reuter, Grahammer, Andersen and Eckstein. It's time you claim some of that money for yourself, Dieter Reiber told Heinz Höher, who had worked in professional football for three decades, always signing whatever contract they put in front of him. Heinz Höher promptly provided Gerd Schmelzer with a list of just how much a dozen players had risen in value under his guidance: Köpke, bought for 200,000 marks, value today: 2.5 million. Grahammer, bought for 200,000 marks, sold for 2.4 million. Reuter, signed for free from their own youth team, sold for exactly the same as Eckstein: 3.4 million marks ... Heinz Höher was awarded a bonus of 350,000 marks. Dealing with vast sums of money was becoming an everyday thing at FC Nuremberg. As soon as you got used to it, you stopped worrying about it. After all, it was just a couple of extra zeros on the end.

Dr Rödl, the club's chief accountant, who had been looking after the books at FC Nuremberg for 15 years, announced that in the tax year 1987-88, which had just ended, the club had achieved one of the best results in its history. They could take it for granted that the club was free of all debts. Hidden amid all this good news was the fact that if they hadn't sold all those players, Nuremberg, like almost all Bundesliga clubs, would have made a loss.

Club treasurer, Professor Doktor Doktor Ingo Böbel, who lectured in economics at the universities of Flensburg and Leipzig, was praised in the newspapers for his careful management of their finances. Now Böbel could continue to dedicate himself privately to the club's little secret. In the club accountant's office, he'd stashed away a grey metal box. This was where he kept the money for back-handers. Whenever they played friendlies or indoor tournaments the rule was that they were paid in cash, directly to Böbel. The club's book-keeper, Hanne, who had been a reliable woman throughout her entire career and was soon to retire, itemised income and expenditure to and from the secret box. Item no. 49: 20,000 marks paid out to Dieter Eckstein, cash in hand. Item no. 79: 16,000 marks paid in re: friendly in Scheinfeld. Item, 30 November 1988: 2200 marks to club business manager Manfred Räntsch re: clothing. There was much care taken of the referees, as well. Tracksuits or even, once, a home gym, were ready as presents for them. Everyone was doing it, club president Schmelzer believed.

Everything about Professor Doktor Doktor Böbel was on the grand scale: his head, his throat, and the round glasses with their flesh-coloured frames which reached from the tip of his nose to his eyebrows. With his long hair and his pinstriped suits, he looked like someone who wanted to be an investment banker and a rock-star all at once. When the board sat down to celebrate in the Café Central, or at the Sebold, or, later on in the evening, sometimes in Gerd Schmelzer's very own castle, he would take from his pocket a spiky rubber ball but from a joke shop. This ball could roll about on its own and it would bite you if it ran into your arm or your leg. Everybody laughed, and Ingo Böbel felt a wave of happiness running warmly through his body: he had made everybody laugh. As a child he'd raced to Nuremberg's games every Saturday, what a feeling that had been, to have 30,000 people shouting together after a goal, to feel the power of the masses in his own body, and now he truly belonged, now he was part of the club. One night, in Schmelzer's castle, he pulled out his guitar – he'd once played in a band – to perform '(I Can't Get No) Satisfaction', and then, when the show was over, he stood up and smashed his own guitar to pieces in Schmelzer's living-room. Everybody laughed even more loudly. Ingo's a good man, said Heinz Höher.

As an hourly paid lecturer at the University, Professor Doktor Doktor Böbel earned 4000 marks a month. As treasurer of the club, he dealt with millions, he okayed 35,000 marks as a backhander one moment, and the next he was using the club's credit card to pay over 1000 marks for a heady evening out. He started using the club's Gold Card to buy Davidoff cigarillos for himself. When he paid for flights to his workplaces in Flensburg and Leipzig, they went on the club's Lufthansa AirPlus Card, he got a book of receipts from a taxi-driver and filled them out for himself, 'journey to town 150 marks', then got the club to cover them.

No one at the club's top table wanted to know what little things Ingo was doing on the quiet. When it came to the big things, his work as treasurer was, after all, exemplary.

At Hamburg, Heinz Höher found Dieter Eckstein's successor, in the shape of another man who played his football with his backside. When Under-21 international Bruno Labbadia got to the ball he stuck his buttocks out, using his backside to keep his marker away from him while he himself spun goalwards on his own axis. The children of first-generation immigrant workers were making it into the Bundesliga: Erdal Keser, Maurizio Gaudino and Bruno Labbadia, whose parents had emigrated from south-east of Rome to a dump in Hesse, to feed their seven kids by working as a navvy and a seamstress in the curtain factory. On the last Monday in October, Labbadia, who had only been used as a substitute forward by Hamburg, declared that he was happy that his switch to Nuremberg had been decided. On Tuesday, Heinz Höher called the deal off. Labbadia had broken one of his ribs.

'Labbadia isn't in the right condition to be the player we need to solve our short-term problems,' Heinz Höher explained to the Nuremberg journalists. In actual fact, he still wanted to sign Labbadia. But he was scared of being subjected to vile press attacks again, if he were to bring an injured forward to the club. And he hoped he could beat the transfer fee down if he kept Hamburg hanging on.

But Bruno Labbadia and Hamburg were in no mood to hang on. Instead, Labbadia went to Kaiserslautern. The press-pack pounced on Heinz Höher. Hadn't he heard that Labbadia's broken rib would have been healed within three weeks? How the hell could he have blown the transfer over such a stupid little thing? 'Our general manager: nuts, or useless?' asked the headline in the *Nürnberger Abendzeitung*.

Club president Schmelzer put his head in his hands. What had Heinz Höher done this time? If I were convinced about a player, it wouldn't matter if he was out for three weeks. And as for trying to beat down the transfer fee – Hamburg were asking 800,000 marks for Labbadia. Nuremberg had got 3.4 million for Eckstein.

But Schmelzer let Heinz Höher have his way. He didn't trust himself to go against his general manager when it came to football decisions. He felt that he was too inexperienced. Heinz Höher had so often seen things in players that no one else had seen: Dorfner, Schwabe, Reuter, Grahammer, Köpke, five players plucked from nowhere and given their first chance by him, who'd gone on to the national team. Against the background of this evidence, Schmelzer tried to understand his friend in the case of Labbadia, too. Heinz Höher's thoughts certainly worked in mysterious ways, but when it came to questions of football they took things to another level; usually. Bruno Labbadia, who they had spurned, later won his national caps at a different club.

Anyone who had to make decisions in the Bundesliga made a mistake like that at one time or another. If everything went well, as it had at Nuremberg in the mid-1980s, such failures would one day just be seen as merry anecdotes. But now, in the winter of 1988-89, Nuremberg were left without Eckstein or Labbadia or any other real goalscorer. Hermann Gerland's team were stuck fast in the bottom third of the table.

The newspaper reports got more biting: 'You can tell a lot about the attitude of the players by the way they run to the physio at the smallest scratch, cry their eyes out and bunk off training,' yelled the *Nürnberger Zeitung*. Manager Gerland explained that he couldn't make the lame walk. Heinz Höher snapped back at him that he should stop always bad-mouthing the players, that way they'd never improve. The crowds got smaller: 14,500 against champions Bremen, 12,000 against Hannover, 10,000 against Stuttgart. The club weren't going to get through the season without serious financial losses. The tabloids accused Schmelzer of having given preferential treatment to an architect friend of his during the renovation of the club's site. Rudi Stenzel, the player who had risen swiftly from the local league, found himself at odds with Heinz Höher because the club wasn't paying him bonuses. It was December 1988; please, Heinz, said Gerd Schmelzer, be our manager again.

Heinz Höher felt the hairs on the back of his neck rise. To manage the club again was the one thing he wanted. But he said: I won't do that.

He'd brought Gerland here, he couldn't stab him in the back after six months, no matter how much he'd lost trust in him.

Heinz, please, begged the other board members, Ingo Böbel and Sven Oberhof. You've got to come back.

And what if I do? he asked himself. No, he told Böbel and Overhof, it couldn't be done.

In February 1989, the team and manager Hermann Gerland flew to their winter training camp at Valletta on Malta, and the entire club hoped, as so many Bundesliga clubs had so often hoped, that things would just get better, somehow. In professional football, success or failure were often not a question of planning or tactics, but of the dynamic within the team. Something might occur, a goal, a victory, an experience during training, that brought them all together, and a chain reaction might happen: everything would come good again, their position in the table, the newspaper headlines, the crowds.

Heinz Höher went along with them to the training camp. It would be a good opportunity to have a calm talk with the seven players whose contracts were up for renewal, Gerd Schmelzer told him. Above all, they urgently needed to have a conversation with midfielder Manfred Schwabl. A year after Reuter and Grahammer, he too had been approached by Bayern.

Every evening, at the Hotel Dragonara on the Bay of St George, the sun sank golden before the windows into the Mediterranean Sea. From the balcony, Heinz Höher could hear the waves rolling serenely onto the beach, now and then accompanied by the cry of a seagull. The sounds of the wintry sea could not drown out the voice inside him. Should he have taken over as manager from Gerland? Was he going to have to change his whole way of doing things, was what he called decency really just hesitation? Heinz Höher fretted away with his own thoughts.

On Sunday evening, the day after his arrival, he was supposed go to the hotel bar to have a confidential talk with the four Nuremberg journalists who'd come along. It was to be a good opportunity to clear the decks after all the trouble that had brewed up between him and the press in the last few months. He'd seen the headline in *Bild Zeitung*: 'Höher takes a nap – Nuremberg lose a player.' They claimed he'd incompetently messed up the documentation proving that Johann Kramer was of German descent. But the fact was that the whole business was news to him. And what did these little scribblers know about anything, someone should tell them that the board were on their knees trying to get him back as manager. Heinz Höher appeared at the hotel bar. The four journalists, always the same old faces, were already sitting together in a group. He said that he didn't feel like talking to people who'd already decided that all the troubles at the club were down to him, and he bade them good evening. The journalists were enraged: he'd left them sitting there like they were stupid brats.

Next morning, Heinz Höher phoned home. The *Nürnberger Nachrichten* had run an interview with German international Manfred Schwabl. Schwabl told the paper that it was high time for Heinz Höher to start thinking seriously about renewing his contract: 'In the first half of the season, we've taken stick from the fans because of all the mistakes the club management has made.' Schwabl listed that badly organised trip to Rome and the high price of tickets for the home game against the Italians, as well as the lack of a goalscorer and the fact that before their home game against Karlsruhe, they got stuck in a traffic jam and only arrived at the stadium 35 minutes before kick-off. With insufficient time to warm up, Andreas Köpke and Jörg Dittwar had both been injured in that game. Schwabl's last word was: 'We've got an outstanding president and an excellent manager.' The omission was glaring – he hadn't backed the general manager.

A Bundesliga team who were desperately chasing success always believed that either the manager or the general manager were idiots. Heinz Höher should have been able to remember that, he'd been a player himself. When things went wrong they immediately tried to pin the blame on the manager or the general manager, to make things easier on themselves.

Heinz Höher sat alone at breakfast at his table in the Hotel Dragonara. The orange juice was freshly pressed. He didn't say good morning any longer to the players, the journalists, the manager. At training, he wandered around outside the ground. Then he disappeared for the rest of the day.

He walked beside the sea, he explored the centre of Valletta, he popped into a pub, sat alone at the bar, drinking a couple of beers and no shot. Since becoming general manager, he'd taken care to drink less. Drinking didn't fit in with his own image of a general manager, and he was getting fed up of hearing people saying old Höher can put it away. But no one was watching him now. He went into another bar and had a couple of beers, no shot.

He'd made a plan for how to run the contract negotiations with their international, Schwabl, he wasn't going to be rushed into it by Schwabl or the journalists, no one was going to tell him when he should talk to who. He was going to wait until Wednesday to have the conversation: that was when Uli Bayerschmidt, the defender he had signed on loan from Bayern, was getting in. Bayerschmidt would tell Schwabl how tough it was for a young player at Bayern and let him see how good he had it at Nuremberg. That was the plan, but of course, the journalists and Schwabl didn't know it.

He lost any sense of exactly what was so enraging him, it just turned into a generalised rage against the whole world. He called Gerd Schmelzer to report on the rubbish work Gerland was doing in training – after all, it was his job to report to the president. He listened to the seven players talking about what they planned to do when their contracts were up in the summer, but didn't tell them what he planned to do with them. He didn't ask the manager which players he wanted to keep or sell. He had no desire to talk to the manager. What Gerland was doing just couldn't go on any longer, he was trying to remake forward Rudi Stenzel as a defender, he was just getting them running round and round at this late stage in their preparation. Heinz Höher shouted it all out, alone in the hotel with club official Christian Schmid, while the team were at training.

Schmid was his most loyal follower. But even he ran from the hotel, shaking his head. Heinz had to leave Hermann in peace, once and for all, thought Schmid, and raced straight to the training-ground. He told Gerland that Mr Höher had gone into a rage at the hotel. Mid-training exercise, manager Gerland stood in the centre of the pitch and roared: 'Well, he can just piss off and get lost! That old bastard can't stand anyone, even himself!'

That evening, Heinz Höher gathered the team together in a meeting room at the Hotel Dragonara. I'm back, he told the players. From now on, he was going to keep a careful eye on how each of them was playing – and you, he pointed to Manfred Schwabl, who do you think you are, you think you're our press officer, or what? Heinz Höher had only just got started talking.

Half an hour later, Manfred Schwabl left the meeting-room with his fists clenched and tears in his eyes. Hermann Gerland bumped into him in the hotel corridor. Mr Höher had said nothing to the manager about a team meeting. Gerland ran to Höher, four months, he'd been trying to cope with his general manager's ill humour, trying to just sit it out, but now it had gone too far, Mr Höher, we need to talk. 'Not now,' said Heinz Höher. 'You're too worked up, Hermann.' And he was off, into the night.

If Mr Höher wants to play at stroppy, I can as well, Hermann Gerland said to himself. From now on, he wasn't going to speak a word to the general manager.

Many of the players, like Rudi Stenzel, had up to now got the impression that the manager and the general manager were working together as one, as old friends from Bochum. From that moment on, Heinz Höher and Hermann Gerland swapped icy gazes and not a single word when they met each morning at breakfast at the Hotel Dragonara, where they served fresh-squeezed orange juice and those delicious, sweet pastries. Gerland called his wife. I think it's Höher or me, he said, one of us is for the chop. Maybe both of us, too.

Club president Schmelzer sat in Nuremberg and read the sports pages of the Nuremberg papers, which carried daily reports from the front. On Friday, after they'd been a week at the training camp, the lead article in the *Nürnberger Nachrichten* was bordered in red. The headline said: 'Höher damages Nuremberg.' The subtitle was: 'General manager undermines own authority by inexplicable actions.'

The piece had been written by Rudolf Pilous. He was one of the journalists who were positively inclined towards Heinz Höher. Pilous wrote: 'Instead of dealing with the problems that can always arise in a training camp (people call it camp-fever), instead of covering his manager's back as he prepares the team for the second half of the Bundesliga season – and these preparations will be especially important this year – Heinz Höher simply spreads unease wherever he appears, with his brusque manner and his inability to even say a polite Good Morning.'

Gerd Schmelzer fielded the excited calls from the journalists in Malta, he spoke on the phone with Heinz Höher, with Hermann Gerland, and with the player he trusted most, Andreas Köpke. The expedition to Malta was returning in three days. It began to dawn on Schmelzer that it was too late now for any peace initiative. The only thing anyone wanted now was the judge's verdict.

On their last night in Malta, the team celebrated the end of the training camp. Heinz Höher was the only one absent from the celebration. As happens to any manager, some of the players had been sceptical of Hermann Gerland. Since the strife with Heinz Höher had escalated, almost all the players were on the manager's side. In the end, he was one of them, someone who was being attacked by the general manager, just like they were. During the celebrations, Manfred Schwabl revealed to his team-mates that he was going to Bayern over the summer. Contractual negotiations had been the supposed reason for Heinz Höher's journey, but they had never beyond non-binding chatter.

Werner Haala, football correspondent of the *Nürnberger Abendzeitung*, left the team celebration and went back to the hotel. He found Heinz Höher at the hotel bar. The team feels united again, said Haala, not without enthusiasm. It took Heinz Höher a moment to realise that Haala genuinely didn't understand how it was that the team had become united again: they'd been welded together by turning against him, the general manager.

The day after their return from Malta was Monday, 13 February 1989. Gerd Schmelzer put on a dark suit and a dark tie. He knew that around midday, or maybe not until the afternoon, he was going to have to announce an unfortunate piece of news. He just didn't know yet what that news would be.

In the club's office, the board questioned the manager, the general manager and the team captain about the events in Malta. Then Schmelzer, Oberhof and Böbel withdrew for discussion. The last time they had needed a meeting like this, behind closed doors, had been 4½ years before, after the October rebellion. Heinz Höher and Hermann Gerland waited for the result. That morning, they had greeted one another again for the first time in days.

Good morning, Hermann.

Good morning, Mr Höher.

In the Stuhlfauth-Stuben, the journalists were waiting for a press conference which no one had announced but everybody just knew was going to happen. Even radio reporters had appeared. Was Heinz Höher going to be sacked? Was Hermann Gerland going to be sacked? Would they both have to go?

At about 3pm, Gerd Schmelzer came into the room. Beside him, in a yellow pullover, jacketless, walked Heinz Höher.

They've sacked Hermann Gerland, was the first thought that came into the head of Klaus Westermeyer, sports editor of the *Nürnberger Nachrichten*. Or else it wouldn't be Höher appearing at the president's side.

Heinz Höher's grey-white hair, which had originally been parted over his left temple, had lost all its shape. It was standing up, as if a hand had been passed repeatedly through it. The radio reporter from Bavarian Broadcasting set his microphone in front of Heinz Höher.

They didn't have a press officer to lead the conference. For five years, Gerd Schmelzer and Heinz Höher had done everything themselves, they signed players, led the team, taken public question-and-answer sessions. Gerd Schmelzer said he welcomed them to this improvised press conference, in which he had sadly to announce the 'immediate parting of the ways between the club and the manager'.

They really had sacked Gerland!

'I beg your pardon,' said Schmelzer, 'I mean, the immediate parting of the ways between the club and the former manager and present general manager, Heinz Höher.'

Höher had always remained the manager, to him. Now he wrote the word 'ex' in front of it.

Over the last six months, things had got out of hand, said the president, both the general manager and the manager had allowed things to escalate at the training camp. However, the driving force behind the conflict in Malta had undoubtedly been Heinz Höher, he said. 'Lately, he's seemed to me rather like an elderly married man who's been cuckolded.'

Heinz Höher was sitting next to him. He and Schmelzer hadn't discussed what exactly he was supposed to do at a press conference whose point was to announce his own sacking. They'd just had a sort of feeling that he should say farewell in a proper manner, that they would take this final step together.

Heinz Höher started the ball rolling by attacking the club's manager right there on the club's own premises: 'The club's three sizes too big for Gerland.' Throughout the press conference he held his car-keys in his left hand, as if he was already almost gone. He had interfered in the manager's business a total of five times, said Heinz Höher. 'And I should have done it earlier, none of the players have improved this season, we could have kept hold of Eckstein, but the manager ruined his reputation with the fans.' He turned the official press conference at FC Nuremberg, called to announce his dismissal, into a grand plea about why it was actually the manager who should have had to go, rather than him. Club president Schmelzer sat next to Heinz Höher, looking at him with his famously calm gaze, but this time he was looking out of the corners of his eyes, and his moustache drooped low. He didn't interrupt. Later, Hermann Gerland had to face the reporters out on the cold training-ground and defend himself off the cuff against the ex-general manager's charges. No one thought that this was the sign of a world gone crazy, maybe it wasn't quite the best way to do things, but then again, they'd had to improvise.

The longer Heinz Höher spoke at the press conference, the calmer he became, and the better he himself understood what had happened. What he'd done on Malta had been, he said, 'an act of pure self-destruction'. He had felt himself backed into a corner: 'The team loves Gerland, the journalists love Gerland, everyone loves Gerland. There's no love left over for me.' Heinz Höher stood up. He wanted to put a bit of distance between himself and the club, at least in a geographical sense. He was going off to Sylt on the spot, for a few days, maybe for weeks. It came out more melodramatically than he intended: 'I am leaving the city.'

If Heinz Höher had shown before that he had such a way with words, and such insights, he could have avoided this whole business, and this farewell, thought Klaus Westermayer, sports editor of the *Nürnberger Nachrichten*.

On the horizon, the sky and the the sea became one. The longer Heinz Höher stared out at the North Sea, the stronger grew that feeling that he was miles away from everything. The colours of sky and sea were washed out, all that was blue seemed a shade of grey, and the yellow of the sand on the beach beneath his feet seemed a shade of brown. North Germany in February is a place where all shades are pastel. Here on the beach, at any rate, he was the only person on earth. The feeling calmed him.

He started running. Just straight along the beach, on and on, heading from Westerland towards Hörnum. He'd been coming to Sylt for 15 years, to let the fresh air cleanse his mind and body. He'd even brought his teams to Sylt. In the 1970s, in summer, when they were preparing for the coming season, the bus had dropped off the Bochum XI in Westerland and then they had to run, right to the end of the island, 18 or 19km with no chance of stopping early because the bus was only waiting for them at the red-and-white striped light tower, there at the end of the world, where all that was left was the blue vastness. At Nuremberg, he'd brought them to a training camp on Sylt right in the middle of the season; no doubt the old, conservative hands in the Bundesliga, Otto Rehhagel and the rest of them, had shaken their heads – what, a training camp on Sylt, right in the middle of the season? But that was his strength: to have ideas, to do things differently. The season after their promotion, he'd come to Sylt with Nuremberg, it was September 1985, they'd still been young, Eckstein, Reuter, Grahammer, Dorfner. They'd all still believed implicitly that it would go on like this for ever; onwards and upwards.

On Sylt, your thoughts grow more placid. He ran along the beach, his gaze rested on the wide open spaces, and he saw the whole picture.

If Hermann Gerland had listened to me, if I'd talked reasonably with him, we could've made a success of things together. But the truth is, I was never able to talk reasonably to anybody. I always just tried to control things.

I thought that Hermann would listen to me. I mean, I'd been his manager, he'd been my player, back in the day. If I'd just thought about things a little bit, I'd surely have realised that we couldn't just slip back into our old roles again, teacher and pupil, after 16 years, that in those 16 years Hermann had developed his own ideas, ideas that were different from mine.

Mind you, I still believe that I could have prevented a lot of the things that went wrong between him and the team in the first six months. Hermann believes that it's all about work-rate. What he wanted from his players was hard graft and dedication. But players like Dieter Eckstein and Rudi Stenzel only get worse when he tries to beat their weaknesses out of them. If you make Dieter Eckstein graft, it just uses up all his energy – and Rudi Stenzel's never going to make a tough-nut defender good enough for the Bundesliga. You've got to accept their weaknesses and play to their strengths. Then they'd both be bloody good forwards.

But the real problem wasn't Hermann, of course, it was me. As general manager, I just wasn't needed. Basically, I was just jealous. He had my job. I'd given it to him myself. That just made it worse.

Heinz Höher ran the whole length of the beaches on Sylt, from north to south. The winter wind played with the grass on the dunes. When he was running, Heinz Höher didn't care a bit if the wind blew straight into his face. He knew that on the way home, he would have the wind behind him.

Officially, he'd been sacked. But since FC Nuremberg were going to have to give him a severance package anyway, he might as well work for the money, Gerd Schmelzer had told him. In absolute secrecy, as the president's private talent-spotter, Heinz Höher watched and judged players who might strengthen the club. Schmelzer was convinced that nobody had an eye for players like the man he'd just fired.

From Sylt, Heinz Höher travelled to Edenkoben, deep in the Rhineland countryside, to take a look at a third-division player. He did it because it was 1150km there and back. So he'd make some decent mileage-money. Anyone who worked in the Bundesliga, anyone who was used to always having their status judged, and judging other people's status, inevitably found themselves often thinking about things in terms of money.

Two weeks later, Heinz Höher drove from Nuremberg to the Westerwald, to watch that semi-professional from Edenkoben playing away from home as well. He took Thomas with him. On car journeys, he always thought of some quiz or other for the children: who could name the 50 states of America, who could name the most footballers beginning with an O? On this journey, he suddenly invented the number-plate game. He had to note the registration numbers of the cars they overtook, Thomas wrote them down and asked: what were the numbers of the red Passat? Then he had to remember them: MTK-AR 250. Or: the grey BMW, what was the fourth letter on the plate? W. He could remember more than 50 number-plates, even two hours after they'd overtaken those cars.

For the following season, club president Gerd Schmelzer signed a player from FC Edenkoben by the name of Uwe Wolf. Neither the manager, Gerland, nor anyone else at the club, had ever seen him. Wolf was to play in Nuremberg's defence for five years. When journalists asked where they got him from, Gerd Schmelzer said that someone had recommended him, he really couldn't remember who.

After his six years at Nuremberg, the old managers' roundabout started again in summer 1989. Wait for it, and take what you get. A club from Saudi Arabia contacted him, it was called Al-Ittihad. Heinz Höher said yes immediately. Dettmar Cramer had already been manager there.

His team played in front of stands built of marble which seldom held more than 500 spectators. On Monday evenings, Heinz Höher had to train the veterans of the club, about 60 players on a single pitch, all of them over 40 and not all of them still able to sprint. When his team played an away game at Mecca, he, as a Christian, had to get out of the team bus before they reached the gates of the holy city and was chauffered around the walls into the stadium.

In his apartment in Jeddah, he turned on his satellite TV intending to watch the Bundesliga, and saw the fall of the Berlin Wall. He hadn't thought at all about the reunification of Germany for years, he hadn't thought seriously about politics at all, and suddenly that seemed a bad thing to him. As an 18-year-old, he'd wanted to volunteer to help the Hungarians in their rebellion against the Soviet occupation, he hadn't understood why there was no office where volunteers could report. He'd been naive back then, but wasn't being naively passionate better than just not caring? And that was the way he'd come to be, focused exclusively on football and the Bundesliga.

In the Bundesliga, they'd lived with their backs to The Wall. East German football simply didn't exist, as far as they were concerned.

Once, in 1986, Gerd Schmelzer had introduced him to a new player, Frank Lippmann. He'd fled from Dresden. Heinz Höher wanted to do something to give him a welcome, and he couldn't think what. He took Lippmann to the zoo.

In Jeddah, Heinz Höher went snorkelling and shopping. There wasn't much to do in a city which seemed to consist only of stone, trapped in the heat of the desert. It was as though the city was mocking him for how little he'd cared about things: was he now stuck in a city especially created for people who'd lost all interest in things?

And yet, he found a healing power in this absence of any change, in this distance from everything that was supposedly interesting and important. It was as though the monotony of life in the desert was a cure for the inner exhaustion which had befallen him, he didn't know why, in the last couple of years. He made it his mission to do nothing. Just as he had often set himself missions simply to see if he could fulfil them, he decided that here, in the land of abstinence, he would drink no alcohol. It would have been easy for him, as a foreigner, to get a beer in certain hotels.

He got Doris to send him the records of the numbers that had come up recently at roulette in the casinos at Bad Kissingen, Bad Reichenhall and Bad Kötzing. He spent his afternoons in the shade of his flat in Saudi Arabia, going through the roulette records, trying to see if the numbers yielded any kind of a pattern.

17 May 1990:

ONE SINGLE MOMENT

His wife is on the phone and trying to speak calmly. The police have called, says Doris to him.

He only picks up his jacket and his wallet, not even his toothbrush, and leaves the spa in Wiesbaden. He thought he'd be able to relax here for a couple of weeks, he'd never been to a health farm, he thought this would be the ideal time, after his sacking from Al-Ittihad, before hopefully getting a new club for next season in the Bundesliga.

Where do you think you're going, one of the nurses calls after him, curtly. You can't just leave the health farm without informing someone. He explains it to her in a single sentence. Her head drops, she stands aside and murmurs, I'm sorry.

He reaches the University Hospital at Marburg in an hour and a half. You can't see Markus just now, says the doctor. Doris arrives from Nuremberg. I can get his bones back into shape, says the doctor, who's an American. But his head.

In Marburg, they are able to stay with friends of their neighbours in Nuremberg. So they aren't sitting alone in a hotel. Look, have a dram, says the host. Heinz Höher shakes his head.

They go back to the hospital, even though there's nothing they can do there. It took the rescue paramedics a long time to get Markus out, says the doctor, he was trapped under the lorry. It was no fault of Markus's, says the doctor, as though that were some consolation, and it is a consolation, although it makes no difference at all. The lorry broke through the barrier and tipped over on the opposite carriageway, the driver probably fell asleep for a second, it was on the A5 at Alsfeld, Markus was driving from Hamburg to a presentation in Karlsruhe. The HGV tipped over at the precise moment that Markus was driving by from the north in his VW Golf, he had no time to brake – no one could have braked – and he went head-on into the HGV just as it was tipping over. The lorry-driver died instantly.

On Sunday, three days after the accident, the doctor says, you have to decide. As a medical man, it's his duty to keep his patient artificially alive on the heart and lung machine, even if there's no prospect of him of ever being able to breathe on his own again. Only the parents can ask for the machine to be turned off.

If Markus had only taken the journey on the A5 at Alsfeld one instant more slowly, maybe to turn the dial on the car radio, thinks Heinz Höher. If the radio presenter had only put on a song that Markus didn't like, so that he went to change channels, and drove more slowly, just for one second. One second on the autobahn, that's 33 metres, what if Markus had turned the dial on the radio and been 33 metres further back when the lorry flew out onto the road in front of him? All it would have taken was for just one single moment to have been different, thinks Heinz Höher, one single moment out of the 86,400 seconds that we live through every day. Heinz Höher talks to Doris about things that can't be spoken of. Then he nods to the doctor.

'Try holding the phone in your hand for the shot,' said the photographer, 'that way it'll look as if you're pretty busy.' Then the photographer was gone and Heinz Höher's life went back to looking very different.

WAYS TO TRY KEEPING ON LIVING

Heinz Höher moved into the cellar. They kept the old furniture there: the cupboards made of teak, the carpet and the bed from their years at Bochum, 20 years old. The light of day, and life, couldn't get in here. He lay on the old bed without any sense of time. In the cellar, the minutes didn't pass.

Sometimes he cried out, at the top of his voice, so loudly that Doris heard him up in the house. But the pain wouldn't be driven out of his body. He saw Markus, sitting at his homework, paralysed by the fear of disappointing his father, he saw Markus coming home downcast when the youth team at VfL Bochum told him they were sorry, but he wasn't good enough any more, and the scream inside him got louder again: what kind of idiot had he been to not have helped Markus with his homework, how could he have been such an idiot not to order them to keep Markus in the youth team, as manager of Bochum he certainly could have done that easily. He picked up the bottle of whisky and drank, without putting it down, drank, until the bottle was empty, opened the cans of beer, drank until he could crush the tin cans in his hand. He closed his fist around the tin and squeezed till his fingers hurt. Then he squeezed some more.

When there was nothing left to drink, he had to leave the cellar. He went to the supermarket, there was no problem, he wasn't actually there, not in this life, he walked past people, wrapped in a bullet-proof layer of air.

Around midday, he had visitors in the cellar: Thomas, Susanne's boyfriend Michael and the neighbours.

I'm such an idiot, why didn't I just order them to keep Markus in the youth team at Bochum, why didn't I . . .

No, Dad, you were a good father to Markus, Thomas interrupted him. Silently, their neighbour dealt out the cards.

They played poker every day until deep into the night, the stakes rose insanely, at one point Thomas owed 2000 marks to his sister's boyfriend, they played on. Nobody said, look, Thomas is only 15. Next day, the boy was sitting in his biology lesson. He looked at the exercise in front of him and all he could see was Ace, Jack, Eight of Spades. Faced with Markus's death, their own lives meant nothing.

Doris didn't touch a drop. She was scared that if she took a drink now, she would go crazy. She let her husband do what he had to do in the cellar. There are no rules for mourning.

At the funeral, Heinz Höher mostly kept his gaze fixed firmly on nothing. Then he disappeared into the cellar for days again.

They had to liberate him from his mental isolation. The best way to tempt him back to life was through football. The 1990 World Cup in Italy was coming up. Why didn't he and Doris go to it, they all said. He refused. He wasn't interested in anything carrying on, in his life carrying on. We've already got tickets for the round of 16 and the quarter-finals in Milan, they said, you can watch Germany at their training camp at Lake Como, after all, your own players are there, Stefan Reuter and Andy Köpke. He had no idea who had organised it all for him. Was it Susanne's boyfriend Michael, who was touchingly concerned, was it Gerd Schmelzer, or had it all arranged itself, just like that? He was still insisting I don't want to go when he was already sitting at the steering wheel, heading to Italy.

Five weeks after Markus's death, he watched a football match again. Germany won 2-1 against Holland in the round of 16, Jürgen Klinsmann played the game of his life, and something inside Heinz Höher kicked in automatically. Was it just an instinct honed over the decades that made him sit up immediately at a football match, or was it a genuine passion re-awakening? Heinz Höher felt that some part of him was still deaf.

The boss, Franz Beckenbauer, invited him to visit the national team at their hotel in Erba. He chatted with Stefan Reuter and Andy Köpke, and no doubt they realised that the most important things were the things left between the words, unsaid. Köpke had been named third-choice keeper for the World Cup. The number one was Bodo Illgner, the man Heinz Höher had signed to Nuremberg in 1986 as competition for Köpke. If Illgner had actually come to Nuremberg, he would have had the two best keepers in Germany in his team, and most probably no one would have noticed, because one of the two would have fretted himself away on the subs' bench. At the hotel in Erba, he was approached by forward Pierre Littbarski. Heinz Höher managed to force a stiff smile from himself. Littbarski was going around with a movie camera. He was wearing a baseball cap and training shoes with football socks – and nothing else. Heinz Höher didn't ask what this costume was supposed to mean. When they were locked up for weeks on end, football players had the wildest ideas. But all the same, without wanting to, he'd smiled again for the first time in weeks.

We're quite safe financially, he told himself, and he told Doris, it seemed strange to act as though money mattered at all, after Markus's death. But it helped to know that at least something was still secure.

He'd opened a hotel in the Old Town in Nuremberg. Helmut Schmelzer, Gerd's brother, had told him that there was insufficient overnight accommodation in Nuremberg, and hardly any sites where new hotels could be built. You'd have to build them under the river Pegnitz. They'd laughed at the idea. At night, when he was lying awake, Mr Winzlinger said to him, okay, that was a good joke, 'under the river Pegnitz' – but why not take a look on the other side of the Pegnitz, in the Old Town, maybe you can find an old building there and convert it into a hotel. So he converted a three-storey 18th-century house on the Unschlittplatz into the Hotel Merian, at a cost of over 4 million marks. Heinz Höher had no fear of dealing with large sums of money. He saw what you could make, not what you could lose. It worked out that he had to pay 22,000 marks a month for the credit and the interest, and would take in 30,000 marks a month from the tenancy of the hotel and restaurant. He could afford to do nothing, and he'd have around 8000 marks before tax to play with. It was supposed to sound reassuring. The weeks passed, and doing nothing started to weary him. In the morning he'd drink a beer or two, then it would feel a bit better. At midday he'd drink a beer or two to keep the feeling going.

His wife and his daughter gave him funny looks. But what was the problem, if he wanted, he could stop drinking, just like that. To prove it to them, he said I won't touch a drop for seven whole days, until next Sunday at midday. The first day without alcohol, he felt as though his whole body was shivering with cold, although he was warm, the shivering must just be a mental thing, an imagined thing, he thought, until he looked at his fingers. He had to lie down on the sofa, he thought he'd never be able to stand up again, and he pretended to be asleep so that no one would notice. But after a couple of days, the withdrawal symptoms disappeared. For an entire week he didn't touch a drop and on Sunday, at precisely 12 midday, he opened a beer. Well, he'd proved that he could stop any time he wanted.

He thought about Markus and said to himself, in his condition there was no way he could manage a Bundesliga club anyway. But at the same time he waited, and yearned, for an offer.

At the end of 1990, Gerd Schmelzer said to him, get yourself ready. I'll get you back as manager.

Hermann Gerland had already been sacked in April 1990 even though he'd stabilised the club's position once more, mid-table in the Bundesliga. But in some strange way, the relationship between Gerland and Gerd Schmelzer had just got worse ever since the day when the club president theoretically buttressed his manager's position by sacking Heinz Höher. They were at odds, as if Schmelzer unconsciously held it against Gerland that he'd had to sack his friend Höher, and as if Gerland didn't trust Schmelzer because of his friendship with Höher, the man who'd just been kicked out. For six months, they didn't speak a word to each other.

Sometimes, Gerland awoke at six in the morning, asking himself, what am I doing wrong, am I really doing something wrong? The president began to believe that the papers had declared Class War on him: in the eyes of the public, what chance did he, a property developer who lived in a castle, have against that honest working-class chap, Hermann Gerland? The final straw came when the manager did an interview with *Der Spiegel*, in which he claimed that the club president was clumsily plotting against him: according to Gerland, Schmelzer had once even tried to alter the team's tactics. Gerland was sacked for giving an interview, which was something rare, even in the Bundesliga.

*

Nuremberg were now hopelessly off balance. All it took was for three or four transfers to go wrong, and for the State of Bavaria to make a retrospective demand for a million marks regarding the rebuilding of the stadium, and the club's finances got completely out of hand. Schmelzer still clove to his principle of acting steadily, with a cool regard for the facts, but in practice he was now just fire-fighting. By New Year 1990-91, now under Gerland's successor, Arie Haan, Nuremberg were lying second to bottom. Heinz Höher went to Sylt to ready himself for his comeback.

He was a manager of 52, but he went for it as though he was still a player. He ran long distances along the beach, he did sprint-work up the dunes. He cut back on alcohol, he stayed away from the Westerland Casino. Two years earlier, he'd won about 5000 marks five nights in a row at the roulette wheel there. He shivered at the memory: even back then, he'd thought how such shameless luck would have to be terribly repaid one day. That was 15 months before Markus died.

In his head, he went through the Nuremberg team he'd create as soon as Gerd Schmelzer got the board to agree his re-appointment. Eckstein and Dorfner, his favourites, were back at the club and were joined by Reiner Wirschling, a 28-year-old medical student who he'd discovered shortly before his dismissal, still playing as a semi-professional in Schweinfurt. The media and the fans were suddenly treating it as sensational that a student in his mid-20s could still make the leap into the Bundesliga. But the fact was that Heinz Höher discovered players in local and regional leagues all through his managerial career. Yeah, back in the day, people said. Heinz Höher didn't want to believe that things had changed that much by 1991.

He set down a list of all the players he'd nurtured at Nuremberg, and entitled it 'Heinz Höher – managerial achievements from 1984-1988 with sporting and financial data'. When he was presented to the media as manager, he would hand this list to the newspaper reporters, who saw him only as the failed general manager. '1986-88: played the most attractive and attacking game in the Bundesliga,' it said in the list. But it wasn't without self-mockery: '1984: defended our position at the bottom of the table in grand style.'

On 10 January 1991 he got the longed-for call from Gerd Schmelzer. Heinz, said the club president, and it seemed to Heinz Höher that Gerd Schmelzer took an age to draw breath. It's not going to happen. Vice-president Sven Oberhof, Ingo Böbel and the rest of the board had outvoted Schmelzer. Arie Haan was going to remain manager. Oberhof and Böbel considered that following the death of his son, Heinz Höher was too fragile to win the relegation battle.

But since when had Gerd Schmelzer let himself just be outvoted by those two? In their day, Schmelzer and he had always made the big decisions on their own; to be successful, a Bundesliga club needed a strong man at the helm.

Gerd Schmelzer said that just for a minute, all the fight went out of him. His father had died shortly before, his marriage was threatening to fall apart. For that one moment, being allowed to just give up felt like liberation. After his fellow board members refused to have Heinz Höher back, Gerd Schmelzer stepped down as president of FC Nuremberg. In the newsagents, the football weekly *Kicker* from 10 January was still on the shelves. It carried an interview in which Gerd Schmelzer said: 'The team needs Höher.'

Life didn't want to go on. Doris had always been sure that her husband would work as a football manager until the day he dropped down dead on the pitch aged 89. Now he was 52, sitting at home with his beer-bottles and making the whole family nervous. Their thoughts flew back for a moment to Heinz Höher's 50th birthday. Anyone who was anyone in Nuremberg, anyone who wanted to be anyone, was at the party, the club board presented him with a reclining chair that must have cost at least 5000 marks, Gerd Schmelzer himself surprised Heinz Höher by giving him the first chess-computer that moved the pieces with a robotic arm – and added a book, too: 'Sex after 50'. All its pages were blank.

Gerd was the only one of all those people who had the time of day for Heinz Höher now.

In secret, Gerd Schmelzer became a sort of professional advisor for Heinz Höher. He tried to find him a berth in the Bundesliga. In the summer of 1991, Borussia Dortmund found themselves looking for a new manager. Their general manager, Michael Meier, liked a candidate from Switzerland, but club president Gerd Niebaum had some reservations about this Swiss fellow. Actually, the Swiss was really a German who worked in Switzerland, but that wasn't the point. Heinz Höher went to Dortmund. On the car journey he got his son Thomas to recite every bit of information about Borussia's players in the special edition of *Kicker*. He spent an entire working day talking with Niebaum and Meier.

It's between you and the Swiss, Schmelzer told him next day. They chose the German from Switzerland, Ottmar Hitzfeld.

Heinz Höher became the Bundesliga's nearly-man. Aachen called him – and as soon as they did, the man already in the job, Norbert Wagner, started winning; Aachen didn't need a new manager any more. Bayer Uerdingen got in touch – and no sooner had they done so, than Timo Konietzka, their current manager, conjured a win and two draws from his relegation-haunted team; Uerdingen decided they wanted to give Konietzka a bit more time.

Let's have a chat on the phone after the game, said Borussia Mönchengladbach's president Karl-Heinz Drygalsky to Heinz Höher, as they sat in the stand at Nuremberg before his team played their Bundesliga game there.

You won't call anyway, replied Heinz Höher to Drygalsky.

What do you mean?

You'll see.

To everyone's surprise, Borussia Mönchengladbach beat Nuremberg 1-0.

Well, let's have a think about it, said Drygalsky to Heinz Höher.

You see, that's what I meant: you won't call anyway, because as soon as I'm in the frame as manager, whatever team it is, it always starts winning.

By now it was already December 1992, Heinz Höher had been out of Bundesliga football for almost two years. He decided to have a go at being a writer.

He had another read-through of the story of young Tommo, which he'd written in Greece for Thomas. He developed it into a children's book. Tommo, the boy with no parents who can talk with the animals of Ulmenhof, goes off with them to the Canine European Championships on Sylt. A hundred and fifty-eight pages later, Heinz Höher ended the story with the following sentence: 'Timmi the collie looks admiringly at Heini the tomcat. And Heini feels himself swell with pride, because to be praised by the blue-black collie is the greatest thing in Heini's life.' To feel that you have friends, to be near your friends, was more important than winning – that was the message of the book. He thought that was something children really should learn, but could he say that of himself: that friends were more important to him than winning?

Since the book had been written, it had to be published, too. He'd truly enjoyed writing it, and he would have agreed that the true happiness of writing lay in the moment the sentences came alive on the paper before him, but he still wanted the book to be held in people's hands. Obviously, he didn't go as far as Peter Handke, who sniffed and stroked away at his newly published books, but still, the feeling that you'd created a book, a real book, depended on being able to see it between two covers and take hold of it in your hands. Heinz Höher knew a man who'd surely be able to help him find a publisher: Franz Beckenbauer. The Kaiser had contacts all over heaven and earth, and you could always give him a ring, he was always ready to help. Apart from that, Franz owed him a favour. When Beckenbauer was in charge of the national team in the 1980s, Dieter Eckstein came back to Nuremberg from an international game with a muscle injury, and was unable to play in the Bundesliga that Saturday. Heinz Höher really tore Franz off a strip for that.

Still, Beckenbauer seemed totally unsurprised by Heinz Höher's request. While they were on the phone, he talked out loud about what he could do for Heinz. A book. Of course! He'd ask Middelhoff. Thomas Middelhoff was the chairman of Bertelsmann. Bertelsmann was one of the biggest media groups in the world, they owned RTL TV, dozens of newspapers, and a few publishers.

As arranged by Beckenbauer, Heinz Höher called Middelhoff at his office one weekday at 12. He seemed to be in a meeting at that very moment, and at any rate he didn't sound like a man who'd been waiting all morning to take a call from a football manager who'd written a book for children. Heinz Höher could tell that much by the tone of his voice. But he asked Heinz Höher to send him the manuscript, he said he would get it to the right people.

Sadly, a few weeks later Heinz Höher received a rejection letter from C. Bertelsmann Young People's Publishing. He sent the manuscript to further publishers by himself, but had no more success with them. So, what if he self-published the book? He recalled a certain Nuremberg fan who he'd occasionally played cards with at their training camps – he was a typesetter, wan't he? He got hold of the man and had his book printed at his works. Heinz Höher's nephew, Bernd, produced the title picture, in which a line-drawn dog shot a football into the net with its back foot as the keeper, a black tomcat, dived vainly. Heinz Höher picked up the books personally from the printing-works. His work looked splendid, the shining cover, the unusually large format, he'd had it produced in hardcover. He'd be able to knock out the paperback quickly later, when the hardcover version was sold out. It took him two car-journeys to get all the boxes of books back home. He'd had 5000 copies printed. It had cost him 15,000 marks.

He went knocking personally on the doors of the booksellers. Good morning, he would say, he was Heinz Höher the football manager and he's written a children's book. Many booksellers blushed. That was a rather unusual move, publishing your own book. Well, okay, he might as well leave 20 copies with them and come back in two or three months to see how it had done. He drove to Leverkusen, to Bochum and right up to Sylt, delivering his books by car, he even had some of them put out on a stand at the Christmas market in Nuremberg. The only bookshop that turned his books down was Jakob's on the Hefnerplatz in Nuremberg. Unfortunately, it was their company policy not to stock self-published books.

He had a book-launch, and invited the four Nuremberg football writers who'd always reported on his activities. Next morning, on his way to school, his son Thomas saw the headline on the *Nürnberger Abendzeitung*: Football, farewell – Heinz Höher's writing children's books.

His school-friends laughed. Thomas could feel his face turning bright red. His dad asked him to ask the headmaster sometime if he couldn't come and give a reading in the school. Never! snarled Thomas. He was 17.

Once Heinz Höher had delivered his book and presented it to the Nuremberg press, a deafening silence descended. In January 1993, the woman who had the stand at the Christmas market rang at his door to give him his money, and to give him back his unsold books. Heinz Höher felt ashamed as he accepted the pile of books. He had no reason to be ashamed, he told himself, but he couldn't get rid of the vague feeling that he'd disgraced himself. He probably hadn't gone about the whole business with the book very professionally. He never went back to all the bookshops to collect his money and his left-over books. In his cellar in the Elbinger Straße, 4000 Tommo books were still lying there.

Managers become walking adverts: Udo Lattek, 1992.

In the Midst of the 1990s:

THE BUNDESLIGA CLAIMS IT'S MODERN, NOW

After finding no work in the Bundesliga for three years, Heinz Höher decided to become a completely normal person. Every morning, he placed two sandwiches and a fruit yoghurt in his briefcase. He pulled his tie straight and said goodbye to Doris. At almost 55 years of age, he started with the Blumenauer property group, training to become an estate agent.

Property, he thought, interested him. It was a business where you could find at least a hint of the thrill which he so loved in professional football or card-playing: you bluffed and raised, you played.

In the afternoons, after work, he stood with the telephone in hand and talked with Mr Unger from the Deutsche Bank. Mr Unger advised him in his share-trading. Heinz Höher didn't simply buy shares, that would have been too boring. He purchased Put and Call Options. It was the stock-market equivalent of betting on horses. He betted on prices rising or falling, by buying Options which he could either convert into shares (the Call) or give up (the Put). Thomas eavesdropped on his father's telephone conversations with Mr Unger and thought to himself, oh Lord. Neither of them has a clue what they're doing.

On Saturdays, like many other estate agents and their sons, father and son watched Bundesliga football on the new Saturday night football show *ran*. He saw the old faces, Otto Rehhagel managing Werder

Bremen, Udo Lattek, lately become manager at Schalke, but he had trouble recognising them. They were wearing shockingly bright track-suits all plastered over with company logos. Lattek also had on a baseball cap which he pulled down over his face so that instead of his eyes, all you could see was the advert for buttermilk on the cap. After the final whistle, still filled with the stress and aggression of the game, they appeared for TV interview with Reinhold Beckmann, presenter of *ran,* who was beamed to pitchside live from the studio, red denim jacket and all. Nothing was too gaudy for the Bundesliga. On *ran,* some of the interviews with managers were carried out by Günna. Günna was a talking glove-puppet.

What would you look like in this Bundesliga, Heinz Höher asked himself nervously, and the next time Nuremberg were on *ran,* he analysed play as if he were being allowed to take over at the club immediately.

Overnight, the Bundesliga had become the New Rich. For the 1992-93 season, the private television channel Sat 1 paid 74 million marks to win the broadcasting rights for the first time. That was an increase of 700 per cent from the 9.2 million which the public stations had spent five years before on the same rights. The Bundesliga was also getting more tempting as a platform for the advertising industry thanks to the bright, long football programmes produced by the com-mercial channels. Only half its income now came from ticket sales. The Bundesliga clubs took the money and only a few presidents and managers, never mind players, stopped to think what television was turning them into.

Media entrepreneurs like Leo Kirsch, who counted Sat 1 as part of his empire, or Rupert Murdoch in Britain, knew that their football pro-grammes on their own could never bring in the money they spent on the broadcasting rights. The point was to tie people who wanted to watch football into the channel. Football was, as Murdoch put it, the battering ram that would give the new channels their breakthrough. Cameras raced on tracks through the stadiums and caught the game from innumerable angles. Football became more dramatic, more human. They didn't need the quality of the play itself to improve.

Little things on the periphery, such as the lucky blue jumper worn by a manager, the rivalry between two keepers, or a forward kicking an advertising hoarding in rage, were as important as the goals. You didn't have to understand the way zonal marking worked to sit there every

Saturday, chair pulled up close to the TV, to watch, fascinated, as Bundesliga players went through triumph and disaster.

At *Das aktuelle Sportstudio*, many of the editors hated the shrill tones of this new TV era. Few of them wanted to admit that *ran* had just taken the original format of *Sportstudio* further. Sport was entertainment. Heinz Höher rarely watched *Sportstudio* these days. After two hours of *ran* early on a Saturday evening, you'd already seen it all anyway.

Heinz Höher and Gerd Schmelzer watched from the middle distance and were astonished at how much football could take and still survive. Bundesliga games were shown live on pay-TV, Bundesliga games were changed to Sundays, so that Sat 1 still had something to talk about then. The German Football Union allowed teams to field three rather than two foreign players, and the *Münchener Merkur* newspaper asked whether there would soon be any real Munich men at all at Bayern, what with all those Brazilians, Hessens and Karlsruhers. According to decades of received wisdom, they were doing everything to drive spectators away from the stadiums: games on TV all the time, teams with scarcely any regional roots any more. But the crowds kept growing. In the 1992-93 season, the average gate at Bundesliga matches was over the 25,000 mark for the first time in 13 years. Was it the pictures from *ran* that were tempting people into the stadiums? Were spectators looking for the thrilling and spectacular football they saw on TV? There didn't seem to be any other explanation.

The Bundesliga declared that it was now modern. In the twinkling of an eye, that slogan was everywhere. Managers praised their style of play as 'modern football', Sat 1 congratulated its own programme, *ran*, as being the expression of modern football, newspaper reporters wrote about players' advisors, merchandising gurus and VIP boxes as the signs of modern football, and some fans held up banners in the stadiums saying 'Down with modern football'. No doubt they meant boxes filled with directors of car companies and games being played on Monday evenings for the sake of TV. Even the lumbering football authorities suddenly wanted to belong to modern football. FIFA banned keepers from handling back-passes, and awarded three points instead of two for a victory, to encourage offensive play. UEFA founded the Champions League. And Heinz Höher published an essay in the broadsheet *Welt am Sonntag*, to explain how football could become truly modern.

For years, he wrote, people had been shutting their eyes to the fact that football – the actual game itself – was no longer up to date. 'People want action. But what are we offering them in football?' A sport in which defending, breaking down, and boredom had long gained the upper hand over skill and spectacle. 'So elephants are led around the pitch at half-time, and 50 glamour girls flick their skirts up – it doesn't make our sport any better. We need rules that can scupper the tacticians and the brick-layers.' Reducing teams to eight men would make room once again for inspired players, demanded Heinz Höher. Instant substitutions at the centre-line should be brought in, like in ice hockey. If you back-passed three times, it should be a free kick to the opposition. Passing back to the keeper should be absolutely banned. There should be no more walls allowed at free kicks; if free kicks were more dangerous, players would foul less.

Lots of people thought his ideas were clever but after a passing glance at his proposals, modern football raced onwards and Heinz Höher was left behind, without a managerial job. Well, has he found anything? Doris's acquaintances asked, when she took the dog for a walk. Nobody asked Heinz Höher himself. They were too afraid that by asking, they'd open up the wound again.

Experienced as he was in the difficult art of understanding his father, Thomas came to the conclusion that his dad's interest in football was ebbing. On Saturdays, he opened the *Nürnberger Nachrichten* at 'property for sale' before looking at the sports pages; he gave Thomas his German Football Union manager's ID so his son could sneak for free into the stadium. He didn't want to go any more himself, he said.

One Saturday at 4pm, Heinz Höher was standing in his suit and tie in a detached house in Wilhelmsdorf, a good way out of Nuremberg on the B8, waiting for a potential buyer who'd been slightly delayed. Heinz Höher had time to stare out of the windows. He was trying to distance himself from Bundesliga football, so that his own absence from it wouldn't hurt so much. But when he looked at the clock, his thoughts couldn't help travelling 40km to the east, to the other side of Nuremberg. It was 4.05. Right now, the club was playing in their shiny new stadium, the Frankenstadion. And you're standing here in the wilderness waiting for someone who's not going to buy this wretched detached house in any case. What kind of a pathetic bastard are you.

In his 14 months as an estate agent he sold four flats. Two of them to Helmut Schmelzer, two of them to his lawyer. He began buying houses and flats himself, instead.

On his way to school, Thomas saw the *Nürnberger Abendzeitung* in the newsagents. His school-friends laughed. Thomas blushed. The advertising poster for the paper said, 'Football, farewell – Heinz Höher is now a hotelier in Dresden'.

His Hotel Merian on the Unschlittplatz ran itself, without him having to do anything. But he wanted to do something, that was the point. At Blumenauer's estate agency, his boss told him, I was doing business with your friend Gerd Schmelzer today, I offered him a property in Dresden, but he didn't want it. Heinz Höher pricked up his ears. He'd only recently bought a villa with a swimming pool in Herzogenaurach for 750,000 marks, then sold it six months later and made half a million profit. His friends were telling him he had a feeling for property. It was true that he'd quickly lost most of his profit on the Herzogenaurach villa playing Put and Call on the stock market, but that was nothing to do with it. He bought the property, a restaurant and flats in the Dresden suburb of Heidenau, and converted it into a hotel, Die Alte Reichskrone. The property, and the rebuilding, cost him virtually 6 million marks. While he was at it, he bought another three blocks of flats in Heidenau, as well as an office building in nearby Pirna. Putting all his hotels and houses together, he had to pay a good million marks a year on credit and interest. What he saw above all was how much he could make, probably over 1.2 million. Doris couldn't understand why the banks were giving him such big loans. Maybe because he was a Bundesliga manager. People were happy to do favours for heroes from the Bundesliga.

He used his old contacts to invite teams to stay at the freshly renovated Reichskrone when they came to play Dynamo Dresden away. Nuremberg, Kaiserslautern, Bremen and Schalke all stayed at his place. But he couldn't find a tenant who'd pay more than 30,000 marks a month. The hotel was a good way from the city centre, and other investors had saturated the market in Dresden before he got there. He'd reckoned on 50,000 marks a month. Well, he'd have to see how he managed. He'd manage, somehow. He ordered another Radeberger Pilsener for himself and Schalke's general manager Rudi Assauer, at his own bar in the Reichskrone. It was April 1994, the evening before the game against Dresden, the players had already had to retire to their rooms, but as their general manager, Assauer could still have a drink with him, or two.

Christ, that Zobel's an idiot, said Rudi Assauer, he goes and gets Zarate warming up an hour into the game! Assauer had been at Friday's game, when Nuremberg beat Leipzig 2-0. Sergio Zarate, Nuremberg's little goalscorer, the one they called 'Magic Mouse', had been out injured for weeks. Heinz Höher refused to believe that their manager, Zobel, would bring an injured player along to Leipzig, never mind warm him up for a possible substitution.

Seriously, I'm telling you, that's what an idiot Zobel is!

Bet on it?

Heinz Höher was convinced that Assauer was mixing Zarate up with Nuremberg's other Argentinian, Sergio Bustos.

They shook on the bet – for the entire cost of Schalke's stay at the Reichskrone, a good 2500 marks. The question was, who could dispel the uncertainty. It was 12.30 on the night before the game, and they dragged Schalke forward Dieter Eckstein out of bed. As a former Nuremberg player, Eckstein would surely have seen the team-sheets on the TV.

Of course Zarate wasn't there at Leipzig, said Eckstein, standing half-awake in front of them at the hotel bar. You don't want to bet against that one, he added for Assauer's benefit, and nodded at Heinz Höher. Heinz Höher felt reassured that he always won his bets, including the ones on leases and loans.

When he had appointments with the lawyers or bank officials, Heinz Höher sometimes appeared with a bright yellow Adidas backpack, which seemed a surprising choice for the business in hand as well as for the decade, this being the middle of the 1990s. What he didn't tell anyone was that it was Markus's backpack.

Just like Markus back then at Bochum, Thomas was thrown out of the Nuremberg youth team. And now he was no longer the manager who could put a word in for his son.

One day around midday, Thomas came home with a few friends and found his father, who had taken Nuremberg to such success, lying rather than sitting on the sofa, watching a daytime TV agony-aunt. Doris found a half-empty whisky bottle behind the books in the bookcase. Thomas found a bottle of schnapps behind his football boots. Heinz Höher said, if I want to stop I can stop, just like that.

On Whit Sunday 1995, he decided to do something for his health. He went off on his bike for a 70 or 80km trip into the hills of the Fränkische Schweiz. The basket on his handlebars was well stocked with beer and schnapps. Around midday, already beyond Gräfenberg, he sat down in the rich green grass to take a break. He said he'd be back for lunch. He cycled onwards, passing through Ermreuth and Schlichenreuth with their half-timbered houses and red-painted wooden balconies, without knowing exactly where he was; he could drink just as easily while pedalling. Back at the Elbinger Straße, Susanne and her husband Michael had appeared for Sunday lunch. He said he'd be back for lunch, said Doris, so I'm starting to get worried.

It was already gone 4pm, maybe 5pm, when he returned to the town from a northerly direction via the Äußere Bayreuther Straße. He stopped at the Leipziger Hof. The flat front roof made the pub look as though it was bowed down. There was a red chewing-gum machine hanging on the turquoise wall. The Greek landlord greeted Heinz Höher as a well-known guest. Later, he'd start talking to him about how he had taken Olympiakos to victory over Ajax in the year 1983. Every time Heinz Höher came in there, the landlord started talking about that victory. Heinz Höher didn't go to bars to talk to the landlord or the customers. He went there to knock himself out.

When he got home that evening, he didn't understand why everyone was so excited and why they were also angry with him. It was only when he was sitting on the sofa and they were still all having a go at him, telling him it couldn't go on like this, that they were going to call a doctor right now, that a blocked passageway opened up in his mind and their words got through to him at last, my God, what have you done, how have you let yourself go like this, they're right, how can you torture your wife and your children like this with your boozing; you've already lost Markus. His son-in-law called their doctor. It was Whit Sunday, in the evening. Their doctor, Dr Schütte, appeared after a short while. He could have him signed in to a residential rehab clinic first thing in the morning. Heinz Höher nodded.

Next morning, without saying a thing to one another, Doris and Thomas each had ready a whole list of reasons to convince him to go, in case he woke up and didn't want to know anything about it. But he just said: let's go.

Engelthal lay beyond the final stop on the Nuremberg suburban railway. It was a place for anyone who didn't want to see anybody. Walkers strode along a footpath, the Ulrich von Königstein Way, crossed a few fields, and were soon lost in the thick forest. Heinz Höher remembered the place. On Ascension Day 1988, he'd brought his team to go for a stroll and drink a coffee here in Engelthal. It was two days before the decisive game against Kaiserslautern to qualify for the UEFA Cup, and he wanted to give them a bit of relaxation. And now he was coming back to Engelthal in this state.

The Frankenalb Clinic lay outside the village, already hedged in by the forest. He'd rarely felt at ease without alcohol in a group of people, apart from football teams; he was plagued by the feeling that he had to say something. Now he found himself in a group of people consisting entirely of alcoholics. He was haunted by thoughts of escape. The therapist questioned him: how much do you drink, how regularly do you drink? Do you drink in binges, do you drink when you're angry or sad? Heinz Höher answered politely. But he could sort himself out, couldn't he, he didn't need any doctors.

In the afternoons, they were supposed to go as a group for a walk into the village. Maybe someone or other would strike up a conversation, maybe it would help someone or other to hear that he wasn't alone in his addiction. They were like prisoners on furlough, thought Heinz Höher to himself, as he strolled along with the group. He kept facing straight forward, so that hopefully none of the others would talk to him. When Doris came to visit him on the second day he said, I'm going home, I've got the point, I've got to watch my drinking.

Doris felt herself falling apart, without moving an inch from her chair. Heinz, I can't take any more, she said: if you walk away from this therapy too, I'm leaving you.

He looked at her, and something in him seemed to come to life.

An hour or two later, Doris left the clinic in the forest of Engelthal. She drove straight to a Nuremberg jeweller, and bought herself a ring. She had the date engraved on it: 6 June 1995. It was the happiest day of her life, she said to herself. She'd done it. She'd really made him commit to rehab; she'd finally made him say goodbye to alcohol.

Heinz Höher stayed until Saturday. He'd spent six days at the clinic. The specialists said that his therapy required two or three weeks of residential treatment. They couldn't force anyone stay against his wishes.

Back home, Heinz Höher declared to his son, Thomas, that he had to stop smoking. Any addiction could be cured with determination. He felt new strength, a new desire for life. Thomas looked at him and didn't say what he was thinking.

Heinz Höher was waiting for news from a certain Mr Kett. Mr Kett was interested in the Alte Reichskrone hotel in the Heidenau suburb of Dresden. If he could just get shot of the hotel, he could re-orientate himself in peace. He wasn't at home when Mr Kett's lawyer called. The lawyer told Doris that Mr Kett had died of a heart attack.

Heinz Höher couldn't take any bad news, he's never been able to take bad news, why did everyone have to come at him with bad news, he cursed inwardly. He tried to remember the places he'd hidden a bottle of schnapps, behind books, behind boxes in the garage. He'd drink carefully, he hadn't forgotten that he must not drink, but he was strong enough to drink carefully. Every Sunday, he set down the days of the week he was allowing himself to drink.

It was getting hard to make the regular repayments on his property portfolio. The banks wrote to him formally, requesting meetings to resolve the situation. When Heinz Höher simply binned their letters and demands, it wasn't because he actually thought his troubles would solve themselves. It was just that he couldn't think of any other way out.

Well, has he found anything, asked Thomas's friends?

Heinz Höher was waiting for the call from FC Nuremberg. He knew that it was pointless: Gerd Schmelzer's rival, Michael A. Roth, was back as club president and was never going to call the man who'd been manager under Schmelzer. He waited, despite knowing this. May 1996, Nuremberg went down into the third division, even Roth would surely have to think of him now, the man who'd made them such a storming, fighting club. Or maybe Roth would be toppled and Gerd Schmelzer elevated to the presidency again? He knew that it could never come to this. The club was financially dependent on Roth, and Schmelzer's good name had suffered after hints came out about the mismanagement that flourished during the last years of his term in office. Club treasurer Professor Dr Dr Böbel, having begun by forging taxi receipts, had later put 11 private journeys to Monte Carlo through the club books. On one of those 11 journeys, he claimed 26,800 marks expenses. He became the image of how the club had ruined itself by bad behaviour. Since Böbel was a ready-made scapegoat, there was no need to dig any deeper to see what had gone wrong, and how. FC Nuremberg, which the accountants had officially declared free of debt in 1989, had, within three years, piled up debts to the tune of 23 million marks.

And yet, Heinz Höher kept on waiting for the call from the club. He had nothing else to do, anyway.

If only he had something to do, then it'd be easier to keep his drinking under control, the best thing would be just one beer in the mornings, one beer and a shot at lunchtimes, and a couple of glasses in the evenings, then he'd be on the right path.

The Bundesliga was still his whole world, yet he no longer belonged to it. Hundreds of former players and managers lived trapped in this dilemma for decades – never truly happy, but never truly unhappy enough to really break free of that gravitational pull. Was he going to have to get used to a life so close to the Bundesliga, yet so far from it? He didn't think it through.

He could still see the traces of his own life in the Bundesliga: Otto Rehhagel, whose career had run parallel to his for so long, was now *the* manager in the Bundesliga, at European Cup Winners' Cup holders and German champions Werder Bremen. At Bundesliga press conferences, Rehhagel was suddenly spouting quotes from Goethe and Schiller, he was allowed to spread wisdom and predict trends, such as that the real way to achieve success was with players over 30. Even though that didn't really fit at all into modern football.

Beyond the Bundesliga, everyone at the top of the game was now playing zonal marking, but the Germans kept on with their *liberos* and their man-to-man marking, that was the German way. In 100 years there'd still be these national differences, the Italians might have their tactics, and the English their pace, but the Germans had willpower and players who knew how to lead. Hadn't everyone seen that in Euro 1996? Matthias Sammer and Jürgen Klinsmann could stimulate a team and rip it along with them.

On the pitch, away from the pictures on *ran*, Heinz Höher couldn't see anything in the Bundesliga of 1996 that he hadn't already seen in 1989; he didn't want to even say the words, back in his day.

He said to himself, I'm just waiting for the call, and yet he was taken utterly aback when, in October 1996, a friend did call. Dieter Reiber had something for him.

There's something not quite right with him, thought the VfB Lübeck team, as they listened to Heinz Höher for the first time.

THE BREAK

The final curve of his signature made a jaunty, upward sweep. It was as if the joy of it was guiding his hand. Heinz Höher looked up from the contract that he'd just signed with VfB Lübeck, and said to one of their board members: wait till I tell my son about this.

Every week, Thomas phoned up from Kempten, where he was studying business management at the technical university, and every week he asked his mum: well, has he found something? At last, Heinz Höher could answer his son.

His job was to save Lübeck from relegation from the Bundesliga 2. He had had to wait seven years for a new mission as a manager.

In modern football, the idea was that talent scouts would systematically supply Bundesliga clubs with players and managers. Even so, in the late 1990s many clubs still found their players or managers the same way VfB Lübeck got Heinz Höher: Julius Rießen, a member of Lübeck's business management team, had been on holiday when he'd met a Nuremberg businessman who knew the manager who'd once taken FC Nuremberg from the Bundesliga 2 into the UEFA Cup. If you need a new manager, he's the man for you, said the Nuremberg businessman Dieter Reiber to Rießen.

Julius Rießen was a landowner in a village with five streets through which the wind blew down from the Baltic Sea. He'd specialised in wind-power, and he knew the footballing world by virtue of having been for many years boss of the amateur first-division club Pansdorf.

He had been at VfB Lübeck for three and a half months. In the middle of October 1996, when *Kicker* magazine said that Lübeck manager Michael Lorkowski was on the verge of being kicked out, Rießen called his holiday acquaintance Dieter Reiber. Heinz Höher flew to Lübeck the next day. Günther Schütt, chairman of Lübeck's business management committee, patriarch of the club, took him out to dinner. Let's hope he doesn't notice that I'm not eating much but I'm already drinking my fourth beer to make up for it, thought Heinz Höher.

Right now, said Günther Schütt, Molle to his friends, tomorrow was Wednesday, and that meant no training, so he'd lay things before the business management committee. And then Heinz Höher might as well start work on Thursday. 'I'm not going to waste time beating about the bush' was a phrase Molle Schütt liked to use. He led the club the same way he led his building firm, in the absolute conviction that he could make all the right decisions for himself. Lübeck hadn't had anyone on their books who was a proper football expert since their general manager Helmut Schulte had left in the summer of 1996.

Heinz Höher had to pass the time all Wednesday in Lübeck. In his children's book, Tommo the hero went to school in Lübeck. Was it just an entertaining coincidence, or was it actually fate, that meant he'd got his unexpected break in Tommo's very city? His children's book would actually sell at last; if he achieved success with VfB Lübeck, he could market it here in Lübeck. He went to the fitness studio at his hotel in Lübeck to jog on the running-machine. You could still run those 19-year-olds into the ground, he said to himself. Heinz Höher was 58. His friends thought that for a while he'd been turning his head very slowly. He had another couple of beers at the hotel bar.

From tomorrow, he wouldn't allow himself to touch another drop of alcohol. When training began, he had to be fit, Lübeck was his last chance. Over the past year he'd done three radical stints of abstinence, each of them six weeks, he controlled his drinking, he'd said to himself on 1 January 1996, I'm not going to drink anything until 11 February, and he opened his first beer after that on 12 February. On the days he wasn't abstaining, the level of alcohol in his blood hovered permanently between 1 and 1.5 per thousand. Outside his family, almost nobody thought that Heinz Höher's alcohol consumption was a problem. After all, he never got lary or behaved unusually.

From tomorrow, he absolutely could not drink at all. But how was he going to make it through the first days of training if he was going through cold turkey?

He had a clear picture of himself: he was stronger than other alcoholics, he could do cold turkey all alone and quicker than most people, after only two days he had thrown off the trembling in his body, the chattering of his teeth, the whirling in his head. But this time, he didn't have two days.

He had to jump straight into training, on Sunday he already had his first game, against FC Gütersloh, a relegation duel; if he lost it the players would immediately start to distrust him, and that was something many managers never got over. He imagined what would happen if he won; everything would fall into place all by itself. He knew almost nothing about his new team. It was true that by now Bundesliga 2 games were covered well on German sports TV, in fact there was a live game shown every Monday evening. But he'd just let those televised games go in one ear and out the other.

He couldn't keep on drinking tonight if he was going to start work in the morning. And he couldn't start the first training day when he was in cold turkey. And there was no way that he could screw up this last chance, this gift. Desperate, he called his family doctor in Nuremberg.

There were such things as appetite-suppressants, the doctor told him, and since March 1996 there'd been an alchohol-suppressant, Campral, on the market in Germany too. He faxed Heinz Höher a prescription to his hotel in Lübeck. Heinz Höher didn't tell him that he was already taking sleeping tablets as well as Aponal, a mood-enhancing drug prescribed in cases of depression.

They'd have to order Campral in for him, said the pharmacist in Lübeck. She said they'd definitely have the medicine there by 9.30 in the morning. The first training session was scheduled for 3pm tomorrow. Before that, at midday, he was going to have to introduce himself to the team and the press. Heinz Höher went back to the Senator Hotel and drank another couple of beers at the hotel bar, the last for a very long time, he told himself.

On Thursday, 17 October 1996, he got up early. He wanted to go into the fitness room to sweat out the alcohol before he went to the pharmacy. He was there at the door at 9.30am sharp. Unfortunately, the delivery hadn't come in yet, said the pharmacist, but it was sure to arrive in the next few minutes. Heinz Höher walked round and round the pharmacy.

At 10.30am, he at last got the package of Campral. He straight away washed four tablets down with tap-water. He'd had nothing for breakfast. For the first time in days, he hadn't had a beer all morning. Before presenting himself before the press at 1pm, he took another two tablets. He didn't read the instructions about dosages.

Instead of gathering as usual on the small training-pitch at Im Burgfeld, the team had been summoned for 2pm to their stadium at Lohmühle. A new main stand with 22 boxes had been built there for the Bundesliga 2. They thought that if Heinz Höher met the team here, he'd straight away realise that he hadn't come to just any old club, and the unusual nature of the meeting would make the team feel that something special was beginning.

The new man's name had already spread around among the players: Heinz Höher. It meant something to most of them, after all, he'd been manager at Nuremberg. Some of them had never heard of him. In the team, the whispers had already started. Where we are, we need a man who knows our team and knows the Bundesliga 2, said defender Jörn Schwinkendorf.

Heinz Höher addressed the team about fighting against relegation, courage, a new chance for every one of them. Andre Golke, Lübeck's *libero*, wondered what was up with him. Heinz Höher's speech just didn't hang together. His eyes flicked this way and that. Was he trembling? As the players made their way down the steps of the main stand, to drive to the training-ground in their own cars, there was no time to talk about it, just time for the one thought: he's a weird one, thought Andre Golke to himself. Before the training session, Heinz Höher took another two tablets of Campral.

The training-ground was noticeably narrower than most pitches. It only took a careless shot or a full-blooded clearance to send the ball flying over the main road next door. Heinz Höher was in too much turmoil to be surprised at this, never mind get worked up about it. He fell back on the training exercises he'd used for decades, which meant he could spend most of the time standing on the pitch, watching in silence. But his body just wouldn't stop shivering, ice-cold microwaves were shooting clean through him. He wanted to lie down and shut his eyes. Soon, he told himself, after training, you can give them just an hour's training today, it's the first time, no one will notice, then you can lie down in the hotel.

At least 300 spectators had come, just to see a training session. In modern football, everyday things had become events. To finish off, Heinz Höher got the team to play a game without goal-posts. Then he called them to him, there was just a warm-down to go. They approached him from all sides. The first of them had actually reached him when Heinz Höher collapsed. He himself could no longer feel the way he writhed on the ground.

A heart attack at his first training session, was how presenter Dagmar Berghoff described it on Germany's biggest TV news programme, *Tagesschau*. The doctors knew better. It wasn't his heart that had given up, but his circulation. One of the Lübeck officials had fetched Heinz Höher's clothes from the dressing-room and brought them to the hospital. The doctors had found the tablets.

By the time Heinz Höher woke up in intensive care, it was already Friday.

He hadn't felt his collapse at the training session coming. He'd only wanted to send the players out for a warm-down, and then the session would have been over. Then he would have been able to lie down in bed at the hotel. A sleep would have calmed the trembling and those icy waves. If he'd held out for five minutes longer, Heinz Höher said to himself, no one would have noticed a thing.

Thomas raced from Kempten to Lübeck, the whole length of Germany, picking up his dad's car at Nuremberg. When he saw him, he was horrified. His face was all bloated, his skin a fiery red, his nerves shattered by the anger, sadness and fear which were shaking him through and through. They want to throw me out, they absolutely can't throw me out, it was just a one-off, a slip-up, that's all, I've got a contract haven't I, you've got to talk with them.

Thomas Höher, who was 21 years young and studying management, met Molle Schütt and another member of the club management team in the main stand of the Lohmühle Stadium, to plead for his father. He could see for himself that Lübeck could hardly keep his father on, now. He said the opposite, with all the conviction he had. This was the break his dad had been waiting for so long, his dad was the manager who'd taken Nuremberg into the UEFA Cup, collapsing like that was something that would never happen again. Look, lad, said Molle Schütt, in a calm and friendly way – and Schütt didn't need to say another word. Thomas could feel that the chairman of Lübeck had already come to his decision. They agreed that Thomas would take his father home and that they would phone when he was better.

Thomas drove to the Senator Hotel to gather up his father's stuff, you could look through the windows of the expansive lobby right down onto the calm waters of the Lübeck Canal. He drove his father back to Nuremberg in his father's own black Mercedes SL. You couldn't fail to see the contrast: the five-star hotel and the Mercedes limousine made a mockery of the life that his father really led, and which awaited him once more.

He was okay again, thought Heinz Höher, three days after his collapse. He told the journalists who called him in Nuremberg that he'd been signed off sick until Tuesday, and he'd be taking training again at Lübeck on Wednesday. 'I just took the wrong medication and it gave me a sort of collapse,' he told *Kicker*. 'But I'm fit as a fiddle now. I'm raring to go.'

He hoped against hope that the management team at Lübeck would believe him. He called the boss, Molle Schütt. The conversation began with Heinz Höher presenting rational arguments, and it ended with him pleading and begging. He said that Schütt had to give him another chance, of course he'd made himself look idiotic but he wasn't a boozer, he could control his drinking. The Lübeck management team decided by ten votes to zero not to continue working with Heinz Höher. 'Anyone who needs to take pills can't be healthy,' Molle Schütt told *Bild Zeitung*.

Heinz Höher chose attack as the best method of defence. He gave half a dozen interviews in which he spoke with apparent honesty about his relationship to alcohol. 'It's well known that I have to take care with the drink.' – 'I'm certainly no teetotaller.' – 'Sure, I drink more than the average person.' In all his interviews he added: 'But I'm no alcoholic.' Wasn't there still a difference between a Hemingway who could put it away, who could hold his drink, and a drunk who slept in the bushes in the park? Couldn't people see which class he belonged in?

He learned from the papers that Lübeck were about to appoint a new manager. Molle Schütt declared: 'Our principle is that life goes on.'

In the hallway at Heinz Höher's home in Nuremberg, a week after his collapse, it was still standing there: the suitcase he'd taken with him up to Lübeck. The suitcase he'd wanted to take back up again to Lübeck.

On TV in 1998, Ulm manager Ralf Rangnick explains to the Germans how the rest of the world plays football.

At the Turn of the Millennium:

THE UNBEARABLE DISCOVERY OF ZONAL MARKING

It was left to Doris to tidy up his life. Heinz Höher himself could never be parted from things. In the cellar, which was kitted out with their old furniture, there were complete years' worths of football magazines and thousands of Tommo books. When it finally got too much for Doris yet again, she went at it full on, it was time for all that crap to be chucked out, into the street and ready for the council to take to the dump.

In the spring of 1997 she threw the dummy books out of his bookcase, he had enough books already, why did he need dummy books as well.

Where are my dummy books, Doris, he asked when he saw the decluttered bookcase. He tried to keep the panic out of his voice.

Outside the front door, waiting for the council to take them. What do you want with all that rubbish?

Heinz Höher charged out into the Elbinger Straße and started rummaging through the rubbish. From the dummy books he produced several thousand marks.

He'd hidden away his card-playing money inside the fake books.

Cards were his replacement for football. His own self-image, even after the last-chance saloon at Lübeck, was still of himself as a Bundesliga manager, but Heinz Höher knew, even as he fought the knowledge down, that in a world that came to snap decisions, he was now 'the one with the drink problem'. He was 59. No one asked any longer: well, has he found something?

He could have tried to get a job in the senior semi-professional league. But he wasn't going to go chasing his own relegation. He'd never gone after a job yet. He was too proud for that.

At some time or another the Bundesliga spat all its children out, whether they were players or managers, at sometime or another the sports reporters put an 'ex-' in front of your name, ex-Bundesliga professional, ex-Bundesliga manager, most people had to come to terms with the fact that they still felt to themselves like Bundesliga players or Bundesliga managers, even though they no longer were.

Once a month he played cards with Dieter Reiber's school. After seven or eight hands, the others couldn't remember properly which cards had already been played. He made an exact note in his mind of who had played which card and which cards were therefore still in the game. Years before, when he'd been playing the numberplate-memory game with Thomas on the autobahn, Heinz Höher had realised that he obviously had an unusual ability to remember numbers. On those evenings playing cards with Dieter Reiber and his colleagues, he usually won somewhere between 300 and 2000 marks. That was enough for his everyday expenses.

He been trying for years to get shot of the hotel in Dresden, but who wanted an 80-bedroom hotel in a suburb of Dresden? The Alte Reichskrone was losing him 20,000 marks a month. Several floors of his office building in Pirna stood empty, because Pirna, like most small towns in the former GDR, had shrunk in population since reunification. Its inhabitants had gone down from 48,000 to 39,000. Who was going to rent office space in a shrivelling small town?

The bailiff rang at the door. He took the trouble to sound understanding, he didn't confiscate any items of value. He was just a menace made flesh, a reminder that it might soon come to that.

When it was a question of having to make an immediate payment to the banks, Heinz Höher's son-in-law helped him out. A few weeks later, the bailiff appeared again. His son-in-law stepped into the breach once again. Heinz Höher had taken out loans with the Hypobank, the Deutsche Bank, the Postsparkasse and the Deutsche Kreditbank. The sums rolled over his head like an avalanche.

In June 1997, the Dresden court declared officially that with regard to the hotel-management company 'Alte Reichskrone' GmbH, Dresdener Straße 84, 01809 Heidenau, represented by the chief executive Heinz Höher, the aforementioned company was hereby declared to be in administration. A long, complicated sentence to deliver a short, sharp blow. The hotel was bankrupt.

Heinz Höher let his lawyer take care of the matter, to spare himself the details. All he got was the big news. The Reichskrone was forcibly sold. Then the flats in Heidenau were taken back. Finally, the office block in Pirna was signed over to the banks. All he had left was the debts. So long as his feelings were thoroughly dulled by 1 to 1.5 per thousand parts of alcohol, reality was quite easy to live with. If it hadn't been for the looks on the faces of his wife and the children.

Doris looked at the ring she'd bought on 6 June 1995. She had thought it was the happiest day of her life. How wide-eyed and innocent she'd been, she thought now. Then, she'd really believed that he'd manage to give up the drinking.

One Sunday evening, at the end of the weekend visit, Thomas said to him: Dad, stick to it, you'll make it, you can stop drinking. So then, Heinz Höher felt obliged to have a go. He just couldn't cut so wretched a figure in front of his own son. But after just five hours without a drink, the trembling awoke inside him, he was scared of the trembling, of the icy coldness of body and the rawness of nerves that came along with the trembling. The squeak of a door, every word spoken by a person, it all became unbearable. What the hell was he doing, letting his son dictate his life to him, he was only 22, still half a boy. Heinz Höher had his bottles hidden away all over the house.

He went to the card game with Dieter Reiber and his friends in Altmühltal, he had an unbelievable hand, a sure-fire full house. One of them kept raising him. Well, the other guys sometimes betted on an absurd chance. They could afford to lose. Heinz Höher couldn't lose with this hand. He was still thinking that, even after he lost. He asked his fellow card-players to at least lend him the money for the taxi. In a single hand he'd just lost 7380 marks.

Now and then, journalists still called him. In this modern football, journalists were obsessed with getting quotes from behind the scenes in the Bundesliga. Quotations were more important than your own observations. News agencies' reports on Bundesliga matches were often no more than a list of quotations. Quotations suggested that you were up close and authentic. With this in mind, professional press offices of the 1990s, like those at Bayern or Werder Bremen, provided local reporters with lists containing the private telephone numbers of their entire teams. One time, Bayern manager Erich Ribbeck's phone rang at 3am. A student who worked as a freelancer at the *Süddeutsche Zeitung* was having a party, and to entertain the other partygoers one of the guests used the list of phone numbers to tell Ribbeck: 'Erich, it's Uli here, we're having trouble with Lothar again.' Uli being Hoeneß, Lothar being Matthäus, obviously.

But those were glitches you could put up with. Everyone involved in the Bundesliga in the 1990s thought it was incredibly important to see themselves quoted in the papers. They thought that anyone who wanted to cut a figure in the team had to make a noise off the pitch too. After all, if you looked at what was on *ran*, and because of them in the other media too, the ballyhoo was at least as important as the game. Footballers who wanted to be leaders of the pack, like Matthäus, Effenberg and Klinsmann, marked out their territory with quotations; players who were dissatisfied with their supporting roles put pressure on their managers by making pointed remarks to the media. To which the managers retorted by making colourful statements to the media. After being substituted, Bayern midfielder Thomas Strunz moaned sourly into *ran*'s microphone that you had to question his manager's tactics, and manager Giovanni Trapattoni answered two days later: 'Struuunz? Who this Strunz thinking he is? In thees game are two, three players they are so weak like the bottle empty!'

Since the daily spectacle of people actually involved in the Bundesliga wasn't enough for the tabloids, they also liked to call ex-managers, who were always up for a juicy quote, obliged as they were to use the media to position themselves for a new job. 'Nuremberg are combing Germany to find some assistant coach to be their next manager, and all the time the best manager in Germany's living right here, not five km from their ground. I ask myself what kind of a strategy that is,' Heinz Höher told the *Nürnberger Abendzeitung*. When he saw the interview in the paper next day, complete with a portrait photograph of him in his finest days as Nuremberg manager he thought, maybe someone will still think about me, after all.

It was his hairdresser who took him back into football. Toni, at his salon in the Sankt Jobst district, thought it important that he should personally trim the hair of any customer who was a somebody, and he possessed the quality most vital to any hairdresser: he got on with everybody. His hairdressing-chair welcomed Heinz Höher as warmly as it welcomed Reinhold Hintermaier, who Höher had kicked off the team at Nuremberg. Toni talked with everyone about everyone. At the end of the day, even in the era of commercial television and mobile phones, one of the most important sources of information was still your hairdresser.

Couldn't he do something for Heinz Höher, he really wasn't in a good way, in health or in wealth, warbled Toni, as he pruned the 42-year-old Hintermaier's hair, which he no longer wore quite so long these days. For the first time since the 1960s, modern Bundesliga professionals were wearing their hair cut short to the neck again.

He didn't want anything to do with Mr Höher, answered Hintermaier: he'd chucked him out of the club, back in the day.

In 1984, Heinz Höher's first season at Nuremberg, Hintermaier, their Austrian international with the southern European colouring, had been fighting to get back his old place at the heart of the team after breaking his leg. To the outside world, Hintermaier was the best mannered of players, but behind the scenes there was friction, football was all about conflicts, especially in your own team, it was always a question of power, of status, that was the way Hintermaier had learned his football in the 1980s. It was all too stressful for Heinz Höher, he'd sooner get rid of a player like that than have all this tension turn into aggro on the pitch.

But after Toni had warbled three or four times that things really weren't going well for Heinz Höher, he was already looking bent down as he walked, Reinhold Hintermaier thought about letting bygones be bygones. After all, it was nearly 14 years since Mr Höher had chased him out of the club. And whatever had happened between them as people, Mr Höher did have his qualities as a manager. In the late autumn of 1997, Reinhold Hintermaier invited him to train a group of children at his private football school.

Just ten years earlier, children hadn't had the time to go to private football schools. They'd been too busy playing football in the street all afternoon. But now that football had become modern, it seemed a logical necessity that on top of what the football clubs were doing, children should be offered private football training to go along with their private piano lessons and their private tennis coaching.

Up till now, the youth teams at Bundesliga clubs had trained three or four times a week in the evenings after school, completely separated from the professionals; if one or two of their talented young players made the breakthrough now and then, that was great, and if not, that was fine too. No Bundesliga manager had to rely on mere 18- or 19-year-olds. There was enough money there to buy proven players. For the 1997-98 season, Sat 1 paid 128 million marks for the broadcasting rights, 12 times as much as it had cost them ten years before. In 1995 the average Bundesliga gate had gone over the 30,000 mark for the first time and had never dropped below since. Thanks to the Bosman Ruling, the borders within the EU were open, so Bundesliga general managers could speedily buy in a left-back from Bulgaria or the Czech Republic whenever they needed to, and meanwhile they were swapping established Bundesliga players this way and that among themselves. The German national side had been victorious in Euro 1996, Borussia Dortmund won the Champions League in 1997, Bayern took the UEFA Cup in 1996 and Schalke did so the year after. On Planet Bundesliga there were only a few quiet voices whispering that at the very moment German football apparently stood at its zenith, it was already in decline. Those lone voices, who travelled the world in search of new ideas, said that German teams were too fixated on battling it out man to man, meaning they'd be playing more slowly, and leaving their opponents more room, than French, Italian or even Norwegian teams. But they were just the moaning minnies, who always thought the grass was greener somewhere else.

These whispers were strongest in the dusty cellar of professional football – the youth programmes. The more alert among the youth coaches were prophesying that in the next five or six years there'd be few exceptional talents coming up from the junior sides. The trouble was that when it came to training children, which surely wasn't that important, most German clubs had just kept on doing things the way they always had: endurance and power were relentlessly pursued, but just on their own terms, not specifically for football. Interplay and tactics were ignored in the belief that there was always enough talent about and it didn't need nurturing, it just needed to be moulded by strong wills forged in the school of hard training.

The Bundesliga was too busy celebrating itself and its thrilling image (as seen on *ran*) to notice that a few men, such as Helmut Groß, youth coordinator of VfB Stuttgart, a bridge engineer by trade, were modernising things their own way at the grass roots: they got their youth sides to practise zonal marking, and they used lots of new small-pitch exercises to prioritise ball skills. The thought behind it was as simple as it was revolutionary: the more touches of the ball a young player actually got, the better he'd become.

Reinhold Hintermaier had merely been going with the flow of the Bundesliga when he had the idea of starting up a private football school at the end of his own playing career: everything was getting more professional, and there was money to be made out of it all. But it meant that as fate would have it, when Heinz Höher landed at Hintermaier's Football Academy at the end of the 1990s, he did so at the very time when youth sides were the most interesting places in German football: it was here, in mentoring the players of the future, that the German way of football was being turned on its head.

Heinz Höher's new team stood in front of him in the gym hall. The kids' eyes gazed at him cheekily, or remained fixed on the floor to avoid catching the eye of this white-haired man in his tracksuit. Heinz Höher had played manager at 434 Bundesliga games. Now, a group of 12-year-olds from Hintermaier's Football Academy were waiting for him. He could hear his own heart beating. His eyes began to water. He tried to keep control of the sheer happiness that was filling his whole body, yet at the same time to enjoy it. He just wanted to suck the air in deep. He was a manager again.

He reminded himself about his old dream, to take a club side of 12-year-olds and train them up for seven years. He would spend every afternoon with them, at team training sessions at the ground, at their private training sessions in the park, he would watch them grow and then, after seven years, when the best three or four of them were making their Bundesliga debuts, he would sit in the stand and allow himself to be overpowered by the memory of the journey they'd made together. Reinhold Hintermaier smiled cautiously every time Heinz Höher told him about this dream yet again.

Just come along one Saturday, Hintermaier told Heinz Höher in 1998, it was spring already. Then you can meet Mr Hack.

Alongside his private football school, Hintermaier was boss of the youth programme at second-division side Greuther Fürth. Mr Hack was their president.

One Saturday, at 9am, the three of them were stood bunched close together under a tree in the grounds of Nuremberg Tennis & Hockey Club. It was pouring with rain. Hintermaier and Helmut Hack were looking for a training ground for their youth teams. Around 1998, plans for nurturing the next generation were being made and initiated on every side: residential schools were being built for talented youths, papers about co-operation with schools and new ways of training were being written – but the reality was that many youth teams at professional clubs still trained on cinder pitches or, like here in Fürth, they played each week on different pitches rented from amateur teams.

Standing under the tree, they watched the rain. They talked of unimportant things, What do you think about the pitch at the Tennis & Hockey Club then, there are real differences in the quality of artificial grass pitches, these days, yes indeed. Trust could often be built through simple physical nearness, rather than through words; by standing together under a tree in the rain. A few weeks later, Mr Hack asked to see him. He said he was interested in involving Heinz Höher in the club's work; that was if he, as an experienced Bundesliga manager, could even start to imagine working with the youth organisation of a modest Bundesliga 2 outfit. He might be able to offer him the reserve team. That was a job second only in importance to the first-team manager. No, said Heinz Höher, he wanted the Under-13s.

The Under-13s? But, look, forgive me, we can't take on a man with your qualifications and then send him off to the 12-year-olds. Why don't you take the Over-17s, they play in the youth Bundesliga?

Heinz Höher said he would take on the Over-17s if he could have the Under-13s too. He had a dream.

Mr Hack said if Heinz Höher called spending his time with teams below his rightful level his dream, he wasn't going to hold him back from it. He held out his hand to Heinz Höher.

Just one thing, said Helmut Hack. You'll be working with children and youths, now, Mr Höher. Please, never come to work drunk. Or I'll have to throw you out.

Heinz Höher tried to act outraged. He knew what discipline was. He never drank before training sessions.

He trained them on a football pitch called Sportpark Ziegelstein where the only flag that waved was the blue one hanging above the door of the club-house, advertising ice-cream. The park lay directly under the approach-path of Nuremberg airport, but usually, all you heard was the birds. Planes only took off or landed at Nuremberg every now and again. When the weather was bad, Heinz Höher took the Under-13s of

Greuther Fürth for a run to the end of a forest path, to train them on the cinder pitch belonging to Franken Concordia, the Catholic youth sports association. He laid out little orange-and-white plastic cones to make three goals in line next to one another. In front of these goals, his boys played three against three. The three goals were unguarded, but a seventh boy ran backwards and forwards behind them. A score only counted if the seventh boy wasn't behind that particular goal when the ball went in. This meant that, without noticing it, the seventh boy was practising starting quickly and stopping abruptly, because he was always sprinting backwards and forwards behind the goals, to stop the others scoring. The others were learning how to swiftly change the direction of play when on the ball, because all of a sudden they had to aim for a different goal. Heinz Höher was inventing training exercises once more.

Some days, he drove to three different pitches. As well as managing the Over-17s and Under-13s at Fürth, and the boys at Reinhold Hintermaier's Football Academy, he was also in charge of a team of mentally and physically handicapped sportsmen. He'd been given this team by a lady judge. Heinz Höher had been sentenced to 250 hours of community service. A friend of his had tried to help him out with a cute little move. This friend had purchased a property and put Heinz Höher down as the estate agent, in order to shove an imaginary estate agent's percentage of 450,000 marks his way; money that would otherwise just have been gobbled up by the taxman. Sadly, the Inland Revenue found it somewhat too interesting that Heinz Höher, who hadn't worked as an estate agent for so long, was suddenly getting such high fees. Heinz Höher swiftly confessed all. The lady judge had no idea that she was doing him such a favour when she handed down his sentence. What with his four different teams, he was busy on the football pitch every day from midday until early evening. He was learning how to be happy once again.

In the evenings, to reward himself, he went to some pub in Nuremberg – he found a different one every day. By never going to the same bar, he hoped to keep other people and himself believing that he wasn't a drunk. His two beers and a shot tasted differently now than a year ago. Being satisfied at the end of a day's work well done gave the drinks a fuller flavour. Doris was happy with him, too. He was just drinking his couple of beers and his one shot in the evening, as his reward. That was practically nothing, really.

In the mornings, he went straight out with the dog for a walk in the Volkspark Marienberg. He thought like a manager here, too. The mere sight of a path that led up a small hill and then straight down again could make him feel euphoric. It would be a perfect place to get his boys doing interval-training. He stood in a clearing by the lake and dreamed of having his young Nuremberg side of 1985 here, doing sprints of increasing lengths in the grass, Reuter, Grahammer, Dorfner, Eckstein – all of them there together in their red training-shirts, they would fill the whole clearing and then, backlit by the morning sun, they would sprint towards him. He could imagine nothing more beautiful. When he came home from the park, there were only two, two and a half hours, and then, after his siesta, he had to be up and doing. Could it be that at 60 years of age he was learning all over again what the word 'fulfilled' meant?

His sister and her husband came to visit. He managed to resist trying the old one of asking them if they'd come to talk to his dog. That joke was long dead, now. His old closeness to Hilla couldn't be restored just on demand, but he made an effort. His brother-in-law Heinz Wachtmeister, who'd cheered him on 40 years before when he was playing for Bayer 04 Leverkusen, came along to the training-ground with him. His brother-in-law was amazed.

Blimey, Heinz, he said, they may be just little kids, but there's real spirit and discipline in them.

His brother-in-law still had in his head a picture of the young Heinz Höher, who lived his life in the firm belief that everything was going to turn out all right for him.

During the years he'd spent in mental darkness, Heinz Höher had developed a simple trick to protect himself from the fact that he was now just orbiting around the Bundesliga, instead of belonging to it. He loudly claimed that the others, the ones still involved in the Bundesliga, hadn't the faintest idea about football, so it followed – without him having to actually say it – that in their ignorance they overlooked him, too. He hasn't got the faintest idea, he'd say to Thomas, when they saw a Bundesliga player blow an attempted dribble. He hasn't got the faintest idea, he'd say, when a Bundesliga manager appeared on the TV screen. The TV commentators had the faintest ideas of all.

Now that he was working to full capacity with his four teams, his judgements became a little milder. However, he still grew mistrustful whenever he heard journalists or fans use the word 'tactics'. The fact was that Heinz Höher had been one of the deepest tactical thinkers of the 1970s and 1980s: the offside trap at Bochum, the mix of man-marking and zonal marking, playing with no centre-forward, these were all unusual tactical variations which he brought into the Bundesliga. But that didn't stop him thinking the same way almost everyone in the Bundesliga had thought for over 30 years – that tactics was of secondary importance in the German game. What mattered, it was thought, was the class, the physicality, and the leadership qualities of individual players. 'It's not the best tactics that win games, but the team with the best players,' was an article of faith in the Bundesliga, and it was stoically insisted on by people like Uli Hoeneß. What was behind this sporting religion? Was it just a question of football, or did it also secretly have to do with 40 years of ever-present conflict between East and West, between capitalism and communism? The communist vision was a collectivist one; by contrast, the capitalist vision was that a citizen's individuality, creativity and hard work were what led to prosperity for all. A tactic like zonal marking placed collective action higher than individual inspiration, and for 30 years the Bundesliga thought it at best something for Italians and Communists; and at worst, the blather of theoreticians.

As regularly as the waves on the shore, the debate about zonal marking had splashed up into West Germany again and again. Even back in the early 1950s, it had been discussed after the impact of the fabulous Hungarian team. Gyula Lóránt's influence in the 1970s, or Arrigo Sacchi's Milan side of the late 1980s got the debate blazing again. It soon blew out. The truth was that German teams had long been playing a simplified form of zonal marking: the man-marker didn't just run after his opponent the whole time, every defender took care of a particular zone; within that particular zone he could, indeed had to, play as a passionate man-marker. In their own eyes, though, German teams never won thanks to tactics, but thanks to the inspirational power of outstanding personalities like Fritz Walter, Uwe Seeler, Franz Beckenbauer, Lothar Matthäus or Matthias Sammer. The German language had invented a single word for it: 'Führungsspieler' – 'players who can lead'.

In 1994, SC Freiburg came third in the Bundesliga by playing a prophetic version of zonal marking under manager Volker Finke: when an opponent was in possession, they systematically sent two or three men racing in to close him down. People stood amazed. 'It was as if Freiburg were playing an extra man,' said Bayern midfielder Thomas Strunz. But it was written off as a freak result, and soon forgotten. At the 1998 World Cup, the national team played wretchedly right up to their knock-out in the quarter-final and for the first time, many people got the vague feeling that something was no longer quite right in German football. Young newspaper reporters met young Bundesliga professionals and debated Saachi's zonal marking or how to defend with no *libero*, without any of them really understanding how that kind of football worked. Until that moment, 19 December 1998 at 10.01pm when, in a TV studio on the Lerchenberg in Mainz, a railway-station clock ticked inexorably forward.

On the dot of the third beat of the accompanying jingle, the camera panned onto a noticeboard of space-ship grey which bore the title *Aktuelles Sportstudio*, at which point a cartoon squirrel bounded into frame in order to announce 'Top sports and great entertainment presented by OBI warehouses'. Presenter Michael Steinbrecher said good evening. The studio audience clapped, whistled and hollered as though they were off their heads. A warm-up act had got them into the mood before the start of the programme. Steinbrecher, his long blond curls down over his shoulders, wore a heavily ribbed dark-green roll-neck sweater under his brown suit. The studio audience were dressed in pin-striped shirts or generously cut pullovers; their clothing paled in comparison with what people had worn in the 1970s and 1980s. At least half of them were over 50 years old.

Steinbrecher calmed the applause-to-order and welcomed the first of our guests in today's *Aktuelle Sportstudio*, our Manager of the Season, Ralf Rangnick. Not everybody in the studio, or at home in front of the TV, actually knew who on earth he was. But despite this, he was greeted with another burst of thunderous applause.

Rangnick took his place beside Steinbrecher at a glass coffee table; with his sharp face behind his rimless glasses, he was a newcomer to the Bundesliga 2 and was already top of the table with SSV Ulm. On the table there stood two glasses of still water. Rangnick was wearing a shiny brown shirt and a brown tie with his brown suit. Across the TV screen rolled the headlines which had been dedicated to Rangnick over the past few months, 'Ulm – playing like the world champions', 'The future of German football is called Ulm', 'The German Football Union has done nothing for tactics since 1974'. A commentator pulled it all together: 'Ralf Ragnick has revolutionised German football.' The studio audience in *Sportstudio* applauded ecstatically. Rangnick, sitting at the glass coffee table, with his glass of water untouched, looked down at the ground.

What he'd essentially done was, he'd copied football. As Under-17 coach at Stuttgart, he'd spent hours in the early 1990s sitting beside Helmut Groß, the youth-team coordinator with the sharp eyes of a bridge engineer. Groß had bought an ultra-modern video-recorder for more than 3000 marks so that he could study videotapes of the way Milan played under Sacchi. Even this top-quality machine was soon worn out, because Ragnick and Groß were permanently rewinding and suddenly stopping, so that they could note the exact zonal dispositions of Sacchi's team – or at least, given the picture quality, get some idea of them.

'We've been talking for years about zonal marking and the back four,' said the presenter, Steinbrecher, 'and you almost get the feeling that people are in awe of the idea. But even today, many viewers still don't know what it means: the back four.' Steinbrecher had got up from the table with the untouched glasses of water on it. Rangnick stood beside him. He was almost a head shorter. Steinbrecher indicated a blackboard standing directly behind them. 'We've got a tactics board here,' he said. 'Could you explain zonal marking and the back four to our viewers?'

On the green tactics board were 11 yellow magnets representing the defending side. Eleven red magnets were attacking, with the ball currently on the right of midfield. 'Our aim is superiority over the ball-carrier,' began Rangnick. He moved three yellow magnets so that they surrounded the man on the ball in a triangle, 'Oops, the ball just went out of play.' The magnet representing the ball had just fallen off. His zonal marking was oriented on the ball, Rangnick continued, that meant that his players always moved around the pitch so they really closed down the space 30 or 40 metres all around the ball-carrier, and risked leaving the more distant areas of the pitch open. The usual German system of man-to-man marking, on the other hand, meant that every player concentrated on his individual opponent, meaning that the defence was spread out as little islands all over the pitch, leaving the opponent more space between them. No one had ever talked about football this way on German TV: ball-carrier, oriented on the ball, creating triangles, moving.

'Let me try to put it simply,' said Steinbrecher, who seemed to be concentrating hard. 'You don't think in terms of team positions, but in terms of the danger in the zone where the ball is.'

'Have you got any time to spare?' asked Rangnick. 'If you have, I'll give you a job.'

'The question is,' said Steinbrecher, 'if we can explain it so easily here, why is it still such a big deal in Germany, why do we still treat the whole thing with such awe?'

Ralf Rangnick believed he was just giving a friendly little bit of a lesson to the general public. It couldn't have been more than two days later when the Monday papers were delivered, that he saw what he'd really done. He'd declared cultural war within football. The German football establishment felt itself to be under personal attack. As if it wasn't bad enough for a football manager to wear glasses anyway. And then he went on as if Germany – with three World Cups! – was some kind of tactical Third World country! When *Kicker* asked him what had most disappointed him in his first 100 days as national manager, Erich Ribbeck replied: 'I'm disappointed in all these exaggerated discussions about tactical systems, like on Saturday evening in Channel 2's *Sportstudio*, we got a colleague dishing out platitudes as if every manager in the Bundesliga was a complete moron.' Rangnick hadn't actually said anything about Bundesliga managers or morons, but Ribbeck still obviously felt it was aimed at him. Franz Beckenbauer, by now manager at Bayern, had already told *Kicker* the week previously: 'All this talk about systems – it's a load of crap. Foreign players can just do more with the ball. Ours can't. Back four, zonal marking, *libero*, it all doesn't matter a damn. The back four is actually a fatal mistake.'

Two and a half million viewers had tuned in to Ralf Rangnick's appearance on *Das aktuelle Sportstudio*. In the 1980s, they'd regularly got 8 million. Back then, *Sportstudio* had been the first, and basically the only, medium where you couldn't just see the Bundesliga, but feel it as well. In 1998, by the time it got to 10pm, five hours after the final whistle, almost everyone had seen almost everything on *ran* already.

Channel 2's sports editors tried to find a cure. They tried opening with skiing, and in their items on the Bundesliga they hardly reported on the actual match, but focused on a theme thrown up by the game, a star-player possibly changing club or an unhappy substitute rebelling against the manager. Instead of running their interviews at the end of the game, they showed them before the actual clips from the match.

But they remained just a more upmarket copy of *ran*, doing the same things by other means. 'It hurts to see that you're just not going to win any more,' said Karl Senne, the programme's long-time boss. 'All that's left for *Sportstudio* is trying not to lose too heavily.'

Heinz Höher had early on promised himself never to become one of those people who say that everything used to be better. But when he heard the way they were talking in modern football – movement, ball-oriented play – one phrase always used to shock him: working against the ball. That was a crime! How could any manager get his team to *work against the ball*? Maybe he didn't teach his young footballers to play a perfect version of Arrigo Saachi's collective pressure, but he did teach them to play *with* the *ball*.

Mr Höher really ought to take a look at the Bayern Kickers' Under-13s next time they played, said Reinhold Hintermaier in November 1998. He'd got a tip from a sports teacher, who said that there was a boy playing there who'd be perfect for Heinz Höher's youth team at Fürth.

One Saturday morning, Heinz Höher drove along a grass track to the club-house of local-league team FC Bayern Kickers. They had two grass pitches out on the edge of Nuremberg, where the town gave way to meadows and small detached houses, and where the streets were called things like Am Schweigeracker.

The boy took the ball and off he dribbled, the parents standing round the touchline cheered, it was obvious that they seen it all before, the boy twisted and turned, his right foot controlled the ball with per-fect caresses, the boy dribbled around six players and, with a generous pass, set up one of his team-mates to score. He was 12. His name was Juri Judt.

The moment Heinz Höher saw Juri Judt, he stopped thinking of himself as out of the Bundesliga. He was on his way back.

They looked like a team from the past. Under Lothar Matthäus, Germany have a dreadful Euro 2000, and suddenly everyone starts thinking, we need a better youth system.

1999-2002:

HIS BOYS

The houses in the Schäufeleinstraße were painted white, yellow or light brown but really their colours all looked the same: flat. Almost every day, Heinz Höher stopped his car in front of this old workers' housing-estate. He never had to wait. Juri was already standing there, with that dependability of a boy who wants to do his own thing the right way. In the car, Juri answered when Mr Höher asked him a question. Otherwise, he stayed quiet.

He'd been six years old when his parents emigrated to Nuremberg. Their country had ceased to exist. After the collapse of the Soviet Union, many of their neighbours in the town of Karaganda said that they were now Kazakhs. In Karaganda, it was nothing unusual for the winter temperature to get down to −25°C. In the 1940s, 70 per cent of the town's inhabitants had been ethnic Germans, settled there for generations. Fifty years later, people of German descent, like Juri's parents, were returning to Germany. There, people called them Russian-Germans. In Karaganda, Juri's mother had been a doctor. In Nuremberg, she had to begin again as a care-worker in an old people's home. Her Soviet medical qualifications were not recognised. His father, a trained lathe-operator, found work in a transport company, doing shift-work loading lorries. They made do with these jobs in the hope that they could work their way to a new life; in the belief that whatever happened, they had to be an example of hard work and guts for their three children.

Heinz Höher took Juri to whatever kind of football training he could possibly find. He brought him to the Fürth club sessions and to Reinhold Hintermaier's Football Academy. During the holidays, he took him to the Schafhofstraße to train with his team of people with learning difficulties. At Easter, one of them wished Juri a Happy Christmas. Juri told his mum about it, but he never told Mr Höher. He didn't want to say anything to Mr Höher that might make him think he was mocking them.

The Under-13 team at Greuther Fürth could train only twice a week because the pitches were always busy, so Heinz Höher rented a sports hall from the local church on his own account, to give them extra sessions. He had the place from 8pm to 9.30pm, for his 11- and 12-year-old boys. Hardly any of them ever missed a session. To be allowed along to his group in the little sports hall was a special accolade, he invited the five or six most talented members of the Fürth Under-13s there for special mentoring. He called it 'Höher's Higher School of Football'. He told the other coaches in Fürth that he was going to train these boys every day till they were 19, and by then he'd have made professionals of at least five of them, and two would make the national team.

Each Tuesday felt to him like a celebration. He held his training sessions in the old gym-hall, which dated from early in the century. The parents sat around the edge of the hall on low gym-benches as he drove the boys on through circuit-training and repeated sprints, and then it was football. Twelve-year-old children flitted through the hall with the aesthetically perfect movement of top players. Heinz Höher watched them and felt a strangely unbearable longing, like a prophet who is ready to spread his message but can find no audience for it. His boys, Daniel Adlung, Samil Cinaz, Sascha Amtmann, Chhunly Pagenburg, had all it took to become professionals. But for him, the most talented was Juri Judt. Heinz Höher was aware that the the other parents noticed him spending more time on Juri. He didn't care.

Heinz Höher absorbed every move the boy made, his finesse as he drew his foot softly backwards so as to make sure that the ball didn't bounce even a centimetre back when he stopped it, his triple-step, the explosive tension in his body when he went into a one-on-one duel, the way he read the game visually when he created space with a pass. Greuther Fürth had had to pay Bayern Kickers 750 marks to transfer him – a transfer fee for a 12-year-old. Greuther Fürth wanted to pay only 500. Heinz Höher's son-in-law had put up the other 250 marks. Had he been infected by Heinz Höher's infatuation, or was it just to put an end to Heinz Höher's never-ending insistence that he simply had to train this boy?

Juri stroked the top of the ball with the sole of his foot, like one of those Brazilian indoor players. Leave that out, growled Heinz Höher, it's just show-off stuff. Heinz Höher had been just as strict with one of the other boys, Daniel Adlung, when telling him that he mustn't forget when it was the right moment for a pass. In the next game, Adlung cheekily kept right on dribbling, whatever – but Juri Judt immediately stopped trying to perform tricks.

Heinz Höher believed that he had to be strict with children. At his sessions, they all had to tie their football boots on with double knots. During an indoor tournament, one of the boys' laces inevitably came loose all the same. Heinz Höher cut his laces off.

Juri grew scared of Heinz Höher's umbrella. The only reason he seemed to have an umbrella was so that he could smash it onto the ground in a full-on rage over some mistake his boys had made. Juri didn't want Heinz Höher to have to throw his umbrella to the floor on account of him.

During games, outraged parents regularly came up to Heinz Höher. The tips of his shoes were marked with white chalk from treading on the touchline so often. His team were only kids, couldn't he stop shouting at them for once, pleaded the parents – the parents of the opposing team. The kids, and their parents, on his own team thought the same. But they kept quiet. Despite everything, they were delighted to have this man as coach.

He got his kids to play in every position, forwards, full-backs, even in goal, they were to become complete footballers. When Juri and Daniel Adlung were invited to play in the Mid-Franconia regional select team, he kept it from them; he thought that a training session or a game with the regional select team was one training-day less with him. In spring of 1999, his Under-13 team played against FC Nuremberg's Under-13s. Nuremberg always won every youth game, because as the only Bundesliga team in Franconia it was easy for them to get all the most strikingly talented boys. Heinz Höher's boys beat Nuremberg 5-0.

He drove Juri to Bochum and to Leverkusen, to train for a day with each of their youth teams. He wanted to see how his boy compared to other talented players. But would he really have taken it on board if some boy at Bayer 04 Leverkusen or VfL Bochum had been better than Juri? Heinz Höher had long since made up his mind that Juri was the best.

On the early afternoon of 29 May 2000 he was, as usual, training the children at Reinhold Hintermaier's Football Academy in Ziegelstein; he had to be at the Hans Lohnert Sportplatz at 7pm to train Fürth's Under-17s. Hintermaier wanted to pay him 1000 marks a month for the work he did at his private school. Heinz Höher had refused a monthly salary so that Juri would be allowed to train there for free.

Did he have a moment, said Hintermaier after the training session, there was something they needed to talk about.

They sat down at one of the tables in the club-house of the Catholic youth sports club Franken Concordia, with the blue ice-cream flag hanging above the door, and Heinz Höher could never remember if he even ordered anything at all. Reinhold Hintermaier handed him a letter which had been folded twice and hole-punched. The letterhead had been stamped, as an afterthought: 'News! We're on the web: www.greuther-fuerth.de'. Hintermaier gave Heinz Höher time to read the letter.

Dear Mr Höher,
The existing contract between us for your service as youth team manager ends on 30.06.2000.
As Mr Hintermaier, sporting coordinator of Greuther Fürth, will explain to you personally, we will not be extending this agreement beyond the above-mentioned date.
However, we take this opportunity to thank you heartily for the work you have done in the two foregoing years and remain,
Sincerely
Spielvereinigung Greuther Fürth
Edgar Burkart
Vice-President.

Heinz Höher couldn't understand the letter. Reinhold Hintermaier talked it over with him, but, being a man who always liked to be sensitive in face-to-face conversations, he was unable to explain to Heinz Höher why he'd been sacked as youth-manager. To have done that, he'd have had to say: I helped get you chucked out.

For a while now, Fürth's youth-coordinator and their other youth coaches had been casting suspiscious glances in the direction of Höher's Higher School of Football. Heinz Höher had bound his Under-13s so closely to him that it was as though they were playing for FC Höher rather than for Greuther Fürth. What was going to happen when the players went up to the Under-15s under Hintermaier but spent half the week training privately with Heinz Höher? Wasn't there inevitably going to be a conflict? What if Heinz Höher decided, one fine day, to persuade his players to switch to Nuremberg or Stuttgart? Hadn't he already been heard to say that he was going to get at least two of his boys into Bayern Munich? What if, on top of it all, he tempted players from Fürth's other youth teams into his private elite programme, and interfered in the way the other youth-coaches worked?

Nobody had tried to talk it over with Heinz Höher. After all, he gave the impression of a man who couldn't be talked to.

In professional football, what counts is the story that's put about afterwards. People whisper behind your back and slag you off, and then, sometime or other later, you find out at least part of the truth.

Still he couldn't understand it. How could people complain about him doing everything he could for the kids? And even if Juri or Daniel Adlung did go to Bayern Munich some day, the club would get a pretty penny for them.

Whenever he'd been fired as a Bundesliga manager, he'd never gone out looking for another job. He found the idea too shameful. In the summer of 2000, he fought like a man possessed for his job as coach of an Under-13 side. He brought the law firm Lovells Boesbeck Droste in to dispute his sacking, but in vain. He got Doris to write a letter to the club president: 'Dear Mr Hack, You can have no idea what grief you are causing us by giving my husband notice. He was devoted to his young players with his heart and soul, I have never seen him happier.' He got Juri's mother to give him a free hand to transfer Juri to local rivals FC Quelle Fürth if need be. Daniel Adlung and Samil Cinaz had already gone over to FC Nuremberg after his sacking. He knocked at the doors of the sports editors of the Nuremberg papers, to make his case go public. For the first and probably the last time, a story about an Under-13 coach appeared as a huge headline on the front page of the *Nürnberger Abendzeitung*: 'Sacked and sickened: Heinz Höher's dramatic story.' The first thing that the editor of the *Abendzeitung* noticed was how bent Heinz Höher looked.

Heinz Höher had been observing an acquaintance of his, a paediatrician, who had recently retired. Each morning, the children's doctor was dragged a step further into lethargy by the endlessly empty day ahead. He didn't want to end up like that.

He watched TV to distract himself, and suddenly, even the pictures on television seemed to have some connection with his sacking from the Under-13s: bottom of their group at Euro 2000 in Belgium and the Netherlands, the German national side looked like a team from the past, without spirit, without talent – and he could have trained up that talent! 'German football is flat on its back,' he wrote once more to club president Hack. 'Everyone is bemoaning the lack of work being done with youth, yet you have just trodden down a delicate shoot of hope.'

The hopelessness of the national team at Euro 2000 troubled the German public. National manager Erich Ribbeck, the man who had gone off on one about Ralf Rangnick's popular introduction to zonal marking on *Das aktuelle Sportstudio*, played the 39-year-old Lothar Matthäus as *libero*, deep behind the defence, the way that German teams, according to Ribbeck, had always done – and suddenly, smaller nations like Portugal, Romania or Norway looked more refined and lively. And thus Euro 2000 became a watershed in the history of the Bundesliga; the point at which one kind of German football collapsed, and a new one was born. To stand out from the crowd once again, German footballers had to play with more technique, and more speed. Playing as a unit, defending space as a team, automatically going over to the attack, all this had to be more conscientiously studied. In fact, footballing thinkers like Volker Finke at Freiburg or Helmut Groß at Stuttgart had already begun to move in this direction half a decade before. Now, at last, they were noticed. One green shoot seemed to have managed to survive through 37 years of Bundesliga football: back at the start of the Bundesliga, when Germany still thought of itself as a footballing nation with a clear regional divide, the south of the Republic had always claimed that it embraced a more stylish way of play. And now the way back to a more elegant, more tactically demanding style of play was being led from the south, from Freiburg, Stuttgart, Ulm, and soon from Mainz as well – was this just coincidence at work, or was it a kind of tradition?

Heinz Höher having talked him round by an incessant barrage of letters and newspaper articles, Fürth club president Helmut Hack invited him to come back for talks to clarify the matter, although as far as he was concerned the matter was clarified already. Hack invited Reinhold Hintermaier along too.

Hintermaier picked Heinz Höher up from his house in the Elbinger Straße and they drove into the countryside, sitting side by side, to visit Mr Hack in Vestenbergsgreuth. Hintermaier was thinking to himself, old Höher chucked me out of the club in 1984 and now he's been trying to go behind my back again and get players from my youth teams under his personal control. Heinz Höher was thinking to himself, that Hintermaier was a troublemaker back in 1984, and now he's stabbed me in the back again because he was jealous of what I achieved with the Under-13s. And off they drove, sitting in peace, as if they were two partners cooperating happily.

Thanks to Helmut Hack, Swedes, Egyptians and Guatemalans tried to pronounce the name Vestenbergsgreuth; they did this when they were trying to describe the location of the tea company from whom they got their wares, or to whom they delivered their spices. As CEO, Hack had played his part in building up the tea company founded by his grandfather, Martin Bauer, into a business with worldwide interests. In his spare time, he'd united his village team, FC Vestenbergsgreuth, with Fürth and established them in the Bundesliga 2. Hack always told his wife she was a lucky woman. Because he was there so little. He left her to work out for herself whether he was telling the truth or just joking. Even now they were in the Bundesliga 2, she herself baked the cake they handed round at every home game for the journalists to snack on at half-time.

After reaching 40 years of age, Helmut Hack didn't grow any older. At 51, he looked just the same as at 42: below his glasses there was a hint of a smile and his thick brown hair was combed back in exactly the same, unchanging style. Give us a laugh, for once, said Mr Hack, as he greeted him at his door, I've never seen you laugh yet. Heinz Höher nodded grimly.

They stuck to the facts, the arguments were all well known. Heinz Höher said that he didn't understand why he was being sacked for having done his work so very conscientiously. Helmut Hack said that he couldn't open a 'club within a club'. Heinz Höher found his gaze drifting off to the holy pictures which hung on Mr Hack's wall, Jesus, Mary, Benedict of Nursia or whoever they were, all these preachers of religion. As the club president talked on, Heinz Höher imagined the saints were shaking their heads.

Mr Höher, said Hack, you can't go building up a private training pro-gramme running parallel to club training without consulting us – if you do, we at the club can't help fearing that sometime or other, you're going to take the players to another club behind our backs. Heinz Höher saw the saints on the wall furiously shaking their heads. He could feel a laugh welling up inside of him, he tried to control it but the saints kept on shaking their heads and – well, now Helmut Hack saw him laughing, for once. Even though he didn't understand why.

A few days afterwards, Helmut Hack wrote to Heinz Höher, saying that it had been a serious conversation for which he was grateful; obvi-ously, that laugh had just been caused by a momentary irritation. He was not at present in a position to alter the dismissal, Hack continued, but they should remain on such terms as would enable them to discuss the matter again in a year's time.

It was an olive branch. But all it did was increase Heinz Höher's sense of desperation. A year stretched before him, meaningless and empty. Like a fan, or a stalker, he drove to Bad Wörishofen, where Nuremberg were holding their summer training camp. He buttonholed Klaus Augenthaler, the Nuremberg manager; he, an experienced Bundesliga manager, was making up to a man only just starting out in the business of managing a Bundesliga side. Heinz Höher asked Augenthaler if he didn't have some kind of volunteer job for him, or could put a word in for him with the youth-team coordinator. To Heinz Höher, it didn't feel like asking. In his own eyes, he was begging. Augenthaler said that he was sorry, but he wasn't the right man to talk to.

Heinz Höher sat on a park bench in Marienberg and called Edgar Geenen, the sports director at Nuremberg. Haven't you got anything at all for me, he said to Geenen, I'll even set out the plastic cones for the Under-9s. Geenen said there might be something for him with the Under-11s. But it turned out that the job with the Under-11s was already taken.

Elektro Hoffman got in touch with him. As well as selling washing machines and toasters, Hans Hoffman was a sponsor of the women's team at FC Nuremberg. He'd read in the papers about Heinz Höher's desperate search for employment. How about he trained the women?

Women's football. To put it mildly, Heinz Höher had never had any-thing to do with it. To put it objectively, he didn't have much choice, now. It was January 2001 and he'd been without a team for six months.

On a winter's morning, he set foot on the property of FC Nuremberg for the first time in 12 years, dressed in his tracksuit and football boots, and was immediately greeted by a striking image of where he now stood. The modern stadium and the lush grass of the professionals' training pitches were simply a backdrop for his own session: he had to take the women out onto the muddy cinder pitch.

No Bundesliga manager had ever yet trained a women's XI.

Twenty-eight years after Carmen Thomas said 'Schalke 05', it was still a curiosity to talk of women and football. After Carmen Thomas, only four women had presented on *Das aktuelle Sportstudio*, and all of them only briefly. At Channel 1 it took until 1999 for a woman, Anne Will, to anchor *Sportschau*. No women had ever yet been permitted to commentate on a live football game. Women's football only managed to get onto the front pages of the newspapers thanks to an upper-body that was naked but for a sports-bra: in her sheer joy at scoring the winner at the women's European Championship in the pouring rain, Claudia Müller pulled her top over her head – and *Bild Zeitung* ran the headline: 'This is how good women's football can look!' Attention like this felt like progress: when they won the European Championship for the first time in 1989, the German women's team was awarded a coffee-service by the German Football Union. Maybe the sporting world was still rather stuck in the Neanderthal age, thought Carmen Thomas to herself, and maybe you could even understand it? Maybe men wanted to at least keep the football all to themselves, since it was the women who got to have the children?

As a women's coach, Heinz Höher was once again national news in the side-columns of the sports pages: 'Women-power with Heinz: the ball's the same,' 'Heinz Höher chooses his girls,' 'Höher: don't be mean, let their charms be seen.'

He wanted to take his new team up from the second division into the Bundesliga and thus become the first man to manage both men and women in the Bundesliga; he'd always liked off-beat titles like that. He got Juri to train with the women. The boy was 14. Heinz Höher always repeated one instruction to his women; take a look at what he's doing, and then you'll know what football's all about.

When the women played a training-match against the male Under-16s of Quelle Fürth, many of Nuremberg's youth players stood leaning on the railings and watched them inquisitively. They laughed. There was Juri, playing on a women's team. He tried to act as if he hadn't noticed his contemporaries up there on the railings.

When Mr Höher explained something, Juri listened to him, tight-lipped. He could laugh with his eyes.

At the end of the day, Juri had stayed at Greuther Fürth. So as to watch him play in the Under-15s, Heinz Höher drove to Ronhof, to the very club who had kicked him out without a thank-you. Maybe it was the wisdom of old age, or maybe it was the boy who'd managed it: Heinz Höher's pride no longer got in his way.

You'll definitely make it as a pro, he told Juri, again and again. Juri's parents said school's the most important thing. Juri came home from school at midday and set off for training in Fürth, it was a journey of more than an hour, involving three changes of bus, he got back at about 10pm, did his homework and fell into bed, day after day.

Elektro Hoffman paid Heinz Höher 1000 marks a month for training the women's XI. Most of what he made from the Hotel Merian disappeared into his debt repayments. His son-in-law, who was boss of an advertising agency, helped out generously, but somehow, soon, he was going to have to earn some serious money again.

He was 62. In May 2001 he watched as Ottmar Hitzfeld, the man who'd pipped him to the manager's job at Borussia Dortmund ten years before, won the Champions League with Bayern Munich. He himself narrowly missed promotion to the Bundesliga with the women's XI of FC Nuremberg.

Heinz Höher listened, fascinated to Hitzfeld's TV interviews. Never mind what question the reporter asked, Hitzfeld elegantly turned it around so that he could say what he himself wanted to say, not what the journalist wanted to hear. In modern football, managers sounded like politicians, thought Heinz Höher and asked himself: How would he sound, these days?

Fürth president Helmut Hack had put it in writing that they would talk again in a year's time, and when the year was up, Heinz Höher got a shock: he'd been serious. Helmut Hack, who had strengthened Reinhold Hintermaier's position in the summer of 2000 when he kicked Heinz Höher out, didn't renew Hintermaier's contract when it ran out in the summer of 2001, and brought Heinz Höher back as youth-coach. A feeling re-awoke in Heinz Höher, one that had been buried for so long that he didn't even know he still had it in him: the unfounded but absolute conviction that everything was going to be all right.

He was given charge of the Under-14 and Under-16 teams. This time, he talked over his plans for Höher's Higher School of Football with the club president, and got his son-in-law to back him by renting an artificial grass pitch at Marienberg for his private training sessions. He brought Daniel Adlung back from Nuremberg, the 15-year-old had now swapped twice between Fürth and Nuremberg; talent was no longer taken for granted in modern football, it was a precious thing.

Heinz Höher trained his boys in the park, he got them running intervals on the course with that little hill, he stood at the bottom of the hill and watched the boys, his boys, charge up the slope and take the hill.

The drinking, Heinz Höher persuaded himself, was under control, two beers and a shot in the evening, okay, sometimes a beer and a Campari soda for lunch as well, and a glass of champagne for breakfast and four beers and two shots if there was a party. Other people noticed that above the elegant pullovers Doris bought for him, his face was chronically red.

In the holidays, when there was no training, he trained alone with Juri in Marienberg Park on a normal recreational ground, he hit passes that sent him on runs down the wing, even though pain shot through his right knee with every pass. The next day he took the boy on an 80km endurance training bike ride through the hills of the Fränkische Schweiz. The furthest Juri had ever been on a bike was to the supermarket or the underground station. After the bike trip, he couldn't sit down for days, his backside hurt so badly. But he said nothing about it to Mr Höher.

Whatever kids you gave him, he coached them. Heinz Höher at the Greuther Fürth summer camp.

The Noughties:

GOOSE PIMPLES

The sports desk of the *Nürnberger Abendzeitung* received a lengthy piece about a hornet. The paper employed Heinz Höher as a columnist. Usually, his copy did indeed stick to the world of Franconian football, but now and again he offered short fictional pieces in which any relationship to sport could be discerned only with the greatest goodwill. The hornet in this case was a peloton of amateur cyclists in red-brown tops, charging down a mountain road at 70km/h while Heinz Höher cycled up towards them, his open-topped handlebar-basket full of banknotes, he having just been to the bank. Sucked up into the air by the slipstream of the passing hornet, the notes flew from the basket – and the *Nürnberger Abendzeitung* decided that they would prefer not to publish what happened when it started raining money.

Heinz Höher carefully cut out and kept his newspaper columns. Then he immediately put them in any old order into a chest and never looked at them again, but while he was cutting them out and holding them in his hands, the pieces he'd written about FC Nuremberg or Greuther Fürth made him still feel connected to the world of professional sport. In 2003, he had turned 65 and was officially a pensioner. But short-story writers and football-managers don't know what retirement means. Old Otto had won Euro 2004 at 66.

Otto Rehhagel's sensational victory with the Greek national side at the European Championship 2004 in Portugal left the public with a slightly crazed smile on their faces, expressive of disbelief and irritation in equal measure. At the very moment the Bundesliga scene had just persuaded itself that playing a *libero* and man-marking were medieval ideas, up popped Rehhagel to win the greatest coup of the decade by employing a *libero* and the most elementally ruthless man-marking. One particular moment from the Euro semi-final between Greece and the Czech Republic was unforgettable: Czech Republic striker Jan Koller, all 6 foot 8 of him, retreated into his own half, worn down by the ceaseless man-marking, simply to be alone for a moment. The moment Koller took a step over the centre-line again, his shadow, Michaelis Kapsis, raced down upon him, to follow him step for step, hip tight to hip. Koller threw back his head and cried aloud to the heavens in his desperation.

Rehhagel's Greece proved that if every team played the same system, as they all did in Euro 2004 – zonal marking with the back four in a straight row – a team with completely different ideas could confuse and stretch them all, even if the way they played was theoretically outdated.

While Otto was winning Euro 2004, Heinz Höher was training Juri in the park. He'd had to loosen his grip on the boy. At Greuther Fürth, Juri had other coaches, Heinz Höher had to take care of the 14-year-olds, while Juri was now playing in the Under-19s. He'd turned 18 in July 2004. Within the year the decision would be made as to whether Juri would make it as a professional footballer.

His new youth-coaches had fixed on playing Juri as a holding midfielder. Heinz Höher could second that decision: Juri had a wonderful ability to read the game, allowing him to win the ball and start a counter-attack with a clean pass. It was as a holding midfielder that he was called up to the German Under-19 team in autumn 2004. But even so, Heinz Höher was troubled at his being fixed in this position. Young players could only truly develop their potential in offensive positions, where they had to dribble, pass and find creative solutions in the tightest of spaces and the shortest of moments. Heinz Höher hoped that Juri had not slipped too far downfield too early, but he said nothing to the boy.

Thomas had tried to get Juri's mother a job, through the father of a friend of his who was chief doctor at Erlangen University Hospital, but there was nothing doing. Her Soviet medical qualifications were not recognised in Germany. Thanks to the former CEO of FC Nuremberg, Heinz Höher got Juri's father a job doing what he had been trained for, operating a lathe, to free him from having to do late shifts as a lorry-loader. A few months later, Juri's father came back to the transport company. As a lathe operator, he was no longer up to speed with the job, he'd had to ask his colleagues every five minutes how they did this or that, these days. Juri could feel that his father was like him. Neither of them liked having to ask other people's advice, or wanting things of other people.

On the outskirts of Erlangen, Greuther Fürth players were trying to drive the excess tension out of their bodies. As he did before each game, their manager, Benno Möhlmann, had sent his team off for a morning walk around the hotel in Erlangen. Carefully making it look like a coincidence, the manager made sure that after a few minutes, he ended up strolling beside Juri Judt. It was 29 August 2005. Two months earlier, Juri had passed his Advanced Vocational Certificate of Education, and four weeks ago he'd turned 19. Are you up for playing this evening? asked the manager.

A hundred Bundesliga managers had asked precisely this question to 100 young players before their debuts. As if any footballer was ever going to answer: no, I'm not up for it. Of course I'm up for it, answered Juri, as the unwritten script demanded.

The little stadium with its low stands and and its green-and-white-striped floodlight-towers was humming and buzzing. Almost 11,000 spectators had come to Fürth's Ronhof ground. The Ronhof was nowadays called the Playmobil Stadium. Juri wore a short-sleeved top, the all-white strip showed up how brown his skin was, he hadn't been to the barbers for weeks, his black hair curled up at the ends. He looked like summer itself.

The stadium was lit by the final glow of a mild August day. Their opponents, 1860 Munich, were top of the table of Bundesliga 2 two weeks into the new season, the Monday evening game was being shown live on *Deutsches Sportfernsehen*. Heinz Höher turned on the TV at home and felt a shock pass through his body. Juri was playing! The boy hadn't even known it himself when they spoke on the phone yesterday.

The referee's whistle blew and the game thundered down upon Juri. Everything was faster, tighter, tougher than he was used to in the Under-19s. He felt that he was always chasing the game, and what with all the stress, he hardly noticed how much he was doing right. In the holding midfield position, he ran to the left and to the right, he closed down space, he went full-on into tackles, sometimes he got the ball, sometimes he got an opponent's legs, and occasionally the ball and the opponent's legs were both already gone. When his manager called time on Juri Judt's first professional game by substituting him after 81 minutes, the applause pattered down around him like warm summer rain. Greuther Fürth fought their way to an honourable 2-2 to draw with the league leaders. The *Nürnberger Zeitung* wrote: 'Juri Judt paid back the trust of his manager with a resolute and irreverent performance as holding midfielder.' Above the match report stood a photo: 1860 Munich's Marcel Schäfer was flying high through the air, half of his face consisting of a mouth opened wide in pain. Beneath him, on the left, Juri Judt was sliding across the grass, his body pure dynamism, his right foot, which had just taken Schäfer's legs away, still stretched out before him.

At home, having turned off the TV, Heinz Höher decided that he and Juri had no time to be proud of things. They had to analyse the points of the game, they had to keep on training. All he could feel was a certain headiness he hadn't felt for ages, you might almost have called it arrogance.

Juri's parents presented Mr Höher with a smile and a single word: Thanks. Like most people who've found someone to help them in a foreign country, they believed that their gratitude should last for ever. All these years, they'd felt a sort of bad conscience when they watched how Mr Höher busied himself with Juri. Shouldn't that have been their job?

Heinz Höher would like to have seen Juri's grandfather. It had always been his grandfather who took the young Juri to training sessions and games at Bayern Kickers, three times a week he came out on the underground from Nürnberg-Langwasser to the Schäufeleinstraße, where he picked up the boy and then walked to the sports ground at the edge of town. When Juri switched to Greuther Fürth, his grandfather stopped coming. Why don't you come any more? Juri's mother asked him, Juri's playing brilliantly. Ah, said his grandfather, it used to be better. When Juri could beat a whole team all on his own.

It sounded as if he meant: when Juri still played like a little child. Before Juri started getting all those instructions and rules that were shaping him up for a professional career.

If some thought came into Heinz Höher's head, he'd call Juri at 11pm. He didn't think about how late it was, simply that he'd just seen

Barcelona playing in the Champions League on TV, and had noted how skilfully their holding midfielder Rafael Marquez had snuck up into the attack. If Juri played in Koblenz or Jena on a Friday night, Heinz Höher would phone him on Saturday at 7am. Doris said, think about the boy for once. She and Thomas were worried that he was making too many demands of Juri.

Juri never said a word. After all, he had so many reasons to be grateful to Mr Höher.

In the dressing-room, Juri laughed long when the others cracked jokes. He never made jokes. He was simply present. He had been given his place in the team in September 2005 as try-out and he made it his own in a perfectly matter-of-fact way, as extraordinarily talented players do. By the end of his debut season, he already looked like an old hand: the keystone of the defensive midfield.

As soon as he started earning professional money, he gave his parents 500 euros a month without them having asked for it, so that they could move out of the Schäufeleinstraße.

Players in the Bundesliga 2 had always regarded it as quite an achievement if they didn't have to go to work any more, if they could do nothing but play football for a couple of years and make a living from it. In modern football, even being second class was something worth aiming for. A decent Bundesliga 2 player made 8000 euros a month, the best of them might make 20,000. By the time of the World Cup of 2006, at the latest, the footballing boom ignited by the private TV stations had trickled down from out of the Bundesliga itself. In the lexicon of German football a new word had appeared: *Das Event*. You went along to the stadium 'for the atmosphere'. Spectators wanted to feel part of a group, to rejoice, to scream, to embrace each other, to suffer together. The main point of the game itself was to make all this possible. In the 2005-06 season the average Bundesliga gate rose above 40,000 for the first time. And yet the money made from selling those tickets played a smaller role than ever. By now, gate-receipts accounted for only about 30 per cent of club budgets. The TV stations paid over 300 million euros per season for the broadcasting rights. But one thing had remained unchanged since the very first Bundesliga season in 1963: the clubs always took things right to the financial edge; they agreed to wages in the full knowledge that they wouldn't be able to pay them unless real success came along. Since 1963, the debts had risen in pace with the takings.

From August 2006, Heinz Höher was no longer alone with his dreams. Jürgen Köper called to tell him that Rudi Theimert, up till now vice-president of VfL Bochum, was moving to Nuremberg at the weekend, maybe Heinz Höher would like to meet him, he was sure they'd get on well. On the Monday morning, Heinz Höher called Theimert, and on the Monday evening the late vice-president of VfL Bochum arrived punctually at FC Möhrendorf's pitch in a suburb of Erlangen – punctuality was always a golden rule to Rudi Theimert. He watched the Under-16 game between Möhrendorf and Greuther Fürth, standing on the opposite side of the pitch so as not to disturb Heinz Höher in his work as coach. After the game, Rudi Theimert said they should call each other by their Christian names. Heinz Höher could never bring himself to be the one to suggest first-name terms. An hour later, Rudi Theimert was officially advisor of Heinz Höher's youth XI.

Advisor is a technical term. They had to find some new way to accurately express Rudi Theimert's role: he became Heinz Höher's fellow-dreamer. Together, as coach, advisor, guardian and father-figure all rolled into one, they would make boys into professional footballers. Juri Judt was Heinz Höher's alpha and omega, an example for many who would follow after him.

Rudi Theimert, stocky of build and still wearing a bushy moustache at 66 from force of habit, rolled his shoulders as he walked. It looked as if he was being shaken by an excess of energy and heartiness. The Theimerts had moved from the Ruhr area to Nuremberg, so as to be close to their daughter in their retirement. Theimert had sold his share in a wholesale roofing supplies business where he'd been a partner and the boss, well, everyone's work has to come to an end one day, never mind how fulfilling it's been. The one thing he still needed was to be close to football.

A cup of coffee tasted quite different in the stadium from in town: one of the pros could walk past at any moment. Rudi Theimert was reminded of his own time in the game; in 1959 he'd been in the reserve team at Schwarz-Weiss Essen when the first team won the German Cup. On Saturdays, at the Ronhof ground, when Juri and Fürth were playing in the Bundesliga 2, he and Heinz Höher went into the white VIP tent in front of the stadium, there was no room in the crowded stadium itself for the vital business of showing hospitality to guests more than happy to open their wallets. The crush of bodies and the buzz of voices in the VIP tent gave Rudi Theimert an agreeable feeling of dizziness, the sense of expectation before the match, the feeling that he belonged in football, hey, look there, that was Kon Schramm, agent to Lukas Podolski and David Odonkor, the heroes of Germany's dream summer, 2006, and there was Reza Fazheli, agent to a really hot young player called Mesut Özil. Theimert introduced Heinz Höher to the agents who he knew from his days as vice-president at Bochum. God, Heinz, said Rudi Theimert after these conversations, why don't we open a players' agency, you've got the knowledge, I've got the contacts, the players will come flocking to us, Heinz Höher already had two of them in the shape of Juri and Daniel Adlung, who'd also successfully made it into the Bundesliga 2 team at Fürth.

Over 250 German players' agents were officially registered with FIFA. No one knew how many of them actually made a living at it and how many of them just wanted to. There were agents who didn't have one single client, who just phoned up a player and claimed 'maybe I could get you taken on by Greuther Fürth'. If the player expressed an interest, the agent would then call Greuther Fürth and say, 'I could get you this player.' Heinz Höher left Rudi Theimert's enthusiastic idea of starting an agency unanswered, the words hanging in the air. Rudi Theimert liked the sound of his own voice, but he didn't dare push a thing if Heinz Höher stayed silent.

Rudi Theimert planned the training camp for their Under-15s, he organised residential places at the Berthold Brecht sports school in Nuremberg. Once, as vice-president at Bochum, when they were playing in the UEFA Cup against Trabzonspor, he'd waited for an hour at the airport in order to present Turkish Prime Minister Mesut Yilmaz with a bouquet of flowers which had doubltess been handed without a second thought to some gofer or other the moment he got round the next corner. The phrase 'that's beneath me' was one that Rudi Theimert never used. The satisfaction lay in getting the details right, didn't it? When he noticed that the boys at their residential school were always eating McDonald's burgers and chips, he got five of them to stay with host families in Fürth instead. These were boys who had used to come three times a week to train at Fürth from their villages way out beyond Würzburg or even Passau, over 170km each way. No bridge was too far these days for a 14-year-old who wanted to become a professional footballer. No unusually talented 14-year-old still played in his village team, the Bundesliga clubs fetched the most talented boys off to their own academies.

At home, Rudi Theimert wrote reports on every match the Under-15s played, simply for himself. He wanted to document the path they'd taken. They had an outside-left, Adrian Swiechowitz, a head shorter than all the others, incredibly spontaneous with his dribbling, who simply had to go professional. Adrian's dad told Rudi Theimert, you just stay out of this, we've already got an agent and he's in contact with Stuttgart. Adrian was 13.

Saturdays with Rudi Theimert became part of Heinz Höher's routine and the high point of his week: the Under-15 game at midday, if they were lucky a home game for the second-division side in the afternoon, with Juri playing, then a couple of beers and a shot in the evening in the Glubb bar. When Rudi Theimert went out for a couple of beers, he really did only drink a couple of beers, and so when Heinz Höher went to the Glubb on Saturdays, he kept himself to that too. When he drank so little, there was no taste in it. He didn't feel any effect. So he might as well drink nothing at all.

I used to drink a lot, he said to Rudi Theimert in the Glubb.

Yeah?

Yeah.

Rudi Theimert understood what Heinz Höher was trying to tell him. After a few weeks, he already knew Heinz Höher well enough to know that he didn't talk about unpleasant realities, only hinted at them.

One time, Rudi Theimert was on the touchline at an U-15 game and thought he heard the parents talking. He drinks, you know, you could smell it on his breath the other day. But the parents were proud that their boys were allowed to train with Heinz Höher, the way he trained them was just the best, keeping hold of the ball, games of three against two on mini-pitches, the way he noticed things, accelerating away after winning the ball, your foot's at an angle, you've got to lift off from the tips of your toes, you've got to take longer steps when you break out from a tussle for the ball if you want to lose your opponent.

At the end of their first season together, in the summer of 2007, Heinz Höher was walking back to the dressing-room with Rudi Theimert after training, one of those walks where the chat is about nothing much and punctuated by silences, when he said: it's over. They're not extending my contract.

What?

Yeah.

Rudi Theimert thought it would be impolite to ask any more; he thought Heinz Höher would have time later to explain why he'd suddenly been forced to quit as youth coach at Fürth for the second time. They never spoke about it again. At Rudi Theimert's house, the notebook with all the match reports of the Under-15 side lay on the writing table, with many pages still blank.

Heinz Höher had advised Juri Judt that he should on no account renew his contract at Fürth beyond its current date of 2008. You're too good, he said, you can play in the Bundesliga. The conflict of interests, which club president Helmut Hack had feared seven years previously, had now arisen: Heinz Höher, employed as a youth coach by Greuther Fürth, was deploying his influence to ensure that the club would lose one of its most important players. That was not on.

Heinz Höher refused to see the conflict: he felt that he had continued to work loyally for the club as youth coach. Juri would leave at some time in any case, he'd been called up for the national Under-21 team, the ultimate pool of talent; he was getting too big for the Bundesliga 2.

Compared to the last time, in 2000, this departure from the club didn't hurt Heinz Höher so much. He still had his most important team, his one-man XI, Juri Judt.

Actually, it wasn't just Juri. Three other kids from Höher's Higher School of Football had become professionals: Chhunly Pegenburg played in the Bundesliga at Nuremberg, Daniel Adlung was one of the driving forces at Greuther Fürth and Samil Cinaz had found a berth at Erfurt in the newly founded third tier of the Bundesliga. But the link between him and those three had become more distant as they grew from boys to men.

Heinz Höher considered how best to fulfil his role as a one-man coach. In the autumn of 2007 he suddenly told Rudi Theimert that he was driving to Frankfurt. He had applied to the German Football Union to be accepted by them as a players' agent. He never afterwards mentioned this to Rudi Theimert again. So Theimert knew that Heinz Höher had failed the exam.

To say that it was a sore point was putting it mildly. Failing an exam, him! You could twist the facts however you liked, it just didn't fit in with Heinz Höher's self-image. Naturally, he'd made no sort of preparations whatever for the exam.

He made a deal with Fritz Popp. Popp had been his assistant manager at Nuremberg back in the 1980s and was now a successful agent.

Popp would act as Juri Judt's official agent, and Heinz Höher would stay in the background as Juri's coach/mentor/footballing godfather. Popp suggested that he would take only 20 per cent of whatever fee they got for him changing club or extending his contract, with Heinz Höher keeping the other 80 per cent.

For God's sake no, we'll do it 50/50, said Heinz Höher. He wanted to avoid giving the impression that he needed the money.

He'd had to move out of his house in the Elbinger Straße in 2007. What with his debts to banks and the taxman, the result of his ventures into property in Saxony, he could hardly afford to rent a place to live. Thomas used his savings to pay for a three-room flat in the Rudolfstraße where his parents could live. Thomas was by now working in modern football as well, he was with a UEFA company, selling the broadcasting rights to the Champions League all over Europe. The flat in the Rudolfstraße even had a little patch of garden for the tortoises.

Doris ordered her husband to throw out all those old books and magazines from the cellar when they moved, there'd be no room for them in the new flat. It was her way of transferring her rage at his property gambling onto the books, onto dumb objects. He carried hundreds of Tommo books to the recycling depot and wrote a short story about the book-murders of Elbinger Straße. On the day of the move, Heinz Höher employed his oldest trick. He drank himself into insensibility so as not to feel how he was leaving behind the last relics of success in life.

When he woke up from the drink, he told himself that it would be okay. Things really were okay for him. The income he had left from his pension and life assurance was henceforth going to be administered by Thomas, who was going to give his parents housekeeping money every month. Heinz Höher busied himself with finding a Bundesliga club for Juri. Greuther Fürth were certainly in the running for promotion themselves, at the high point of their 2007-08 season they were lurking fifth in the Bundesliga 2.

But Heinz Höher swore to Fritz Popp, to Rudi Theimert, to Doris, to everybody he spoke to that Juri had to go to a bigger club, that he was the perfect footballer. Heinz Höher got the feeling that during his eulogies to Juri, Fritz Popp just lowered his eyes and waited till it was over. But this unspoken resistance simply fired Heinz Höher up even more. They simply had to get Juri into the Bundesliga, in a first-rate team! Thomas asked himself how his father's obsession with Juri could have become so excessive: was it the uncontrollable enthusiasm of a coach for his star pupil? Or did his father just want to show them all in the Bundesliga? Was he – horrible though it sounded – using Juri as his last way of doing it? Maybe you could never really draw the line between a coach's adoration of his star pupil and a coach's obsession with showing them all.

Heinz Höher didn't change with the advent of the e-mail. He kept writing letters. In November 2007 he addressed himself to 'Dear Klaus', his former player Klaus Allofs, now become general manager at Werder Bremen: 'I've coached the very finest players, Kurt Jara, Bernard Dietz, you and your brother Thomas, Reuter, Eckstein, Dorfner and Greece's player of the century, Georgios Koudas. But, as one footballer to another, I would have loved to take player A's header and give it to player B, or take player B's strength one-on-one, or his speed, and give it to player A, to create the perfect footballer. In 1998, I was working for Greuther Fürth when, by the Grace of God, that perfect footballer crossed my path in the shape of a 12-year-old, Juri Judt ... Take a look at Juri Judt, if possible at an away game against a strong opponent, or send your finest scout.'

Klaus Allofs rang back and promised to get someone to take a look at Juri. Meanwhile, Fürth president Helmut Hack invited Juri to discuss things at the Transmar Hotel in Erlangen over the Christmas holiday period of 2007. Hotel cafés handily situated for the motorway or the airport had replaced motorway service stations as the favoured places for Bundesliga doers and shakers to hold their confidential meetings. Helmut Hack was still fighting to get Juri to extend his contract. He said he would offer him the kind of contract no player at Fürth had ever got before. Nobody knew how often Helmut Hack had already said the same thing to other players.

Heinz Höher drove Juri to the hotel and waited in his car. He had no part to play in an official discussion. It was going to get cold in the car, he wouldn't be able to keep the motor and the heating running for as long the meeting was probably going to take, it would surely be an hour or two, given the way Hack was ready to fight to keep Juri. After 15 minutes, Juri came back.

What happened, asked Heinz Höher.

Nothing, said Juri. I told him there was no way I was going to extend my contract, and that was the end of the conversation.

Heinz Höher started his car, suffused with a heady feeling that the great journey could now begin. Two games later, with Greuther Fürth now having advanced into one of the promotion spots, their manager Bruno Labbadia took his key player, Juri Judt – who according to his team-mates and the football writers had been playing perfectly – off the team-sheet and left him off.

The manager gave no explanation to Juri. Juri didn't ask. A professional accepted such decisions, he told himself, and was content with this unwritten law. Juri found it easier to take setbacks without complaint than to start conflicts. The newspapers devoted two sentences to the change in the team: 'After the one-nil defeat against Kaiserslautern, it was only to be expected that manager Labbadia would re-jig his team. But it's surprising that the fall-guy is Juri Judt,' wrote the *Nürnberger Nachrichten*. As far as the media was concerned, that was that. The Bundesliga 2 wasn't reported on in enough detail to make an issue out of some player who was no longer being played and wasn't even complaining about it. For Juri to be sitting on the subs' bench was just one man's fate in a team sport. Greuther Fürth tumbled down again out of the promotion-chasers, the team captain went to the manager to tell him that we feel safer with Juri there in front of the defence. But in the remaining 14 games, Labbadia called Juri back only once, when a ban on his other vital midfielder, Martin Lanig, made it unavoidable. Greuther Fürth won that single game, 3-1 against 1860 Munich and according to his team-mates and the newspaper critics, Juri Judt performed as perfectly as ever. He rejoiced inwardly, I've got over the jinx, I'm back in the team. But he sat the whole of the next match out on the bench again.

Heinz Höher was sure that it was all about making an example of him. Anyone who won't extend his contract here, doesn't get a game here, either.

Since 1995, when Belgian midfielder Jean-Marc Bosman won a judgement in the European Court meaning that players could get free transfers to other clubs when their contracts were up, the movers and shakers of the Bundesliga had been regularly complaining that they were now helpless in the face of player-power. If they didn't raise wages, a player could leave the club at the end of his contract without the club getting a penny for him.

In fact, the balance of power between the clubs and their employees had just been somewhat equalised. For example, in the 1960s, at the time the Bundesliga was founded, professional footballers in France were forbidden from changing clubs before they were 35 years old, and as late as 1980, SV Hamburg refused to renew the contract for their keeper, Rudi Kargus, while still blocking his move to Düsseldorf because they didn't think the transfer fee high enough. Kargus ended up unemployed for six months. After the Bosman ruling, modern football was full of hysterical reports about player-power, such as when German national captain Michael Ballack left Bayern Munich hanging despite a fat new offer, and ended up going to Chelsea on a free transfer. But there were more cases of players being forced out of existing contracts by their clubs, or cases like that of Juri Judt, where the club was obviously trying to punish the player for wanting to move.

Klaus Allofs called back: sadly, Werder Bremen were in no need of a holding midfielder, they had one of the best in Germany, the international Torsten Frings, and plenty of back-up too. Enraged, Heinz Höher asked himself what Bundesliga club was ever going to want a player who was stuck on the subs' bench in the second division.

Twenty years before, as a player, Bruno Labbadia, the manager who'd taken Juri out of the game at Greuther Fürth, had himself been treated as a piece of goods. In the autumn of 1988 FC Nuremberg's manager, Heinz Höher, had more or less agreed Labbadia's move to them, then suddenly blocked the transfer without even calling up and telling him why. But Heinz Höher didn't think of that. When you feel you're being wrongly done by, you seldom remember the wrongs you've done to others.

The manager did himself no favours by banishing Juri; with the loss of their backbone in the holding midfield role, Gruether Fürth also lost touch with the promotion spots. Many players' agents would have sought a dialogue with the manager or the club president. Heinz Höher wrote a short story. The B-L Syndrome. B-L stood for Bruno Labbadia. Heinz Höher struck out and told the story of a boy who was playing football in the park while his friends were lying around at the swimming-pool, but before he got to the point, and showed how a man with B-L syndrome robbed the boy of his innocent dreams, he broke off. This time, unlike so many times before, writing couldn't calm him.

Football was a sport where people enthusiastically made fools of themselves again and again: managers could plan everything exactly, players could rehearse everything conscientiously, journalists could

analyse everything profoundly, spectators could see everything precisely – and then a single irrational moment in the game meant that
everything happened quite differently than had been planned and predicted. The sport's incalculable nature often infected the movers and
shakers of the Bundesliga: now and then, something unforeseeable
would happen off the pitch as well. Fritz Popp, the agent, managed to
get Juri Judt, a player banished to the subs' bench at the small-time
Greuther Fürth, taken on by their grand neighbour, FC Nuremberg.

When Juri signed his contract with them in April 2008, Nuremberg
were in the Bundesliga. In May 2008, six weeks before Juri actually
joined them, Nuremberg were relegated.

But even down in Bundesliga 2, the club felt like a Bundesliga team.
Nothing changed in the size of the club, the 30,000 in the stadium, the
fantastic training-pitches, the daily excitement in the pages of four
newspapers. Juri accepted without complaint that his job here was
simply to help out, sometimes defending on the right, sometimes
defending on the left, then back into the right of the midfield, he was
shifted in, and shifted out, a pro had to play whatever position the manager put him, he thought, even though he himself knew that he'd be
far more use as a holding midfielder. Juri Judt appeared in almost every
game as Nuremberg won immediate promotion back up in their first
season.

On 12 September 2009, the fifth matchday of the Bundesliga season
2009-10, Nuremberg's ground was a 47,000 sell-out for the game
against Borussia Mönchengladbach. Selling out a Bundesliga stadium
no longer demanded an electrifying opponent, it was enough now that
the thermometer didn't fall to 10° below and the home side weren't
having their worst season ever.

Judt's starting the game, said the reporters in the stand.

Well, that's a surprise.

Juri had already come on as a substitute for nine minutes at
Frankfurt and 25 at Stuttgart; but a player felt like a real Bundesliga
man only when he'd seen out his first game from kick-off to final whistle. The players assembled themselves on the walk from the
dressing-room, the stadium's PA played the club anthem 'A Rock in
Wildest Oceans'. In the stand, Heinz Höher got goose-pimples, he
thought he could see his own team down there, his Eckstein, Reuter,
Dorfner, Grahammer long ago, he tried to work out how many years it
was since he'd been in the stadium. Twenty years after his sacking as

manager of Nuremberg – *a rock in wildest oceans/we stand there still unbowed*, the anthem echoed round the ground – Heinz Höher felt that he once again belonged.

When Mönchengladbach attacked down the opposite flank, Juri cut infield; when full-back Javier Pinola went into a one-on-one with Matmour, he stayed close, securing his left flank. That was the way his generation had learned to play football: always be on the move, even if you weren't close to the ball, tactical awareness was all-important. When Gladbach's Juan Arango broke from midfield, Juri shadowed him, trying to make him drift out to the wing through his positioning, just don't go for your man too early, the great thing was not to make a mistake, that's what his coaches had hammered home for years. At last, Juri gave it a lash. He started going in hard against Arango, wanting the ball; Juri was only 5 foot 9 and lightly built, but he always shone in a real fight for the ball. Having won it, he played a simple pass to the full-back beside him or a short diagonal ball to the holding midfielder. After hanging on nervily, Nuremberg beat Borussia Mönchengladbach 1-0 for their first victory of the season. Juri Judt had done nothing to draw further attention to himself in his Bundesliga debut – which meant he could be very happy with himself: he hadn't made a single error.

After the game he drove home, his parents' faces were glowing with pride, Heinz Höher phoned as he did every day but his voice, too, sounded brighter than usual. It made Juri happy to give pleasure to other people. He stayed at home that evening just as on any normal evening. He liked it when he could be quiet and alone in his happiness.

By the end of the season he had played in 18 Bundesliga games. Juri could step into almost any position, said the manager. Juri had the ultimate quality of a professional in the modern game: he was reliable.

And still he turned up conscientiously to the training sessions which Heinz Höher organised for him in the summer break. Heinz Höher's 12-year-old nephew took up position between the thick iron posts which served as a goal as Juri Judt, a Bundesliga professional of 23, trained with Heinz Höher in the local park at Marienberg, working on taking the ball past an opponent.

Juri Judt battles it out with Bayern's Franck Ribery.

DOUBLE KNOTS FOR EVER

Three-quarters of an hour before kick-off, Juri Judt always sat there in the dressing-rooms of the Bundesliga, which these days looked rather like wellness spas, tying on his boots with double knots. The way he'd learned it from Mr Höher as a 12-year-old boy.

At 24, Juri was married and the father of a two-year-old daughter. Mr Höher still called him daily. Juri shouldn't touch the ball so often with his foot while dribbling, it acted as a brake on him, and he should never dribble off from a standing start, he'd never get past an opponent from a standing start. Juri agreed with Mr Höher, in an understanding manner. But what, he thought quietly, if I just can't do it better?

In the late summer of 2010, under manager Dieter Hecking, he'd for the first time become a fixture at Nuremberg, a fixture in the Bundesliga. Game after game, for the whole first half of the season, he played as right-back. Things were going well for the team, they were maintaining their place mid-table. Juri defended solidly and sometimes, as in their 2-1 victory over Schalke, he did it excellently. He himself was more and more aware of his limitations. No one was complaining about his performances, but Juri thought he could detect a silent grumbling from the manager, from the fans and even from Mr Höher, because he hardly ever came out of his defensive position to join the attack. Superb full-backs like Barcelona's Dani Alves took the public by storm with their surging breaks up the touchline: and because everyone could admire this stuff on Internet clips now, most of them thought that a Bundesliga defender should play the same way. I can't do that, said Juri Judt. I can cover my side, no one gets past me, and now and again I can dare to go forward if I'm going full-steam at an opponent and simply run straight past him. But I'm not a player who can take it round an opponent at Bundesliga level, at the end of the day I'm a holding midfielder, my job is to break down the opponents' build-up, to play quick clean passes, to run the tempo of the game. His managers had always valued his reliability. Suddenly, Juri thought he could feel them thinking that 'reliable' was a polite way of saying 'middle of the road'.

Juri, said Heinz Höher, I've been taking a close look at Uchida, Schalke's right-back, on the TV: the things he does, you've been doing them for ages, you understand the right position and the correct decision much better than him – just get forward a bit more often, like Uchida.

Heinz Höher thought he was encouraging Juri.

Mr Höher, said Juri, don't you think you overrate me?

Heinz Höher thought he should worry about Juri. There was a good side to this. It gave him something to do. Now he once again had no team to coach, the days dragged by. For Juri's sake, he fell back on his old way of dealing with problems. He wrote a letter, this time to Nuremberg manager Dieter Hecking:

Hello Mr Hecking,

I'll just introduce myself: I'm Heinz Höher, I've been manager for a good 400 Bundesliga games, had the privilege of playing in all three European knockout competitions – European Cup, Cup Winners' Cup, UEFA Cup – have given Nuremberg five members of the national team, whereas for 20 years before me and for 20 years after me, no Nuremberg player wore the national colours. In Lübeck, where you also used to work, I had a collapse in 1996.' He was aware, Heinz Höher continued, that Juri was said to lack an offensive game, 'but that is sheer rubbish. Juri Judt has a feel like no one else for the decisive pass at high speed, at the right moment, in the right place.' He said that Juri lacked only one quality: 'He quite simply doesn't have that egotistical mind-set, the kind that makes players like Kahn and Effenberg parade about the place, and with which I, too, was plentifully blessed.' Juri knew how to play for the good of the team. Heinz Höher advised Dieter Hecking that a player like this needed the manager's support more than others. And to be played as a holding midfielder. He signed off with friendly greetings to Hecking and waited expectantly for the manager's answer.

Meanwhile, in his search for a way to fill up his days, he discovered the Internet. He left opening emails and suchlike rubbish to Doris. He used the Internet to bet on football matches. After all, he knew what was what in football, it would be a piece of cake to swipe a bit of cash from the bookies. Every month, he secretly put 200 of their 2000 euros housekeeping money aside for betting. He thought to himself, I'll change that 200 into 2000 every month.

He bought himself a second monitor so that he could compare the quotes from the online bookies Bwin and Betfair in real time and bet on the best odds. He never managed to get the second monitor set up, but left it standing there on his desk. His plan was to sit in front of his computers for an hour or two after his siesta on Sundays, and at midnight he was still sitting there. He bet on ten or 20 live games at the same time, Lazio vs Inter, Amkar vs Volga Nizhnyi Novgorod, Slavia Sofia vs Svetkavitsa. He sometimes didn't even know the teams. He relied on his feeling for the dynamics of a football game, and his theory that after a 1-1 draw a 2-1 victory often came next. But a victory, for whom? In the 75th minute of the game he bet 100 euros that Villareal were still going to lose against Atletico Madrid, next minute he bet 300 euros that there would be another goal in St Johnstone vs Rangers. He won 320 euros and a couple of minutes later lost 300. He didn't get angry when he lost, and it didn't make him happy when he won. His pulse didn't rise as he gambled. At the end of the day, Heinz Höher found that the thrill of gambling only kicked in when it was a question of financial survival, when you were betting right to the edge of existence.

Dieter Hecking didn't answer his letter. Heinz Höher was surprised at this. He went to the club's ground, the Valznerweiher, and button-holed the manager. Hecking said vaguely that he must still have the letter somewhere. He declared himself ready to meet Heinz Höher, the best time would be tomorrow after training in the club bar, the Stuhlfauth-Stube.

The following day, Heinz Höher watched the final minutes of the training session and then went to the Stuhlfauth-Stube. He waited 20 minutes. Of course, Hecking had to shower, he might need to have a couple of conversations, a modern Bundesliga manager was always having to talk to someone or other, the team psychologist, the video analyst, agents, reporters. Heinz Höher could easily see that. But he didn't feel like waiting any longer. *After training*, that had been his arrangement with Hecking. He stood up, told the landlady that she should tell the manager he'd been there, and went home. He never again tried to make contact with Dieter Hecking.

In October 2010, Heinz Höher felt as if his own foot had run away. He took a step but he couldn't feel his right foot any more, he looked down, the foot was still there, but it didn't seem to belong to his body any more. He couldn't feel it any more.

He was sent to see a neurologist.

Do you drink alcohol, asked the neurologist.

Now and then, said Heinz Höher.

He was suffering from toxic polyneuropathy. Drink was destroying his nervous system. Polyneuropathy often starts on the outer extremities, the hands and feet, because the longest nerve-fibres are the first to suffer. First you feel a tickling in the toes, then a numbness, and finally nothing at all. If he kept on drinking, he was in danger of soon becoming a cripple. Bit by bit, his whole body would become numb, the way the right foot already had.

Imagine the illness in your foot slowly working its way up, said the neurologist. Someday, it'll reach your heart.

Heinz Höher left the clinic and thought: now you've got the reason you've been seeking for years; a reason to force you to stop drinking. At home, he collected all the beer and took it back to claim the deposits on the bottles. He claimed the deposits on full bottles.

Juri was teetotal. He preferred going for ice-cream in the mall with his wife and daughter. He'd bought a flat for his young family in a newly built block in Langwasser, on the ground floor so that they'd have a bit of a garden. Langwasser didn't have a good reputation in Nuremberg, it consisted almost entirely of monotonous blocks of flats, home to many poor people and to some who had trouble with the law. Juri thought it was an ideal spot, near to the training ground, beside the mall, and a meadow right behind the block of flats, with majestic trees for the children to play in. On a Saturday, he was still gardening shortly before the Bundesliga kicked off at 3.30pm. The fans passed by on their way to the stadium and greeted him, astonished. He was out with an injury.

He'd torn a muscle fibre in his upper thigh in February 2011. He wanted to get back into the game as quickly as possible. Ten days after tearing the muscle, he'd started training again. The stress of it really tore the wounded muscle open, and he was out for five weeks. It was an everyday peril for a Bundesliga player. With minor injuries, you took painkillers and hoped that it would go away. If the injury got worse, that was bad luck. Taking the time out to get a minor niggle properly cured wasn't an option. There was always someone in the team who'd been lurking there for months, his eye on your place in the starting line-up.

After five weeks out with injury, Juri Judt was able to take up his place in the team again, seamlessly. Now, though, he was no longer a fixture, but a player under observation. At his comeback game in April 2011, Nuremberg lost 1-0 to a last-minute goal from Cologne. In his manager's eyes, he was to blame.

Juri met Heinz Höher in the Marienberg Park, the trees were already in bloom. Mr Höher insisted vehemently that the goal at Cologne had been no fault of his: they took you out with a one-two, no one would have stood a chance. Juri, you've got to say it out loud in the dressing-room, you've got to defend yourself: it wasn't my fault!

Juri waited until Mr Höher had finished his impassioned address. They sat on the bench in front of the playing-field where they trained in the holidays. The grass was worn clean away in front of the goals. Heinz Höher had parked his new electric bicycle beside the bench. They'd had to give him an artificial knee. Bundesliga football only really started to take its toll 40 years later.

He had something to tell him, said Juri. Heinz Höher jumped. He realised that Juri had never spoken to him without first being spoken to.

For days now, youths had been plaguing him and his wife at their flat in Langwasser. They chucked stones at his windows at night, they growled insults and threatened to climb into the flat. He was scared when he had to play away, leaving his wife and daughter alone at home.

Heinz Höher drove to Langwasser. In the Salzbrunnerstraße, Juri's block stood out as the only new building amid the six-storey blocks of flats. At the front of the neighbouring block, the lawn was neatly mown, the facades of the flats nicely painted. At the rear of the block, the balconies were of bare concrete, a shopping-trolley and a rusting grill were leaning against the wall, among other rubbish.

Heinz Höher set to work as a detective. He discovered that these little runts were evidently a group of youths who experimented with alcohol at night in the cellar of a neighbouring block. Had they deliberately targetted Juri, did they know who he was, had he become an interesting victim because of his local fame? That had to be it.

Mr Höher took a walk with Juri's wife, up and down the meadow behind their flat. She was determined to move away; to the countryside, if life in the town was like this. Mr Höher listened attentively, here and there he imparted a word of consolation and was happily surprised at himself: he could actually do this after all – talk to other people, listen to them, be understanding.

The day afterwards, Juri wasn't in the starting line-up. Timothy Chandler, a speedy 20-year-old, took over his position. Chandler played the way people expected a right-back to play, he was always racing forward down the wing. The thought came into Heinz Höher's head: it never rains but it pours.

Within four weeks, Juri had sold his flat and moved out to the countryside, to Zirndorf. In the night, someone keyed his car. It must be fans who didn't like the way he played, thought Juri, the fans never really liked me because I came from Fürth.

Heinz Höher limped off into town on his newly operated knee, to buy a notebook for Juri. Juri should write down all his thoughts and order them, writing helped, thought Heinz Höher. Doris grew angry: Why hadn't he said that he needed a notebook, she could have got it in town just as well as him, but no, he had to march off with his wrecked knee, and without his crutches at that, naturally, because he was too vain to let himself be seen with crutches!

Of course, she actually guessed why Heinz Höher had limped into town himself. It hadn't been just about getting a notebook, but about the need to feel he was doing all he could to help Juri.

His place as the team's right-back was truly lost. For two years, Juri Judt had played in this position and that in the Bundesliga as a utility defender, then played three-quarters of the season as an established player – and after a single injury and a single unlucky game, he'd become a sub who hardly got a run-out any more. By the year 2011, that was a classic career-arc in the Bundesliga.

In the 1970s, there'd been about 250 footballers who could really call themselves Bundesliga professionals; 14 per team. Once you were part of this magic circle, you usually stayed in it for years. Thirty-five years later there were at least 600 pros who could call themselves Bundesliga players, 25 per club, and at least a further 100 who had had two or three half-way hopeful years in the Bundesliga and were now in the lower divisions, in foreign leagues, or unemployed, waiting for the chance to get back in. But there was still only room for 250 of them to actually play. So there was now a class of professionals who, after an often long and steady rise, made it in the Bundesliga – only to find themselves, before long, suddenly dropping into obscurity for some minor failing. There were so many little things that could turn a brilliant footballer overnight into an only averagely successful professional: tactical questions, injuries, a moment of weakness, a competitor who was in form, a manager's preference for a certain kind of player; luck.

Every summer there were players like Andreas Hinkel, who had won plaudits as a member of the national team and just a couple of years later was struggling to find a club. They were only 23 or 27, they felt themselves to be in their best years and yet were having to come to terms with what looked like their own failure. Failure: that was how the newspapers always presented it, and that was how the players themselves always felt it, when you lost your role in the Bundesliga in your early or mid-20s. Because they all measured professional footballers according to the long-outdated values of the pre-modern Bundesliga, when a regular player usually held onto his place for a decade. In reality it wasn't just logical, it was inevitable, that the modern Bundesliga should kick fine players out each year: the place was so awash with TV money that if a player showed the slightest chink in his armour, a Bundesliga club could always buy themselves a new player from somewhere or other. And that same TV money had also professionalised youth training so much that every year, dozens of high-class 19-year-olds were flooding into a market where one fact hadn't changed in 30 years: come Saturdays at 3.30pm, there were still jobs for only 250 of them.

Heinz Höher had seen it for himself: of the kids he'd coached in 1999, four had become professionals. Of the kids he'd coached just as enthusiastically in 2006 with Rudi Theimert, just one had managed to make it into a Bundesliga reserve team. Adrian Swiechowitz, with his angelic dribble, who surely had to become a professional, ended up in division six. For a long time now, children across the country were being trained with the same dedication that Heinz Höher had shown so unusually in 1999. The more first-class footballers were trained up, the more of them would never actually make it into the Bundesliga. That was the iron law of the boom.

When the public of 2011 thought about Bundesliga players, it thought of Neuer, Lahm and Schweinsteiger, but the reality for most Bundesliga players had long been very different: playing in the Bundesliga was now only a half-career with many gaps. Most of them could keep it up at the highest level for two to seven years, and after that it was a case of somehow muddling through the final seven to 12 years of a career. As in any booming part of the economy, what sociologists call a *precariat* had been born in football: professionals who played for 1200 euros a month in the third division, managers who suffered unemployment for months at a time, agents who had no players on their books; all of them united in a hope that sometimes looked like desperation, the hope that somehow, someday, they'd make it into the Bundesliga.

Juri had one more year to protect his status as a Bundesliga player. His contract at Nuremberg was going to run out in June 2012. He didn't need anyone to tell him that in that remaining year he'd at the very least have to get back his role as a utility player. If not, he'd be out.

The decisive season began in August 2011 with Nuremberg playing Hertha, Hannover, Dortmund, Augsburg. Juri was on the bench for each of those games. He wasn't brought on in any of them.

At midday, after training, he'd lie down in bed. Bad thoughts could never get at him when he was asleep.

He just didn't have enough egoism, Heinz Höher said to the neurologist who he was visiting for his polyneuropathy and with whom he regularly discussed Juri in the consulting-room. Imagine now, for a minute, said Heinz Höher, four Bundesliga players are sitting in a café together after training: every player builds himself up to be more than he is, the substitute slags off the manager, who's got no idea, and his rivals, who've got no talent. But Juri would never do that! Juri would never say: ha! that Chandler, he's always charging upfield, but that means he's always leaving gaps in the defence behind him.

'Why should I say that?' Juri said, when we talked about it. 'Chandler's a better full-back than me. I haven't got a problem with taking reality as it is.'

In September 2011, Nuremberg played Cologne, Bremen, Mainz. Juri was on the bench for each of those games. He wasn't brought on in any of them.

Doris Höher couldn't stand watching the TV broadcasts of Nuremberg's games any longer. She'd been through it all with her husband for long enough now, there she was off again, worrying about Juri, was he going to play, or wasn't he, and then that impotent rage against the manager who didn't bring Juri on. Doris felt that her nerves were like brake-shoes with the pads worn right away.

Heinz Höher changed his tactics. He had to make Juri truly see what being a professional footballer meant, he had to reawaken the boy's passion for the game, then he'd fight for his place. And when Juri really fought, nothing could stop him.

Juri, said Heinz Höher, how much money would it take for you to give up football?

Dunno, said Juri. Maybe a million.

Christ, just stop it, Juri! You've probably already earned a million, you'll easily earn another million if you just play another couple of years in the Bundesliga! I, said Heinz Höher, and he stressed the word, I wouldn't give up football for all the money in the world.

Juri didn't answer.

Heinz Höher tried again: when I hear the club anthem before a game, it gives me goose-pimples.

Yeah? said Juri. You know what it does to me? It makes me want to throw up. It makes me want to throw up, the training, the coach-journeys, the hanging about in hotels.

Juri, said Heinz Höher, and couldn't think what else to say: Juri.

Two years previously, German national keeper Robert Enke had committed suicide while suffering from severe depression, and even though many in the Bundesliga still had only a vague understanding of what depression was, it was now broadly agreed that psychological problems in players should be treated seriously. Heinz Höher thought about informing Nuremberg's sports director, Martin Bader, about Juri's inability to take pleasure in the game; maybe he, too, was suffering from a depressive condition? Jesus, Juri thought to himself, I'm not depressed. I just don't enjoy it any more! Like anyone else who sometimes can't be bothered when it's all crap. It'll soon blow over.

In October 2011, Nuremberg played Stuttgart. Juri Judt was brought on as sub. After three months and ten games of waiting, he got 21 minutes of play. He'd been on for a minute when Nuremberg scored to make it 2-1. Now they had to defend, Chandler on the right of midfield, Juri in behind him, a double-lock, no one was going to get through them. It's amazing how few touches of the ball a football player, never mind a full-back, gets in 21 minutes, maybe half a dozen, yet every moment he's working away at top concentration, moving in, moving out, moving back, blocking, offering himself and not getting the ball. Nuremberg gave a goal away to make it 2-2, but the cross came in from the opposite wing. Juri Judt had defended reliably.

After showering, he had to walk past the reporters in the tunnel. They were separated from the players by a railing. Twenty or 30 journalists were standing packed close together, as if they were marking each other so as not to miss a single quotation. The players didn't know most of their names. They stretched microphones and recording equipment at them through the railings.

Juri Judt was hardly questioned. He was known for saying nothing much of any interest in an ever-friendly manner. He had taught himself some empty phrases to say to them. The result was that every newspaper article about Juri, who was in fact a reflective player well able to formulate his thoughts, called him uncommunicative. He thought he was being professional by giving nothing away.

The excesses of the 1990s were a thing of the past. Back then, playing the big mouth in the media, openly attacking your opponents, whether that meant the manager or your team-mates, had been thought of as a cunning battle-plan. By 2011, professionals in the Bundesliga despised such chav-talk. Now, Channel 1's *Sportschau* had the rights to the Bundesliga again, it was no longer Sat 1's *ran*. The presenters and commentators from *ran* had simply joined *Sportschau*. Apparently, the TV public needed well-known voices and faces to feel comfortable. But glove-puppets, pop-hits and acrobats no longer featured on the programme. Everything had got more sensible.

Those 20 minutes against Stuttgart, with Chandler and Juri on the right wing, deserved a repetition. For the next game, faced with the extravagant ball-skills of Bayern's Franck Ribery, playing two defenders on the wing seemed to be just the right solution.

Ribery swung out his left hip, the outside one, but almost in the same instant he headed right, passing Juri on the inside. It all happened so quickly, it was as if Ribery could move simultaneously in two opposing directions, dummying and then going past you. Chandler knew he ought to support Juri in his duel with Ribery, but Bayern's full-back Philipp Lahm was already surging up from deep, and Chandler really had to shadow him, too. They went through the game in a state of constant over-stretch. Juri grasped at Ribery's hip to try to stop him somehow, he got the yellow card and 69,000 spectators thought: he'll soon be getting red. And now Ribery sprinted loose again, he cut hard back inside, he could run faster with the ball than other people could run without it, he shot from 20 metres out. They were 39 minutes in and already it was the third goal for Bayern. At half-time, the manager took Juri off.

Ribery frequently showed full-backs the true extent of their own impotence. In the games that now followed, Juri wasn't even on the bench.

You're just tagging along, the manager told him. Juri didn't defend himself. 'The manager had it right: I went to training, did what was down in the programme, and drove home. I was just tagging along, by then.'

Back home, Juri asked himself what it would be like to have a perfectly normal job, to go off each morning and come back each afternoon free of it all, no worries, no sadness, no stress because of his stupid job. As well as being a professional footballer, he was a qualified dietary advisor.

Juri, he could play for Barcelona, seriously, that's how good he is, said Heinz Höher to whoever he was talking to. The further Juri got from a secure place in the Bundesliga, the more Heinz Höher built him up.

You're burdening him too much with your own expectations, his neurologist told him: if you always go on to him about Barcelona, he's bound to suffer from the feeling that he's disappointing those expectations.

Heinz Höher distracted himself by turning on the computer. Genoa vs Palermo, a goal will be scored, he betted, Estoril will lose against Arouca, he typed, he lost 78 euros and lost 200 euros. He had his secret savings of 25,000 euros, from wins on the betting and from his fee for the extension of Juri's contract at Nuremberg 18 months before. He put 10,000 euros on Bayern to be German champions and 12,000 euros on Barcelona to be Spanish champions.

Modern football, which was speed made flesh, could give its players chances as unexpectedly as it took them away. Chandler was red-carded in December 2011 for a nasty foul and was banned for two games. The newspapers reported that Juri Judt would replace him against Bayer Leverkusen. Christ, Juri, said Heinz Höher and then he just laughed instead of talking.

Two days before the match against Leverkusen, Juri was sprinting in training when he prepared to play the ball and felt a resistance followed by a sudden stab of pain. His studs had jammed in the pitch. With a powerful jolt, his boot twisted. He had torn several ligaments in his ankle. He'd be out for a good two months, the doctor predicted.

When Juri returned to team-training at the end of January 2012, there were still 15 league games remaining before his contract was up. But he didn't believe in luck any more, or that fate was going to help out. He already felt that his time here was over.

It had taken him eight months to come to terms with the loss of his regular place in the team. Like most sports people who, after long resistance, have finally accepted that something has come to an end, Juri now felt a kind of relief. This summer he could go somewhere else, anywhere else, and start over; he could leave things behind him. He went to his manager and asked on his own account to be put back into the reserve side. He wanted to feel that he was a truly valued part of some kind of team again, to play every weekend again, so as to be in good playing form in summer when he got to his new team, whoever that might be.

He played for the reserves in front of 222 or 127 spectators, among 19-year-olds who were living off the dream that they would one day run out onto the pitch in the Bundesliga; they looked up to him because they thought, he must be living the dream. Slowly, his pleasure in the game returned. He was allowed to play holding midfielder, though not always, even the reserves' manager had his tactical obsessions, but often enough for him to feel he had a goal again: that he would one day play in his best position again and show what a good player he could be.

In April 2012, agent Fritz Popp reported that Bundesliga 2 side FC Ingolstadt wanted him. Ingolstadt would be ideal, thought Juri, a quiet, prosperous club only 70km away from Nuremberg, from home. And Bundesliga 2 was just the right platform to get him feeling good again. But Mr Höher told him that he should only allow himself to go down into the second division if they played him as a holding midfielder again at last. Mr Popp imagined that he'd certainly be able to play in the midfield at Ingolstadt, they'd surely be happy just to get a player like him. The three of them drove down for contractual discussions with Ingolstadt's sports director, Thomas Linke. Their manager, Tomas Oral, joined them.

I really want to play holding midfielder, said Juri. I feel that's my best position.

The sports director and the manager listened attentively. Heinz Höher felt proud of Juri, knowing as he did what Juri used to be like, in times gone by: Juri, who had difficulty making any demands at all, had said straight out what he wanted. If he could just get back to playing holding midfielder, he would certainly make it from Ingolstadt back into the Bundesliga, thought Heinz Höher.

As contractual discussions went on, they seemed to get a little vaguer. Fritz Popp several times asked the sports director, so we'll talk the financial details over between the two of us, yeah? Every time, the sports director hinted that he should wait. Then, at some stage, the sports director began to ask about other players who Popp represented. Finally, the sports director showed Juri and Heinz Höher round the stadium. It was a little gem, square-shaped, small and narrow, completely roofed in, the spectators near to the touchline, lots of steel and glass. In the four years since Juri had last played in the Bundesliga 2, it had taken on some aspects of the top flight. The wages had gone up again too, between 12,000 and 33,000 euros a month for a player who was good enough for the Bundesliga but couldn't find a berth there.

Basketball players and athletes complained that football was gobbling up all the money and attention, *Das aktuelle Sportstudio* now showed 70 minutes of football, including two Bundesliga 2 matches. The whole programme only lasted 75 minutes.

Very few people understood the cause and effect that was going on here: since the beginning of the 1990s, the TV stations had poured immense sums into getting the broadcasting rights to football. So now they had to show more and more football, for it to make even halfway financial sense. And because football was now almost the only sport on television, fewer and fewer viewers were interested in other sports.

Television had made the Bundesliga rich and potent. After a while, football began to dictate prices and the rules to TV. The TV stations were helpless, they needed football, they'd trained the public to be greedy for the game. When they signed their contract with the Bundesliga, Channel 2 were forced to show Saturday matches from Bundesliga 2 as well as all the Bundesliga games on *Sportstudio*. No one on *Das aktuelle Sportstudio* was keen on showing Bundesliga 2 matches every week. But they had no choice.

The programme had been shifted by Channel 2 to Saturday at 11am. And still 2.5 million viewers tuned in. After haemorrhaging viewers in the 1990s to their competitor, *ran*, the programme was now holding its own. It seemed that so long as it showed football, a TV station just couldn't fail.

Heinz Höher and Juri Judt drove from Ingolsdtadt back to Nuremberg, feeling that things had gone well. Next day, Ingolstadt's sports director, Thomas Linke, called. They were looking for a full-back, and now it turned out that Juri Judt only wanted to play holding midfield, they didn't understand it. And they didn't need a player for that position. He wished Juri all the best in his search for a club.

Every morning, before 9am, Heinz Höher went out with the dog to the meadows at Wöhrd or the park at Marienberg. Summer had come early. If he was lucky, and Doris didn't catch him at it, he could wear shorts. Doris couldn't abide him wearing shorts at his age, almost 74.

In the park café at Marienberg he drank a latte macchiato and gazed at other people's beer-glasses. He could feel the pull of it, the bitter coolness of the beer in his throat, the relaxation alcohol sent out into your whole body. He forced himself to bear the sight of that forbidden beer until he finished his latte macchiato and went back out into the park. Tomorrow he would come here again, and then he would have to pass that test yet again, and the test was never going to end.

There just had to be some club for Juri, he thought, as he let his dog run free, for such a fine boy with such quality. He'd think of something, he always had the right ideas, somehow or other. Or did he? Borussia Dortmund, not Bayern, were German champions; Real Madrid, not Barcelona, had won the Spanish Liga. Heinz Höher's 22,000 euros of savings disappeared from his gambling account with the click of a mouse.

Heinz Höher at 74, bearing tidings of eternal truth: Coaches Never Lie.

ALWAYS HIGHER,
ALWAYS HÖHER

Doris leaves him on his own for a week. She's off with her sister to Majorca, on holiday. In the attempt to limit the catastrophic consequences to their home, she writes him a long list before she leaves, with all the things he has to do on a daily basis. Give the dog fresh water, water the lawn, recharge the cordless phone at night, buy salad for the tortoises because the parks are all mown and you can hardly find dandelions there. Drink lots of water yourself!

Heinz Höher works his way conscientiously through the list, it's summer in the city, 2012, and because his wife isn't there he wears shorts the whole time, he likes putting on his white, short-sleeve shirt to go with them, it lends him a certain elegance, even at 74. So as to have something to do, he even goes to the supermarket twice a day to buy lettuce for the tortoises. But that can't be all there is to life, passing the day buying salads. He gets an idea.

In the morning, he buys a lettuce at the supermarket and pays with a 100 euro note. In the afternoon, he goes back just in time to get the same check-out girl before she changes shift, buys another lettuce and pays with another 100 euro note. The next day he turns up the tempo, he appears at the supermarket four times, each time paying for a lettuce with a 100 euro note, more salad than any tortoise could ever eat. In between visits he goes to the bank to get his change converted back into 100 euro notes. He just wants to see how the check-out girl reacts, how long it will be before she explodes. The eighth time that he pays for a lettuce with a 100 euro note, the check-out girl says: 'Do you print this stuff at home? I must come and see you some day.' Not bad, as reactions go, thinks Heinz Höher to himself, but let's see how long she can stand it. The ninth time, the check-out girl says, with a sigh: 'A lettuce and 100 euro note.' Heinz Höher calls it off then. Somehow or other, he'd hoped for some more extraordinary reaction.

This may not be the way that most 74-year-olds spend their time, but for him, it's an achievement: to find satisfaction in such harmless little games. From the day in October 2010 when the neurologist diagnosed polyneuropathy in him, he hasn't touched a drop of alcohol. He himself has got himself blocked by the online gambling companies.

Heinz Höher always thought of life as a game, and the Bundesliga let him feel that the world really was one big pitch for playing on. Fifty years ago, on 24 August 1963, he appeared in the Bundesliga on its very first day. Today, none of those pioneers is around any more, even Otto Rehhagel stepped down for good in the summer of 2012, his final act having been to get relegated once again, this time with Hertha. Thanks to Juri Judt, Heinz Höher is still on the ball in this 50th year. After his planned move to Ingolstadt fell through, Juri went to Leipzig, a brand-new club conjured out of thin air by Red Bull with the aim of reaching the Bundesliga in four or five years. Fired by this hope, Bundesliga professionals like Juri or sports director Ralf Rangnick took the plunge down to the fourth division, where newly born Red Bull Leipzig were obliged to start.

An epochal gulf separates the Bundesliga of 1963, a place where a few young men from a suburb called Meiderich could be runners-up, from the Bundesliga of 2013, a place where firms like Red Bull elbow their way in as part of a carefully planned marketing strategy. If you just look at the raw data, it's easy to think you could detect a clear, straight line showing the rise of a league in which everything was always going faster, higher, onward. But our journey with Heinz Höher through 50 years of the Bundesliga has shown that there never was such continuity, and that its rise was never so inevitable. In the course of those years, professional football in Germany was several times at risk of playing itself offside. The match-fixing scandal of 1971 threatened the reputation of the Bundesliga in wider society, and it happened again in the 1980s, when football seemed to be degenerating into a hyper-physical, cynically defensive sport, the stomping-ground of thugs. For most clubs, being in the Bundesliga in those days meant certain financial ruin.

It wasn't the beauty of the game, or its power, which made the Bundesliga fly ever higher, but one single, external factor: television. On that first matchday in 1963, *Das aktuelle Sportstudio* began, in all innocence, to present the Bundesliga not just a sport, but as entertainment. Around 1990, the private TV stations took up the notion with commercial chutzpah. Over the following 20 years, by pumping millions into the Bundesliga, TV created the sort of football which it wanted, and which it needed: speedy and dynamic, spectacular and stylish at the top level. The mountains of data which info-tech firms like Opta and Impire nowadays supply on every Bundesliga match give a striking picture of just how much faster and more skilful play has become: in 1990, a world-class striker like Rudi Völler averaged 29 touches of the ball per match, and converted 22 per cent of his chances. Twenty years later, German international striker Miroslav Klose averaged 41 touches per match and converted 47 per cent of his chances. In 1990, a world-class defender like Jürgen Kohler won an average of 46 per cent of his one-on-one battles per match, with 80 per cent of his passes on target. In 2012, Bayern defender Holger Badstuber won 77 per cent of his one-on-ones and 93 per cent of his passes reached the intended recipient. That doesn't necessarily mean that Klose, Badstuber and their generation are technically better as individual players than their predecessors Völler and Kohler; it is, rather, that teamwork and patterns of play have become so perfect that it's easier to win a one-on-one or get a pass away to a team-mate.

With change happening at such pace, it's easy to overlook the fact that much in football, perhaps its true heart, has remained unaltered from 1963 to 2013. In 2012, Barcelona and Spain scored great successes playing with no centre-forward, and this was spoken of as if it was the hottest, newest development. It was splendidly irritating to learn that Heinz Höher had already tried out the tactic at Bochum back in 1977. It's an example that should teach us to be a bit more modest, and to resist that common human instinct to treat the old days with amused condescension.

Heinz Höher's friend and club president at Nuremberg, Gerd Schmelzer, believes 'sure, everything's got better, the money coming in, the quality and attractiveness of the game, sure, everything's multiplied beyond belief, the number of reporters, agents, club employees – but when you get down to the bare bones, it's still the same game as ever.' If you put newspaper articles from 1970, 1986 and 2013 side by side, says Schmelzer, it's always the same stories. It's all about the dynamic of victory or defeat. Managers are sacked in exactly the same circumstances, be it 1970, 1986 or 2013, club presidents are under exactly the same pressures, or just as arrogant, and they make the same mistakes. Individual players rise through the ranks or are out of the game, depending on the results, clubs are always taking things right to the financial edge, never mind how much or how little money they have. When you come down to it, the cast of the Bundesliga from 1963 to 2013 have always been characters at the mercy of the game itself.

Despite this, or maybe because of this, hardly anyone who was ever part of the Bundesliga can let go of it. It's late at night now, after a lively evening with Heinz Höher in Gerd Schmelzer's castle. Heinz Höher's friend and club president drives me back to my hotel through the empty streets of Nuremberg. 'President of the club again,' Gerd Schmelzer dreams out loud, against his better judgement, 'that would really be something.' The headlights of our car are reflected in the shop-windows. At 62, Schmelzer looks younger today than he did back then in his mid-30s. The moustache is gone, along with what was left of his hair, his checked jackets have been replaced with a fashionable pullover, his glasses are now broad and horn-rimmed. Heinz Höher has already gone back home to bed. For him, sleep is still a holy thing. Gerd Schmelzer's thoughts drift back to him. 'When I try to work out where life went wrong for Heinz, I come down to this: Heinz had it too much on a plate. His mind was as sharp as a razor, he was a great-looking guy, as a player and a manager he could do it all without breaking sweat. Life was just too easy for him. I suppose that's when you get wild ideas.'

In his room in the flat in the Rudolfstraße, which he has equipped with those 40-year-old pieces of furniture from Bochum, Heinz Höher spreads a sheet out onto the floor.

'What on earth are you doing this time?' asks Doris and then shouts: 'Oh God!' when she sees what he's up to. The 50th anniversary of the Bundesliga means it's also exactly 50 years she's spent with Heinz Höher. In that time she has created 'a box inside of me, where I put everything I've had to repress,' as she calls it, 'and it's pretty well full'.

Heinz Höher isn't about to be put off. He continues writing on the bedsheet with red and black marker-pens. At 74, he's about to slip into a new role in German professional football: for the first time, he's a fan.

He's been thinking for ages about anything he could do to support Juri in Leipzig. It's clear to him that Juri has to march with Red Bull straight from the fourth division into the Bundesliga. If that's to happen, if Juri is to stay an irreplaceable part of the team for four or five years, which is an eternity in modern football, it has to go beyond sport, Juri has to become an iconic figure in the city of Leipzig. So what he needs first of all is his own personal fan club, thinks Heinz Höher. He drives to Langwasser, where he still knows a few Russian-Germans, who Juri used to play football-tennis with, once upon a time, behind the block of flats. He offers them a free trip and free tickets to Red Bull Leipzig's first game of the season, on 12 August 2012. If Juri really does make it up into the Bundesliga with Red Bull in years to come, Heinz Höher says he'll give every member of Juri's first fan club a bonus of 1000 euros. Seven Russian-Germans from Langwasser turn up for the Sunday trip to Leipzig. Heinz Höher rents a minibus, ropes in his son-in-law as chauffeur, and writes on a bedsheet, to give the Juri Judt Fan Club colours to fly.

Juri knows nothing of all this. Well, it's supposed to be a surprise. And in any case, Heinz Höher thinks he's the one who knows best what's good for the boy.

In Juri's kitchen in Leipzig, the cans of Red Bull energy drink are piling up. The club gifted each player a dedicated fridge for their supplies of Red Bull, but it turned out to be too small. Every player gets that many cans free per month. Juri can't drink them down as fast as they come in.

He's rented a three-room flat in a renovated Russian barracks. He intended to move in with his wife and daughter, but now the child's room stands empty. They couldn't find a place in a kindergarten in Leipzig, which is an especially brutal irony considering the fact that his wife is a kindergarten teacher. So his wife and daughter are still living in Nuremberg. When he talks about the distance between them that football has caused, the muscles in his face draw his mouth downwards. But he quickly adds: 'Still, I'm lucky that I found a club relatively near to Nuremberg. I'm content with things.'

He uses the word 'content' very often, like somebody who has to remind himself now and again not to forget that the word exists. But

still, you can't help feeling that Juri Judt has found a sort of content-
ment in his work once again.

He has to play right-back at Leipzig too, not holding midfielder, and
once he had to spend a couple of games on the bench even in the
fourth division; at first it irritated him, but then he tried to keep his eye
on the bigger picture. At 26 – the papers always say: the best age for a
footballer – he's beginning his second football career; modern footballers can't help having many lives. Unlike Heinz Höher, Juri Judt
doesn't think that he's absolutely got to make it back into the
Bundesliga, of course it's his aim, his dream, but he's learned to take
pleasure in the moment rather than chase abstract goals. Modern professional football has so few completely happy moments.

At Red Bull Leipzig he almost always wins. They're just a tad
overqualified. This is a team that would probably do reasonably well in
Bundesliga 2, and they're turning out in the fourth division, in small
towns called Torgelow, Neustrelitz or Meuselwitz, where the spectators
stand behind steel railings with the paint peeling off them, the way
they used to at FC Bayern Kickers back when he was ten. While the
players in Torgelow or Meuselwitz have to go to work during the week,
at Red Bull Leipzig they have the levels of creatine and kinase in their
blood measured before training, which is supposed to give information
about their energy-levels. Their body fat index is checked every week,
every training session is filmed and analysed and every opponent is
shown to them twice on video, whether it's Torgelow or Germania
Halberstadt. The morning before a game, they all go for a walk. This
ritual has remained the same since 1963. On their walk before the away
game in Magdeburg, Juri's team is accompanied by the police.
Opposing fans just love to hate Red Bull Leipzig for being an artficial
construct. As far as they're concerned, the way companies or oligarchs
just pull teams out of the hat for their own purposes is one of the worst
excesses of the entertainment industry that football has become. For
a footballer like Juri, Red Bull Leipzig is a professional's dream: excellent conditions, perfect specialist support, sporting success. For Heinz
Höher, the club is an excuse to start getting ideas again.

As his son-in-law steers the minibus along the A9 towards Leipzig,
Heinz Höher, sitting on the passenger seat beside him, says: 'Just don't
look round.' In the back seats, the seven members of the Juri Judt Fan
Club are passing vodka bottles round, they yell and sing and bring forth
other noises from their bodies. At the service station, Heinz Höher and

his son-in-law watch, struck dumb with astonishment, as their fellow passengers help themselves to stalks of corn on the cob from the neighbouring field and then beat each other up. It's really hot today, thinks his son-in-law.

Despite the racket behind him as they journey onwards, Heinz Höher is able, as so often before, to isolate himself from the world about him and sink down into his own reality. Since he gave up drinking, Winzlinger has appeared again, that fictional friend with whom he holds conversations to order his thoughts. For years, his mind was too foggy for him to be able to carry on a dialogue with Winzlinger. 'A book about you? That'll only be a success if Juri really does make the national squad after all, or if you end up in the gutter,' says Winzlinger to him, 'and you don't need me to tell you which of those is most likely.'

Winzlinger might be right, maybe the book won't be a success, but it's been a help to Heinz Höher anyway. While he was holding those conversations for the book, he realised what he'd been like for all those 50 years. 'And I have to say that I've pretty well lost any respect for myself,' he says. 'The way I treated other people; my wife, when I simply told her back in 1966 that we were going on holiday without our new-born daughter. Or my children, when I just sat next to them when they were doing their homework, like a silent menace, instead of helping them.' He slaps the flat of his hand to his forehead and lets the hand slide, very slowly, down over his eyes.

Not long ago, he was sitting on a park bench in Marienberg with his dog, Pauli, beside him, when a woman came by with her dog, and Heinz Höher started talking to her, he asked, what sort of a mongrel is yours. It was the start of an interesting conversation, the woman told him that her husband's job had made him move from North Germany to Nuremberg, what a thing it is to live split between two places. Christ, why did you never talk to people like this before, Heinz Höher asked himself. But he's doing it now, at 74, and that's something, at least.

Mind you, there are still certain situations when he absolutely thinks the right thing to do is ignore the outside world. 'Don't turn around,' he reminds himself, in the minibus, shortly before they get to Leipzig.

More than 7000 fans have turned up to the fourth-division match between Red Bull Leipzig and Union Berlin's reserve team. There may be many fans who abhor the notion of teams created out of the blue by firms, but there are many other fans attracted by these very teams, new, shining with ambition and the promise of success. Heinz Höher hadn't really thought it through: how was anyone going to hear the seven-strong Juri Judt Fan Club amid 7000 other spectators?

'I think a couple of fans are yelling for you in that block up there,' says one of the team officials to Juri Judt after the final whistle.

'What, me?' says Juri. 'No way. No one knows me here in Leipzig.' And off he goes, to the dressing-room.

Sometimes, it's true, Juri finds Mr Höher's ideas a bit, well, how should he put it: surprising. But he'd never tell him so. He hasn't forgotten what he owes him. They are roped fast together by that double-knot Heinz Höher taught to a boy of 12.

On the terrace at Leipzig, the fan club hoists their home-made banner aloft. 'You can do it, Juri,' it says. And right now, Heinz Höher absolutely believes it: that Juri and he will make it back into the Bundesliga. Even if nobody can read the message. The drunken fan club are holding the banner upside down.

Heinz Höher thinks it's funny. For 50 years, many of his travelling companions in the Bundesliga have thought he sort of sees the world the wrong way around, but none of them has seen the things he's seen.